# DECOLONIZING MANAGEMENT AND ORGANIZATION STUDIES

# RESEARCH IN THE SOCIOLOGY OF ORGANIZATIONS

## Series Editor: Michael Lounsbury

# RESEARCH IN THE SOCIOLOGY OF ORGANIZATIONS ADVISORY BOARD

RESEARCH IN THE SOCIOLOGY OF
ORGANIZATIONS   VOLUME 93

# DECOLONIZING MANAGEMENT AND ORGANIZATION STUDIES: WHY, HOW, AND WHAT

EDITED BY

## EMAMDEEN FOHIM
*University of Bern, Switzerland*

emerald
PUBLISHING

United Kingdom – North America – Japan
India – Malaysia – China

Emerald Publishing Limited
Emerald Publishing, Floor 5, Northspring, 21-23 Wellington Street, Leeds LS1 4DL.

First edition 2025

**Reprints and permissions service**
Contact: www.copyright.com

**British Library Cataloguing in Publication Data**
A catalogue record for this book is available from the British Library

ISBN: 978-1-83608-641-3 (Print)
ISBN: 978-1-83608-638-3 (Online)
ISBN: 978-1-83608-640-6 (Epub)

ISSN: 0733-558X (Series)

INVESTOR IN PEOPLE

# CONTENTS

# ABOUT THE EDITOR

**Emamdeen Fohim** is a Postdoctoral Research Fellow at the KPM Center for Public Management (University of Bern) and Co-founder of the Centre for African Smart Public Value Governance (www.c4sp.org). From an organizational theory perspective, his research examines measures public sector organizations take to address the challenges of a constantly complex environment.

# ABOUT THE CONTRIBUTORS

**Diane-Laure Arjaliès** is a French settler who joined what is now Canada in 2015. She has been working with Indigenous communities in Southwestern Ontario on the development of financial instruments aimed at stewarding the land from Indigenous and Western perspectives. She is a mother, a spouse, a daughter, a sister, an aunt, a granddaughter, a niece, a friend, a teacher, and a researcher.

**Michael Asiedu** is a Doctoral Researcher at the Institute of Political Science, University of St. Gallen, Switzerland. His research focuses on Technology and Society in Africa with interests in civil society, institutions (judiciary), and authoritarianism in Africa.

**Sandiso Bazana** is a Doctoral Researcher as well as a Teaching and Research Assistant at Grenoble Ecole de Management in France. Sandiso is also a Lecturer in organizational psychology at Rhodes University in South Africa.

**Julie Bernard** has been working with responsible investment professionals since 2012—including as one herself— and Indigenous communities in Southwestern Ontario on developing financial instruments (e.g., Conversation Impact Bond) and accountability tools since 2020. She is a researcher and a new mother who enjoys canoeing on rivers and cross-country skiing on cold winter days.

**Oana Branzei** is a Romanian-born and raised, dual citizenship first-generation immigrant settler who has lived, studied, and worked on unceded and treaty lands in Canada for half of her life. She has collaborated on intergenerational Indigenous-led health, well-being, entrepreneurship, restoration and regeneration projects in Brazil, Canada, Chile, and South Africa.

**Luciana Cezarino** is a Brazilian researcher who delves into the heart of sustainability, intertwining her work with the lives of those often overlooked – teenage mothers, quilombolas, riverside communities, and Indigenous peoples. Beyond her academic pursuits, Luciana carries the profound role of being a mother, weaving her journey with compassion and understanding for the communities she holds close to in the context of emerging economies.

**Myrto Chliova** is Associate Professor of Entrepreneurship at Aalto University. She holds a Ph.D. from ESADE Business School. Her research focuses on how entrepreneurship and organizing can help tackle grand challenges such as poverty, inequality, refugee crises, and rising authoritarianism.

**Snehanjali Chrispal** is a Lecturer in the Department of Management, Monash University, Australia. Her research interests include inequality and organizations focusing primarily on gender and caste, and decolonial and postcolonial studies. She has published in leading management journals.

**Luciano Barin Cruz** is Professor of Management at HEC Montréal. He is also Director of the Sustainability Transition and the Center on Social Impact (Ideos). He researches the role of organizations in transition, entrepreneurship in marginalized communities and institutional change.

**Leanne Cutcher** is a proud Awabakal woman whose research is motivated by a desire to be a good ancestor. Leanne's research aims to enrich our understanding of the role of culture, kinship, and country in shaping ways of organizing in and for Aboriginal communities. Leanne spends as much time as she can as a guest on the land of the Worimi people on the Barrington River, where she battles the harsh Australian climate as she seeks to regenerate a few acres of land.

**Léo-Paul Dana**, formerly tenured at the University of Canterbury, is Professor at Dalhousie University and Visiting Professor at LUT School of Business and Management, Lappeenranta University of Technology.

**Sarah De Smet** holds a Master in Applied Economic Sciences and Conflict and Development. After working for many years in international development, she embarked on a Ph.D. in women's entrepreneurship in the Global South. She is a Lecturer and Researcher at the Artevelde University of Applied Sciences (Belgium).

**Natalia Aguilar Delgado** is an Associate Professor in International Business at HEC Montreal. She is also the Associate Director of the Center on Social Impact (Ideos). Her research examines sustainable and inclusive value chains, social innovation in marginalized communities and institutional change.

**Luke Fiske** grew up in a white English-speaking community in Cape Town, South Africa, near where the contested Amazon headquarters is being built. An Assistant Professor of International Business at Erasmus University in the Netherlands, Luke's work focuses on sustainable global value chains and the impact of policy and regulation on multinational enterprise strategy.

**Carmelita Euline Ginting-Carlström** is Postdoctoral Researcher in Entrepreneurship at Aalto University. She employs feminist theories and various discourse analysis approaches to critically examine the emancipatory potential of entrepreneurship.

**Bernadetta Aloina Ginting-Szczesny** is Postdoctoral Researcher in Entrepreneurship at Aalto University School of Business, Finland. Her research focuses on the sociopsychological dimensions of entrepreneurship in different contexts. She also seeks to develop innovative visual methodological approaches for entrepreneurship research.

**Ali Aslan Gümüsay** is Professor of Innovation, Entrepreneurship & Sustainability at LMU Munich and Head of Research Group Innovation, Entrepreneurship & Society at the Humboldt Institute for Internet & Society Berlin.

**Leanne Hedberg** (she/her) received a Ph.D. in organizational sociology from the University of Alberta after many years in leadership and organizational development consulting positions. Her research focuses on the role of organizations in creating a more socially and environmentally just future.

**Ella Henry** (Ngātikahu ki Whangaroa, Te Rārawa, Ngāti Kuri), a Māori woman from Aotearoa New Zealand, with tribal affiliations to the Far North, is a Professor of Entrepreneurship, in the Faculty of Business Economics & Law, Auckland University of Technology.

**Markus A. Höllerer** is Professor in Organization and Management at UNSW Business School, Sydney, Australia. He is also Senior Research Fellow at WU Vienna, Austria, as well as Professorial Research Fellow at IAE Business School, Argentina.

**Jean-Pierre Imbrogiano** holds a Ph.D. from the University of Queensland, Australia, and is now based at the University of Helsinki, Finland. His research focuses on businesses' sustainability performance, the governance of business sustainability, and socio-cultural foundations of (un-)sustainable development.

**Claus D. Jacobs** is Professor of Public Management and Organization at KPM Center for Public Management, University of Bern in Switzerland. His research focuses on strategy work in pluralistic settings, organizational change, and identity.

**Jess Auerbach Jahajeeah** is an Associate Professor at the Graduate School of Business at the University of Cape Town. She is the Director of the Inclusive Innovation Program and directs the research group Light Lab: African Digital Infrastructure.

**Albert E. James** is an Associate professor of Family Business and Entrepreneurship at Dalhousie University. He learned the ropes of business renting vehicles across Canada. He is also the father of four children, who opened his eyes to rethinking his assumptions and relationship with Indigenous people.

**Tauriq Jenkins** is a human rights defender and active member of the South African civil society. He is the Convener of the Save Our Sacred Lands campaign and, as an accredited South African Human Rights Commission monitor, has done work on Anti-Repression. He is the High Commissioner of the Goringhaicona Khoi Khoin Traditional Indigenous Council, founding chair of the AIXARRA Restorative Justice Forum and interim chair of the South African Palestinian Arts and Culture Coalition.

**Lehlohonolo Kekana** is a Ph.D. student at the Graduate School of Business, University of Cape Town. His thesis explores the career trajectories of low-income humanities graduates in South Africa.

**Chintan Kella** is a Lecturer at the Rotterdam School of Management, Erasmus University, where he teaches courses such as Diversity, Inclusion & the Future of Work, and Managing Socio-economic Dilemmas. He holds a Ph.D. in Management from LUISS Guido Carli University. His research focuses on social & migrant entrepreneurship and institutional change.

**Shaista E. Khilji** is Professor of Human and Organizational Learning & International Affairs at George Washington University. She teaches graduate-level courses in leadership and change. Her recent work focuses on paradoxes, macro talent management, decolonizing, and neoliberalism within universities.

**Ewald Kibler** is Associate Professor of Entrepreneurship at Aalto University's School of Business in Finland. He obtained his M.A. in Sociology from the University of Graz, Austria, and his Ph.D. in Economic Geography at the University of Turku, Finland.

**Moses N. Kiggundu** is Distinguished Research Professor and Professor Emeritus, International Business, Sprott School of Business, Carleton University, Ottawa, Ontario, Canada. Founding Editor, *Africa Journal of Management.*

**Anupama Kondayya** is an Assistant Professor in the Organizational Behavior group at the Indian Institute of Management (IIM) Calcutta in India. She is interested in studying organizational and institutional change initiated by marginalized actors toward fostering diversity, inclusion, and pluralism.

**Mogopodi Lekorwe** is an Associate Professor in Public Administration at the University of Botswana. His research interests are in development administration, democracy, local government, organization development, public policy, public systems management, governance and leadership, and public enterprise management.

**Lara Liboni** is a Brazilian-Italian citizen who immigrated to Canada with a full heart and a spirit committed to honoring the land and its stories. She has worked on systems change and sustainability for over two decades and collaborates with Indigenous Communities in different regions of the Amazon Rainforest.

**Michael Lounsbury** is a Professor, A.F (Chip) Collins Chair, and Chair of the Strategy, Entrepreneurship and Management Department at the Alberta School of Business. He is also a Professor of Business Strategy and Entrepreneurship at the Australian National University, and the Series Editor of Research in the Sociology of Organizations.

**Dorothy Mpabanga** is an Associate Professor in the Department of Political and Administrative Studies, University of Botswana. Her research interests are HRM, HRD, Public Sector Management and Innovation, Strategic Management, NGO Management, ICT, Higher Education Management, Leadership and Governance, and Democracy.

**Abhishek Nagaraj** is a Faculty Research Fellow at NBER and an Assistant Professor at the Haas School of Business at the University of California, Berkeley. His research focused on innovation, entrepreneurship management, and the digital economy.

**Stella M. Nkomo** is a Professor in the Department of Human Resource Management at the University of Pretoria. Her research on DEI, race and gender in organizations, and management in Africa has been published in leading journals, book chapters and books.

**Aidin Salamzadeh** is the Vice Dean of the Faculty of Business Management (University of Tehran), the Cofounder of the Innovation and Entrepreneurship Research Lab (UK), and an Integrated Researcher at CIICESI (Portugal). His interests are new venture creation and entrepreneurship.

**Esther Salvi** is Postdoctoral Research Fellow at IMD Business School. She conducts qualitative and quantitative research at the intersection of entrepreneurship, culture, and sustainable development. Her work spans the individual, organizational, regional, and national levels of analysis.

**Tapiwa Seremani** is an Associate Professor in Sustainability and Business Ethics at IESEG School of Management in France and Member of IESEG's Center for Organizational Responsibility (ICOR). His research explores how colonialism has shaped knowledge in management and organization scholarship.

**Lucas Stocco** is a Latin American researcher from Brazil dedicated to exploring Indigenous entrepreneurship focused on non-timber Amazonian bioactives. His work emphasizes these enterprises' environmental and social impacts, rooted in traditional knowledge and deep connections to nature.

**Gasodá Suruí** earned his PhD in Geography from the Federal University of Rondônia. He is now the superintendent of the State Superintendency of Indigenous Peoples of Rondônia, Brazil. He is one of the leaders of the Paiter Suruí People in Brazil and was the coordinator of the Wagoh Pakob Cultural Center.

**Tadashi Uda** is an Associate Professor at the Faculty of Economics and Business, Hokkaido University. He mainly focuses on the emergence and transformation of work practices in organizations, the management of contemporary flexible workspaces, and the sociocultural context of entrepreneurial process.

**Georg von Richthofen** is Senior Researcher in the Innovation, Entrepreneurship & Society Research Group at the Humboldt Institute for Internet and Society (HIIG). His research focuses on AI and the future of work, the sharing economy, and corporate digital responsibility.

**Medina Williams** is a current Purdue Doctoral student and an Adjunct Business Professor at South Puget Sound Community College. Ms Williams has years of public and private sector experience and currently works as a Security Analyst helping to protect a complex agency from cybersecurity threats.

**Hongyu Yao** is a Ph.D. student in the Technological Innovation, Entrepreneurship, and Strategic Management group at MIT Sloan School of Management. His research focused on innovation, the economics of science, and development economics.

**Charlene Zietsma** is Faculty Director of the Erb Institute and Max McGraw Professor of Sustainable Enterprise at the University of Michigan's School for Environment & Sustainability and Ross School of Business. She researches sustainable/social entrepreneurship and innovation, and institutional change.

**Baniyelme D. Zoogah** is a Professor in the Department of Human Resource Management and Management at McMaster University, Hamilton, Ontario, Canada. His research is broadly on development of individuals, groups, organizations and societies with emphasis on strategic followership, sustainability, and Africa Management. He has published articles in leading journals, book chapters, and books.

# FOREWORD: RESEARCH IN THE SOCIOLOGY OF ORGANIZATIONS

*Research in the Sociology of Organizations* (RSO) publishes cutting-edge empirical research and theoretical papers that seek to enhance our understanding of organizations and organizing as pervasive and fundamental aspects of society and economy. We seek provocative papers that push the frontiers of current conversations, that help to revive old ones, or that incubate and develop new perspectives. Given its successes in this regard, RSO has become an impactful and indispensable fount of knowledge for scholars interested in organizational phenomena and theories. RSO is indexed and ranks highly in Scopus/SCImago as well as in the *Academic Journal Guide* published by the Chartered Association of Business Schools.

As one of the most vibrant areas in the social sciences, the sociology of organizations engages a plurality of empirical and theoretical approaches to enhance our understanding of the varied imperatives and challenges that these organizations and their organizers face. Of course, there is a diversity of formal and informal organizations – from for-profit entities to nonprofits, state and public agencies, social enterprises, communal forms of organizing, non-governmental associations, trade associations, publicly traded, family owned and managed, private firms – the list goes on! Organizations, moreover, can vary dramatically in size from small entrepreneurial ventures to large multinational conglomerates to international governing bodies such as the United Nations.

Empirical topics addressed by RSO include the formation, survival, and growth of organizations; collaboration and competition between organizations; the accumulation and management of resources and legitimacy; and how organizations or organizing efforts cope with a multitude of internal and external challenges and pressures. Particular interest is growing in the complexities of contemporary organizations as they cope with changing social expectations and as they seek to address societal problems related to corporate social responsibility, inequality, corruption and wrongdoing, and the challenge of new technologies. As a result, levels of analysis reach from the individual to the organization, industry, community and field, and even the nation-state or world society. Much research is multilevel and embraces both qualitative and quantitative forms of data.

Diverse theory is employed or constructed to enhance our understanding of these topics. While anchored in the discipline of sociology and the field of management, RSO also welcomes theoretical engagement that draws on other disciplinary conversations – such as those in political science or economics, as well as work from diverse philosophical traditions. RSO scholarship has helped push forward a plethora of theoretical conversations on institutions and institutional change, networks, practice, culture, power, inequality, social movements, categories, routines, organization design and change, configurational dynamics, and many other topics.

Each volume of RSO tends to be thematically focused on a particular empirical phenomenon (e.g., creative industries, multinational corporations, and entrepreneurship) or theoretical conversation (e.g., institutional logics, actors and agency, and microfoundations). The series publishes papers by junior as well as leading international scholars and embraces diversity on all dimensions. If you are scholar interested in organizations or organizing, I hope you find RSO to be an invaluable resource as you develop your work.

Professor Michael Lounsbury
Series Editor, *Research in the Sociology of Organizations*
Canada Research Chair in Entrepreneurship & Innovation
University of Alberta

# ACKNOWLEDGMENTS

When I reconnected with Michael Lounsbury, the series editor of *Research in the Sociology of Organizations,* to ask him whether I still have a GO to edit a volume on "Decolonizing Management and Organization Studies," his answer was: "Yes! Go Go Go! This is important!". I want to extend my sincere appreciation to Mike for having received his trust and for having given me the opportunity to edit this volume. I also want to thank all 48 contributors for their collaboration and the several steps they took to reach this achievement. I am grateful to the Swiss National Science Foundation for covering the book processing fees necessary to publish this volume open-access. I want to thank the anonymous reviewers and the end-to-end reviewers who commented and gave valuable feedback on each paper, helping to improve the quality of this volume. Furthermore, I want to express my gratitude to Ronja Federspiel, who helped me format the entire manuscript before its submission. Finally, special thanks also go to Chintan Kella, Adeelah Kodabux, Smita Ramloll, and Metkel Yosief for their support and listening when needed.

# EMBARKING ON A JOURNEY TOWARD DECOLONIZATION

Emamdeen Fohim

*University of Bern, Switzerland*

## ABSTRACT

*In this paper, I introduce the Decolonizing Management and Organization Studies (MOS) volume from the* Research in the Sociology of Organizations *series. This volume invites scholars to embark on a journey toward decolonization, aiming to correct knowledge shaped by colonial legacies through integrating perspectives from the colonized in pursuit of human emancipation and dignity for the common good. Created as a collaborative and reflective journey, the volume is based on an open dialogue among diverse MOS scholars from across the globe. By summarizing these contributions, I illustrate how they address the main aspects of decolonization and subsequently derive a provisional list of principles that I believe are essential for advancing this critical endeavor. I call on fellow scholars to engage with these insights and join us on this journey!*

**Keywords:** Decolonizing; impactful research; journey; knowledge production; management and organization studies

## INTRODUCTION

Antenór Firmin was a Haitian anthropologist who lived from 1850 to 1910. Raised in a working-class family in the first country in Latin America to achieve independence from European colonial rule, he became a member of the Paris

Decolonizing Management and Organization Studies: Why, How, and What
Research in the Sociology of Organizations, Volume 93, 1–14
ISSN: 0733-558X/doi:10.1108/S0733-558X20250000093001

Anthropology Society in 1884 (Fluehr-Lobban, 2005). Recognized as the first black anthropologist in the Western world (Joseph, 2021), Firmin can also be seen as a decolonization scholar (Allen & Jobson, 2016). Drawing from his upbringing in Haiti, he understood that decolonization – the undoing of colonialism – requires actions beyond the political to include other domains, such as science (Holley, 2024). In his book, *The Equality of the Human Races* (Firmin, 1885), Firmin challenged Arthur de Gobineau's (1853) *Essay on the Inequality of Human Races*, which sought to legitimize racism and slavery by proclaiming the superiority of the white race. Firmin deconstructed Gobineau's arguments by exposing the lack of empirical evidence behind them and emphasizing the contributions of pre-colonial Africa to civilization (Williams, 2014). His work thus epitomizes scholarship aiming to decolonize knowledge (Joseph, 2021): *In pursuit of human emancipation and dignity for the common good, introducing perspectives from the colonized to correct knowledge that has been shaped by colonial legacies.*

This notion of the "coloniality of knowledge" has been raised by Peruvian sociologist Anibal Quijano, among other scholars. Quijano (2007) argued that since the colonization of the Americas, the prevailing system of knowledge has been dominated by a Eurocentric paradigm that is based on a Cartesian subject-object divide and claims universal truth. He views this as a colonial legacy that perpetuates the exploitation of former colonial regions, such as Latin America and Africa. Similarly, scholars such as Said (1978) have explored how concepts like Orientalism are rooted in Eurocentric prejudices and biases established during colonial times, reinforcing a sense of Western superiority. In line with these arguments, Fanon (1952) addressed the psychological effects of colonialism on the colonized. Spivak (1988) elaborates on the term "epistemic violence" to highlight how a "coloniality of knowledge" can lead to indirect violence when ignoring subalterns' voices in the production of knowledge. Thus, the decolonization of knowledge must consider the lived experiences of colonized peoples and legitimize non-Eurocentric ontologies, epistemologies, and methodologies (Maldonado-Torres, 2007). This process also calls for transforming established academic norms and structures, such as the university itself (Joseph Mbembe, 2016).

Within Management and Organization Studies (MOS), these ideas have found acceptance, particularly among scholars from Critical Management Studies (CMS) (e.g., Bruton et al., 2022; Filatotchev et al., 2021; Ibarra-Colado, 2006; Jaya, 2001; Nkomo, 2011; Yousfi, 2021). They have examined a range of subjects, including the challenges faced by "periphery-based" scholars aiming to publish in top management journals (Barros & Alcadipani, 2023), the importance of political reflexivity when researching contexts affected by colonial violence (Abdelnour & Abu Moghli, 2021), the critical reassessment of theoretical concepts that perpetuate ethnocentric biases (Bothello et al., 2019), and the decolonization of business schools by creating intellectual spaces for Indigenous Peoples (Woods et al., 2022). In doing so, scholars have found that emancipatory measures extending beyond the embrace of non-Western contexts (Wickert et al., 2024) are necessary to overcome institutional barriers in academia that hamper the heterogenization of insights in MOS (Banerjee, 2021).

The decolonization of knowledge is not only a metaphor (Tuck & Yang, 2012); it embodies a political agenda (Abdelnour, 2022) while striving to achieve the fundamental scientific goals of creating, expanding, and correcting knowledge. Firmin's work exemplifies this by detailing the pre-colonial history of Africa – an account that not only delegitimizes the false notion of racial inequality but also offers a fuller depiction of the continent, countering the Eurocentric hegemony in knowledge production. In psychology, the concept of "WEIRD bias" critiques the predominance of theories derived from Western, educated, industrialized, rich, and democratic countries (Henrich et al., 2010). This bias is particularly problematic in our field that seeks to conduct impactful research (Wickert et al., 2021; Williams & Whiteman, 2021) for addressing grand challenges (Gümüsay et al., 2022; Seelos et al., 2023). As MOS scholars aiming to generate impactful knowledge on management and organizing, we must recognize that many of the current insights are limited to the Western sphere. Decolonizing MOS is thus an urgent imperative for all scholars within the discipline.

This volume of *Research in the Sociology of Organizations* (RSO) on Decolonizing MOS is an invitation to all MOS scholars to join in the journey toward decolonization, with the aim of creating impactful knowledge that contributes to universal dignity and the common good. In this volume, we endeavor to explain *why* decolonizing our discipline is needed, to provide ideas on *how* we, as scholars, can approach this task, and to discuss *what* aspects should be decolonized in academia. We view the decolonization of MOS not merely as a niche area for a small number of experts but as a reflective journey among all interested scholars. As illustrated by Mauritian artist Evan Sohun (www.evansohun.com) in Fig. 1, created specifically for this publication, this volume seeks to initiate a dialogue among the community of scholars (represented by the four figures in the illustration). This dialogue aims to critically reflect on entrenched academic institutions, norms, and rules (depicted as square boxes in the upper right of the image). Our goal is to redirect the flow of our field (symbolized by the river on the bottom right) toward new institutions that contain fresh and creative norms and rules while considering old elements where needed (depicted as the modified boxes in the form of a briefcase and the stairs at the bottom). In this introductory paper, I outline how this volume was created in the spirit of a reflective journey, the ways in which it can be read through this lens, and how we, as scholars, can continue to move forward along this path.

## ESTABLISHING THE VOLUME AS A JOURNEY

When developing this RSO volume, we committed ourselves to the idea of a reflective journey promoting open dialogue among a variety of MOS scholars while meeting on equal footing. We acknowledge that our efforts were not flawless, and setbacks formed this process, too. For instance, because the RSO is an English-language publication, the contributors had to know English, excluding other scholars. Furthermore, most contributors were affiliated with universities,

*Fig. 1.* **"Passarelle" by Evan Sohun**.

thus excluding other people who could have contributed equally to this discussion. Nevertheless, in our pursuit of an inclusive approach toward decolonization, we made concerted efforts to diversify our contributor base. This included incorporating the work of scholars from different parts of the world, though we acknowledge that we still fall short of capturing the cultural diversity of global society. Our efforts also included welcoming scholars from different stages of their careers, from PhD students to seasoned scholars, and embraced scholars with a range of views on what the decolonization of MOS might entail. We also included scholars at different stages of engagement with decolonization, from those newly encountering the literature to those deeply familiar with it.

Some might question our inclusion of less experienced voices in this debate, as well as scholars immersed in the Western academic tradition, which may seem disconnected from decolonizing efforts. However, I contend that if we want to effect institutional change in academia, we must invite all scholars on this journey regardless of their academic or cultural socialization, while being aware this approach might cause some to prefer staying away from this project. In my view, genuine transformation begins only when we engage in dialogue, see the humanity behind each other's arguments, are open to listening to each other, and take others' perspectives into account. By establishing such a dialogue, we aimed to foster what Mignolo (2000) describes as "border thinking," a practice that involves learning from and experiencing other forms of knowing, thinking, and becoming. What can unite us, in the words of Gümüsay (2023), is a shared commitment to conduct impactful research and a recognition that our current approaches allow us to understand only a fraction of the world and perpetuate a colonial legacy that contradicts our goals. This shared commitment and awareness encouraged the contributors to this volume to courageously and collectively embark on the journey toward decolonization, learning, and advancing together.

To move as contributors along this journey, we prioritized an open dialogue while developing this volume. We organized two rounds of online workshops in which all contributors could present their initial ideas and drafts to their peers, accommodating different time zones to facilitate participation. These meetings provided an opportunity for participants to learn from each other by exchanging cultural understandings and different approaches to decolonization in scholarship and knowledge production more broadly. Furthermore, many papers in the volume were collaboratively written by a diverse team of authors, enabling lively internal dialogues. Lastly, the first drafts of all papers were read and commented on by anonymous external reviewers, many of whom are experts in the literature on decolonizing MOS. This valuable feedback helped the authors refine their perspectives and reflect on their previous assumptions about academia.

## READING THE VOLUME AS A JOURNEY

This volume of the RSO series has been designed to provide readers with the experience of embarking on a journey toward the decolonization of MOS. To reach a global audience, we have made the volume available as an open-access publication. We extend our gratitude to the Swiss National Science Foundation for covering the book processing fees necessary for this open-access initiative.

We begin by laying out the basics and taking stock of the literature on decolonizing MOS (Section I). We then discuss the reasons *why* decolonization is imperative for our discipline (Section II), *how* this might be done (Section III), and *what* aspects of academia need decolonization (Section IV). The volume concludes with three explorations inviting further discussion on continuing this important work (Section V). Below, I summarize each paper and subsequently illustrate how we, as scholars, can move forward on this journey.

### Section I: Opening

Lounsbury (2025) opens the volume by introducing the concept of "Decolonizing Ourselves." By elaborating on his personal story as the son of a Palestinian refugee, he outlines the institutional constraints somebody can experience when one's background is associated with a stigmatized identity. Through decolonizing ourselves, he exemplifies that we can learn and understand what the debate on decolonizing MOS can mean for ourselves as a starting point for broadening the discussion. As he points out, many of us have stories of dispossession and exploitation, more or less proximate. He thus calls on the scholarly community to work on this topic together and to find ways that allow for institutional change in our field.

The second paper of this volume, by Seremani and Bazana (2025), take stock of the literature on decolonizing MOS and then proposing future directions. The authors identify four main streams of decolonization thought, each associated with certain geographic regions: (i) postcolonial studies and postcolonialism emerging from Southeast Asia and the Middle East; (ii) neo-colonialism and African perspectives; (iii) decoloniality from Latin America, and (iv) Indigenous perspectives. Advocating for a forward-looking approach, Seremani and Bazana suggest acknowledging the different perspectives of decolonial approaches by integrating hybridity. They propose knowledge production that allows a "mixture of what existed before and after colonization." They emphasize revising epistemology and methodology to find new forms of knowledge production. Recognizing the importance of intersectionality, they argue for a deeper consideration of how multiple forms of discrimination intersect and interact. Lastly, they call on scholars to work as an academic community to develop "practical strategies for decolonizing MOS.

### Section II: Why Should We Decolonize Management and Organization Studies?

In the second section of this volume, Nagaraj and Yao (2025) explore the reasons for decolonizing MOS. Using a machine-learning approach that incorporates natural language processing (NLP), they analyze the geographical origins and focus of academic articles published in six leading management journals. Their findings show a persistent Western-centric bias in MOS despite frequent claims of increasing diversity. The evidence they provide shows several substantial disparities: (i) only 15% of the studies were conducted in the context of a middle- or low-income country; (ii) as many as 67% of the articles were authored by teams based entirely in the United States (US); and (iii) the US remains one of the most frequently studied contexts, even by researchers outside the country. Their findings suggest that knowledge production if it is to be truly impactful beyond the

Western sphere, requires fundamental institutional changes like those discussed by decolonization scholars.

James et al. (2025) further explore the imperative for decolonizing entrepreneurship studies. Contrary to the prevalent economic focus in Western entrepreneurship literature, the authors propose understanding entrepreneurship as a universal human desire to discover and innovate by evolving from the old. They argue that Western theories may not fit the needs of Indigenous people. To address this, the authors suggest opening both eyes by combining elements of existing entrepreneurship insights with Indigenous knowledge. Through examples of Indigenous conceptual frameworks, they shed light on alternative models of entrepreneurship that are effective in Indigenous contexts. They emphasize how collaborating with Indigenous people on equal footing can lead to knowledge that finally matters for the communities – an approach they understand as a "moral imperative to redress harms of colonization."

Driven by a similar ambition, Auerbach Jahajeeah et al. (2025) argue that conducting impactful research to address today's grand challenges – such as climate change, digitalization, and conflicts – requires the decolonization of research partnerships. Introducing the concepts of the "minority world" (covering regions usually viewed as the West) and the "majority world" (covering regions traditionally referred to as the Global South), they highlight the discrepancy that, while grand challenges are universal, the knowledge typical used to tackle them mostly originates from minority world scholars. For this reason, they call for rethinking research partnerships and provide examples of how inclusive partnerships among minority and majority world scholars could be designed. Drawing on their own experiences, they describe a process for developing such partnerships that evolves from ignorance to awareness and integration, ultimately leading to elevation.

### Section III: How Can We Decolonize Management and Organization Studies?

Chrispal (2025) continues the thoughts on decolonizing MOS by critically examining how research practices might be complicit in perpetuating epistemic violence, particularly when working with often silenced and marginalized people. Reflecting on her fieldwork with women in India who have faced gendered violence, she realized the risk of epistemic violence inherent in applying research standards from the Global North to a Global South context. Chrispal shows how standards of ensuring safe spaces during interviews, anonymizing interview participants, adhering to strict interview protocols and procedures, and translating interviews must be adapted so that they function ethically when working with marginalized people. While she stops short of providing a one-size-fits-all methodological toolkit, she urges MOS scholars to be reflective when conducting research in such critical contexts to ensure they do not inadvertently cause harm.

Considering that decolonizing knowledge requires understanding people's lived experiences, Uda (2025) introduces phenomenology as a methodological approach, focusing on the first-person perspective to understand how people experience a phenomenon. Uda outlines which ingredients of this approach differ from those of a positivist one, emphasizing how, instead of objectivity, phenomenology strives for intersubjectivity. Using the Japanese workplace concept of *sasshi* – anticipating others' intentions even if they do not communicate them explicitly – as an example, Uda demonstrates how phenomenology can deliver insights within cultural contexts that might initially be unfamiliar to researchers. Thus, phenomenology can serve not only as an approach to deepening understanding without Western lenses but also as a means to challenge and expand MOS theories beyond Western paradigms, contributing to the decolonization of knowledge.

Ginting-Szczesny et al. (2025) further develop this phenomenological approach by conceptualizing place within a specific geographic context. Through their research with home-based women entrepreneurs in rural Central Java, Indonesia, they discovered how "home as a place" is experienced and shaped differently compared to European and North American contexts. The authors show the importance of taking context seriously and provide examples of how this can be done. In doing so, they demonstrate how a phenomenology of place can help avoid the use of Western standards to understand non-Western forms of being, doing, and knowing. Their work calls for the adoption of place-sensitive research methods to prevent epistemic violence and to facilitate the integration of non-Western knowledge and perspectives into MOS theories.

### Section IV: What Aspects of Management and Organization Studies Should Be Decolonized?

In Section IV of this volume, Henry (2025) addresses the need to decolonize institutional arrangements within academia and the field of MOS. She identifies the curriculum as a critical area for decolonization, drawing on her experiences in developing a Māori Indigenous Business minor. By providing a brief historical overview from the Māori perspective, Henry reminds us of the harm done to the Indigenous population and the negative consequences it has had on maintaining local knowledge. Thanks to the newly established program, traditional Māori knowledge (mātauranga) is now taught by aligning it with traditional pedagogy (akonga). Henry attributes the successful implementation of the minor to several factors: strategic academic leadership, the engagement of Māori Indigenous expertise, and consultation with the target communities. She concludes that while the decolonization of knowledge in academia cannot be fully achieved overnight, substantial progress can be achieved by changing the university curriculum.

In turn, Asiedu et al. (2025) examine the role of education in decolonizing MOS through virtual exchange courses connecting students from Global South and Global North contexts. They reflect on the process of designing their joint course "Public Sector Management, Reforms, and Innovation," which connected master's students from the University of Botswana and the University of Bern. Using an Ubuntu framework (Dennis et al., 2018) as an analytical lens, they assessed the decolonializing potential of their educational approach. The authors conclude that such courses can uphold high standards and resemble an epistemological "Third Space" as described by Seremani and Clegg (2016), allowing the coexistence of different worldviews through dialogue. However, these courses also face the challenge of the predominance of Anglocentric knowledge in the field. Thus, while a virtual exchange course is not a complete solution for decolonizing MOS, it can represent an important step toward this goal.

Zoogah et al. (2025) discuss the role of academic journals when decolonizing MOS. They argue that the decolonization of knowledge has several dimensions that affect how journals are designed, governed, and structured. By detailing how the Africa Journal of Management (AJOM), a publication of the Africa Academy of Management (AFAM), was established, the authors illustrate the ways in which a journal can contribute to epistemic pluralism, valuing different forms of knowing. In line with Escobar's (2020) idea of "pluriversal politics", they describe AJOM's approach to fostering pluriversal collaboration through the creation of spaces that "accept different ontological understandings to forge a pluriversal management research agenda." Zoogah, Nkomo, and Kiggundu argue that such a strategy can contribute to the decolonization of MOS journals as the process of "decolonization is not isolated but a collaborative effort with scholars both in and outside Africa."

Lastly, Kondayya et al. (2025) address the relevance of scholarly dialogues such as conferences in the decolonization of MOS. They outline how the institutional arrangements of most MOS conferences perpetuate the colonization of knowledge by serving as barriers to access, such as high registration fees and restrictive visa regimes. Drawing inspiration from selected Indigenous perspectives for scholarly dialogue and learning, the authors propose a 6-R framework to reimagine MOS conferencing. They suggest building conferences around the principles of *Representation, Relationality, Responsibility, Reciprocity, Reflexivity, and Respect*. Through this framework, they seek to clarify how a "Third Space" (Bhabha, 1994) can be designed to give equal voice to all actors, allowing genuine epistemic pluralism. The authors also aim to create awareness among the MOS community to launch practical institutional change regarding conferencing.

*Section V: Further Explorations*

Barin Cruz et al. (2025) draw upon the other papers in this RSO volume to reflect on their own research practices when engaging in market-based approaches to poverty alleviation. They critique a purely decolonial evaluative approach in MOS for addressing power asymmetries without providing impactful solutions. They propose instead a reflexive pragmatist approach consisting of four elements when engaging and collaborating with local actors during research projects: (i) adopting a place-based approach, (ii) engaging in iterative co-construction, (iii) experimenting together, and (iv) learning and scaling. Through this approach, people conducting research in formerly colonized contexts can incrementally change power structures from the bottom up, creating and correcting knowledge to promote human emancipation and dignity.

Arjaliès et al. (2025) sat in a circle to share their research experiences about bringing the colonized and the colonizers together. A critical insight they gained is that "decolonizing is a succession of new beginnings": Each experience is unique, providing an opportunity to relearn and an invitation to sense and sense-make the space-time continuum. The space-time continuum is what they define as the understanding of Indigenous partners' experienced past injustices to find new ways to correct them. They thus conclude that decolonization is a practice in the continuum of space and time, encompassing and reexperiencing the land, the body, the ethics, and the politics: The land that holds us humans together, the body allowing us to see the land holistically, the ethics to ensure respectful interactions with Indigenous partners to begin the politics and political processes again.

At the end of the volume, Kella et al. (2025) remind us that all discussions and literature on decolonization will remain a metaphor (Tuck & Yang, 2012) if we as an academic community do not act. They thus conclude the volume with Toward "a Charta," an invitation to all scholars to recognize and rectify "the complicity of educational and scholarly practices in sustaining colonial structures." They provide a checklist for assessing power imbalances and needs for decoloniza-tion, as well as seven principles for MOS scholars to be aware of and act upon: (i) revising theoretical foundations, (ii) furthering epistemic justice, (iii) adopting ethics of respect and de-anthropocentrism, (iv) ensuring resources and collabo-ration, (v) establishing global networks and accountability, (vi) fostering educa-tional transformation, and (vii) committing to cultural sensitivity. They conclude the volume by a call to join them in the suggested transformative agenda.

# CONCLUSION

In this introductory paper for the RSO volume on Decolonizing MOS, I have argued that we, as MOS scholars, must embark on a journey toward decoloni-zation, recognizing that top management journals produce primarily Western, Anglocentric knowledge and the current body of knowledge in our discipline is limited in its capacity to understand the world beyond the West. To conduct impactful research capable of tackling grand challenges, we need to expand our knowledge of management and organizing beyond that produced by minority world scholars. To do so, we must open both eyes to draw upon and create knowl-edge that serves Indigenous communities and others outside the Western sphere. We must reconsider existing practices in our discipline that perpetuate epistemic violence, and we must strive for fair cross-cultural collaborations that respect first-person perspectives and are sensitive to local contexts. We also must rethink our university curricula, experiment with new teaching formats to foster cross-border and cross-cultural exchanges, redesign journals and their governance structures, and reconfigure scholarly platforms such as conferences. We must change institu-tional practices in our daily work and institutional arrangements to promote an academic environment that produces knowledge reflective of epistemic pluralism.

But how can we, as scholars, embark on and continue this journey? Drawing on insights gained from the papers in this volume and experiences gained in its compilation, I propose a provisional set of five principles to help guide us:

*Engage in pluriversal and cross-cultural conversations.* Zoogah et al. (2025) clarify that "decolonization is not isolated but a collaborative effort." We should, therefore, break out of our professional and social bubbles and engage in spaces where we can encounter scholars from different backgrounds. We should see this as an opportunity to gain new perspectives and learn from each other, allowing us to broaden our horizons. New kinds of research partnerships (Auerbach Jahajeeah et al., 2025) and amended forms of conferencing (Kondayya et al., 2025) can serve as platforms for pluriversal and cross-cultural conversations.

*Attempt to be empathic and see the Others' perspectives.* Lounsbury (2025) calls for integrating the 'Other(ed)' perspectives in our work and being open to distinct ontologies and epistemologies. We should, therefore, ensure that we are sensitized to recognizing new forms of being, doing, and knowing by opening both eyes (James et al., 2025). We should be empathic, not judgmental, and find ways to see phenomena (Uda, 2025) and places (Ginting-Szczesny et al., 2025) from the perspectives of Others.

*Remain critical and reflective.* Arjaliès et al. (2025) shows how decolonization requires a sensitive and self-critical mindset for recognizing the perpetuation of harm coming from colonial legacies. For this reason, we must be reflective, particularly when working with marginalized people (Chrispal, 2025). If we are not reflective and do not actively seek alternative methodologies in data collection or collaboration, we risk complicity in perpetuating epistemic violence.

*Invest time and effort.* Henry (2025) demonstrates that developing a new institution to decolonize MOS – a Māori Indigenous Business minor – is time-consuming. Likewise, the establishment of this volume was not a straightforward journey but equally marked with setbacks and detours. We must be prepared to dedicate substantial time and effort to develop and implement new practices in research, teaching, and the dissemination of MOS insights if we genuinely want to create impactful knowledge and address the biased outputs produced by today's system (Nagaraj & Yao, 2025).

*Make use of virtuality and connectivity.* Asiedu et al. (2025) demonstrated the power of virtual exchange in their course connecting students from Botswana and Switzerland. While not a substitute for on-site exchanges, today's digital communication tools can indeed create "Third Spaces" (Bhabha, 1994), in which people with different worldviews can meet to engage in dialogue on equal footing. We also used these virtual tools to compile this volume, recognizing their potential to facilitate listening and learning across diverse perspectives.

In conclusion, we invite you to build on this provisional list of principles, engage with this RSO volume, and join us on the journey toward decolonization, contributing to human emancipation and upholding the dignity of people worldwide for the common good.

# REFERENCES

Abdelnour, S. (2022). What decolonizing is not. *M@n@gement*, *25*(4), 81–82.

Abdelnour, S., & Abu Moghli, M. (2021). Researching violent contexts: A call for political reflexivity. *Organization*, *0*(0), 1–24.

Allen, J. S., & Jobson, R. C. (2016). The decolonizing generation: (Race and) theory in anthropology since the eighties. *Current anthropology*, *57*(2), 129–148.

Arjaliès, D.-L., Bernard, J., Branzei, O., Cezarino, L., Cutcher, L., Fiske, L., Jenkins, T., Liboni, L., Stocco, L., & Suruí, G. (2025). Decolonizing as an ever beginning. In E. Fohim (Ed.), *Decolonizing management and organization studies: Why, how, and what (Research in the Sociology of Organizations)* (pp. 247–252). Emerald Group Publishing Limited.

Asiedu, M., Mpabanga, D., Jacobs, C. D., & Lekorwe, M. (2025). Decolonizing through virtual exchanges? Reflections on an educational experiment between Botswana and Switzerland. In E. Fohim (Ed.), *Decolonizing management and organization studies: Why, how, and what (Research in the Sociology of Organizations)* (pp. 173–189). Emerald Group Publishing Limited.

Auerbach Jahajeeah, J., Gümüsay, A. A., Salvi, E., von Richthofen, G., & Kekana, L. (2025). Grand challenges, decoloniality and management scholarship. In E. Fohim (Ed.), *Decolonizing management and organization studies: Why, how, and what (Research in the Sociology of Organizations)* (pp. 83–101). Emerald Group Publishing Limited.

Banerjee, S. B. (2021). Decolonizing management theory: A critical perspective. *Journal of Management Studies*, *59*(4), 1074–1087.

Barin Cruz, L., Zietsma, C., Delgado, N. A., & Smet, S. D. (2025). At the risk of not being decolonial enough. In E. Fohim (Ed.), *Decolonizing management and organization studies: Why, how, and what (Research in the Sociology of Organizations)* (pp. 231–245). Emerald Group Publishing Limited.

Barros, A., & Alcadipani, R. (2023). Decolonizing journals in management and organizations? Epistemological colonial encounters and the double translation. *Management Learning*, *54*(4), 576–586.

Bhabha, H. K. (1994). *The location of culture*. Routledge.

Bothello, J., Nason, R. S., & Schnyder, G. (2019). Institutional voids and organization studies: Towards an epistemological rupture. *Organization Studies*, *40*(10), 1499–1512.

Bruton, G. D., Zahra, S. A., Van de Ven, A. H., & Hitt, M. A. (2022). Indigenous theory uses, abuses, and future. *Journal of Management Studies*, *59*(4), 1057–1073.

Chrispal, S. (2025). Reducing epistemic violence in the pursuit of organization studies through reflective praxis: Some reflections. In E. Fohim (Ed.), *Decolonizing management and organization studies: Why, how, and what (Research in the Sociology of Organizations)* (pp. 105–118). Emerald Group Publishing Limited.

Dennis, A. C. (2018). Decolonising education: A pedagogic intervention in Bhambra et al. (2018). *Decolonizing the University*, 190–207.

Escobar, A. (2020). *Pluriversal politics: The real and the possible*. Duke University Press.

Fanon, F. (1952). *Black skin, white masks*. Pluto.

Filatotchev, I., Ireland, R. D., & Stahl, G. K. (2021). Contextualizing management research: An open systems perspective. *Journal of Management Studies*, *59*(4), 1036–1056.

Firmin, A. (1885). *De l'egalité des races humaines (anthropologie positive)*. Librairie Cotillon.

Fluehr-Lobban, C. (2005). Anténor Firmin and Haiti's contribution to anthropology. *Gradhiva. Revue d'anthropologie et d'histoire des arts*, (1), 95–108.

Ginting-Szczesny, B. A., Ginting-Carlström, C. E., Kibler, E., & Chliova, M. (2025). Taking context seriously through a phenomenology of place: An illustration of home-based work. In E. Fohim (Ed.), *Decolonizing management and organization studies: Why, how, and what (Research in the Sociology of Organizations)* (pp. 137–153). Emerald Group Publishing Limited.

Gobineau, A. (1853). *Essai sur l'inégalité des races humaines*. Librairie de F. Didot frères.

Gümüsay, A. A. (2023). Management Scholars of the World, Unite!. *Organization Studies*, *44*(8), 1377–1380.

Gümüsay, A. A., Marti, E., Trittin-Ulbrich, H., & Wickert, C. (2022). *Organizing for societal grand challenges* (p. 320). Emerald Publishing.

Henrich, J., Heine, S. J., & Norenzayan, A. (2010). Beyond WEIRD: Towards a broad-based behavioral science. *Behavioral and Brain Sciences*, *33*(2–3), 111.

Henry, E. (2025). Mātauranga Māori: A case of incorporating indigenous Māori Knowledge in a Business School Minor. In E. Fohim (Ed.), *Decolonizing management and organization studies: Why, how, and what (Research in the Sociology of Organizations)* (pp. 157–172). Emerald Group Publishing Limited.

Holley, J. (2024). Racial equality and anticolonial solidarity: Anténor Firmin's Global Haitian Liberalism. *American Political Science Review, 118*(1), 304–317.

Ibarra-Colado, E. (2006). Organization studies and epistemic coloniality in Latin America: Thinking otherness from the margins. *Organization, 13*(4), 463–488.

James, A. E., Salamzadeh, A., & Dana, L.P. (2025). Decolonizing entrepreneurship: Time to open both eyes. In E. Fohim (Ed.), *Decolonizing management and organization studies: Why, how, and what (Research in the Sociology of Organizations)* (pp. 65–82). Emerald Group Publishing Limited.

Jaya, P. S. (2001). Do we really 'know' and 'profess'? Decolonizing management knowledge. *Organization, 8*(2), 227–233.

Joseph Mbembe, A. (2016). Decolonizing the university: New directions. *Arts and Humanities in Higher Education, 15*(1), 29–45.

Joseph, C. L. (2021). Introduction: Firmin, Global History, and the End of Race. In *Reconstructing the social sciences and humanities* (pp. 1–8). Routledge.

Kella, C., Khilji, S. E., Hedberg, L., Williams, M., & Imbrogiano, J.-P. (2025). Toward "A Charta". In E. Fohim (Ed.), *Decolonizing management and organization studies: Why, how, and what (Research in the Sociology of Organizations)* (pp. 253–263). Emerald Group Publishing Limited.

Kondayya, A., Fohim, E., & Höllerer, M. A. (2025). Curating *open* academic fora: Reimagining institutional arrangements for scholarly dialogue and exchange. In E. Fohim (Ed.), *Decolonizing management and organization studies: Why, how, and what (Research in the Sociology of Organizations)* (pp. 209–227). Emerald Group Publishing Limited.

Lounsbury, M. (2025). Decolonizing ourselves. In Emamdeen Fohim (Ed.), *Decolonizing management and organization studies: Why, how, and what (Research in the Sociology of Organizations)* (pp. 17–22). Emerald Group Publishing Limited.

Maldonado-Torres, N. (2007). On the coloniality of being: Contributions to the development of a concept. *Cultural studies, 21*(2–3), 240–270.

Mignolo, W. J. (2000). *Local histories/global designs: Essays on the coloniality of power, subaltern knowledges and border thinking*. Princeton University Press.

Nagaraj, A., & Yao, H. (2025). Geographic inequality in management scholarship: Data-driven estimates and trends. In E. Fohim (Ed.), *Decolonizing management and organization studies: Why, how, and what (Research in the Sociology of Organizations)* (pp. 39–64). Emerald Group Publishing Limited.

Nkomo, S. M. (2011). A postcolonial and anti-colonial reading of 'African' leadership and management in organization studies: Tensions, contradictions and possibilities. *Organization, 18*(3), 365–386.

Quijano, A. (2007). Coloniality and modernity/rationality. *Cultural studies, 21*(2–3), 168–178.

Said, E. (1978). *Orientalism: Western Conceptions of the Orient*. Penguin.

Seelos, C., Mair, J., & Traeger, C. (2023). The future of grand challenges research: Retiring a hopeful concept and endorsing research principles. *International Journal of Management Reviews, 25*(2), 251–269.

Seremani, T., & Bazana, S. (2025). In Emamdeen Fohim (Ed.), *Decolonizing management and organization studies: Why, how, and what (Research in the Sociology of Organizations)* (pp. 23–36). Emerald Group Publishing Limited.

Seremani, T. W., & Clegg, S. (2016). Postcolonialism, organization, and management theory: the role of "epistemological third spaces". *Journal of Management Inquiry, 25*(2), 171–183.

Spivak, G. C. (1988). Can the subaltern speak? In P. Williams & L. Chrisman (Eds.), *Colonial discourse and post-colonial theory* (pp. 66–111). Colombia University Press.

Tuck, E. & Yang, K.W. (2012). Decolonization is not a metaphor. *Decolonization: Indigeneity, Education & Society, 1*(1), 1–40.

Uda, T. (2025). Access to the local lived experiences: A phenomenological approach to decolonize management and organization studies. In E. Fohim (Ed.), *Decolonizing management and organization studies: Why, how, and what (Research in the Sociology of Organizations)* (pp. 119–135). Emerald Group Publishing Limited.

Wickert, C., Post, C., Doh, J. P., Prescott, J. E., & Prencipe, A. (2021). Management research that makes a difference: Broadening the meaning of impact. *Journal of Management Studies*, *58*(2), 297–320.

Wickert, C., Potočnik, K., Prashantham, S., Shi, W., & Snihur, Y. (2024). Embracing non-Western contexts in management scholarship. *Journal of Management Studies*.

Williams, G. (2014). Deconstructing pseudo-scientific anthropology: Antenor Firmin and the reconceptualization of African humanity. *The Journal of Pan African Studies*, *7*(2), 9–32.

Williams, A., & Whiteman, G. (2021). A call for deep engagement for impact: Addressing the planetary emergency. *Strategic Organization*, *19*(3), 526–537.

Woods, C., Dell, K., & Carroll, B. (2022). Decolonizing the business school: Reconstructing the entrepreneurship classroom through indigenizing pedagogy and learning. *Academy of Management Learning & Education*, *21*(1), 82–100.

Yousfi, H. (2021). Decolonizing Arab organizational knowledge:"Fahlawa" as a research practice. *Organization*, *28*(5), 836–856.

Zoogah, B. D., Nkomo, S. M., & Kiggundu, M. N. (2025). The role of *Africa Journal of Management* in decolonizing management and organization studies. In E. Fohim (Ed.), *Decolonizing management and organization studies: Why, how, and what (Research in the Sociology of Organizations)* (pp. 191–207). Emerald Group Publishing Limited.

# SECTION I
# OPENING

# DECOLONIZING OURSELVES

## Michael Lounsbury

*University of Alberta, Canada*

## ABSTRACT

*Over the past decade, conversations about decolonizing management and organization studies have grown tremendously in scale and scope. In this brief reflective essay, I explore the idea of decolonizing ourselves as an important way we can foster further dialogue and understanding, and hopefully lay the groundwork for more profound and progressive institutional change. I tell a personal story, as a son of a Palestinian refugee, that sketches the suffering journey of my mother, Violet Barakat, and how that has shaped me and my struggle to figure out what decolonization might mean for me. I hope my story further broadens our dialogue on decolonization to enable more voices, accounts, and stories to be heard, and contributes to our effort as a scholarly community to decolonize management and organization studies.*

**Keywords:** Decolonization; dialogue; management; organization studies; Palestine

Emamdeen Fohim invited me, in my capacity as the series editor of Research in the Sociology of Organizations, to consider writing a short reflection piece on the challenges of decolonizing management and organization studies. While I was initially reluctant to do so, I have agreed mainly because of the encouragement of

Decolonizing Management and Organization Studies: Why, How, and What
Research in the Sociology of Organizations, Volume 93, 17–22
ISSN: 0733-558X/doi:10.1108/S0733-558X20250000093002

many colleagues and friends, and my firm belief that the theme and the volume is critically important. I am certainly no expert on decolonization and decolonizing studies, and I am fully cognizant that I am somewhat naively wading into potentially hazardous terrain, and that there is no way for me to string together words that will not be objectionable, perhaps fiercely objectionable, to some people.

I understand decolonizing as going beyond achieving independence of colonized peoples, comprising variegated efforts to address profound problems related to colonial institutions and broader economic, cultural, and psychological maladies created by various forms of colonialism – past and present (e.g., Tuck & Yang, 2012). This includes the structural inequalities that have been created and exacerbated by capitalism and modern corporations that have been made possible by various forms of ongoing violence and appropriation, including slavery. This has resulted in growing poverty, especially in the Global South with many people left with limited access to basic amenities such as water, sanitation, health care, and education. Many have argued that universities have also perpetuated colonization intellectually via the marginalization of Indigenous peoples, as well as non-Western worldviews, knowledge, and pedagogies (e.g., Banerjee & Prasad, 2008). To address this, Smith (2012) and others have emphasized that decolonizing research, scholarship, and education requires efforts to valorize concerns and world views of non-Western individuals and collectives, and respectfully knowing and understanding theory and research from previously "Other(ed)" perspectives.

I believe that to make progress as a community of educators and scholars, we should be inviting a broader and honest dialogue on this topic – to educate each other and enroll sympathetic others as allies across the academy. While many of us may be willing to support decolonization as an abstract institutional project that aims to uplift marginalized or oppressed peoples around the globe (but see Simpson, 2016), it remains unclear to me how this project should, and could, go forward in a concrete way, and what the implications are for extant institutions and people. Even more profoundly, decolonization implies to me the need for deep subjective reflection about how colonially-inflected epistemologies, languages, institutions, and processes have co-constituted all of us, sometimes in violent ways (e.g., Thiong'o, 1986). Given that these subjective understandings and ways of being also undergird the very institutions that we study, and within which we are embedded, and acknowledging the need for this to be changed, I would like to briefly explore the notion of decolonizing ourselves – which might perhaps be understood as a form of personal emancipation, but that I also believe is a precondition for the kinds of emancipatory institutional changes we seek to promulgate (see, e.g., Fanon, 1967). I will tell a personal story – my story – as a vehicle for exploration.

I am a Palestinian American who has also become a Canadian citizen. While I now enjoy the privileges associated with the bourgeois life of a senior academic in North America, and am probably mostly perceived as a middle-aged "white guy," the Palestinian in me has recently been awakened. My mother, Violet Barakat, was a Palestinian refugee, whose family was forcibly removed from their house in Jerusalem by British soldiers in 1948 when she was 6. In the early 1950s, my mother and her family were able to escape to upstate New York thanks to a local church who sponsored them and helped set them up with a place to live. They were poor refugees who were stigmatized and struggled to survive. Palestine was in the process of erasure and was not recognized by the American government – the official papers for Violet and her family actually indicated that they came from Jordan.

As a teenager in a new country, Violet sought to break away from at least two forms of oppression: the stigma of being Palestinian as well as that of being a young woman in a patriarchal Arabic family. Against parental wishes, Violet both went to college and married an American man – these were major cultural transgressions. Before I was born, Violet taught Latin and art at a high school. When I came along, we lived in a trailer. We were poor, my father worked two jobs, and we had governmental aid in the form of food stamps to be able to eat. As I grew up, Violet told me stories of trauma from her childhood in the "old" country, and the struggles she endured in the "new" country. I heard from her stories that everyone is out to get me, and in retrospect, it seems that every effort was made to ensure my brother and I were more assimilated into North American culture for the hope for a better life. I did experience communal gatherings with our extended Arabic family, only limitedly learning the language, but very much enjoying the food. Nonetheless, much effort was made to keep distance from that family, and, in a sense, break away. To "purify" (Douglas, 1966).

In my teens, Violet became afflicted with rheumatoid arthritis, slowly and painfully declining, and tragically died at age 52 during a failed liver transplant operation. A lifetime of suffering. She lives on inside of me, and inculcated in me a great deal of resilience. But, as I grew up, my Palestinian identity remained largely hidden. In retrospect, I think Violet believed it was a liability.

Of course, I grew up learning about and watching the ongoing struggles of Palestinian people. But it seemed so very far away. Depersonalized. Even though there has been such a massive diaspora over the years, with Palestinians now living all over the world, I never felt a strong sense of Palestinian community. However, in recent years, something has changed. A few years ago now, my good friend, Tammar Zilber, invited me to a conference at Hebrew University where she works. It was my first time in Jerusalem. It was a profound experience in many ways – walking the streets where my family once lived. Seeing Palestinian ghettos and marginality. Thinking about all the pain and suffering that has occurred in that land. And then, in 2023, I became transfixed by the shock and horror of the initial Hamas attack on Israelis, and then the resultant Israeli invasion of Gaza which some have labeled a genocidal effort (Short, 2016), with more than 64,000 people (more than half of which were women, children and those over the age of 65) killed between October 7, 2023 and June 30, 2024 according to a recent study by Jamaluddine et al. (2025). As I write this in January 2025, there is a nascent truce that I pray enables a more lasting peace, many more people are feared dead, and much of the infrastructure has been annihilated including most of the educational and healthcare infrastructure.

Last summer at EGOS 2024 in Milan, I had the pleasure of meeting and listening to Zahira Jaser, a Professor at the University of Sussex Business School, give a talk that elaborated on the provocative essay she published in the *Financial Times* entitled, "Coming out as Palestinian." Her words resonated with me. She writes:

> I am Palestinian and Italian, with fair skin, blue eyes and a slight Italian accent. I am not "obviously" Palestinian – many people think I am European when they meet me – so it did feel like a coming out. Do not misunderstand me, being Palestinian is one of the greatest honours of my life. But it can feel like a highly stigmatised identity, reinforced by racist assumptions. This is a reality lived by many Palestinians. (Jaser, 2024, p. 14)

She detailed aspects of Palestinian discrimination, and how she felt the need to proclaim and express her Palestinian identity more pointedly.

I found Zahira to be brave and inspiring; at the same time, my teenage daughter was also amidst a more profound search for her own identity, prompting me with questions and concerns about all the killing and destruction, as well as the silencing of Palestinian voices and protests. Coterminously, many colleges and universities including mine forcibly shut down and removed Palestinian encampment protests (e.g., Kent, 2024). It is amidst all of this that I also began reading about and thinking about decolonization, and began to contemplate how my biographical journey has been imprinted by colonialism. This has left me tied up in knots – at different times, I have felt confused, depressed, fearful, filled with guilt, empowered, paralyzed…

I despise all forms of racism and discrimination – those against the Jewish people (i.e., antisemitism in all its forms) and those against Arabs in general and Palestinians in particular. But I remain deeply troubled by the globally supported efforts to erase Palestine and silence Palestinian voices. While some have referred to this as part of an ongoing settler-colonial process (see, e.g., Cavanaugh & Veracini, 2020), I am sympathetic to the argument that such labeling may do more harm than good if we aim to create a more progressive and peaceful world (Kirsch, 2024). Perhaps less inflammatory is to acknowledge that this is a complicated historical process that was enabled by colonial powers, and marked by the Balfour Declaration in 1917, the "Nakba" at the conclusion of World War II, and ongoing conflict every since – unfolding over generations including my entire life. What could decolonization mean in this context? History cannot be undone. But could a decolonizing process enable Palestinians to exist with more perceived dignity? Could it enable Palestinian voices to be heard? For Palestinian advocacy to be legitimated in our universities, in Western society, and around the world? And if so, how?

What are the implications for decolonizing ourselves? I am not sure. For me, I have increasingly become more aware and embracing of my Palestinian heritage, and am trying to find a way to effectively use my voice as a Palestinian American/Canadian. I am more mindful of how Western institutions, including our academic environment, has a stifling effect. I think about what it might feel like for scholars of organization and management who belong more explicitly and openly to colonized communities. Of course, the Palestinian situation, as well as my story, is not completely unique, and only scratches the surface of problems stemming from colonialism. Colonial regimes across time and space have embraced slavery, the forced exodus of people, the murder, rape and torture of dissidents, the destruction of the environment, genocide, and the extermination of Indigenous populations, as well as the destruction of various cultures and forms of knowledge (e.g., Saeed, 2024). Many of us have stories of dispossession and exploitation – some more proximate than others.

Given that the volume I am writing this for is focused on decolonizing management and organization studies, it seems that a key implication is the need for reflecting on how what we do as educators and scholars in management and organization research has been shaped by and interpenetrated with the broader colonial project and political economy. Certainly, I would like to see more studies of decolonization efforts as well as a deeper unpacking of the colonial nature of our institutions, including the role of universities, corporations, and other organizations in perpetuating the physical and symbolic violence of colonialism. Such research should also work its way into our classrooms; for instance, where are the Harvard Business School cases on Palestinian entrepreneurs? However, such efforts should go hand in hand with mindful efforts to decolonize ourselves. In doing so, I believe we need to be open to a wider variety of epistemologies and ontologies. We need to be more sensitive to intersectionality, systemic power, cultural marginality, and oppression (Sasaki & Baba, 2024). We need to hear more voices, accounts, and stories. We need to listen to, stand up for, and help each other. As a scholarly community, we should work together on this – not against each other. And ultimately, I would like to see management and organization studies evolve in a way that can reflect these concerns, and even have an impact in addressing some of the profound problems associated with the legacy of colonialism. I would like to be hopeful. I am enthusiastic about this volume as a conversation starter and amplifier. My hope is that it enables further, and broader, dialogue.

## ACKNOWLEDGMENTS

I am grateful to Zahira Jaser for suggesting this title given the text I had drafted.

## REFERENCES

Banerjee, S., & Prasad, A. (2008). Introduction to the special issue on "Critical reflections on management and organizations: A postcolonial perspective." *Critical Perspectives on International Business, 4*, 90–98.

Cavanaugh, E., & Veracini, L. (Eds.). (2020). *The Routledge handbook of the history of settler colonialism*. Routledge.

Douglas, M. (1966). *Purity and danger: An analysis of concepts of pollution and taboo*. Frederick A. Praeger, Inc.

Fanon, F. (1967 [1952]). *Black skin, white masks*. Grove Press.

Jamaluddine, Z., Abukmail, H., Aly, S., Campbell, O. M., & Checchi, F. (2025, January 09). Traumatic injury mortality in the Gaza Strip from Oct 7, 2023, to June 30, 2024: A capture–recapture analysis. *The Lancet, 405*(10477), 469–477.

Jaser, Z. (2024). Coming out as Palestinian. *FT.COM/MAGAZINE MARCH 30/31*: 14–15.

Kent, A. (2024). The Encampment Report. University of Alberta. Retrieved February 24, 2025, from https://www.ualberta.ca/en/governance/media-library/documents/final-encampment-report.pdf

Kirsch, A. (2024). *On settler colonialism: Ideology, violence, and justice*. W. W. Norton & Company.

Saeed, R. (2024). So, what's wrong with colonialism? – Understanding colonialism's political, territorial and epistemic injustice. *International Journal of Law in Context, 21*(1), 99–117. https://
doi.org/10.1017/S1744552324000326

Sasaki, I., & Baba, S. (2024). Shades of cultural marginalization: Cultural survival and autonomy processes. *Organization Theory, 5*(1). https://doi.org/10.1177/26317877231221552

Short, D. (2016). *Redefining genocide: Settler colonialism, social death and ecocide.* Bloomsbury
Publishing.

Simpson, A. (2016). The state is a man: Theresa Spence, Loretta Saunders and the gender of settler
sovereignty. *Theory & Event, 19*(4), 136–162. https://doi.org/10.3138/9781487532048-004

Smith, L. T. (2012). *Decolonizing methodologies: Research and indigenous peoples.* Zed Books.

Thiong'o, N. (1986). *Decolonising the mind: The politics of language in African literature.* J. Currey.

Tuck, E., & Yang, K. W. (2012). Decolonization is not a metaphor. *Decolonization: Indigeneity,
Education & Society, 1*(1), 1–40.

# DECOLONIZING MANAGEMENT AND ORGANIZATION STUDIES: TAKING STOCK AND LOOKING FORWARD

Tapiwa Seremani[a] and Sandiso Bazana[b]

[a]IÉSEG School of Management, France
[b]Grenoble Ecole De Management, France

## ABSTRACT

*Calls to "decolonize" management and organization studies (MOS) have become increasingly louder within the field. These calls stem from an understanding that MOS, in its current form, has been shaped primarily by European and North American perspectives and world views and continues to be dominated by them. Decolonial approaches seek to dismantle colonial legacies and the Eurocentric and North American domination of the body of knowledge of MOS, advocating for inclusivity and diversity of knowledge traditions that have been excluded and silenced by colonialism. This paper provides an overview of these decolonial approaches that are increasingly embraced by MOS scholarship. We outline the diversity of these approaches and their various origins. We take stock of how decolonial approaches have been mobilized within MOS as well as suggest some avenues that we believe to be fertile for the continued growth of decolonial approaches in MOS.*

**Keywords:** Coloniality; decolonizing; Indigenous; MOS; postcolonial

Decolonizing Management and Organization Studies: Why, How, and What
Research in the Sociology of Organizations, Volume 93, 23–37
ISSN: 0733-558X/doi:10.1108/S0733-558X20250000093003

# INTRODUCTION

Calls to "decolonize" management and organization studies (MOS) have become increasingly louder within the field (e.g.: Banerjee, 2022; Barros & Alcadipani, 2022; Coronil, 2016; Jammulamadaka et al., 2021; Maldonado-Torres, 2011). These calls stem from an understanding that MOS in its current form has been shaped primarily by European and North American perspectives, world views, and concerns in relation to management, organizing, and organizations (Ibarra-Colado, 2006; Mignolo, 2002; Nkomo, 2011; Quijano, 2000). Similar to other academic domains and bodies of knowledge, MOS is colonial. It has been profoundly defined by intellectual currents emanating from Europe and North America, shaping its language, theories, methodologies, and epistemologies, perpetuating a conspicuous Eurocentric and North American bias in the field (Barros & Alcadipani, 2022; Ibarra-Colado, 2006; Nkomo, 2011; Quijano, 2007; Weston & Imas, 2019). Other perspectives have been historically marginalized and silenced as a result of colonialism. With colonialism, the world became anchored around Europe and North America and their ways of knowing (see Coronil, 2016; Fanon, 2007; Quijano, 2007; Said, 2003). Decolonial approaches seek to redress this, tracing the origin of this problem back to colonialism and the manner it structured a world centered around Europe and North America, deeming other worldviews irrelevant or lacking reason (Ibarra-Colado, 2006; Mignolo, 2002; Quijano, 2007). Decolonial approaches seek to bring to the fore understanding of organizations, organizing, managing, and management that were put in a backseat by colonialism (Ibarra-Colado, 2006; A. J. Mbembe, 2016; A. Mbembe, 2021; Mignolo, 2002).

In this paper, we attempt to do several things. First, we outline the origins of decolonial thinking in the context of MOS, capturing the different dimensions that constitute the approach, highlighting their diverse geopolitical origins, orientations, and how they have been mobilized in the field. In so doing, we take stock. We present a historical perspective on the emergence and evolution of MOS knowledge, drawing attention to the colonially structured domination of the field by Europe and North America. We highlight how decolonial approaches that emerged from South East Asia and the Middle East, anchored in culture and literature studies, began making inroads in the field aligned with the critical management studies (CMS), "Postcolonial Studies/Postcolonialism" (see Bhabha, 1994; Said, 2003; Spivak, 1988; Young, 2001). We also draw attention to approaches that originated in Africa, which also have strong influences from literary studies (e.g., Achebe, 1958; Nkrumah, 1966; Thiong'o, 1998). We discuss the approaches that emerged from Latin America that place a particular emphasis on the notion of "modernity" and how it served to legitimize colonial subjugation and the knowledge systems of the colonized (see Dussel, 1993; Ibarra-Colado, 2006; Quijano, 2000). We also draw attention to the growing interest in the field in what has been labeled as "Indigenous perspectives" (see Bastien et al., 2022; Bruton et al., 2022; Cutcher & Dale, 2022; Smith, 2012).

We conclude the paper by discussing and proposing ways in which more impetus and momentum could be given to drive the decolonization of the field. In particular, we draw attention to the importance of the notion of hybridity in decolonial approaches in the field (see Bhabha, 1994; Frenkel & Shenhav, 2006; Seremani & Clegg, 2016). We also call for more attention to be given to epistemology and intersectionality (Bothello et al., 2019; Grosfoguel, 2007; Ibarra-Colado, 2006). We also suggest more practical steps that need to be taken into account in the endeavor to decolonize MOS.

## THE COLONIALITY OF MOS: TAKING STOCK

### *The Emergence of MOS as a Field and Its Colonial Foundations*

MOS as a body of knowledge originated in the late 19th and early 20th centuries, during a period marked by industrialization and the emergence of large corporations, necessitating systematic management approaches. Figures such as Frederick Taylor and Henri Fayol significantly influenced and shaped the body of knowledge that we refer to MOS today. Yet, the origins of the field are intricately linked to colonialism. Colonialism that sought to legitimize colonial oppression by arguing that the colonized were incapable of reason, morality, and constructing credible knowledge (Dussel, 1993; Ibarra-Colado, 2006). This has left us with a field that is morally tainted and often struggles with relevance and engaging organization and management realities outside of Europe and North America. For example, Taylor's methods and "Principles of Management" were shaped by practices on slave plantations that sought to achieve forced docility and domination of slaves (Cooke, 2003) and later extended to the US military (Bruce & Nyland, 2011). Furthermore, the approaches to management and organizations that anchor the field are centered on realities, concerns, theories, methods, and epistemologies that originated primarily in Western Europe.

Prasad argue that this stems from the distinct traditions of xenology. European xenology, shaped by historical events like European conquests and religious conflicts, tended to compare and rank different cultural and political systems while viewing "difference" as perilous. Such distinct traditions of xenology have left a colonial imprint in MOS. The historical trends of imperialism and colonialism marginalized knowledge systems that did not originate from the proverbial "center," Europe and North America (Ibarra-Colado, 2006; Mbembe, 2016; Mignolo, 2002; Quijano, 2000). This is something scholarship in MOS is increasingly aware of and has seen a growing interest in decolonial approaches. In sum, momentum has built around decolonizing MOS based on the growing acknowledgment that the core of the field has been defined and shaped by colonialism.

### *What Has Been Done So Far in Terms of Decolonial Approaches?*

Initially, decolonial approaches found a home in MOS within CMS. In recent times, scholars have pushed decolonial approaches to more central spaces in MOS. For example, Frenkel and Shenhav (2006) use the decolonial notion of hybridity, coined by Bhabha (1994) to argue that MOS needs to pay greater attention to how the formerly colonized and their colonizers mutually influenced each other understandings of organizational and management knowledge. Barros and Alcadipani (2022) problematize the dominance of the English language in the production of knowledge in MOS.

The drive to decolonize MOS needs to be understood as a project that seeks to decenter Europe and North America, which have traditionally dominated the field as a result of colonialism (A. Mbembe, 2021). It is an effort to push for voices and perspectives that were silenced by colonialism to be heard on their own terms. This entails confronting and dismantling the European and North American knowledge hegemony in MOS and the associated colonial power structures that created this state of affairs (Jammulamadaka et al., 2021). It is an attempt to create spaces within MOS that integrate, accommodate, and appreciate alternative perspectives and worldviews that have historically been silenced by colonialism. Yet, decolonizing MOS is not only about allowing colonially silenced perspectives to be heard. It is also about "provincializing" Europe and the United States and the knowledge produced within these geographies that have claimed to have universal relevance, creating space for previously suppressed voices to speak and be heard (Ibarra-Colado, 2006). There are worlds that exist outside of Europe and North America that have a great deal to say about organizing and management that were silenced or annihilated by colonialism (Banerjee, 2022; Mbembe, 2016; Thiong'o, 1998; Yousfi, 2021).

However, decolonial approaches are not a single theory nor a homogenous approach, having diverse geo-political origins, theoretical orientations, and spheres of emphasis (Banerjee, 2022; Young, 2001). Below, we outline some of these diverse approaches that have laid the foundations for the decolonization of MOS, which is gaining momentum. Our review is by no means exhaustive, but we try to illustrate the diverse origins of the perspectives gathered now under "decolonial approaches" that forged epistemological, theoretical, and methodological tools that scholars increasingly adopt in the quest to decolonize MOS. While we try to distinguish these approaches, they often refer to and build on each other.

### Postcolonial Studies, Postcolonialism, Southeast Asia, and the Middle East

One of the foundational pillars of decolonial approaches in MOS today is "postcolonial theory," which is sometimes referred to as "postcolonialism" or "postcolonial studies" within the field (see Young, 2001). This critique of colonialism emerged primarily from South East Asia and the Middle East. This colonial critique emerged from literary and cultural studies of the impacts of colonialism, the roles played by scholarship in Europe and North America in instilling colonial hierarchies as well as engaging the manifestations of these hierarchies on questions such as identity and representations (see Bhabha, 1994, 1998; Fanon, 2007; Said, 2003). The intellectual pillars of this approach include the likes of Homi Bhabha (see Bhabha, 1994, 1998), Edward Said (see Said, 2003), Aime Cesaire (see Césaire, 2001) and Gayatri Spivak (see Spivak, 1988). For example, Bhabha's work has done a great deal to shed light on the questions of identity and culture among the former colonized, coining the important notion of "hybridity" which has garnered appeal in International Business where it has been used to explore the relationships and tensions between European and North American multinational corporations and the those in other parts of the globe that work for such organizations or consume their products (see Frenkel & Shenhav, 2006; Yousfi, 2014; Zohdi, 2017). In the context of the ongoing efforts to decolonize MOS, Bhabha's view becomes important as he argues that the formerly colonized exist in an interstitial space of hybridity, a fluid mixture between the ideals of the colonizers and their own. This suggests that efforts to reconstruct perspectives that were annihilated by colonialism may be in vain because the views that exist in the Global South are largely of a hybrid nature. Said (2003) took a different approach and argued for a binary understanding of the relationship between the colonizers and the colonized, drawing attention to representations of the "non-westerns"/the (former) colonized, highlighting how skewed representations of them are constructed in the media and social sciences and ultimately organization and management knowledge. Closely affiliated with this approach is the work by Frantz Fanon (see Fanon, 2007, 2015), which had a particular emphasis on the psychological dimensions of colonialism. Fanon's work also sometimes appears in decoloniality approaches from Latin America and in the neo-colonial perspectives that emerged from Africa.

### *"Neo-colonialism" and African Perspectives*

Similar to postcolonial approaches, in Africa, critiques of colonialism emerged centered around the question of culture, identity, and nationhood following the formal end(s) of colonialism in Africa. A significant portion of the work that emerged from Africa was in the space of literature in which writers such as Achebe and Ngugi questioned the dominance of "Western" ideals, culture, and languages in the former colonies despite the formal end of colonialism (see Achebe, 1958; Thiong'o, 1998) and how this restricted the colonized from being able to articulate their perspectives in their own terms. For example, Thiong'o problematizes the dominance of the English language in Kenya, arguing that there are many things about Kenyan culture and knowledge that cannot be articulated in English (Thiong'o, 1998). He argues that this linguistic dominance is not mundane, stating that "the choice of language and the use to which language is put is central to a people's definition of themselves in relation to the natural and social environment, indeed in relation to the entire universe" … Even at their most radical and pro-African position in their sentiments and articulation of problems, they still took it as axiomatic that the renaissance of African cultures lay in the languages of Europe" (Thiong'o, 1998, pp. 4–5). Reflecting on his experiences in Rhodesia, present-day Zimbabwe, Dambudzo Marechera (2009) concurs with Thiong'o, stating, "For a black writer, the language is very racist; you have to have harrowing fights and hair-rising panga duals with the language before you can make it do all that you want it to do." In the context of MOS and the drive to decolonize, this argument was recently picked up and reiterated by Barros and Alcadipani (2022). They question the dominance of English as the lingua franca of the field, highlighting how this impedes the integration of scholarship and

ideas from non-Anglo-Saxon regions of the globe. They target this important critique to publication outlets and the overall colonial structure of the field. In that
sense, MOS finds itself in a quandary. For the ideas from the (former) colonized
to be heard, they need to be framed in languages that are alien to the realities and
rationalities of the (former) colonized. Coming from the tradition of postcolonial and Subaltern Studies, Spivak (1988) makes a similar argument, questioning how and if subalterns can articulate their worldviews and perspectives whilst
relying on hegemonic world views and languages. The very same that were used
to subjugate them.

Nkrumah (see Nkrumah, 1966) questioned what the newly freed African
nations could become given the continued domination of European powers in
Africa despite the formal ends of colonialism. He coins the term "neo-colonialism"
to depict the predicament of these newly independent African nations. The
terminology of "neo-colonialism" has gone on to gain currency in the African
framing, critique, and engagement with colonialism within MOS and more
broadly. More recently, Mbembe added impetus to this African critique of colonialism (see Mbembe), drawing attention to the coloniality of the field and universities and institutions of tertiary education more broadly.

### Decoloniality and Latin America

For Latin American approaches, the colonial problem is dated to the initial
encounter between Europeans and South America in the 1600s (see Coronil,
2016; Lugones, 2010; Mignolo, 2002; Quijano, 2007). They place an important
emphasis on the role played by the notion of "modernity" in legitimizing the
brutality of colonialism and silencing the voices, ideas, and perspectives of the
colonized (Dussel, 1993; Quijano, 2000). Since the initial colonial encounters, this
modernity has been framed in many different terms. In the case of MOS in its current form, it is understood as a part of a colonial matrix of power (Coronil, 2016;
Quijano, 2007) that perpetuates that belief the "real" management and organization knowledge, modernity, can only come from Europe and North America. This
scholarship problematizes neo-liberalism and the role it has played in perpetuating colonial power relations (e.g., Faria et al., 2010). Ibarra-Colado (2006) labels
the domination of European and North American ways of knowing in the field
of "epistemic colonialism." A field of knowledge that claims universal relevance,
yet its theories, concepts, methods, and epistemologies originate from a small part
of the globe because of colonialism. He goes further and questions why it should
be of any surprise that these theories of management and organization often find
themselves in a jam when confronted with the realities of regions that are not
Europe and North America. From this approach in Latin America emerged the
terminology of "(de)coloniality." A school of thought that seeks to delink from
Eurocentric knowledge hierarchies and ways of being in the world and advocate
and normalize alternative forms of knowing and being. From this perspective,
decolonizing must entail delegitimating the monopoly that the Global North
has had on what is perceived as relevant knowledge. The key to doing this is
deconstructing and questioning notions of modernity that have allowed Europe

and North America to occupy a high seat in the construction of knowledge. In contemporary MOS and the push to decolonize, emerging from this school of thought are scholars such as Faria and Hemais (2017) and Coronil (2016).

### Indigenous Perspectives

The interest in decolonial approaches has also seen growing attempts to include the views and perspectives of the original or "Indigenous populations" in places such as Australia, Canada, the USA, parts of Africa, and Latin America (e.g., Bastien et al., 2022; Bruton et al., 2022; Cutcher & Dale, 2022; Domínguez & Luoma, 2020). These approaches seek to carve out a space in MOS that addresses the realities, concerns, perspectives, and knowledge that were muted by settler colonialism of "Indigenous peoples." For conceptual clarity, the "Indigenous" here does not refer to the general connotation of the term in which any country and its people, as well as their way of knowing and being, can be classified as "Indigenous." It refers to the people subjected to colonial oppression by settler colonialism, and this approach to decolonizing seeks to give them a voice. Recognizing the significance of Indigenous knowledge expands our understanding of organizations, organizing, and managing beyond Euro and North America-centric perspectives that dominate MOS. For example, Maori scholar Linda Tuhiwai Smith fervently advocates for incorporating Indigenous epistemologies in research methodology, highlighting their potential to challenge dominant knowledge paradigms (Smith, 2012). The inclusion of Indigenous knowledge offers a more inclusive perspective that respects diverse worldviews and organizational methods, which is the core of the push to decolonize MOS.

In sum, decolonial approaches have gathered momentum within MOS. They are diverse in terms of their origins and concerns and are centered on trying to carve out spaces in the field in which the perspectives, views, and lived experiences of those excluded by colonialism and the coloniality of MOS can heard in their own terms. In essence, this is an attempt to restructure the power dynamics, a field that is increasingly aware that it is colonial. Whilst decolonial approaches have begun making important inroads into MOS, we believe that there are a number of unexplored avenues that would give decolonial efforts in MOS greater momentum. We discuss these below.

## ADVANCING DECOLONIZATION IN MOS
### Strategies and Challenges

The growing interest in decolonial approaches has succeeded in drawing attention to the reality that MOS is colonial. It is a field embedded in colonial power relations and dynamics that are manifest in its theories, methods, epistemologies, and ontologies being centered in Europe and North America. Implicit in this is that knowledge of organizations, organizing, and management is the privy of the Global North. This is a colonial myth that, nonetheless, continues to be perpetuated in the field. Decolonial approaches take issue with this state of affairs.

Yet, despite the emerging interest and attention drawn to decolonial approaches, the way forward is blurry. There is no one fixed solution to addressing the field's coloniality. Different propositions have come forward, reflecting the diversity of thought within the field and the multiple dimensions and faces of the coloniality of MOS. In the section that follows, we discuss some of these propositions and how they could play a role in decolonizing MOS, as well as draw attention to approaches and perspectives that have currently gone under the radar that could play an important role. In so doing, we do not target these proposals at a specific strain of approaches given how the streams have cross-pollinated historically and have continued to do so to create what we are calling decolonial approaches in MOS today. As such, our proposals speak to decolonial approaches understood as products of postcolonial, neocolonial, coloniality, indigenous, and other perspectives that seek to challenge the coloniality of the field.

### Diverse Perspectives on the Future of Decolonial Approaches in MOS

Whilst decolonial approaches converge on the goal of problematizing the colonial power relations that have shaped the field and carving out spaces that allow the colonially excluded to be integrated, there are diverse perspectives on how this can be achieved. Some have argued that the DNA of the field is colonial, and, as such, it cannot engage in decolonizing beyond a surface-level adoption of decolonial language and terminology (e.g., Banerjee, 2022). Others have argued that more attention needs to be paid to methodology given that the methods that dominate MOS are European and North American and maybe ill-adapted to engage with MOS realities in other parts of the world (Weston & Imas, 2019). Some have argued that a decolonizing MOS is one that takes context more seriously (Filatotchev et al., 2022; Hamann et al., 2020), whilst others have called for greater attention to be given to the epistemological structure of the field and its colonial foundations (Ibarra-Colado, 2006; Seremani & Clegg, 2016). Other scholars have drawn attention to the overall structure of the field, drawing attention to the question of language and the manner in which journals in the field are structured in a colonial manner that makes it difficult for those from the Global South to actively participate in the dialogues and discussions in MOS (Barros & Alcadipani, 2022; Gantman et al., 2015). Some scholars have argued for the decolonization of the curriculum. If such diverse perspectives exist, it is precisely because of the enormity of the task of decolonizing MOS and the multidimensional nature of the coloniality of the field. Below we highlight the importance of taking the notion of "hybridity" (Bhabha, 1994) in the decolonial push.

### Integrating Hybridity

The efforts to decolonize MOS need to be understood not as a drive to excavate "authentic" precolonial perspectives nor "authentic" views of the Global South and their takes on different theories and approaches in MOS. Bhabha (1994) cautioned on this, arguing that we need to embrace the reality that colonialism changed the world in irreversible terms in both the Global North and the Global South.

Spivak (1988) also raises this concern. What we find in the (former) colonies are not untouched precolonial ways of knowing and being but rather hybridity. A mixture of what existed before and after colonization. This is important as the decolonial project needs to avoid the trap of trying to dig up pre-colonial forms of knowledge that no longer exist nor channel its efforts to reconstruct romanticized and purist perspectives in efforts to decolonize MOS. The goal is to restructure that field in a manner that allows diverse perspectives to be integrated, allowing and nurturing perspectives from geo-political and regions of the globe that are silenced by colonialism.

Related to this, a growing body of work on decolonizing has called for efforts to decolonize MOS to escape a binary positioning that pits the "Global North" and "Global South" in opposition or "West" and "East" (Frenkel & Shenhav, 2006; Hamann et al., 2020; Nkomo, 2011; Seremani & Clegg, 2016). Whilst speaking on the colonial nature of leadership studies and its representations of "African" leadership, Nkomo suggests that the key lies in finding spaces of translation and dialogue that move beyond stereotypical colonial images of "African" leadership and management and proposed counter-images that often reflect the excesses of cultural relativism (Nkomo, 2011). Similarly, Hamann et al. (2020) express an unease with efforts in MOS to decolonize framed in this binary manner. Mignolo (2002) makes a similar call, suggesting the decolonizing MOS must move beyond just criticism of Eurocentrism, calling for the embracing of the notion of "transmodernity." Transmodernity means that modernity is not strictly European but a planetary phenomenon to which the "excluded barbarians" have contributed, although their contribution has not been acknowledged (Mignolo, 2002).

The arguments of Gordon (2021) are pertinent in this regard. Gordon (2021) argues for the notion of "creolization." "Creolization" encourages critical thinking about how "worlds" are constantly coming together in their distinctiveness. Unlike the approaches to decolonizing that emphasize the purity of disciplines, creolization highlights the impure nature of disciplines and knowledge, celebrating hybridity. This notion of creolized hybrids celebrates the impure and hybrid nature of knowledge systems, thus enriching the field. Gordon (2021) challenges the notion of MOS knowledge as solely originating in Europe and North America, suggesting that this view fails to recognize the creolized or mixed origins of knowledge systems. Euro-American thought cannot be considered a unilateral "Northern" miracle of thought because knowledge from other parts orts of the globe have influenced it for thousands of years. Gordon's critique of prevailing decolonization paradigms underscores the importance of critically re-evaluating the North-South divide in our decolonization endeavors, which may exist primarily as a conceptual construct while neglecting crucial aspects, such as the emergence of knowledge from both core and periphery regions, with the periphery (South) increasingly assuming a central role in shaping contemporary discourses. The growing efforts to decolonize MOS open a new avenue of inquiry for the approach. This suggests an approach to decolonizing MOS that not only seeks to integrate previously excluded perspectives in the field. But one that also explores the way in which the colonized influenced MOS knowledge.

## The Question of Epistemology and Methodology

A number of scholars have drawn attention to the importance of engaging with the question of epistemology in efforts to decolonize MOS (e.g., Banerjee, 2022; Seremani & Clegg, 2016). This is something we believe to be of great importance for the decolonial push. This is to say that the field needs to engage more seriously with alternative ways of knowing and constructing knowledge. This entails moving away from the increasingly formulaic approaches in the field and finding ways to engage with approaches to knowledge production that do not necessarily align themselves with the canons of knowing that have historically (colonially) dominated the field. In terms of trying to decolonize MOS, this places the spotlight on efforts to decolonize that are anchored in knowledge systems and ways of constructing knowledge from the Global North. Bearing in mind the above-mentioned arguments for appreciating hybridity, the task is not so much to retrieve pure epistemological positions untouched by colonialism but to restructure the field in a manner that makes it receptive to different epistemologies. This is to say that the field needs to have an introspection on how knowledge is constructed as well as how what is considered legitimate knowledge in the field is constructed.

Similar concerns have been raised about research methodology in this drive to decolonize MOS (Weston & Imas, 2019). Encouraging scholars to explore alternative research methodologies that are better suited to non-Western contexts is crucial (Santos, 2014). It requires a willingness to adapt and innovate beyond traditional Western research methods. Recognizing the limitations of these methods in capturing the nuances of non-Western organizational contexts is a fundamental aspect of this shift. The field is dominated by methods forged in the Global North. This means opening the field to broader methodological approaches. If today there are discussions on how and why theories and methods from the Global North fail to capture the realities of the Global South, it has a lot to do with how the field attempts to use methods and ways of knowing from the Global North to try to make sense of the Global South. The rationalities behind the methods that dominate the field may be unable to capture the realities and rationalities in the Global South. Simply applying research methods created in the Global North to empirical settings in the Global South does a disservice to decolonial approaches and what they represent. This means a reorientation of the manner in which the field is structured to allow it to move away from methodological domination by perspectives from the Global North. Sometimes, organizational and management knowledge is considered out of the norm, and yet it simply represents the limitations of the methods constructed in the Global North to capture organizational and management realities in the Global South. This is an important aspect of decolonizing yet can be detrimental to decolonial approaches when such efforts remain centered on theories, methodologies, and epistemologies from the Global North. This means moving away from using the "Global South" as an empirical setting to explore the boundary conditions of theories and ways of knowing from the Global North. It necessitates restructuring the field in a manner that allows the Global South(s) to be integrated in their own theoretical, methodological, and epistemological terms, not just as empirical settings.

## Taking Intersectionality More Seriously

Scholarship has recognized intersectionality and Critical Race Theory as robust frameworks and reference points that potentially add an important dimension to the efforts to decolonize MOS (Abdelnour & Abu Moghli, 2021; Davis & Walsh, 2020). Through an intersectional lens, scholars would be able to unveil the multifaceted dimensions of privilege and marginalization within organizational contexts, emphasizing the importance of considering the experiences of historically excluded individuals. Embracing intersectionality in research is vital, acknowledging that identities and experiences are shaped by a multitude of factors, including race, gender, class, and more (Crenshaw, 1989). This approach allows for a more nuanced understanding of organizational phenomena, acknowledging the complex interplay of multiple dimensions of identity. Furthermore, taking intersectionality more seriously would open an avenue to explore the power dynamics of knowledge production and roles and positions of privilege manifest in decolonial scholars in speaking of and on behalf of those who do not have a voice.

## More "Practical" Suggestions

First, we believe that a first practical step would be pushing for more collaborative research partnerships with marginalized communities for decolonizing management and organization knowledge. Involving community members as active participants in the research process challenges traditional power dynamics and ensures that the voices of those directly affected by management practices are heard (Smith, 2012). These partnerships grant researchers access to local knowledge and perspectives that may challenge established narratives, fostering the co-creation of knowledge that respects diverse ways of knowing and questions hierarchical relationships between researchers and the researched.

Furthermore, the journey toward decolonization in MOS also demands a fundamental rethinking of curricula and knowledge production methodologies, diversifying the MOS knowledge that is taught in our business schools and universities. This involves a critical examination of existing curricula, identifying areas dominated by Euro and North America-centric paradigms, and devising methods to alternative viewpoints. This includes revising course descriptions, reading lists, and learning outcomes to prioritize a more global outlook on management and organizations (Mbembe, 2001). A key part of this is developing courses that intentionally incorporate non-European and North American case studies, theories, and practices. Such an approach would challenge and encourage students to explore alternative viewpoints (Quijano, 2000). Faculty development programs can facilitate this transition. Establishing safe spaces within academic institutions where students and scholars can openly discuss issues related to decolonization, diversity, and inclusion is crucial (Spivak, 1988). These spaces should encourage open dialogue and the exchange of ideas, fostering a culture of inclusivity and mutual respect. Furthermore, training faculty in inclusive pedagogical practices that create welcoming learning environments for all students is foundational (Hooks, 1994). This includes being attentive to diverse learning styles, cultural sensitivities, and the use of inclusive language.

To decolonize MOS, active efforts also need to be made to seek out and support scholarship from the Global South within the academic community. Establishing platforms for their research and ensuring that their voices are heard are essential steps. Organizing conferences or research symposia that specifically highlight the work of scholars from underrepresented regions can facilitate this (Quijano, 2000). Kondayya et al. (2025) draw attention to academic conferences and how they are structured in ways that silence alternative and potentially important perspectives from the Global South. Zoogah et al. (2025) target their colonial critique on the academic journals that dominate the field, highlighting the role played by the *Africa Journal of Management* in advocating greater inclusivity in terms of ways of knowing. This key if decolonial scholarship is to challenge traditional/colonial publication practices that favor Western-centric research, which is a significant step in decolonization (Mbembe, 2016). It is essential to actively encourage journals and academic publishers to seek out and publish research from diverse geographical and cultural contexts. Additionally, re-evaluating peer review processes to ensure fairness and inclusivity in evaluating research from different perspectives is imperative (Spivak, 1988). Encouraging and facilitating collaborative research projects that involve scholars from different regions and backgrounds is essential (Comaroff & Comaroff, 2015). Such collaborations can lead to more holistic and contextually relevant research outcomes. By embracing diversity in research teams, MOS can shed light on the multifaceted nature of organizational phenomena.

# CONCLUSION

Decolonizing MOS is a moral and intellectual imperative. It requires a comprehensive and sustained effort to reimagine curricula, diversify knowledge production, and create inclusive academic spaces. These practical steps are vital for breaking free from disciplinary decadence, embracing diverse perspectives, and contributing to a more equitable and globally relevant field. Decolonization opens doors to alternative ways of understanding management and organizations, acknowledging their complexity and contextuality. In embracing this journey, MOS honors the plurality of knowledge and recognizes that true excellence emerges when we celebrate the diversity of voices shaping our discipline. It is a commitment to a more inclusive, just, and relevant future for the study of management and organizations. Through decolonization, we actively engage with the world beyond the confines of Western-centric thinking, enriching our discipline and contributing to a more equitable global academic landscape. Creating inclusive academic spaces is pivotal in promoting decolonization within MOS. These spaces should not merely tolerate diverse perspectives but actively celebrate them, ensuring that all scholars and students have an equal opportunity to thrive. Encouraging research teams to be diverse in terms of cultural backgrounds, experiences, and perspectives is foundational (Nkomo, 2019). These diverse teams can bring a richer array of insights to research projects, challenging preconceived notions and enriching the quality of academic inquiry.

# REFERENCES

Abdelnour, S., & Abu Moghli, M. (2021). Researching violent contexts: A call for political reflexivity. *Organization*, 13505084211030646.

Achebe, C. (1958). *Things fall apart*. Heinemann.

Banerjee, S. B. (2022). Decolonizing management theory: A critical perspective. *Journal of Management Studies*, *59*(4), 1074–1087. https://doi.org/10.1111/joms.12756

Barros, A., & Alcadipani, R. (2022). Decolonizing journals in management and organizations? Epistemological colonial encounters and the double translation. *Management Learning*, 13505076221083204. https://doi.org/10.1177/13505076221083204

Bastien, F., Coraiola, D. M., & Foster, W. M. (2022). Indigenous peoples and organization studies. *Organization Studies*, 01708406221141545. https://doi.org/10.1177/01708406221141545

Bhabha, H. K. (1994). *The location of culture*. Routledge.

Bothello, J., Nason, R. S., & Schnyder, G. (2019). Institutional voids and organization studies: Towards an epistemological rupture. *Organization Studies*, *40*(10), 1499–1512.

Bruce, K., & Nyland, C. (2011). Elton mayo and the deification of human relations. *Organization Studies*, *32*(3), 383–405. https://doi.org/10.1177/0170840610397478

Bruton, G. D., Zahra, S. A., Van de Ven, A. H., & Hitt, M. A. (2022). Indigenous theory uses, abuses, and future. *Journal of Management Studies*, *59*(4), 1057–1073. https://doi.org/10.1111/joms.12755

Césaire, A. (2001). *Discourse on colonialism* (J. Pinkham, Trans.). Monthly Review Press.

Cooke, B. (2003). The denial of slavery in management studies. *Journal of Management Studies*, *40*(8), 1895–1918. https://doi.org/10.1046/j.1467-6486.2003.00405.x

Comaroff, J., & Comaroff, J. L. (2015). *Theory from the south: Or, how Euro-America is evolving toward Africa*. Routledge.

Coronil, F. (2016). *Latin American postcolonial studies and global decolonization* (pp. 175–192). https://doi.org/10.1002/9781119118589.ch11

Crenshaw, K. (1989). Demarginalizing the intersection of race and sex: A black feminist critique of antidiscrimination doctrine, feminist theory and antiracist politics. *University of Chicago Legal Forum*, *1989*(1). https://chicagounbound.uchicago.edu/uclf/vol1989/iss1/8

Cutcher, L., & Dale, K. (2022). 'We're Not a White Fella Organization': Hybridity and friction in the contact zone between local kinship relations and audit culture in an Indigenous organization. *Organization Studies*, 01708406221128376. https://doi.org/10.1177/01708406221128376

Davis, B. P., & Walsh, J. (2020). The politics of positionality: The difference between post-, anti-, and de-colonial methods. *Culture, Theory and Critique*, *61*(4), 374–388. https://doi.org/10.1080/14735784.2020.1808801

Domínguez, L., & Luoma, C. (2020). Decolonising conservation policy: How colonial land and conservation ideologies persist and perpetuate indigenous injustices at the expense of the environment. *Land*, *9*(3), Article 3. https://doi.org/10.3390/land9030065

Dussel, E. (1993). Eurocentrism and modernity (Introduction to the Frankfurt Lectures). *Boundary 2*, *20*(3), 65–76. https://doi.org/10.2307/303341

Fanon, F. (2007). *The Wretched of the Earth*. Grove/Atlantic, Inc.

Faria, A., & Hemais, M. (2017). Rethinking the bottom of the pyramid: A critical perspective from an emerging economy. *Web of Science*. https://doi.org/10.1177/1470593117704283

Faria, A., Ibarra-Colado, E., & Guedes, A. (2010). Internationalization of management, neoliberalism and the Latin America challenge. *Critical Perspectives on International Business*, *6*(2/3), 97–115.

Filatotchev, I., Ireland, R. D., & Stahl, G. K. (2022). Contextualizing management research: An open systems perspective. *Journal of Management Studies*, *59*(4), 1036–1056.

Frenkel, M., & Shenhav, Y. (2006). From binarism back to hybridity: A postcolonial reading of management and organization studies. *Organization Studies*, *27*(6), 855–876. https://doi.org/10.1177/0170840606064086

Gantman, E. R., Yousfi, H., & Alcadipani, R. (2015). Challenging Anglo-Saxon dominance in management and organizational knowledge. *Revista de Administração de Empresas*, *55*, 126–129.

Gordon, T. (2021). Tribal casino labor relations and settler colonialism. *Critical Gambling Studies*, *2*(2), Article 2. https://doi.org/10.29173/cgs73

Grosfoguel, R. (2007). The epistemic decolonial turn. *Cultural Studies*, *21*(2–3), 211–223. https://doi.org/10.1080/09502380601162514

Hamann, R., Luiz, J., Ramaboa, K., Khan, F., Dhlamini, X., & Nilsson, W. (2020). Neither colony nor enclave: Calling for dialogical contextualism in management and organization studies. *Organization Theory*, *1*(1), 2631787719879705.

Hooks, bell. (1994). *Teaching to transgress: education as the practice of freedom*. Routledge.

Ibarra-Colado, E. (2006). Organization studies and epistemic coloniality in Latin America: Thinking otherness from the margins. *Organization*, *13*(4), 463–488. https://doi.org/10.1177/1350508406065851

Jammulamadaka, N., Faria, A., Jack, G., & Ruggunan, S. (2021). Decolonising management and organisational knowledge (MOK): Praxistical theorising for potential worlds. *Organization*, *28*(5), 717–740. https://doi.org/10.1177/13505084211020463

Kondayya, A., Fohim, E., & Höllerer, M. A. (2025). Curating *open* academic fora. In E. Fohim (Ed.), *Decolonizing management and organization studies: Why, how, and what (Research in the Sociology of Organizations)* (pp. 209–227). Emerald Group Publishing Limited.

Lugones, M. (2010). Toward a decolonial feminism. *Hypatia*, *25*(4), 742–759.

Maldonado-Torres, N. G. E. (2011). Thinking through the decolonial turn: Post-continental interventions in theory, philosophy, and critique—An introduction. *TRANSMODERNITY: Journal of Peripheral Cultural Production of the Luso-Hispanic World*, *1*(2). https://doi.org/10.5070/T412011805

Marechera, D. (2009). *The house of hunger* (2nd ed.). Heinemann.

Mbembe, A. (2001). *On the postcolony* (1st ed.). University of California Press. https://www.jstor.org/stable/10.1525/j.ctt1ppkxs

Mbembe, A. J. (2016). *Decolonizing the university: New directions: Arts and humanities in higher education*. https://doi.org/10.1177/1474022215618513

Mbembe, A. (2021). *Out of the dark night: Essays on decolonization*. Columbia University Press.

Mbembe, A. J. (2016). Decolonizing the university: New directions. *Arts and Humanities in Higher Education*. https://doi.org/10.1177/1474022215618513

Mignolo, W. (2002). The geopolitics of knowledge and the colonial difference. *South Atlantic Quarterly*, *101*, 57–96. https://doi.org/10.1215/00382876-101-1-57

Nkomo, S. M. (2011). A postcolonial and anti-colonial reading of 'African' leadership and management in organization studies: Tensions, contradictions and possibilities. *Organization*, *18*(3), 365–386.

Nkomo, S. M. (2019). The emperor has no clothes: Rewriting "Race in organizations". In *Postmodern management theory* (pp. 463–489). Routledge.

Nkrumah, K. (1966). *Neo-colonialism: The last stage of imperialism* (Later Printing edition). International Publishers.

Quijano, A. (2000). Coloniality of power and eurocentrism in Latin America. *International Sociology*, *15*(2), 215–232. https://doi.org/10.1177/0268580900015002005

Quijano, A. (2007). Coloniality and modernity/rationality. *Cultural Studies*, *21*(2–3), 168–178. https://doi.org/10.1080/09502380601164353

Santos, B. de S. (2014). *Epistemologies of the south: Justice against epistemicide*. Routledge.

Said, E. W. (2003). *Orientalism* (25th Anniversary Ed with 1995 Afterword Ed). Penguin Classics.

Seremani, T. W., & Clegg, S. (2016). Postcolonialism, organization, and management theory. *Journal of Management Inquiry*, *25*(2), 171–183. https://doi.org/10.1177/1056492615589973

Smith, L. T. (2012). *Decolonizing methodologies: Research and indigenous peoples* (2nd ed.). Zed Books Ltd.

Spivak, G. C. (1988). *Can the subaltern speak?* Macmillan.

Thiong'o, N. (1998). Decolonising the mind. *Diogenes*, *46*(184), 101–104. https://doi.org/10.1177/039219219804618409

Weston, A., & Imas, J. M. (2019). *The SAGE handbook of qualitative business and management research methods: History and traditions* (pp. 119–135). SAGE Publications Ltd. https://doi.org/10.4135/9781526430212

Young, R. J. C. (2001). *Postcolonialism: An historical introduction* (1st ed.). Wiley-Blackwell.

Yousfi, H. (2014). Rethinking hybridity in postcolonial contexts: What changes and what persists? The Tunisian case of Poulina's managers. *Organization Studies*, *35*(3), 393–421. https://doi.org/10.1177/0170840613499751

Yousfi, H. (2021). Decolonizing Arab organizational knowledge: "Fahlawa" as a research practice. *Organization, 28*(5), 836–856. https://doi.org/10.1177/13505084211015371

Zohdi, E. (2017). Lost-identity; A result of "Hybridity" and "Ambivalence" in Tayeb Salih's season of migration to the north. *International Journal of Applied Linguistics and English Literature, 7*(1), Article 1. https://doi.org/10.7575/aiac.ijalel.v.7n.1p.146

Zoogah, B. D., Nkomo, S. M., & Kiggundu, M. N. (2025). The role of *Africa Journal of Management* in decolonizing management and organization studies. In E. Fohim (Ed.), *Decolonizing management and organization studies: Why, how, and what (Research in the Sociology of Organizations)* (pp. 191–207). Emerald Group Publishing Limited.

# SECTION II

# WHY SHOULD WE DECOLONIZE MANAGEMENT AND ORGANIZATION STUDIES?

# GEOGRAPHIC INEQUALITY IN MANAGEMENT SCHOLARSHIP: DATA-DRIVEN ESTIMATES AND TRENDS

Abhishek Nagaraj[a] and Hongyu Yao[b]

[a]Haas School of Business, University of California, Berkeley, USA
[b]MIT Sloan School of Management, USA

## ABSTRACT

*Top management scholarship struggles to be globally relevant as it fails to reflect the diversity of global business phenomena. While this issue is informally recognized, the field lacks systematic estimates that detail the level (and trend) of geographic bias favoring the West. Using unique data from over 21,000 articles in six leading management journals, we find that only 3% of authors and 15% of study regions come from mid- or low-income countries. Worryingly, these trends are not improving much over time. Our findings raise serious questions about the extent to which management scholarship truly represents the global business landscape.*

**Keywords:** Geographic bias; global management; management scholarship; science of science; WEIRD Bias

Decolonizing Management and Organization Studies: Why, How, and What
Research in the Sociology of Organizations, Volume 93, 41–66
ISSN: 0733-558X/doi:10.1108/S0733-558X20250000093004

# INTRODUCTION

Social science enables evidence-based practice for a broad range of economic and social phenomena (Cole et al., 2020). Scholarship in the field of management, for example, increasingly makes practical recommendations to both private and public sector actors (Nembhard et al., 2009; Nishii, 2013; Whitley, 1984; Wickert & de Bakker, 2018). Given the potentially high stakes of management research, it is therefore concerning that some regions around the world might be severely over-represented, as many researchers suspect. Without a solid base of locally relevant social-scientific evidence, policy-making in the non-Western world could remain evidence-free, which would create a key impediment to closing the development gap between high and low-income regions of the world (Yamey & Volmink, 2014).

Despite informal awareness surrounding these facts, we currently lack systematic evidence of geographic inequality embedded in management research. Wickert et al. (2024) call on management scholars to embrace more non-Western contexts in their research and, in doing so, to unleash the explanatory potential of these contexts. However, we know little about the magnitude of such geographic inequality in management and how these levels have been changing over time. A major barrier has been the lack of systematic meta-data linking papers to the geographic location of their authors and the geographic focus of the study. Given the sundry challenges, existing analyses of geographic bias tend to produce estimates only for a few issues of single journals or a limited number of time periods (Baruch, 2001; Murphy & Zhu, 2012; Pitesa & Gelfand, 2022).

To overcome these challenges, we develop a novel machine-learning-based method that can systematically enable rigorous meta-science in a wide range of journals and over many time periods. The heart of this method leverages geo-parsing, a Natural Language Processing (NLP) technique that locates specific geographies from text, to measure two dimensions of geographic bias: (1) the frequency of geographic locations studied and (2) the frequency of the author's physical locations. We start by scraping data from the official websites of six top journals we focus on. We supplement this with institutional affiliation data from Dimensions, a research platform developed by Digital Science that has strong coverage dating back to the 1950s. We then clean, standardize, and geo-parse the data to match papers with the locations. Altogether, this enables us to look at long-term trends in the inequality of top management scholarship over the past seven decades.

Our analysis yields three main findings. First, among articles with a geographic focus, over 58% tend to focus exclusively on the United States (US), while only about 15% have at least a part of their focus on mid- or low-income countries, a trend that has been stable since the 1970s. Second, a similar inequality is seen in the geography of the author's locations. Over the full sample period, 67% of publications feature an entirely US-based team. Across all articles, over 74% of researchers are affiliated with the US. Notably, there has been a steady rise in representation from researchers in non-US high-income countries, reaching 30% as of 2022. However, the rise in researchers in mid- or low-income countries (including those in India and China) is minimal and only started in the recent decade.

Finally, there is concordance between the study region and the authors' home regions. US researchers primarily study the US and other high-income countries, while researchers in other high-income countries mainly study their home countries and the US Such matching accounts for more than 80% of all publications. Altogether, these findings paint a worrying picture of the state of geographic representation in top management scholarship and the lack of meaningful progress in the last few decades.

This study makes several contributions. First, we contribute to the growing literature on the "colonization" of management (Banerjee, 2021; Bruton et al., 2022; Filatotchev et al., 2022; Jammulamadaka et al., 2021). While prior work has scrutinized the Western-centric nature of management theory, we are the first to provide broad quantitative estimates covering key top management scholarship since its inception. Second, we contribute to the broader literature on the WEIRD bias across the social sciences (Arnett, 2008; Linxen et al., 2021; Wilson & Knutsen, 2022) by extending these methods and ideas to the field of management research. Our contribution is also to introduce the idea of geographic inequality in the focus of study beyond simply the author's location or the nationality of experimental subjects. Third, we contribute to the nascent literature in the science of science and innovation more broadly on inferring geographic entities from publication texts (Nagaraj et al., 2020; Wilson, 2017; Wilson & Knutsen, 2022) and systematically relating authors' physical locations to regions studied (Briggs & Weathers, 2016). Here, we contribute a new machine-learning-based methodology and hope to make publicly available an open-source database to enable further meta-science on geographic inequality in social science research.

The remainder of this paper proceeds as follows: The next section provides background on measuring geographic inequality across the social sciences. The data and method section describes how the data are collected and processed and the methods used to conduct the analysis. The result section reports several stylized facts concerning the geographic distribution of management scholars and the regions they study. The final section concludes.

## BACKGROUND

The social and behavioral sciences aim to uncover fundamental insights about the underlying drivers of human and organizational actions, as well as to distill these insights into practical strategies to shape behavior (Whitley, 1984; Zand & Sorensen, 1975). Yet, across its many sub-fields, scientists are often confronted with the vast diversity of human behavior, organizational systems, and phenomena (Earley, 2006; Haire et al., 1966; Rosenzweig & Singh, 1991). Ideally, social scientists should strive to make sense of this diversity and collectively chart out a complete map of human experience (Black et al., 1991; Boyacigiller & Adler, 1991; Doktor et al., 1991). In practice, however, there are large gaps in our scholarship, which are oftentimes systematically related to culture and geography.

In particular, existing theories, models, and concepts rely heavily on samples that are WEIRD: Western, Educated, Industrialized, Rich, and Democratic

(Henrich et al., 2010), which are rarely representative of the diversity seen across the world. As a result, scholars warn that mainstream social science has implicitly treated Western theories as universal while overlooking important differences in other settings (Bruton et al., 2022; Doktor et al., 1991; Usunier, 1998). This can be especially problematic when these theories are subsequently applied to non-Western contexts, where existing findings may not apply (Tiokhin et al., 2019). It could also mean that research questions of particular relevance to non-WEIRD geographies (e.g., the one-child policy in China, apartheid in South Africa, and the caste system in India) are not sufficiently covered by mainstream scholarship (Bruton et al., 2022; George et al., 2016). Closely tied to this issue is the fact that researchers themselves are often deeply WEIRD (Baruch, 2001; Meadon & Spurrett, 2010). Not only does this mean they are less likely to focus on non-WEIRD subjects (Meadon & Spurrett, 2010; Nagaraj et al., 2020), but also that the social sciences are drawing from a limited talent pool and being deprived of the benefits of diversity and openness (Clancy & Davis, 2019; Hong & Page, 2004; Lakhani et al., 2007). All of this has led to growing calls to "decolonize" the social sciences (Banerjee, 2021; Clancy & Davis, 2019; Murphy & Zhu, 2012).

In the context of management research, this could lead researchers to miss noteworthy organizational phenomena from understudied regions, such as Chinese family firms navigating succession planning amid the absence of any sibling rivalry due to the One Child Policy (Li & Piezunka, 2019). Alternatively, it may cause researchers to overlook regional contingencies to general theories calibrated in Western contexts, for instance, why firms engage in corporate venture capital (Dushnitsky & Yug, 2022). Perhaps most severely, the field may fail to see competing or contradictory evidence to hypotheses developed in the West, for instance, the negative relationship between resource availability and Corporate Social Responsibility (CSR) observed in Sub-Sahara Africa but not in developed countries (Julian & Ofori-dankwa, 2013). In short, an overt focus on a handful of regions threatens to impoverish the field by leaving important (generalizable) insights on the table and by preventing the applicability of management research to large and important phenomena that are not observed in the West. This has led some of the most influential journals in the field (e.g., the *Academy of Management Journal*) to explicitly call for more research focusing on non-WEIRD contexts (George et al., 2016).

Besides the geographic focus of the study, there is an additional layer contributing to the geographic inequality of social science research: the researchers themselves (Meadon & Spurrett, 2010). While the community of management scholars is relatively global – with the Academy of Management's membership extending to 110 countries[1] – scholars who are able to publish in top journals generally hail from Western contexts. To be sure, these journals are themselves mostly located in the West. For example, the UT Dallas top journal list, widely regarded as the collection of flagship management journals, predominantly includes US journals (Harley & Fleming, 2021; Wei & Zhang, 2020). Nevertheless, these journals have global mandates and actively aspire for geographic representation in their scholarship base (Conlon, 2000). Furthermore, they have extensive international reach and are now factored into hiring and tenure decisions in business schools across the world. For instance, many Chinese universities and the National Science Foundation of China have switched to the UT Dallas journal rankings (Chen et al., 2021). In other words, these influential journals set the tone for the management field globally. If they are indeed excluding large swaths of researchers, then they are potentially missing out on a critical lever to address the geographic inequality in their base of authors, especially in light of evidence that scientists from understudied regions tend to contribute novel insights from their local contexts (Nagaraj et al., 2020).

To address this problem, we need concrete measures of the degree of geographic bias in academic research. While there is a common impression that a geographic bias is widespread, many of the social sciences continue to lack empirical evidence that confirms its existence (Apicella et al., 2020). Of all the disciplines, the field of psychology has arguably made the most progress in identifying the scale of the problem (Linxen et al., 2021). A pioneering analysis of top journals across six psychology sub-disciplines from 2003 to 2007 revealed a significant geographical imbalance, with 68% of study subjects hailing from the United States and a staggering 96% from Western industrialized countries, including North America, Europe, Australia, and Israel (Arnett, 2008). Building on this work, Hendriks et al. (2019) investigate the global reach of positive psychology interventions (PPIs), sourcing data from 187 full-text articles and 188 RCTs across 24 countries between 1998 and 2017, and find that 78.2% of such trials were conducted in Western countries. Finally, Nielsen et al. (2017) meticulously reviewed 1,582 articles published between 2006 and 2010 in three leading psychology journals with high-impact factors, recording the geographical regions of participants and affiliations of authors. The results were striking, with 90.52% of studies involving participants from WEIRD countries and a mere 6.76% from non-WEIRD countries.

Other fields are also beginning to make inroads into measuring geographic bias, revealing similar disparities. In human-centered computing, for instance, Linxen et al. (2021) analyzed 3,269 articles from the CHI Conference on Human Factors in Computing Systems (2016–2020). Their results indicate that only 16% to 30% of studies included participants from non-Western countries. In political science, Wilson and Knutsen (2022) examine a database comprising titles and abstracts from 27,690 publications across eight prominent journals from 1906 to 2019: they find a 1.6:1 ratio of Western to non-Western country references. In conflict studies, Phillips and Greene (2020) review 4,171 articles from five prominent conflict journals between 1990 and 2015 and find that the United States is the most frequently mentioned country in abstracts. In economics, Das et al. (2013) analyze 76,046 economics papers published between 1985 and 2005 and estimate that papers focusing on the US are 2.5 percentage points more likely to be published in the top five journals. Ironically, even the field of geography is not immune to this phenomenon. Graham et al. (2014) look at Wikipedia articles that are "geotagged" and find these articles predominantly reference entities in North America. They find that 564,084 articles concern the United States, while only tens of thousands concern even some European countries, Japan, Australia, and India. Finally, and remarkably, this phenomenon even occurs within the Global South. Looking at two top journals in African politics scholarship during the period 1993 to 2013, Briggs and Weathers (2016) find that former British colonies are far more studied, as are countries where English is the official language.

In contrast, the field of management research has largely not yet begun to scrutinize its geographic bias (Gelfand et al., 2008, 2017). In one early exception, Baruch (2001) studied the geographic origin of the authors of 1,948 articles in the top seven management journals and found minimal representation (20.1%) among authors outside of the North American zone; further, three Western countries (UK, Australia, and Israel) are responsible for over half of the scholarship outside of North America. While useful, the study only considers four discrete time periods, with the most recent sample year being 1995. As a result, it cannot speak to the current state of inequality nor its scope. In addition, the study does not shed any light on the concentration of the regions studied. More recently, Pitesa and Gelfand (2022) provided more context on focal areas by collecting data on a small sample of articles published in the journal *Organizational Behavior and Human Decision Processes (OBHDP)*. Their findings indicate a significant bias toward WEIRD-context publications at 84.21% in 2010, which has since risen to 86.57% in 2020. However, the study is confined to only one journal and two time periods, which may not be representative of the field as a whole. Altogether, this underscores the need for a more comprehensive analysis of management scholarship that considers (1) a larger sample of major journals and research streams, (2) multiple dimensions of geographic bias, including researchers' affiliations and the geographic focus, and (3) all contiguous years of scholarship since the inception of the field.

To make headway on this front, a recent study by Nagaraj et al. (2020) offers a potential roadmap. This study examines the impact of reduced costs and sharing restrictions for satellite imagery data from NASA's Landsat program on the geographic diversity of Landsat-enabled environmental science. To do so, the authors collect 24,000 journal articles from over 34,000 authors from 1975 to 2005. Using machine-learning entity-detection algorithms, they geo-parse the publication titles, abstracts, and institutional affiliations to detect words that represent place names. Finally, these names are geo-coded to obtain latitudes and longitudes. For example, a published author from the "Department of Environmental Science, Tsinghua University" is matched to China, while the publication "A mini-surge on the Ryder Glacier, Greenland, observed by satellite radar interferometry" (Joughin et al., 1996) is matched to Greenland. Using this approach, the authors document how the increased accessibility of Landsat data democratized scientific research by encouraging more research from (and about) developing countries. Not only does this study suggest that both dimensions of geographic inequality are important, but also that current methods enable us to systematically measure these two forms of inequality from publication texts.

In the following sections, we build on these methods and apply them to the field of management with the goal of providing a quantitative assessment of the current status and dynamics of geographic representation in the field. This is important because having data-driven estimates can help assess the severity of the issue, as well as providing a tangible baseline from which ongoing progress can be monitored and managed (Bar-Gill et al., 2023). Further, statistical estimates generally carry more weight in academic and policy circles and can lead to more targeted and effective interventions (Dilnot, 2012; Hjort et al., 2021). Surveying the major journals will help to capture the overall inequality in top management scholarship while also illuminating any heterogeneity by subfield (Arnett, 2008). Understanding long-term dynamics will be beneficial to learn if the field has made progress (and prompt reflection on why), or if it has not and is in need of a wake-up call (Wilson & Knutsen, 2022). Finally, looking at geography in terms of the location of management scholars, the geographies they focus on, and the interaction of these two variables will provide richer dynamics and enable more fine-tuned and nuanced analysis.

## DATA AND METHODS

We focus on six reputable management journals: *Academy of Management Journal, Academy of Management Review, Strategic Management Journal, Administrative Science Quarterly, Organization Science*, and *Management Science*. Such a focus on top journals is standard in scientometric analysis (Baruch, 2001; Birkinshaw et al., 2016; Correa et al., 2013; Wilson & Knutsen, 2022) and makes sense given our focus on top management scholarship. However, one might worry that we only consider publications authored in English, and do not include publications in local and regional journals. This means we will inevitably miss noteworthy scholarship authored in non-Western contexts or by non-Western authors. Nevertheless, our choice is justified in our context because these six journals comprise the upper echelons of the field and set the research direction of management scholarship globally. Local journals, especially non-English language journals, have local audiences and are rarely read by non-native researchers. Indeed, these are the very journals that authors from non-Western contexts strive to publish in and are rewarded for doing so (Chen et al., 2021). They are also the journals from which major practitioner journals (e.g., *Harvard Business Review*) source, which gives them an out-sized role in deciding which management insights are implemented in practice (Birkinshaw et al., 2016). Finally, these journals consider themselves to be hubs of international management scholarship (Conlon, 2000; George et al., 2016). Hence, the decision to focus on the top management scholarship is quite natural; nevertheless, our findings should not be interpreted as representing the totality of management scholarship.

Conceptually, we link science to geography in two distinct ways. Firstly, we look at the distribution of regions studied; this is in line with most systematic reviews of WEIRD bias (Das et al., 2013; Nielsen et al., 2017; Wilson & Knutsen, 2022). The one difference is rather than focus on the nationality of experimental subjects – as is common in Psychology – we measure the geographies where a study is focused: for instance, a quasi-experimental setting or a data set unique to a specific country the study leverages. Further, following a growing literature, we also look at the distribution of management researchers, as given by their institutional affiliations (Baruch, 2001; Briggs & Weathers, 2016). Not only will this help to assess the state of inclusivity in top management publishing – which we hold as intrinsically important – but it will also enable us to shed light on additional empirical questions, such as whether researchers from non-Western countries do indeed tend to focus more on their local contexts, even when publishing in US-based journals (Meadon & Spurrett, 2010; Nagaraj et al., 2020). To facilitate ease of interpretation, we categorize countries into several groups. In particular, following Nagaraj et al. (2020), we establish three regional categories using country income tiers from World Bank data: the United States, high-income countries other than the US, and mid-to-low-income countries. Fig. A2 shows the resulting categorization of countries. Note that this categorization is not a perfect separation of Western and non-Western as some high-income countries like Chile and Saudi Arabia do not belong to the West.

Typically, academic studies in the "Science of Science" and other related meta-science disciplines leverage meta-data procured from existing databases, such as OpenAlex, Scopus, and Web of Science. However, no such systematic meta-data pertaining to detailed and standardized geographical information exists for management publications. Hence, we need to manually obtain this information ourselves, which we do using a suite of machine-learning tools. In the following subsections, we briefly describe how we construct our list of publications, geo-code researchers' affiliations, and conduct geoparsing to identify the focal regions. For more details, see our data appendix[2] (Appendix A).

*Publication List*

To identify the list of papers to be included in our sample, we first draw from the official websites of the journals. We decided to scrape the websites because they contain "Archives" sections, which we believe to have the most comprehensive coverage of publication histories. While the difficulty of this process varies by journal and time period, we are able to obtain the full list of publication titles since inception and, in some cases, further publication-level information like the texts of abstracts. Note that our machine learning tools that process textual data will not identify abstracts if they are made available in non-textual formats like PDFs or images, which is sometimes the case for the official websites. Moreover, the raw texts of the publications will not always contain sufficient information about the authors' institutional affiliations.

As a result, we also obtain additional publication-level information from Dimensions, a new resource that is designed to enable researchers to explore, access, and analyze a wide array of research-related data, including publications, grants, patents, clinical trials, and policy documents, all within a single, interconnected database (Hook et al., 2020). In our specific context, there are several advantages to using Dimensions: first, Dimensions has comprehensive coverage even for old publications dating back to the 1950s, which enables us to analyze long-term trends over the past seven decades. Second, Dimensions has relatively comprehensive information with respect to authors' affiliations, which are raw texts that we can clean, standardize, and geo-code.[3] Third, Dimensions provides strong coverage of paper abstracts. We export publication-level information from the Dimensions API and then match it to our cleaned list of publications based on the Digital Object Identifier (DOI) or title.

## Geographic Focus

Our method enables us to detect any mentions of geographies in the content of the publications, which is defined as a city, state, country, or group of countries on which the paper is focusing. For this method, we focus on a publication's abstract or title to find direct mentions of locations and indirect mentions of country-specific entities; for example, agencies like USPTO are specific to the US. As we elaborate further in the data appendix, our decision to keep only the title and abstract instead of using the full manuscript leads to the highest rate of true positives while keeping false positives to a minimal level. This decision is standard in the literature (Phillips & Greene, 2020; Wilson & Knutsen, 2022). Nevertheless, we acknowledge that our procedure will likely understate the true number of topic mentions: this is especially the case when the publication focuses on the US since such a regional focus is more likely to be omitted in the title or abstract (Kahalon et al., 2022), or when the papers have a focus on three or more countries as country names tend not to be listed explicitly in the abstract. After cleaning the abstracts and titles, we leverage spaCy, an open-source software library for advanced NLP, as our key NLP tool to recognize organizations and geographic information. A detailed illustration of the geoparsing process is provided in the data appendix (see Appendix A).

## Researcher Affiliations

Using the data exported from Dimensions, we are able to identify the names of any institutions authors are affiliated with, as well as the locations of these institutions. However, the data on affiliations are quite raw as there is considerable variability and complexity in their format: while some contain only the (un-standardized) name of the university or organization, others contain city, state, zip code, and in some cases superfluous information like department and position. Hence, we first use spaCy to recognize the names of organizations from the raw text. We clean these names and feed them into Geocodify's API, which searches for a potential match from Geocodify's underlying data sources, primarily OpenStreetMap, Who's On First, and GeoNames. Each match contains information including name, city, region, country, latitude, and longitude. Geocodify will return multiple potential matches for one input, so we filter the potential matches to identify the correct location. Finally, we conduct extensive manual checks to verify the accuracy of the geocoding. Looking forward, we aim to establish a data set of all institutions and their locations together with a matching rule dealing with raw strings of affiliation information to be used as a baseline for future research. A detailed illustration of the cleaning process is provided in Appendix A.

*Summary Statistics*

Table 1 provides summary statistics for our final dataset. We present the descriptive statistics at three levels: the publication-level, the publication-geofocus-level, and the publication-researcher-level. Panel A shows the publication-level statistics. Altogether, *Management Science* has 8,476 publications since 1954; *Organization Science* has 1,950 publications since 1990; *Academy of Management Review* has 2,589 publications since 1976; *Academy of Management Journal* has 3,589 publications since 1958; *Strategic Management Journal* has 3,034 publications since 1980; and *Administrative Science Quarterly* has 1,573 publications since 1956. Across all these journals, we are able to geo-code at least one researcher following our data processing procedures for 96% to 99% of publications, while we are able to identify a geographic focus for about 15% to 25% of publications. The one exception to this is AMR, which is generally a more theory-oriented journal. Our match rate for geographic focus is under 5%. We conducted a validation by manually looking at the title/abstract of a random sample of 250 publications and found that our algorithm fully identifies all the geographic focus we manually tagged: most of the papers without a geographic focus are theory papers. Throughout the paper, we focus on country-level mentions, which count for about 95% of all the geographic focus being identified.[4]

At the publication level, each publication is assigned to one of the three categories: "US Only" indicates that all the researchers (or geographic focuses) that correspond to a given publication are located in the US, "≥1 High Income Non-US" indicates there is at least 1 researcher (or geographic focuses) that located in a high-income country other than the US and there is no researcher (or geographic focuses) located in mid- or low-income countries, and "≥1 Mid-Low Income" indicates at least one researcher (or geographic focus) located in a mid or low-income country. This assignment guarantees that each publication is assigned to only one category while (intentionally) providing more opportunities for non-US publications to gain visibility. Further, since academic research in the US generally leads the world, it is meaningful to look at the relative existence of researchers from non-US countries instead of simply comparing raw numbers. Overall, conditional on any topic being identified, 12% to 19% of publications have at least some focus on mid- or low-income countries. The share of publications with some focus on high-income countries other than the US is comparable at 22% to 32%, while the share of publications focusing entirely on the US is about 51% to 66%. On the other hand, the distribution of researcher affiliations is even more skewed: about 55% to 78% of publications are authored by researchers *all* affiliated with a US institution; about 19% to 40% of the publications have at least one author affiliated with an institution in a high-income country other than the US,[5] and only 1% to 6% of the publications have an author from a mid- or low-income country.

Panel B shows publication-geofocus level statistics, i.e., each observation represents a publication and geofocus pair, as each paper can have multiple geographic focuses. We assign each country-level focus to one of three groups: "United States," "High Income Non-US", or "Mid-Low Income." With each

***Table 1.*** Summary Statistics.

| | MNSC | OrgSci | AMR | AMJ | SMJ | ASQ |
|---|---|---|---|---|---|---|
| **Panel A: Publication Level** | | | | | | |
| Initial Publication Year | 1954 | 1990 | 1976 | 1958 | 1980 | 1956 |
| Number of Publications | 8476 | 1950 | 2589 | 3589 | 3034 | 1573 |
| Percent with Geo-Focus Coded | 14.37 | 24.51 | 3.75 | 16.3 | 28.31 | 26.57 |
| Publications with Geo-Focus Coded | 1218 | 478 | 97 | 585 | 859 | 418 |
| Publications with Country Level Geo-Focus | 1157 | 453 | 92 | 567 | 823 | 408 |
| Only US Focus | 760 | 233 | 52 | 315 | 434 | 240 |
| ≥1 High Income Non-US Focus | 254 | 136 | 29 | 147 | 241 | 106 |
| ≥1 Mid-Low Income Focus | 143 | 84 | 11 | 105 | 148 | 62 |
| Percent with Researcher Geo-coded | 96.02 | 98.31 | 96.25 | 95.54 | 97.92 | 99.75 |
| Publications with Researcher Geo-coded | 8139 | 1917 | 2492 | 3429 | 2971 | 1514 |
| Only US Researcher | 5341 | 1063 | 1945 | 2520 | 1714 | 1165 |
| ≥1 High Income Non-US Researcher | 2296 | 780 | 523 | 766 | 1078 | 295 |
| ≥1 Mid-Low Income Researcher | 502 | 74 | 24 | 143 | 179 | 54 |
| **Panel B: Publication-GeoFocus Level** | | | | | | |
| Number of Geo-Focus Coded | 1537 | 608 | 118 | 711 | 1073 | 513 |
| Country Level Geo-Focus Coded | 1434 | 566 | 108 | 680 | 994 | 491 |
| United States Focus | 963 | 301 | 65 | 386 | 536 | 292 |
| High Income Non-US Focus | 305 | 173 | 32 | 183 | 288 | 132 |
| Mid-Low Income Focus | 166 | 92 | 11 | 111 | 170 | 67 |
| **Panel C: Publication-Researcher Level** | | | | | | |
| Number of Researchers | 18237 | 4388 | 4617 | 7987 | 6763 | 2832 |
| Percent of Researchers Geo-coded | 93.38 | 95.53 | 93.83 | 92.74 | 95 | 95.48 |
| Number of Researchers Geo-coded | 17029 | 4192 | 4332 | 7407 | 6425 | 2684 |
| United States Researchers | 12520 | 2808 | 3500 | 5805 | 4315 | 2188 |
| High Income Non-US Researchers | 3828 | 1298 | 806 | 1404 | 1866 | 432 |
| Mid-Low Income Researchers | 681 | 86 | 26 | 198 | 244 | 64 |

*Notes*: This table lists summary statistics of 6 journals at the publication level (Panel A), the publication-researcher level (Panel B), and the Publication-GeoFocus level (Panel C). One publication can have multiple researchers and/or topics being geo-coded. In Panel A, publications are uniquely assigned to one of the three categories: "only US" means all the researchers or topics are in the US, "≥1 High Income Non-US" means there exists at least 1 researcher or topic that is in a high-income country other than the US and there is no researcher or topic in mid-low income countries, and "≥1 Mid-Low Income" means there exists at least 1 researcher or topic that is in a mid- or low-income country. In Panel B, the number of topics geocoded is the number of regions studied we are able to identify following the procedure illustrated in Appendix A.2. See text for details. In Panel C, the number of researchers is at the publication-researcher level so researchers with multiple publications are counted multiple times. The number of researchers geocoded is the number of researchers whose affiliations we are able to identify and detect the latitude, longitude, city, state, and country information following the procedure illustrated in Appendix A.3.

topic weighted by its propensity to appear in publications, about 53% to 67% of referenced geographies are in the US: 21% to 31% are in high-income countries other than the US, and about 10% to 17% are in mid- or low-income countries.

Finally, Panel C shows the publication-researcher level statistics. On average, the top management journals have about 1.8 to 2.2 authors for each publication, and we are able to geocode about 93% to 96% of researchers. Note that any author with more than one publication in the top six journals would be recorded with multiple observations. Hence, our usage of the term "researchers" in this context does not refer to the unique number of researchers: each researcher is weighted by the number of publications they have or their productivity. Here we can simply assign individual researchers "equitably" to the region of their affiliated institution: "United States," "High Income Non-US," or "Mid-Low Income." About 67% to 81% of researchers are affiliated with a university or organization in the US; 16% to 31% are from high-income countries other than the US; and less than 4% are from mid- or low-income countries.[6] We can see that while the number of researchers from mid- or low-income countries is less than 4%, the percentage of regional focus in mid- or low-income countries can be as high as 17%, which suggests increasing attention to non-Western countries from the Western world.

Fig. 1 plot (i) shows the total number of publications in the six focal journals each year, and plot (ii) shows the number of publications for every year in the sample time frame for each journal. The number of yearly publications is relatively stable for the six journals in the three decades from 1980 to 2010, while some witnessed a growing trend in the most recent decade. Particularly for *Management Science*, there has been a "nearly exponential" growth trend in the past 10 years: the number of yearly publications in *Management Science* has exceeded the number of publications from all five other journals combined since 2018.[7]

## MAIN RESULTS

We aim to shed light on the following three questions: (1) where does management research focus on? (2) where are management researchers located? And (3) how do physical location and geographic focus interact?

### The Geographic Focus of Management Research

We first examine the distribution of geographic focus in the top management publications. Note that only about 20–30% of articles have a geo-coded geographic focus, and the presented results are all conditional based on a regional focus being identified. See Appendix A for a discussion on method and precision.

Fig. 2 shows a choropleth plot of the relative intensity of research focus at the country level on a log scale. It shows a clear US dominance followed by interests in China, Canada, Japan, India, and EU countries, while there is no research focusing on most countries in Africa and the Middle East. The overall results for all publications with an identified research topic in the top six journals are summarized in Fig. 3. Panel A shows the percentages by region, and Panel B shows

## (i) Total Publications by Year

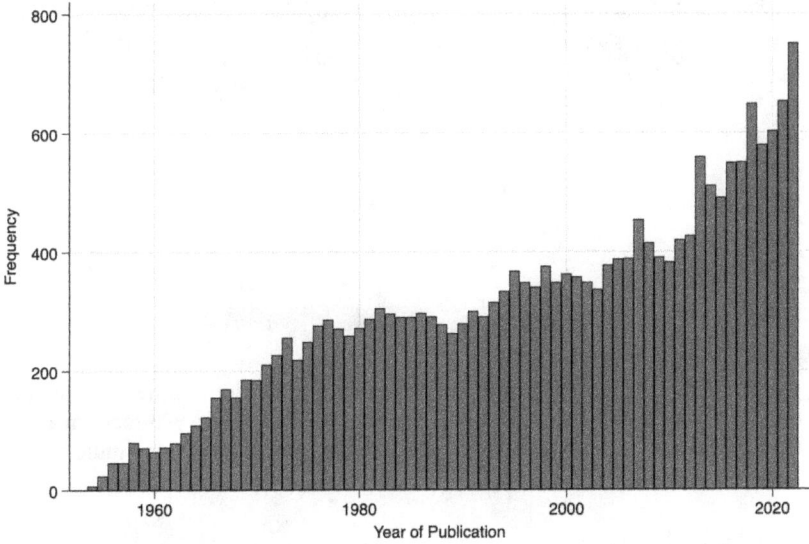

## (ii) Yearly Publications by Journal

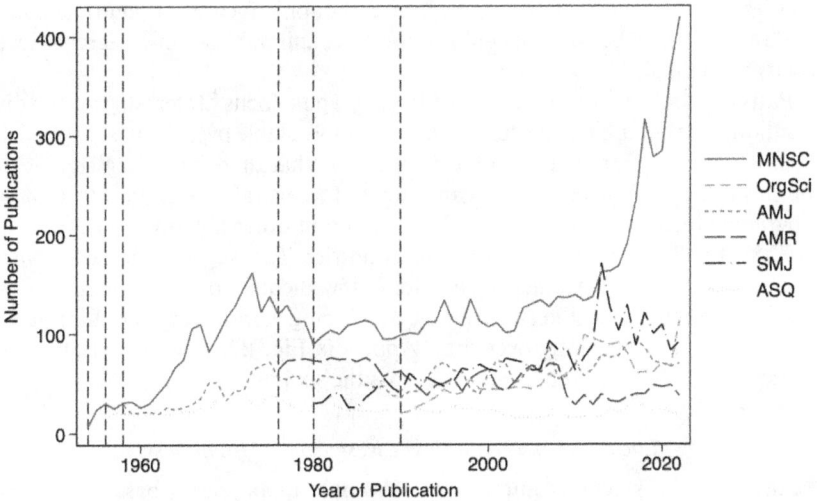

*Fig. 1.* Number of Top Management Publications, 1954–2022.
*Notes*: This figure shows the raw number of publications across the top 6 Management journals over time. Plot (i) depicts the overall count by year, and plot (ii) decomposes the yearly count by journal. See the text for more details.

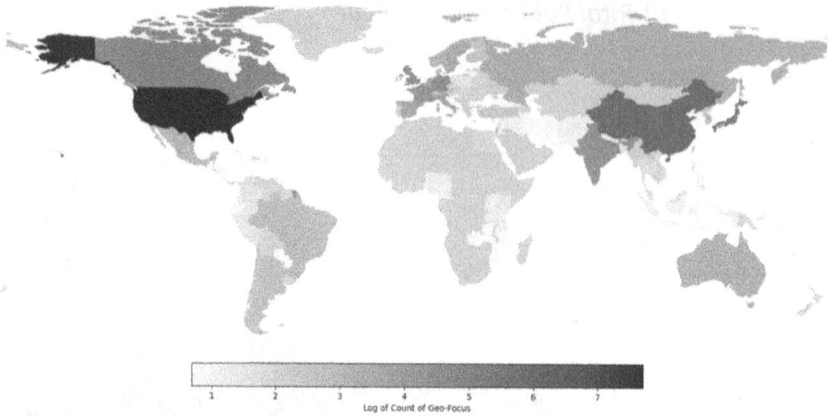

*Fig. 2.* Countries Studied in Top Management Publications. *Notes*: This figure visualizes the frequency of each country being studied as a geo-focus in a choropleth plot. The color coding uses an exponential scale. Gray indicates that no geo-focus is identified based on our method. See text for more details.

how these percentages change over time. Plot (i) is at the publication level and shows that about 58% of the geographic focus is in the US, about 27% in other high-income countries, and about 15% in the mid- or low-income countries. Since only a small number of publications have geographic focuses on multiple countries, the difference between the publication-level and publication-researcher-level results is minimal.

Plots (iii) and (iv) depict the trends in geographic focus.[8] Interestingly, the distribution of geographic focus has been remarkably stable over the past seven decades: this is even more impressive as it turns out that there have been significant compositional changes to the research force. In general, about 55% to 60% of geographic focus is within the US, 20% to 40% in other high-income countries, and 15% to 20% in mid- or low-income countries. This suggests that even when there is a paucity of researchers from mid- or low-income countries, there is nonetheless persistent interest in studying the developing world. However, this interest has not grown significantly over time. Appendix Fig. B2 shows the relative frequency of the three region categories across the six journals.

*Locations of Management Researcher Affiliations*

We then examine where the authors in our sample are physically based. The overall results combining all the six journals are shown in Fig. 4. Panel A shows the percentages by region, and Panel B shows how these percentages change over time. Plot (i) is at the publication-level and shows that 67.34% of all publications in our sample are authored by researchers all affiliated with a US institution, 27.93% of the publications have a combination of researchers from the US and non-US high-income countries, and only 4.72% of the publications have at least one researcher affiliated with an institution in a mid- or low-income country. This inequality is

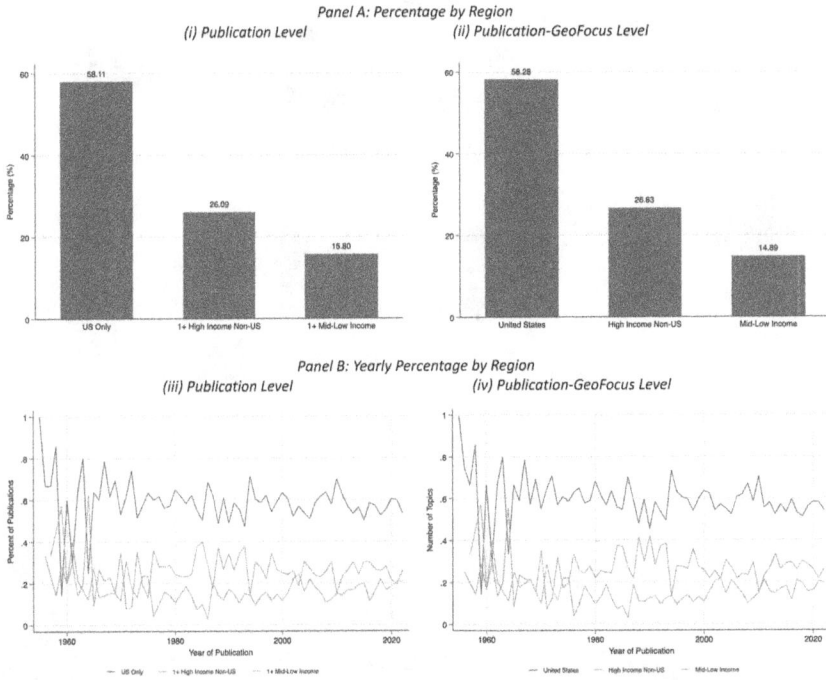

Panel A: Percentage by Region

(i) Publication Level                       (ii) Publication-GeoFocus Level

Panel B: Yearly Percentage by Region

(iii) Publication Level                    (iv) Publication-GeoFocus Level

*Fig. 3.* Distribution of Geo-Focus in Top Management Publications. *Notes*: This figure visualizes the bias to study Western regions in management publications, conditional on a region being identified. Panel A depicts percentages by region over the full sample period and Panel B depicts percentages each year. Plots (i) and (iii) are at the publication level, where each publication is assigned to one of 3 regional categories: "US Only," "≥1 High Income Non-US," and "≥1 Mid-Low Income." "US Only" means all the regions studied are in the US; "≥1 High Income Non-US" means at least one of the regions studied is in a high-income country other than the U.S. and there is no region studied in mid-low income countries; and "≥1 Mid-Low Income" means there is at least one region studied that is in a mid- or low-income country. Plots (ii) and (iv) are at the Publication-GeoFocus level as one publication can have multiple research focuses. Each topic is assigned one of 3 region categories: "United States," "High Income Non-US," and "Mid-Low Income." See text for more details.

even more pronounced when viewed at the publication-researcher level. As plot (ii) shows, 74.14% of researchers are from the US, and only 3.07% are from a mid- or low-income country when weighted by researchers' productivity. Hence, in comparison with the results for research focus, there is significantly more US dominance in management research with respect to researchers.

Turning to trends over time, plots (iii) and (iv) highlight that while management research was completely dominated by the United States in the 1950s and 1960s, its share of both publications and researchers has been gradually declining

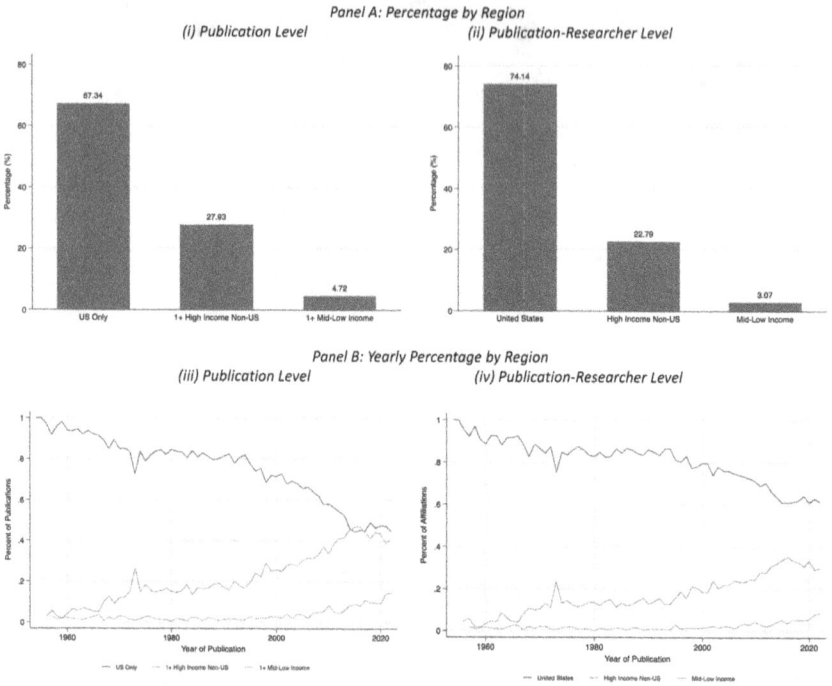

*Fig. 4.* Distribution of Management Scholars in Top Management Publications. *Notes*: This figure visualizes the bias in top scholarship towards authors located in Western regions. Panel A depicts percentages by region over the full sample period, and Panel B depicts percentages each year. Plots (i) and (iii) are at the publication level; due to the potential for multiple co-authors, a publication is considered "US Only' if all co-authors are based in the US, "≥1 High Income Non-US" if at least 1 co-author is based in a high-income country outside the US (and none of the co-authors are based in mid-low income countries), and "≥1 Mid-Low Income" if at least 1 coauthor is based in a mid- or low-income country; Plots (ii) and (iv) are at the publication-researcher level and hence weighted by the productivity of the researcher; individual researchers are assigned to the region of their affiliated institution: "United States," "High Income Non-US," and "Mid-Low Income." See the text for more details.

over time, particularly since the late 1990s.[9] Since then, the representation of researchers from high-income non-US countries has started to increase, peaking around 2018 when nearly 50% of the top management publications involved at least one researcher from high-income non-US countries. Nevertheless, there still exists a large 30% gap in the productivity-weighted share of researchers. On the other hand, the trend for researchers from mid- or low-income countries was nearly flat prior to the late 2000s, and the increase since has been relatively slow. In 2022, about 15% of publications involved a researcher from a mid- or low-income country, whereas the productivity-weighted share of researchers was less than 10%.

We also visualize the trend of affiliated institutions with top management publications. We record the latitude and longitude of each university and aggregate them to the grid level with a size of 1-degree latitude and 1-degree longitude. For each grid point, we record the earliest year that there is a researcher affiliated with any institution inside that grid point published in a top management journal. This measure shows the entry of affiliated institutions into the field of management. The grid points are visualized in Fig. 5. The markers are coded with different shapes according to research publication periods: plus signs for pre-1990, triangles for 1990-2010, and squares for post-2010 entries in top management journals.

This figure shows that the majority of markers in the United States are plus signs, suggesting that most of the US institutions (especially on the coasts) had been actively publishing in top management journals before 1990. After 1990, an increasing number of institutions in the central areas of the US started publishing, as revealed by the triangles and sparsely distributed square markers. In Europe, however, the plus signs are mainly concentrated in the United Kingdom and the Netherlands, and there are clear clusters of triangles and squares, especially in Spain and central Germany. This hints at the rise of high-income non-US institutions since the 1990s. In mid- or low-income countries, there are only a handful of institutions that published before 1990 or even before 2010: the majority of initial publications were after 2010. This trend is especially prominent in China, India, and Argentina. These results align well with Fig. 4 Panel B, where the number of researchers from high-income countries other than the US started to

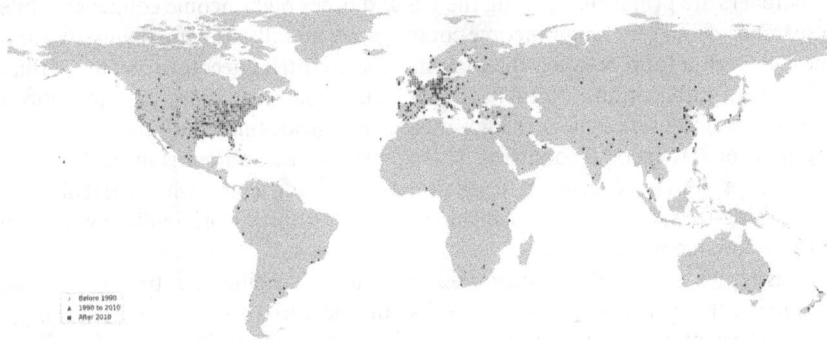

*Fig. 5.* Entry of Affiliated Institutions in Top Management Publications.
*Notes*: This figure visualizes the timing of entry of institutions into the top 6 management journals. Entry means the existence of a publishing researcher affiliated with that institution. Each dot represents one or more institutions with a researcher who has published in a top management journal within the 1-degree latitude × 1-degree longitude grid cell. In total, there are 700 grid points representing 2598 unique institutions. The color of the dot codes the first time an author affiliated with the institution publishes in a top management journal. Plus signs indicate researchers publishing in top journals before 1990. Triangles represent researchers publishing for the first time in between 1990 and 2010. Squares represent the entry of new researchers publishing for the first time since 2010.

rise in the 1990s, while in mid- or low-income countries, the rise has only started in the recent decade.

Finally, having reviewed the overall trends in management research, we decompose these trends by journal. Appendix Fig. B5 shows the results at the publication level for each of the six journals, and Appendix Fig. B6 shows the results at the publication-researcher level. In general, each of the journal follows the same overall trend as described above, however the timing and the extent of increases in non-US representation differs from journal to journal.

### Interaction Between Location and Regional Focus

Finally, we combine the distribution of researcher affiliations and regional focus to reveal the rich dynamics of how researchers decide which regions to study. Fig. 6 shows a scaled heatmap of the joint frequencies. Plot (i) is at the publication level, with a total of 3,357 publications. Plot (ii) is at the publication-researcher-topic level with a total of 7,566 observations: each publication can have multiple researchers and multiple regions (e.g., a publication with three researchers and two regions would yield six observations).

The most common frequency involves US researchers studying US topics: about 40% of all publications consist of only US researchers focusing exclusively on the US. This frequency is even greater when weighted by researcher productivity and the frequency of topics. The second and third related categories consist of US researchers studying other high-income countries and researchers from other high-income countries studying the US, respectively. Altogether, US researchers are primarily studying the US and other high-income countries, while researchers from other high-income countries are mainly studying themselves and the US Such a loop between the high-income countries accounts for more than 80% of all publications. Notably, a small but prominent share of publications (about 15%) are researchers in high-income countries (including the US) studying mid- or low-income countries. This appears to be an important spillover of knowledge from the developed world to the developing world, while most of these developing-focused researchers in high-income countries originally come from mid- or low-income countries.

Lastly, we further decompose these results by specific countries instead of regional categories. We produce one list of the top 10 countries in terms of the number of researchers and another list of the top 10 in terms of regional focus. There are seven countries that overlap: Canada, China, France, Italy, the Netherlands, the United Kingdom, and the United States. The three countries that only feature in the list of researchers are Australia, Singapore, and Spain, while the three countries that only feature in the list of regions are Germany, India, and Japan. Fig. 7 shows a heat plot of the country-level joint frequencies, where the percentage in each cell shows the relative frequency within a row. The union of the 13 countries is included to ensure the symmetry of the heatmap, and we use an exponential scale to color-code the frequencies. There are several clear findings. Firstly, researchers in all countries focus on the US, and for nearly all countries, this is their primary focus. Secondly, researchers from the majority of countries are also interested in studying their home countries. This is most

*(i) Publication Level (N=3,357)*

Researcher Affiliation Category (vertical axis)

| US Only | 9.71 | 14.80 | 39.59 |
| ≥1 High Income Non-US | 4.44 | 10.04 | 15.97 |
| ≥1 Mid-Low Income | 1.91 | 1.22 | 2.32 |

≥1 Mid-Low Income — ≥1 High Income Non-US — US Only
Research Geo-Focus Category

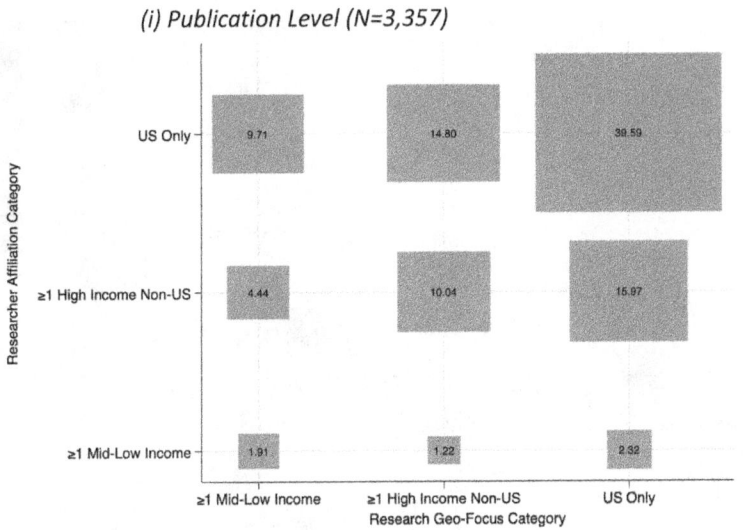

*(ii) Publications-Researcher-GeoFocus Level (N=7,566)*

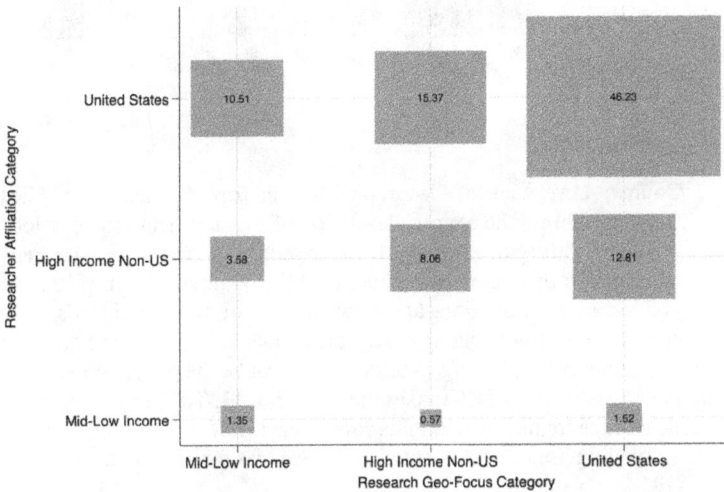

Researcher Affiliation Category (vertical axis)

| United States | 10.51 | 15.37 | 46.23 |
| High Income Non-US | 3.58 | 8.06 | 12.61 |
| Mid-Low Income | 1.35 | 0.57 | 1.52 |

Mid-Low Income — High Income Non-US — United States
Research Geo-Focus Category

*Fig. 6.* Management Scholars and Geo-Focus in Top Management Publications. *Notes*: This figure shows the interaction of management scholars' locations (vertical axis) and the regions they study (horizontal axis) in top Management journals, conditional on the region being identified. Plot (i) is at the publication level, where each publication is assigned to one of 3 regional categories: "US Only," "≥1 High Income Non-US," and "≥1 Mid-Low Income." Each publication is assigned twice: once based on researcher affiliation (vertical axis) and once based on research topic (horizontal axis). Plot (ii) is at the publication-researcher-topic level as one publication can have multiple researchers and multiple regional focuses. Each researcher and each topic is assigned one of 3 region categories: "United States," "High Income Non-US," and "Mid-Low Income." See text for more details.

| Country of Researcher Affiliation | Australia | Canada | China | France | Germany | India | Italy | Japan | Netherlands | Singapore | Spain | United Kingdom | United States |
|---|---|---|---|---|---|---|---|---|---|---|---|---|---|
| Australia | 4.60% | 3.45% | 24.14% | 0.00% | 1.15% | 3.45% | 0.00% | 3.45% | 2.30% | 0.00% | 1.15% | 2.30% | 54.02% |
| Canada | 0.32% | 19.37% | 7.62% | 2.54% | 1.90% | 2.22% | 1.59% | 3.49% | 0.32% | 0.00% | 1.27% | 1.90% | 57.46% |
| China | 0.55% | 2.20% | 45.05% | 0.00% | 1.10% | 0.55% | 0.55% | 2.75% | 0.55% | 1.65% | 2.20% | 0.55% | 42.31% |
| France | 0.69% | 2.08% | 9.72% | 9.03% | 1.39% | 1.39% | 4.17% | 8.33% | 0.00% | 0.69% | 4.17% | 3.47% | 54.86% |
| Germany | 0.00% | 1.41% | 2.82% | 2.82% | 12.68% | 0.00% | 1.41% | 4.23% | 2.82% | 0.00% | 0.00% | 14.08% | 57.75% |
| India | 0.00% | 26.67% | 0.00% | 0.00% | 6.67% | 26.67% | 0.00% | 0.00% | 0.00% | 0.00% | 0.00% | 0.00% | 40.00% |
| Italy | 1.28% | 0.00% | 5.13% | 0.00% | 2.56% | 2.56% | 21.79% | 10.26% | 0.00% | 3.85% | 0.00% | 1.28% | 51.28% |
| Japan | 0.00% | 0.00% | 11.76% | 0.00% | 0.00% | 0.00% | 0.00% | 29.41% | 5.88% | 0.00% | 0.00% | 0.00% | 52.94% |
| Netherlands | 2.00% | 2.00% | 5.00% | 2.00% | 6.00% | 3.00% | 0.00% | 10.00% | 9.00% | 0.00% | 0.00% | 0.00% | 61.00% |
| Singapore | 0.74% | 3.68% | 13.24% | 5.15% | 1.47% | 2.94% | 0.74% | 4.41% | 0.74% | 14.71% | 0.00% | 3.68% | 48.53% |
| Spain | 0.00% | 1.39% | 13.89% | 0.00% | 1.39% | 8.33% | 2.78% | 9.72% | 0.00% | 0.00% | 2.78% | 4.17% | 55.56% |
| United Kingdom | 0.00% | 3.97% | 3.97% | 3.97% | 3.97% | 2.53% | 1.44% | 6.14% | 1.81% | 0.36% | 1.08% | 4.69% | 66.06% |
| United States | 0.72% | 2.51% | 9.23% | 1.83% | 1.93% | 2.39% | 1.12% | 5.52% | 1.16% | 0.42% | 0.64% | 2.23% | 70.30% |

Country of Research Topic

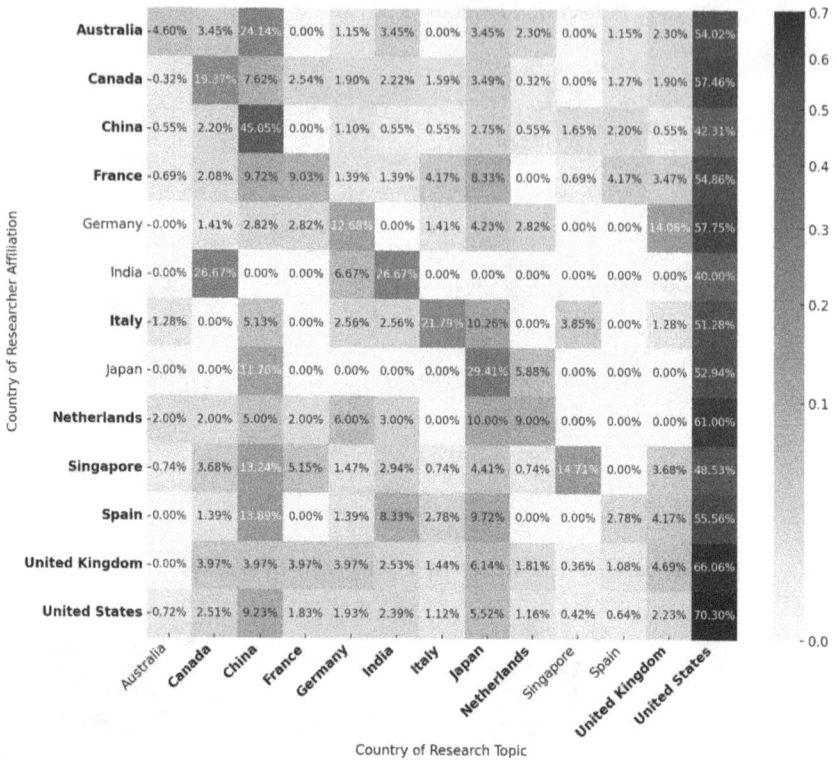

*Fig. 7.*   Country-Level View of Geographic Bias in Top Management Publications. *Notes*: This figure shows the country-level view of management scholars' locations (vertical axis) and the regions they study (horizontal axis) in top management journals, conditional on the region being identified (by country). The top 10 countries in terms of researcher affiliations are shown in bold on the vertical axis, while the top 10 countries in terms of regional focus are shown in bold on the horizontal axis. There are 7 countries that belong to both lists. To make the plot symmetric, we take the union of the two lists, which makes the plot 13 × 13. The percentage in each cell shows the relative frequency within its row, so each row sums to 100%. The color coding uses an exponential scale. See text for more details.

prominent in China, where more researchers focus on their own country (45.05%) than on the US (42.31%). Finally, looking at the vertical columns, there is a general interest in studying China and Japan, as well as other Western countries like Canada and the United Kingdom.

# CONCLUSION

In this paper, we show the extent to which management research is concentrated in and focused on the Western world. To do so, we restrict our attention to scholarship in the top six flagship journals, covering all publications authored in the past seven decades. Because this analysis requires extensive meta-data on the geography of scientific publications – and no such meta-data currently exists – we manually collect all raw publication texts from the journals ourselves and leverage machine-learning-based tools, in particular NLP, to infer the locations of both management scholars and the geographies they study. First and foremost, our findings reveal that the vast majority of top publications are authored by US-based scholars. While researchers from other high-income countries have seen respectable improvements in representation over time, the same cannot be said for researchers from low-income countries: their entry into top journals only started in the last decade and remains minimal. While there is slightly less geographic inequality in terms of the regions studied, a majority of top publications and researchers still focus on US geographies. This distribution is stable over time. Finally, our analysis suggests the location of the authors and their regional focus interact in important ways. In particular, the Western worlds tends to look inward: the majority of papers are authored by researchers in the high-income countries (including the US) focusing on these very countries. While scholars from low-income countries also exhibit inequality in the United States, they contribute additional topics from their own countries.

### Contributions

Our paper contributes to several literatures. Firstly, we contribute to the recent literature on the colonization of management (Banerjee, 2021; Bruton et al., 2022; Filatotchev et al., 2022; Jammulamadaka et al., 2021). This work interrogates the production of knowledge in management scholarship, contending that it largely originated in the West (in particular the Anglo-American world), led by Western voices, and consequently represents Western perspectives, values, and frameworks. Nevertheless, such scholarship is widely considered to be universal, even if it fails to account for theoretical complications that arise from non-Western contexts or neglects such contexts in the first place. Further, scholars worry that efforts to rectify these issues and broaden contexts in management theory may lead to co-opting non-Western knowledge without including non-Western voices, leading to a new form of cultural imperialism (Banerjee, 2021). However, while this literature has revealed important channels for self-critique and growth for management scholars, it has mostly focused on theorizing. We contend that it would benefit from data-driven estimates that contextualize the severity of the problem and enable informed discussion to move the needle. Despite important early advances in this regard (Baruch, 2001), we provide the first to provide such estimates that cover a big slice of top management scholarship since the 1950s.

Secondly, we contribute to a robust literature that documents a general WEIRD bias across the social sciences. Starting with psychology, researchers discovered a significant tendency for experiments to recruit study participants from Western industrialized countries (Arnett, 2008; Henrich et al., 2010). Since then, a number of systematic reviews have been undertaken across the social sciences to understand whether scientists generally over-sample from Western contexts, including in Political Science and International Relations, Economics, Geography, Human-centered computing, etc. We show that management scholarship is no exception to this phenomenon; rather, our estimates suggest it is particularly prone to a Western-centric bias. For instance, Wilson and Knutsen (2022) find that, in Political Science, references to Western countries in titles or abstracts outnumber references to non-Western countries by a factor of 1.6. In management scholarship, the same number is 5.5, over three times worse.

Third, we contribute to a nascent literature that has taken advantage of advances in NLP to determine geographic attributes from the content of publication texts (Nagaraj et al., 2020; Wilson, 2017; Wilson & Knutsen, 2022). This literature has thus far showcased one use-case of this capability: measuring the geographic concentration of regions studied. We go one step further and systematically relate the physical location of management scholars to the regions they study (see Briggs & Weathers, 2016 for another example). We find that scholars based in a given country do generally tend to contribute more research about that country. Beyond these descriptive measures, we envision that these methods can be extended to also study other questions such as the effect of the diversity of journal editorial boards on the geographic diversity of a journal.

Finally, we contribute a new suite of methodological tools to the literature on "Science of Science" and related meta-science disciplines. Our tools overcome a key challenge in this literature – namely that meta-data is not systematically collected and made available for management publications – by using machine-learning and other computing technologies to manually (but efficiently) automate this process. This enables us to obtain all management publications (21,000+) across multiple flagship journals for every year since 1954 and systematically compile geographic meta-data. Our tools and data can potentially enable researchers in other disciplines as well to undertake systematic reviews of the extent of geographic bias and address some of the technical bottlenecks, should the meta-data not already be available.

All in all, our findings should prompt significant concern in the management community. At the highest levels of the field, scholarship has been (and continues to be) highly Western-centric. This raises the question of whether the field can hope to make sense of the global diversity of business phenomena and thereby remain relevant to management practitioners around the world. In an increasingly interconnected world, where multinational companies (MNCs) continue to grow in importance, this should be a matter of concern. Further, as management scholars ourselves, we actively aspire to be members of a field that embraces inclusivity and that reflects the diversity of contexts we study. Yet, even though the management community (including the flagship journals) has admirably shared this commitment, our findings suggest that in practice, this has not yet been realized: representation among lower-income researchers is low, and the trends are not improving much over time. This suggests that the field needs to take more active steps to combat geographic bias.

What are the steps it can take? More research is needed, but Baruch (2001) finds some evidence that the geographical representation of authors is correlated to the geo-origins of the editorial board. In one case study, he finds a particularly strong link at the Academy of Management Journal during the years 1996–1998, when more international scholars were added to its board under the editorship of Professor Anne Tsui. This echoes findings from other fields. For instance, Brogaard et al. (2014) find causal evidence that in economics and finance, the appointment of an editor increases the publication rate of the editor's colleagues by 100%. Further, these "inside" publications garner *increased* citations, which implies that editorial networks enhance the editorial process, not compromise it. Altogether, this suggest interventions at the editorial level are quite promising. As an alternative, Doktor et al. (1991) also recommend special issues and forums as targeted opportunities to broaden the international scope of management thought and practice.

### Limitations

Finally, our study is not without limitations. When looking at the geographic distribution of management scholars, we only consider the location of the institutional affiliations. Future work should also consider the race, ethnicity, or country of birth of scholars to shed more light on what is a multidimensional problem. For instance, many scholars likely grow up in non-Western contexts but are educated at Western institutions and later acquire full-time appointments at these institutions. While our analysis suggests it is quite possible these scholars focus on Western contexts at similar rates to scholars from Western origins, they nevertheless contribute to improved representation and diversity in the field. However, the fact remains that they are socialized into Western systems of knowledge production, which suggests the location of the affiliated institution continues to remain an important vector of geographic bias. In addition, to ascertain a publication's focus geographies, we only consider its titles and abstracts. While this is a standard choice in the literature, future work should consider how best to leverage the full publication texts. Finally, our study does not consider the role of citations in geographic bias. It is possible that even conditional on publishing in the top journals, non-Western scholars are frequently less cited in their work, limiting their ability to influence the field. Our current analysis does not speak to this possibility.

Overall, our study provides quantitative estimates of two important dimensions of geographic bias in top management scholarship. This is the first step toward the broader goal of "decolonizing management studies." Ultimately, our hope is to mark a step forward in addressing the need for a more inclusive and robust academic field with positive externalities for all regions around the world.

## ACKNOWLEDGMENTS

We thank Devanshi Agarwal, Cecil-Francis Brenninkmeijer, Yanqi Cheng, Jai Singh, Sachin Srivastava, and Jiamei Xu for excellent research assistance. We acknowledge the financial support of the Clausen Center for International Business and Policy. Any opinions and conclusions expressed herein are those of the authors only, and any errors are our own.

# NOTES

1. See https://aom.org/membership for more details.

2. The Appendix is available online at https://www.abhishekn.com/publications-all/geographic-bias-management

3. We cross-check all information with other sources, like OpenAlex, Scopus, and Web of Science, to verify the completeness and accuracy of our dataset. Other sources are not primarily used due to data limitations explained in Appendix A.

4. City or state-level focuses are all elevated to country level. The 5% of topic focuses not included in the analysis are at the continental level: for example, Latin America and North America.

5. Based on the definition, this does not include publications with a researcher from a mid- or low-income country.

6. Throughout the article, we use "from a country" to means that the researcher is affiliated with an institution in that country as the time of publication. There is no connection with the researcher's race, ethnicity, or country of birth.

7. Management Science has been producing 12 issues each year since 1966, but the number of articles per issue has been increasing drastically these years. In 2023, there are on average about 30 to 35 articles per issue, while ten years ago in 2013, the average number of articles per issue was about 12 to 13.

8. The raw counts of the line charts over time in Plot B are presented in Appendix Fig. B1.

9. The raw counts of the line charts over time in Plot B are presented in Appendix Fig. B3.

# REFERENCES

Apicella, C., Norenzayan, A., & Henrich, J. (2020). Beyond weird: A review of the last decade and a look ahead to the global laboratory of the future. *Evolution and Human Behavior*, *41*(5), 319–329.

Arnett, J. J. (2008). The neglected 95%: Why American psychology needs to become less American.

Banerjee, S. B. (2021). Decolonizing management theory: A critical perspective. *Journal of Management Studies*, *59*(4), 1074–1087.

Bar-Gill, S., Brynjolfsson, E., & Hak, N. (2023). Helping small businesses become more data-driven: A field experiment on ebay. *NBER Working Papers*, No 31089.

Baruch, Y. (2001). Global or north American?: A geographical based comparative analysis of publications in top management journals. *International Journal of Cross Cultural Management*, *1*(1), 109–126.

Birkinshaw, J., Lecuona, R., & Barwise, P. (2016). The relevance gap in business school research: Which academic papers are cited in managerial bridge journals? *Academy of Management Learning Education*, *15*(4), 686–702.

Black, S. J., Mendenhall, M., & Oddou, G. (1991). Toward a comprehensive model of international adjustment: An integration of multiple theoretical perspectives. *Academy of Management Review*, *16*(2), 291–317.

Boyacigiller, N. A., & Adler, N. J. (1991). The parochial dinosaur: Organizational science in a global context. *Academy of Management Review*, *16*(2), 262–291.

Briggs, R. C., & Weathers, S. (2016). Gender and location in African politics scholarship: The other whiteman's burden? *African Affairs*, *115*(640), 466–489.

Brogaard, J., Engelberg, J., & Parsons, C. A. (2014). Networks and productivity: Causal evidence from editor rotations. *Journal of Financial Economics*, *111*(1), 251–270.

Bruton, G. D., Zahra, S. A., Van de Ven, A. H., & Hitt, M. A. (2022). Indigenous theory uses, abuses, and future. *Journal of Management Studies*, *59*(4), 1057–1073.

Chen, K., Ren, X., & Yang, G. (2021). A novel approach for assessing academic journals: Application of integer DEA model for management science and operations research field. *Journal of Informetrics*, *15*(3), 101176.

Clancy, K. B., & Davis, J. L. (2019). Soylent is people, and weird is white: Biological anthropology, whiteness, and the limits of the weird. *Annual Review of Anthropology*, *48*(1), 169–186.

Cole, S., Dhaliwal, I., Sautmann, A., Vilhuber, L., et al. (2020). *Handbook on using administrative data for research and evidence-based policy*. https://admindatahandbook.mit.edu/book/v1.0-rc5/index.html

Conlon, E. (2000). Editor's comments. *Academy of Management Review*, *25*(1), 7–9.

Correa, M., González-Sabaté, L., & Serrano, I. (2013). Home bias effect in the management literature. *Scientometrics*, *95*(1), 417–433.

Das, J., Quy-Toan, D., Shaines, K., & Srikant, S. (2013). U.s. and them: The geography of academic research. *Journal of Development Economics*, *105*, 112–130.

Dilnot, A. (2012). Numbers and public policy: The power of official statistics and statistical communication in public policymaking. *Fiscal Studies*, *33*(4), 429–448.

Doktor, R., Tung, R. L., & Glinow, M. A. V. (1991). Incorporating international dimensions in management theory building. *Academy of Management Review*, *16*(2), 259–261.

Dushnitsky, G., & Yug, L. (2022). Why do incumbents fund startups? A study of the antecedents of corporate venture capital in China. *Research Policy*, *51*(3).

Earley, C. (2006). Leading cultural research in the future: A matter of paradigms and taste. *Journal of International Business Studies*, *37*(6), 922–931.

Filatotchev, I., Ireland, R. D., & Stahl, G. K. (2022). Contextualizing management research: An open systems perspective. *Journal of Management Studies*, *59*(4), 1036–1056.

Gelfand, M. J., Aycan, Z., Erez, M., & Leung, K. (2017). Cross-cultural industrial organizational psychology and organizational behavior: A hundred-year journey. *Journal of Applied Psychology*, *102*(3), 514.

Gelfand, M. J., Leslie, L. M., & Fehr, R. (2008). To prosper, organizational psychology should … adopt a global perspective. *Journal of Organizational Behavior: The International Journal of Industrial, Occupational and Organizational Psychology and Behavior*, *29*(4), 493–517.

George, G., Corbishley, C., Khayesi, J. N. O., Haas, M. R., & Tihanyi, L. (2016). Bringing Africa in: Promising directions for management research. *Academy of Management Journal*, *59*(2), 377–393.

Graham, M., Hogan, B., Straumann, R. K., & Medhat, A. (2014). Uneven geographies of user-generated information: Patterns of increasing informational poverty. *Annals of the Association of American Geographers*, *104*(4), 746–764.

Haire, M. E., Ghiselli, E., & Porter, L. (1966). *Managerial thinking: An international study*. John Wiley and Sons.

Harley, B., & Fleming, P. (2021). Not even trying to change the world: Why do elite management journals ignore the major problems facing humanity? *The Journal of Applied Behavioral Science*, *57*(2), 133–152.

Hendriks, T., Warren, M. A., Schotanus-Dijkstra, M., Hassankhan, A., Graafsma, T., Bohlmeijer, E., & de Jong, J. (2019). How weird are positive psychology interventions? A bibliometric analysis of randomized controlled trials on the science of well-being. *The Journal of Positive Psychology*, *14*(4), 489–501.

Henrich, J., Heine, S. J., & Norenzayan, A. (2010). The weirdest people in the world? *Behavioral and Brain Sciences*, *33*(2-3), 61–83.

Hjort, J., Moreira, D., Rao, G., & Santini, J. F. (2021). How research affects policy: Experimental evidence from 2,150 Brazilian municipalities. *American Economic Review*, *111*(5), 1442–1480.

Hong, L., & Page, S. E. (2004). Groups of diverse problem solvers can outperform groups of high-ability problem solvers. *Proceedings of the National Academy of Sciences*, *101*(46), 16385–16389.

Hook, D., Porter, S. J., & Draux, H., & Herzog, C. T. (2020). Real-time bibliometrics: Dimensions as a resource for analyzing aspects of covid-19. *Frontiers in Research Metrics and Analytics*, *5*, 595299.

Jammulamadaka, N., Faria, A., Jack, G., & Ruggunan, S. (2021). Decolonising management and organisational knowledge (MOK): Praxistical theorising for potential worlds. *Organisation*, *28*(5), 717–740.

Joughin, I., Slawek, T., Mark, F., & Kwok, R. (1996). A mini-surge on the Ryder Glacier, Greenland, observed by satellite radar interferometrye. *Science*, *105*(5285), 228–230.

Julian, S. D., & Ofori-dankwa, J. C. (2013). Financial resource availability and corporate social responsibility expenditures in a sub-Saharan economy: The institutional difference hypothesis. *Strategic Management Journal*, *34*(11), 1314–13330.

Kahalon, R., Klein, V., Ksenofontov, I., Ullrich, J., & Wright, S. C. (2022). Mentioning the sample's country in the article's title leads Tobias in research evaluation. *Social Psychological and Personality Science, 13*(2), 352–361

Lakhani, K. R., Jeppesen, L. B., Lohse, P. A., & Panetta, J. A. (2007). *The value of openness in scientific problem solving.* Working Papers.

Li, J. B., & Piezunka, H. (2019). The uniplex third: Enabling single-domain role transitions in multiplex relationships. *Administrative Science Quarterly, 65*(2), 314–358.

Linxen, S., Sturm, C., Brühlmann, F., Cassau, V., Opwis, K., & Reinecke, K. (2021). How weird is chi? In *Proceedings of the 2021 CHI Conference on Human Factors in Computing Systems,* pp. 1–14.

Meadon, M., & Spurrett, D. (2010). It's not just the subjects – There are too many weird researchers. *Behavioral and Brain Sciences, 59*(2-3), 104–105.

Murphy, J., & Zhu, J. (2012). Neo-colonialism in the academy? Anglo-American domination in management journals. *Organization, 19*(6), 915–927.

Nagaraj, A., Shears, E., & de Vaan, M. (2020). Improving data access democratizes and diversifies science. *Proceedings of the National Academy of Sciences, 117*(38), 23490–23498.

Nembhard, I. M., Alexander, J. A., Hoff, T. J., & Ramanujam, R. (2009). Why does the quality of health care continue to lag? Insights from management research. *Academy of Management Perspectives, 23*(4), 24–42.

Nielsen, M., Haun, D., Kärtner, J., & Legare, C. H. (2017). The persistent sampling bias in developmental psychology: A call to action. *Journal of Experimental Child Psychology, 162,* 31–38.

Nishii, L. H. (2013). The benefits of climate for inclusion for gender-diverse groups. *Academy of Management Journal, 56*(6), 1754–1774.

Phillips, B. J., & Greene, K. T. (2020). Where is conflict research? western bias in the literature on armed violence. *International Studies Review, 24*(3).

Pitesa, M., & Gelfand, M. J. (2022). Going beyond western, educated, industrialized, rich, and democratic (weird) samples and problems in organizational research. *Organizational Behavior and Human Decision Processes, 174,* 104212.

Rosenzweig, P. M., & Singh, J. V. (1991). Organizational environments and the multinational enterprise. *Academy of Management Review, 16*(2), 340–361.

Tiokhin, L., Hackman, J., Munira, S., Jesmin, K., & Hruschka, D. (2019). Generalizability is not optional: Insights from a cross-cultural study of social discounting. *Royal Society Open Science, 6*(2), 181386.

Usunier, J.-C. (1998). *International and cross-cultural management research.* SAGE Publications Ltd.

Wei, F., & Zhang, G. (2020). Exploring the intellectual structure and evolution of 24 top business journals: A scientometric analysis. *The Electronic Library, 38*(3), 493–511.

Whitley, R. (1984). The scientific status of management research as a practically oriented social science. *Journal of Management Studies, 21*(4), 369–390.

Wickert, C., & de Bakker, F. (2018). Pitching for social change: Towards a relational approach to selling and buying social issues. *Academy of Management Discoveries, 4*(1), 50–73.

Wickert, C., Potočnik, K., Prashantham, S., Shi, W., & Snihur, Y. (2024). Embracing nonwestern contexts in management scholarship.

Wilson, M. (2017). Trends in political science research and the progress of comparative politics. *PS: Political Science Politics, 50*(24), 979–984.

Wilson, M. C., & Knutsen, C. H. (2022). Geographical coverage in political science research. *Perspectives on Politics, 20*(3), 1024–1039.

Yamey, G., & Volmink, J. (2014). An argument for evidence-based policy-making in global health. In *The handbook of global health policy* (pp. 133–155).

Zand, D. E., & Sorensen, R. E. (1975). Theory of change and the effective use of management science. *Administrative Science Quarterly, 20*(4), 532–545.

# DECOLONIZING ENTREPRENEURSHIP: TIME TO OPEN BOTH EYES

Albert E. James[a], Aidin Salamzadeh[b] and Léo-Paul Dana[a]

[a]Dalhousie University, Canada
[b]University of Tehran, Iran

## ABSTRACT

We address our role as educators and researchers of entrepreneurship in ensuring that everything we do today is aimed at reconciling the relationship between Indigenous and non-Indigenous people and restoring balanced relationships. Based on recognition of the importance of Indigenous knowledge for reconciliation and the value of Indigenous knowledge in a more holistic and comprehensive understanding of entrepreneurship to make better scientific and educational decisions, we describe a brief introduction and partial explanation of our lack of attention and offer justification for checking our assumptions about entrepreneurship and decolonizing our research and teaching. We offer a brief introduction to examples of Indigenous conceptual frameworks of ethical and appropriate informed pluralism that allow ways of knowing, being, and doing. Finally, we offer some suggestions for scholars in our field in pursuit of decolonizing their minds and work.

**Keywords:** Decolonization; education; entrepreneurship; indigenous; theory building

Decolonizing Management and Organization Studies: Why, How, and What
Research in the Sociology of Organizations, Volume 93, 67–84
ISSN: 0733-558X/doi:10.1108/S0733-558X20250000093005

# INTRODUCTION

This paper is not meant as a criticism of the scholarship of entrepreneurship but is written in the spirit of something one of the authors read as a Ph.D. student, that we often do not recognize a privileged position until we are made aware of the privilege (Osmund & Thorn, 1993). In the case of decolonizing entrepreneurship research and teaching,[1] recognizing our privilege matters for selfish and unselfish reasons (i) the moral imperative to redress harms of colonization and (ii) insights into what we are missing of the whole of entrepreneurship in our research and teaching. Therefore, this paper is written in an effort to inform and elicit change. We suggest that in this case, the learning and change require a (i) discussion of colonization and the historical as well as the continued impact of colonization on Indigenous people and non-Indigenous people, (ii) learning to recognize that to succeed, our existing theories of entrepreneurship are not necessarily fit for Indigenous people; and (iii) rethink how theories arising from different ways of knowing, understanding, and being can be used together toward greater good.

To provide clarity, we begin by defining the terms and concepts central to our paper, starting with the term Indigenous. *Indigenous* is an umbrella term for those peoples who have been subjected to colonization of their lands and cultures (Tuhiwai Smith, 2008; Wilmer, 1993), and who have retained historically continuous social, economic, and philosophical characteristics distinct from the dominant societies of new societies that grew up around them, and who continue to assert and re-assert their peoples' distinctness (United Nations, 2007). When thinking of Indigenous people, it is critical to keep in mind the distinctness and vibrancy of the differences between each Indigenous nation, people, or community. Each community is reflective of its origins, history, and the impact of place. Common exonyms covered by the umbrella include Aboriginal and Native American, among others; each serves to essentialize and mask the distinctness of a people's distinctness. It is estimated that 500 million Indigenous people live in 90 countries, representing significant parts of most national economies (Anderson et al., 2005). As they continue to recover from the assaults of colonization and recover the economic sovereignty they had before colonization, their economic clout will continue to grow (Anderson et al., 2006). Indigenous people are actively pursuing the reestablishment of their economic self-determination and recognize the role of entrepreneurship in this pursuit (Anderson et al., 2004). As researchers seeking an understanding of entrepreneurship and as educators engaged in sharing knowledge and understanding entrepreneurship, we have the opportunity to participate with Indigenous people in their societal projects.

Put simply, *colonization* is a process of one polity establishing political control and subjugation of a territory and the territory's inhabitants. History demonstrates that colonization is not limited to any single era of history, that there is not one model of colonization, and the experience of colonization is context-specific (Alfred, 2009). Despite this, the history of colonization demonstrates that the subjugation of territory and people is not simply the acquisition and accumulation of territory and people, but it requires the erasure of what was there and replacing it with what the colonizers bring with them (Said, 1994). Colonization's impact on colonized territories is pernicious and long-lasting. The methods of subjugation and impacts of acquisition all remain to some extent, and those who remain in a territory after it acquires its 'freedom' from the colonizing power.

*Decolonization* refers to the intellectual deconstruction of colonial ideologies, narratives, and institutional edifices built up to support the false notion that Western knowledge is universal and the creation of space for Indigenous ways of knowing, being, and doing at the center of academia equal to Western ways of knowing, being, and doing (Moosavi, 2020; Pimbott, 2020). With this understanding of Indigenous and decolonization, it is important to recognize and acknowledge the political nature of Indigeneity through factors such as resistance of the dominant society and assertion of rights to exist according to their choice.

There is no single definition of *Indigenous knowledge* because this is another umbrella term for a set of complex practical and spiritual knowledge systems based on the worldviews of Indigenous Peoples developed through their relationship with the environment and which is the result of Indigenous peoples' adaptations to the land over countless generations (Dybbroe, 1999). Indigenous knowledge encompasses unique cultures, languages, values, histories, governance, and legal systems and is unique to each Indigenous community. Indigenous knowledge cannot be separated from the people inextricably connected to that knowledge and their Knowledge Holders are the only people who can truly define Indigenous Knowledge for their communities. Indigenous knowledge is sometimes referred to as Traditional Knowledge (Canada.ca, 2022; Daniel et al., 2022). We choose not to use this term because it poorly recognizes that much like the Scientific Method upon which academia relies, Indigenous knowledge systems are equally rigorous and are built upon the experiences (hypothesis testing) of earlier generations, informing the practice of current generations (Kimmerer, 2013). We do, however, substitute Indigenous Knowledge with Indigenous ways of being, doing, and knowing as a reminder of the all-encompassing nature of Indigenous and non-Indigenous knowledge systems. Therefore, in our paper, we use the term Indigenous knowledge to represent the ways of knowing, being, and doing that idiosyncratically developed within each Indigenous culture. In the same logic, we use the term Western knowledge to refer to the ways of knowing, being, and doing that developed within the West (defined below).

We draw upon for our definition of *entrepreneurship* and *Indigenous entrepreneurship*. Accordingly, entrepreneurship is "not just a way of conducting business; it is an ideology originating from basic human needs and desires ... entails discovering the new, while changing, adapting and preserving the best of the old" (Kao, 2007, p. 44). This recognizes that there is more to entrepreneurship than being an exclusively economic phenomenon in market societies (Calas et al., 2009). Following from this while also recognizing there is no such thing as a unity that could be called Indigenous Entrepreneurship; instead, it is entrepreneurship whose ideology fits with the ways of being, doing, and knowing of an Indigenous people that entails discovering the new while changing, adapting and preserving the best of the old.

The *moral imperative* we refer to relies on two premises. Those of us who are not Indigenous but who live in or have lived in societies with colonial histories have all benefited from the colonial past. We have benefited from what has been built on lands and resources taken from Indigenous people. To exemplify what we mean by this statement, think of Canada, where two of the authors live. The dominant society in Canada is made up of immigrants. Regardless of when they came, all reside on land and rely on infrastructure funded by colonial actions and with resources taken from Indigenous nations. Canadian universities are located on land taken, often in violation of treaties. As beneficiaries of colonization, we are imbued with a moral imperative to play a meaningful role in reconciliation with Indigenous people. The second premise we propose also represents concrete ways we can participate in reconciliation.

Entrepreneurship is "fundamentally a process of social change" (Calas et al., 2009, p. 553). Although we do not wish to continue the discourse of deficiency in relation to Indigenous people, the fact is that by most measures of economic, health, and welfare measures of well-being, Indigenous communities in every country endure worse outcomes than non-Indigenous communities in the country (e.g., see Fuentes et al., 2020; Gall et al., 2021). Indigenous leaders recognize that revitalizing their entrepreneurial spirit and harnessing entrepreneurship's economic potential is a necessary part of improving their community's well-being while also restoring, rejuvenating, and strengthening themselves from a foundation that is grounded on their traditions, culture, knowledge, and understanding (Anderson, 2002; Peredo et al., 2004). "Become a Chief who creates revenue-generating jobs that make money for your First Nation" (Louie, 2021, p. 131). As academics, we possess knowledge and an understanding of entrepreneurship that results in an ethical obligation to follow the lead of Indigenous leaders and communities and contribute where we can to their entrepreneurial goals.

## COLONIZATION AND ITS CONTINUED IMPACT ON INDIGENOUS PEOPLE AND NON-INDIGENOUS PEOPLE

There is nothing new about colonization. As the Assyrian empire expanded from its heartland, its gods, governance, and knowledge were imposed to replace the culture, gods, and knowledge of the acquired territories, only to be supplanted by the Persian Empire and its ways of knowing, being, and doing. Distinct colonization processes of erasure and replacement can be tracked in the Roman, Mongol, Aztec, Ottoman, and countless other epochs.

Although the Assyrian, Persian, Roman, Mogul, Aztec, and Ottoman empires are ancient history, it could be argued that the world is still living through the impacts of a more recent period of colonization that arose with the expansion of the West. By the West, we refer to the cultural archive that grew out of the Mediterranean Basin and was shaped by the Enlightenment and Renaissance periods to imagine "new worlds, new wealth and new possessions that could be discovered and controlled" (Tuhiwai Smith, 2008, p. 22) by the West's superior ways of knowing, being, and doing (Foucault, 1972; Said, 1994). What differentiates this period of colonization from those that preceded it is that the gods, governance, and knowledge were not those of single polities or empires but of a whole region of the world, the West, and that few regions of the world were spared from direct colonization by Western nations.

The history of the past, roughly 600 years, is one of Western nation-states expanding through establishing colonies and colonial administrations in places geographically, culturally, and epistemologically far removed from Western Europe. As the colonies spread, the colonizers, and in some cases, their successor independent polities, developed systems, institutions, and discourses to subordinate Indigenous populations encountered and to justify the colonization in the colonizers' home countries. Notions such as inferior, less developed, dependent, and peoples desiring and beseeching domination became common aspects of colonization. Indigenous knowledge, their epistemologies, accumulated knowledge, modes of governance, cultures, societies, and economies were delegitimized as undeveloped, unscientific, and irrational and replaced by "legitimate" Western mores. In every colonized territory, the systems, institutions, and discourses of colonization reinforced a discourse of Indigenous people and their ancestors as heathens, pagans, uncivilized, inferior in every way, and the need to give up their way of life and assimilate for their own good. Indigenous people and non-Indigenous populations in the colonies and home countries were subjected to this institutionalized discourse (Sinclair, 2019). The almost universal application of these discourses resulted in historical and current notions of the superiority of Western knowledge and a lack of faith in the legitimacy of Indigenous ways of knowing, being, and doing held by Indigenous individuals about themselves and other Indigenous people, descendants of settlers in former colonies, and recent immigrants to formerly colonized countries (Chakrabarty, 2000).

Even now, it is not difficult to find echoes of colonization's delegitimization practices in the discourses of today when, for example, regions or societies are compared as developed versus less developed, knowledge versus folk knowledge, history versus oral tradition, or tribe, ethnic group, versus nation. Along with the delegitimization, the process of colonization worked physically through things like bounties, politically by not recognizing sovereignty, and culturally erasing Indigenous people from the colonized territory. Cultural erasure is seen in, for example, Canadian governments' use of "systematic, government-sponsored attempt to destroy Aboriginal (*Indigenous*) cultures and languages and to assimilate Aboriginal (*Indigenous*) peoples so that they no longer existed as distinct peoples" (TRC, 2015, p. 107). Cultural erasure is also seen in and perpetuated by less dramatic practices like using one term for all Indigenous people. An example is the use of Aborigine for all Indigenous people of Australia instead of identifying the person as a member of one of the 500 polities, each with distinct languages, cultures, and laws (Map of Indigenous Australia, 2022), thereby erasing cultures in popular discourse.

Why does colonization still matter in the post-colonial era? Our societies remain dramatically influenced by the West's colonization of a large part of the world. Those who live, Indigenous and non-Indigenous, in formerly colonized countries do so in societies where aspects of inherited structures and institutions of colonization remain and continue to reinforce and perpetuate the delegitimizing and erasing of Indigeneity and subjugation. Amnesty International, the

United Nations, and the 148 countries that support the UN Declaration of the Rights of Indigenous Peoples (UNDRIP) acknowledge deleterious effects of this period of colonization and that Indigenous peoples "rights have always been violated. Indigenous Peoples today, are arguably among the most disadvantaged and vulnerable groups of people in the world" (United Nations, 2007).

The effect of colonization is not limited to Indigenous people but also has lingering effects on the descendants of the colonizers and settlers, not questioning the superiority of Western thought and paradigms. The dominant discourse around the past and present of colonization and decolonization affects us all. As briefly pointed out above, the language of colonization's delegitimizing and erasing Indigenous peoples continues in common uses and in ways most of us are unaware of. Most non-Indigenous peoples are unaware of the many ways that their lives remain structured around the continued assumption that the ideas subsumed in what we call the West are right, true, and superior to anything else. Although we live in a decolonized world where the colonization of empire-building has stopped, this unawareness inhibits the decolonization of the minds of non-Indigenous peoples.

We are taught in schools and universities and reminded through various forms of knowledge dissemination that Herodotus, a 5th century BC Greek was the first historian because it is the first (known) written preservation of events of the past (Whitley & Barbour, 2007). Western tradition takes for granted that written histories by trained historians are facts that have not been cleaned up, reshaped, or changed to serve the writer's purposes (Holland, 2012) and takes for granted that non-written forms of history, oral histories are illegitimate and void of fact or truth. This thinking ignores the humanity of both written and oral histories, that Indigenous knowledge keepers also undergo rigorous training, and that all histories take the past out of context to serve the function of supporting a thesis (Sontag, 1962). This attitude is replicated by our continued categorization of the past as "historic" and "prehistoric."

Entrepreneurship, management, and the Academy, in general, are not untouched by the effects of colonization described above in the continued emphasis on Western knowledge as the center of legitimate knowledge (Kemple & Mawani, 2009). From even a superficial survey of our fields, the dominance of Western ways of being, knowing, and doing can be observed in the affiliations and training of authors and Academy of Management members, the reliance on Western literature, theories, and methods as sources in our publications, the location of influential journals and their editors, and the spread of Western pedagogy in business education (Gopinath, 1998). The norms of our academic discipline present Western knowledge as superior, legitimate, and scientific, whilst Indigenous knowledge is categorized as inferior, illegitimate, uncivilized, backward, and superstitious (Jack et al., 2011).

Thus far, we have attempted to raise awareness of the nature and extent of the privileged position many of us have inherited and worked within. In doing so, our message is that despite the discourse of colonization, Indigenous people, their knowledge, and their ways of being, doing, and knowing are no less valid than the knowledge and ways of being, knowing, and doing of Western academia. If we accept this, then we must also accept that understanding the fullness of any phenomena requires the inclusion of Indigenous and non-Indigenous knowledge. As in any phenomena of interest, the distinct differences between Indigenous knowledge extend to entrepreneurship.

# LEARNING TO RECOGNIZE THAT TO SUCCEED, OUR EXISTING THEORIES OF ENTREPRENEURSHIP ARE NOT NECESSARILY FIT FOR THE PURPOSES OF INDIGENOUS PEOPLE

*Entrepreneurship in Indigenous Contexts*

To assume entrepreneurship grew out of the European context or capitalism is wrong-headed. Before colonization, Indigenous societies had economies that allowed their people to prosper and thrive. In comparison to themselves, early European visitors to North America described the people and communities they met as healthy, strong, and vital (Mann, 2005). Evidence abounds of widely dispersed inter-tribal trade networks existing before colonization (Stewart, 2004). In the words of Chief Clarence Louie of the Osoyoos Indian Band of British Columbia, "Every tribe was self-sufficient and had economies based on the land and the water and on inter-tribal trade.... The first entrepreneurs in North America we the First Nations" (Louie, 2021, p. 132). But the colonizers, administrators, researchers, and educators, confident in the superiority of Western ways of knowing, being, and doing entrepreneurship, failed to recognize Indigenous entrepreneurship and learn the lessons offered.

Our literature recognizes that opportunity recognition, innovation, and entrepreneurship are culturally embedded (Dana, 2007). We suggest that the extend of the embeddedness of entrepreneurship extends far beyond culture. Indigenous cultures, ontologies, and epistemologies grew through paths and environments different from those of the West. Indigenous societies developed unique ways of ordering their world (Tuhiwai Smith, 2008), concepts of self and of ethics (Srinivas, 2012), and their ways of knowing, being, and doing (Martin & Mirraboopa, 2003) that can be starkly different from those of the West (Whiteman & Cooper, 2000). Societies developed idiosyncratic questions, applied their theories, and developed knowledge that is novel to the knowledge developed in the context of the West. Indigenous societies found answers to questions we in the West have not thought to exist or to ask.

In a general sense, Indigenous "enterprise-related activities exemplify a distinguishable kind of activity" (Peredo et al., 2004, p. 3). There are also many ways that Indigenous people engage in and understand entrepreneurship. Despite the idiosyncratic reality of Indigenous entrepreneurship, Dana (2007) point out four elements that, to varying degrees and toward various outcomes, distinguish the entrepreneurial activity of Indigenous people: (i) a degree of incompatibility with Western notions of entrepreneurship; (ii) elements of egalitarianism, sharing, and community; (iii) connection to non-economic variables such as land, place, culture, and entrepreneurship as a tool for reinforcing and restoring what was taken; and (iv) a pull toward traditional knowledge and practices of entrepreneurship and the push toward capitalistic entrepreneurial activities.

The distinction and incompatibilities between Indigenous entrepreneurship and entrepreneurship as understood by academia are recalled by Gartner (2001), who draws upon the parable of understanding an elephant to remind us that there are many parts to the whole of entrepreneurship and that understanding requires our being conscious of the assumptions we make and explicit about what we believe we understand of entrepreneurship. We add to this that without including Indigenous knowledge and Indigenous entrepreneurship, the whole of entrepreneurship cannot be known.

## HOW THEORIES ARISING FROM DIFFERENT WAYS OF KNOWING, UNDERSTANDING, AND BEING CAN BE USED TOGETHER TOWARD THE GREATER GOOD

Following along with the recognition of the value and existence of legitimate knowledge and theories outside of that developed in the West and by Western-trained scholarship are questions of the applicability of theories rooted in Western understandings, methods, and expectations. The problem is that theories are rooted in theories developed to understand, explain, and predict in contexts of Western ways of knowing and doing entrepreneurship. The belief in Western-developed theories of entrepreneurship legitimacy and their universal applicability led to the assumption and practice of universally applying the theories regardless of the context. However, Indigenous people and contexts exemplify enterprise-related activities distinct from those of Western societies, which renders mainstream theories and understanding of entrepreneurship less helpful to the questions asked and the outcomes of Indigenous people than previously assumed. How, then, do we go about decolonizing entrepreneurship and developing knowledge that serves to answer the questions and reach the outcomes sought by Indigenous and non-Indigenous people?

We believe the answer lies somewhere within what we know about entrepreneurship, what we are researching and teaching, what Indigenous people know about the ways of knowing, being, and doing, and how these might coexist for the benefit of all.

There is precedence for Indigenous knowledge coexisting with the colonizers' Western knowledge. During the initial stages of colonizing, colonizers were reliant on the munificence of the Indigenous people, followed by a period of mutual interdependence and independence ending in the subjugation of the Indigenous people. Manuel and Posluns (1974) described the relationship, "Both the native people and the visitors developed a mutual dependence that assured that even when relations were not friendly, they would at least be respectful and, for the most part, peaceable" (p. 7). Recreating this sense of mutual dependence and respect is for us, decolonizing entrepreneurship.

How we begin to rebuild mutual interdependence and respect could be answered by starting with Willmott (2008). Willmott reminded us that the value of knowledge ultimately resides in its broad relevance, notably, its capacity to enrich collective self-understanding and thereby provide the basis for sustaining and improving the quality of life; the pursuit of valuable knowledge requires informed pluralism. Informed pluralism "tempers dogmatic claims of sole authority" for any knowledge system by incorporating critical awareness of the limitations of each knowledge claim or contribution while also maintaining an in-depth appreciation of the nature and value of alternative knowledge systems and their ways of being, knowing, and doing. The path to increasingly valuable knowledge is to critically recognize the limits of our knowledge, theories, and claims; accept unreservedly the value of other vaults of knowledge; and incorporate each knowledge system into the puzzles we seek to solve.

Translating Willmott's idea of informed pluralism to a decolonizing project requires the recognition that Indigenous knowledge and theories can complement those of our Academy without repeating the history of researchers and academics expropriating or subsuming Indigenous knowledge into the dominant body of knowledge (Nadasdy, 1999). It also requires changing the assumption that there is one universal knowledge. Western traditions of knowledge have in them inherent belief in there being a universal knowledge, i.e., one way of knowing, being, and doing applicable and pertinent in all contexts. It is within this paradigm most academics in our field were trained and continue to operate within. Indigenous knowledge systems are not thus hampered. There exist multiple Indigenous conceptual frameworks that appreciate the nature and value of alternate knowledge and allow knowledge systems to "speak for themselves in its own context, without assigning one dominant knowledge system" (Reid et al., 2021, p. 248). Although distinct to each Indigenous people, the conceptual frameworks provide paths for the use of multiple knowledge traditions in parallel to each other, neither touching nor subsuming each other but allowing the enrichment of each knowledge system independently. In Reid et al. (2021), four such frameworks are introduced: *Kaswentha, Ganma, Waka-Taurua*, and *Etuaptmumk*. What follows is an attempt to summarize their introductions of the frameworks. To be clear, what follows does not rise to the level of Willmott's "in-depth" understanding and does great harm to the conceptual richness of the frameworks and knowledge on which they are built. We trust the summaries serve to pique the interest of readers so that they seek to develop proper relationships with the appropriate knowledge holders for instruction and guidance.

*Kaswentha,* an example of which is shown in Fig. 1, is Haudenosaunee for the concept of the ongoing negotiation between distinct people in the mutual agreement of coexistence (Parmenter, 2013). *Kaswentha* is often associated with the Two Row Wampum belt, created to record through visual symbols that trigger meanings and details of treaties between the Haudenosaunee and Europeans. The belt records two parallel purple lines of beads in a river of white beads that symbolize each people traveling side by side in cooperation and respect while never attempting to steer the other (Onondaga Nation, n.d.).

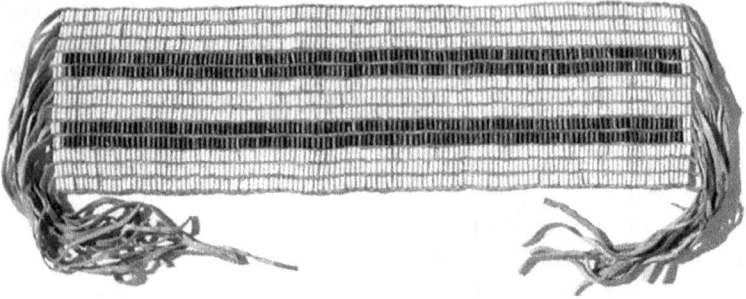

*Fig. 1.*  Two Row Wampum – Gaswéñdah. *Note*: *Kaswentha*, Haudenosaunee
concept of the ongoing negotiation between distinct people and
cooperation.Creator: Darren Bonaparte, *Source*: Southam (2021).

Ganma Theory of Combining Knowledge

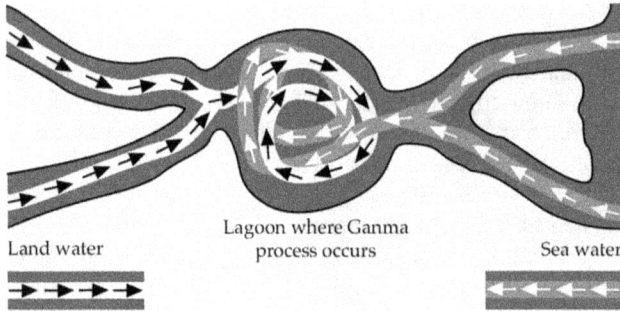

*Fig. 2.*  Ganma Theory of Combining Knowledge. *Notes:* Ganma, the Yolngu
framework that uses the metaphor of two from different sources mixing to
understand the mixing of multiple knowledges to create deeper understandings and
truths. Image is an adaptation of Marika (1999). Milthun latju wäŋa romgu Yolngu:
Valuing Yolngu knowledge in education systems. *Ngoonjook: A Journal of Australian
Indigenous Issues*, *16*, 107–129.

Fig. 2 presents a representation of *Ganma*, the Yolngu framework that uses the
metaphor of two streams, one from the land and the other from the sea, mixing
to theorize about the forces of the waters combining to create deeper understandings and truths. *Ganma* theory provides enabling mechanisms for relating ideas,
concepts, and all perceptions intermingling with tolerance and respect and without privileging one (Watson et al., 1989).

*Waka-Taurua*, illustrated in Fig. 3, is a framework developed by Māori con-
sultations between 2017 and 2018 on how Māori knowledge and non-Maori
knowledge could be lashed together to achieve a common purpose (Maxwell
et al., 2020). This approach is represented as two autonomous canoes, each with
its own set of paddles/*hoe* (tools, actions, knowledge, and theories) temporarily
tied together with a deck representing shared and negotiated engagement space.

He Waka Taurus Lashing Knowledge Together

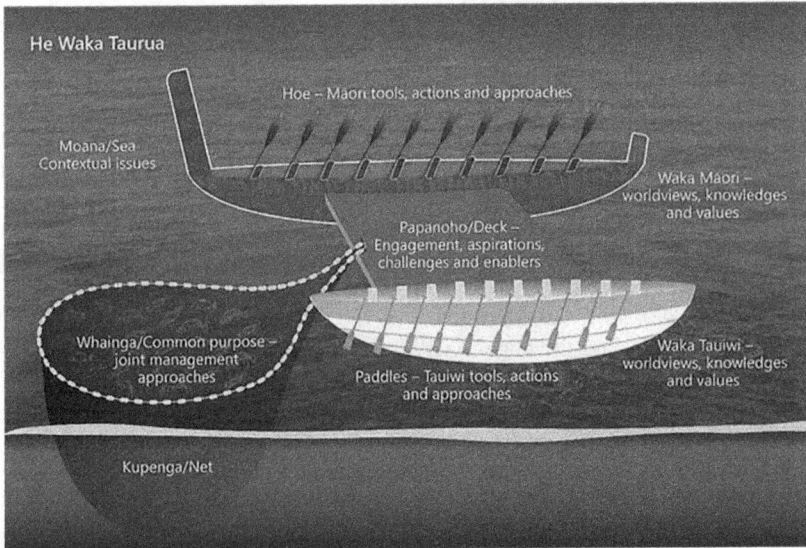

*Fig. 3.* He Waka Taurus Lashing Knowledge Together. *Note: Waka-Taurua* the Māori framework for "lashing" together Māori knowledge and non-Maori knowledge achieve common purposes (Maxwell et al., 2020).

Etuaptmumk: Two Eyed Seeing

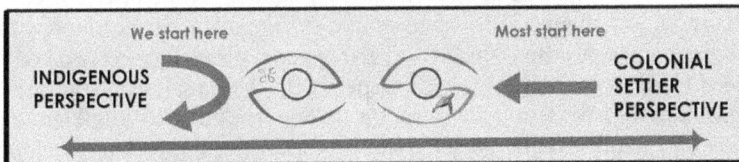

*Fig. 4.* Etuaptmumk: Two Eyed Seeing. *Note: Etuaptmumk* the Mi'kmaw concept of learning to see from one eye the strengths of Indigenous knowledge, from the other eye with the strengths of Western knowledge, and by using both eyes together learn from each other (Weigand & Williams 2024).

Importantly, *Waka-Taurua* allows for more than knowledge exchange, the non-privileged selection between what is determined as most applicable to the question at hand, but it also allows for innovation (Maxwell et al., 2020).

In Fig 4, we present an illustration of *Etuaptmumk* is another example of the living nature of Indigenous knowledge systems, recognizing the interdependence, the need, and the opportunity to learn from each other in unifying knowledge. Respected Mi'kmaw Elder Albert Marshall taught that learning to see from one eye with the strengths of Indigenous knowledge, from the other eye with the strengths of Western knowledge, and to use both these eyes together, for the benefit of all (Reid et al., 2021, p. 246).

An example of Indigenous communities allowing knowledge systems to speak for themselves in their own context can be seen by comparing two Dene communities, the Inuvialuit and the Dene First Nation of the Sahtu Region, and their responses to oil and gas development (Dana et al., 2008, 2009). The Sahtu Dene territory is along the Mackenzie River and Great Bear Lake. The Inuvialuit territory lies further north and encompasses the Mackenzie Delta and the Beaufort Sea. As a result of the differences in place and history, the communities each have distinct Indigenous knowledge and distinct, though related, languages. Outside awareness of the presence of oil and gas reserves along the Mackenzie River dates back to the 1890s, but outside interest in the reserves waxed and waned until the 1970s. This marked the beginning of a period of interest in the fuel reserves in Inuvialuit and Sahtu Dene's territories. Along with the prospectors and oil companies came outside ways of knowing, being, and doing, such as the market economy and maximum resource extraction.

In their research with the communities, Dana et al. (2008, 2009) observed that both communities started with an omnipresent and central understanding of their connection to the land, animals, and environment of their homelands. From that foundation, the researched found distinctions in the knowledge and understanding the communities developed when using both eyes to understand what would be best for their community. In the case of the Inuvialuit, their goal was to strengthen and rebuild their communities by "maintaining their traditional way of life and, at the same time, venture into the market economy" (Dana et al., 2008, p. 158). To this end, the Inuvialuit Development Corp was created to enable involvement and impactful participation in local, polar, and national economies. The development corporation entered joint ventures and development partnerships with the oil and gas companies. By 2000, 70% of the regional oil and gas-related contracts had been made by Inuvialuit-owned businesses. In their analysis of the strengths of Indigenous and Western knowledge, the Sathu Dene came to a different understanding of a path forward. They did not turn away from industrial development but kept it as a junior partner in protecting their lands and traditional renewable resource economy. This was done by agreeing to pipeline routes that avoided culturally significant sites and the creation of cost and revenue-sharing agreements. In both cases, the Indigenous communities were able to strengthen themselves culturally, economically, and their political autonomy. These serve as examples that demonstrate the potential for Indigenous and non-Indigenous ways of being, knowing, and doing collaboratively for the benefit of all.

There is no straightforward procedure for decolonizing. Nothing about this journey is straightforward, quick, or simple. It is a journey that requires patience, humility, reflection, repentance, and a committed willingness to change. Despite this, we suggest a three-part iterative and unending process whereby we, scholars and educators, might proceed with decolonizing entrepreneurship and thereby better fulfill our responsibility to leave the world a better place. Suggesting there is a process as simple as having three parts is both deceptive. Any part of our proposed process is far more complicated, challenging, and time-consuming than we could describe. However, here is our three-part process, which is in no order.

One part of the process surrounds knowledge, including acceptance of Indigenous concepts of multiple knowledge systems working together. Central is the mechanism and understanding that facilitates neither knowledge being subsumed by others nor the enrichment of each knowledge system independently. This step does not end with a scholar accepting there are alternate and valuable knowledge systems. It is not enough to accept the presence of multiple equal knowledge systems because we will often also have to reframe or break our current paradigm of being, knowing, and doing entrepreneurship.

Dana (2007) provide examples of areas where Indigenous knowledge can challenge our entrepreneurship paradigm. The authors identify several understandings that are common among many bodies of Indigenous knowledge. Ones specific to entrepreneurship are the communal and cooperative nature of existence and value creation from entrepreneurship as monetary, cultural, and political. An example of a grander challenge is time. Indigenous conceptions of time in terms of span, interaction with, and simultaneous coexistence of past, present, and future. These examples are the specific bodies of Indigenous knowledge and understandings of entrepreneurship that are the result of each Indigenous community's engagement, and understanding of entrepreneurship is the result of their experience and the influence of the place.

Place leads us to another part of our process, which is honoring and respecting the local or most relevant Indigenous community in your work. Again, in general, Indigenous people's ways of knowing, being, and doing place speak to connections to where they are or have been that are deeper and more pervasive than Western concepts of place and its influence on knowledge. The closest we are aware of is Heidegger's (1962) hermeneutic-phenomenological theory and Ericson's (2021) theory of social material weaving. Indigenous understandings are rooted in place, and all that is there (Dana, 2007). The connection includes symbiotic connections between the people, plants, animals, water, soil, and air. In the symbiotic relationship, Western hierarchies of sentience and intelligence do not hold; humans are not superior to the other entities. Interdependence exists between all people, animals, plants, and physical features of the places they, Indigenous people, have always existed in. As a starting point, Western concepts of embeddedness recognize the influence of place and context on our understanding of and engagement in entrepreneurship, but Indigenous concepts of embeddedness go exponentially deeper than anything we have been taught. Consequently, place and the Indigenous people of a place mean everything in any decolonization path. Whether we are considering the place of your origin, place of your present, or place of your research and teaching, it is necessary to learn at the feet of the Indigenous knowledge holders of the place is an essential part of the decolonization of our minds.

Learning from and being taught by knowledge-holders requires building trusting and reciprocal relationships within the Indigenous communities of the place you are. There are challenges to building relationships. One challenge arises from the fact that Indigenous people have been researched for as long as there have been colonial and post-colonial times and their experience of research, and researchers has predominantly been exploitive and negative (Tuhiwai Smith, 2008). Too often, the practice of researchers has been presenting our work as discovery instead of acknowledging we have extracted, commodified, and distributed Indigenous knowledge, values, and beliefs for our purposes and as our property (Bishop, 1998; Denzin & Lincoln, 2008). Much of the research has not been for the benefit or interest of the Indigenous people but has been for the benefit and advancement of the researchers and funders. At times, the research and researchers have played significant roles in supporting the regulatory mechanisms of subjugation and colonization (Asch, 2014).

Learning from Indigenous knowledge holders and developing the in-depth understanding Willmott referred to requires our overcoming the effects of the history of colonization, and research requires patient and purposeful efforts to establish trusting relationships with local Indigenous communities. How you build relationships depends on the Indigenous people, their protocols, and expectations. In a presentation at the 2023 International Academy of Indigenous Research in Management and Organization (IARIMOS), Algonquin Anishinabe Claudette Commanda, Chancellor of the University of Ottawa, shared guidance, for establishing trusting relationships. She advised audience members to reframe our work from studying Indigenous people to being part of their research. This means working with communities to find answers to the questions they have. It means a commitment that all research is for the benefit, as defined by the community, of the community. It can also mean following knowledge holders in building two-eyed research methods.

Her guidance was to also learn the community's protocols and follow them as you build the necessary relationship. In the case of her community, asking to meet the Chief and Council was an essential protocol. So, too, is recognizing and respecting their status as knowledge holders. She suggested one way to do this is to invite them into your classes and presentations in such a way as to recognize their status and show this respect by inviting them to your university as peers. Ask community leaders to teach you how to be a "good scholar." To build trusting relationships, her admonition was to establish reciprocal relationships that recognize interdependence and interconnectedness where good research and teaching are compatible with what the community wants.

The third part of our suggested process is to incorporate *Kaswentha*, *Ganma*, *Waka-Taurua*, *Etuaptmumk*, or other Indigenous frameworks into our teaching and research. Share with others as you learn and decolonize yourself. Open your students' and colleagues' minds to the possibilities of other ways of knowing, being, and doing entrepreneurship by including Indigenous content in your courses and working with Indigenous researchers. But be aware that incorporating Indigenous knowledge is not as simple as the sentence makes it sound. Learn and follow the local protocols for sharing knowledge that respect the knowledge holder who shared the knowledge.

## CONCLUSION

We attempted to point out a motivation for decolonizing entrepreneurship research and education. We shed light on the realities of our legacies of colonization and argued that there are ethical and scholarly reasons to engage in the decolonization of entrepreneurship. Colonization and its legacies have left us with great inequalities and we can have a role in reconciling these inequalities. Educators have important roles in reconciliation. The "What We Have Learned" report from the groundbreaking Canadian Truth and Reconciliation Commission into the legacy of Canada's residential schools places emphasis on our role: "Reconciliation requires sustained public education and dialogue, including youth engagement, about the history and legacy of residential schools, Treaties, and Aboriginal rights, as well as the historical and contemporary contributions of Aboriginal peoples to Canadian society" (TRC, 2015, p. 126).

To decolonize entrepreneurship research and education, we are being asked to participate in reconciliation by restoring relationships of mutual dependence despite the incompatible aspects of our ways of knowing, being, and doing. As we learn from *Kaswentha, Ganma, Waka-Taurua,* and *Etuaptmumk* there is a need in our research and education to collaborate as equals, become aware of the needs and interests of, and conduct research and education that matters not only to our academic field but also for the Indigenous society with whom we are researching. This will mean we no longer ethnocentrically define the research problem, theories, and methods (Sillitoe et al., 2010). In so doing, not only will we be allies in reconciliation, but by practicing Indigenous multiple knowledge frameworks, we will have available theories and knowledge most applicable to any context and the innovation we need in our ever-changing world.

## NOTE

1. We believe that research and teaching are conjoined twins. What we teach is built from the field's research. Teaching connects our research to practice. Research with broader applicability will result in teaching with broader applicability and visa versa.

## REFERENCES

Alfred, T. (2009). *Peace, power, righteousness: An indigenous manifesto.* Oxford University Press.

Anderson, R. B. (2002). Entrepreneurship and aboriginal Canadians: A case study in economic development. *Journal of Developmental Entrepreneurship, 7*(1), 45–65.

Anderson, R. B., Dana, L., & Dana, T. E. (2006). Indigenous land rights, entrepreneurship, and economic development in Canada: "Opting-in" to the global economy. *Journal of World Business, 41*(1), 45–55. https://doi.org/10.1016/j.jwb.2005.10.005

Anderson, R. B., Kayseas, B., Dana, L., & Hindle, K. (2004). Indigenous land claims and economic development: The Canadian experience. *American Indian Quarterly, 28*(3–4), 634–638.

Anderson, R. B., Camp II, R., Dana, L. P., Honig, B., Nkongolo-Bakenda, J-M., & Peredo, A. M. (2005). Indigenous land rights in Canada: The foundation for development? *International Journal of Entrepreneurship and Small Business, 2*(2), 104–133.

Asch, M. (2014). *On being here to stay: Treaties and Aboriginal rights in Canada.* University of Toronto Press.

Bishop, R. (1998). Freeing ourselves from neo-colonial domination in research: A Maori approach to creating knowledge. *Qualitative Studies in Education, 2*, 199–219.

Calas, M. B., Smircich, L., & Bourne, K. A. (2009). Extending the boundaries "Entrepreneurship as social change." *Academy of Management Review, 34*(3), 552–569. https://doi.org/10.5465/AMR.2009.40633597

Canada.ca. (2022). *Indigenous knowledge: What is Indigenous knowledge.* https://www.canada.ca/en/impact-assessment-agency/programs/aboriginal-consultation-federal-environmental-assessment/indigenous-knowledge-policy-framework-initiative.html

Chakrabarty, D. (2000). *Provincializing Europe: Postcolonial thought and historical difference*. Princeton University Press.

Dana, L. (2007). Toward a multidisciplinary definition of indigenous entrepreneurship. In L. Dana & R. B. Anderson (Eds.), *International handbook of research on indigenous entrepreneurship* (pp. 3–7). Edward Elgar.

Dana, L., & Anderson, R. B. (2007). A multidisciplinary theory of entrepreneurship as a function of cultural perceptions of opportunity. In L. Dana & R. B. Anderson (Eds.), *International handbook of research on Indigenous entrepreneurship* (pp. 595–603). Edward Elgar.

Dana, L., Anderson, R. B., & Meis-Mason, A. (2009). A study of the impact of oil and gas development on the Dene first nations of the Sahtu (great bear lake) region of the Canadian Northwest Territories (NWT). *Journal of Enterprising Communities*, 3(1), 94–117. https://doi.org/10.1108/17506200910943706

Dana, L., Meis-Mason, A., & Anderson, R. B. (2008). Oil and gas and the Inuvialuit people of the Western Arctic. *Journal of Enterprising Communities*, 2(2), 151–167. https://doi.org/10.1108/17506200810879970

Daniel, R. A., Wilhelm, T. 'A., Case-Scott, H., Goldman, G., & Hinzman, L. (2022). *What is "Indigenous Knowledge" and why does it matter? Integrating ancestral wisdom and approaches into federal decision-making*. https://www.whitehouse.gov/ostp/news-updates/2022/12/02/what-is-indigenous-knowledge-and-why-does-it-matter-integrating-ancestral-wisdom-and-approaches-into-federal-decision-making/

Denzin, N. K., & Lincoln, Y. S. (2008). Introduction. In N. K. Denzin, Y. S. Lincoln, & L. Tuhiwai Smith (Eds.), *Handbook of critical indigenous methodologies* (pp. 1–20). Sage.

Dybbroe, S. (1999). Researching knowledge: The terms and scope of a current debate. *Topics in Arctic Social Sciences*, 3, 13–26.

Ericson, M. (2021). *An alternative approach to family business: A theory of socio-material weaving*. Edward Elgar Publishing.

Foucault, M. (1972). The archaeology of knowledge: The discourse on language (A. Sheridan Smith, trans.). In M. Foucault (Ed.), *The archeology of knowledge* (pp. 215–237). Pantheon Books.

Fuentes, L., Asselin, H., Bélisle, A. C., & Labra, O. (2020). Impacts of environmental changes on well-being in indigenous communities in eastern Canada. *International Journal of Environmental Research and Public Health*, 17(2). https://doi.org/10.3390/ijerph17020637

Gall, A., Anderson, K., Howard, K., Diaz, A., King, A., Willing, E., Connolly, M., Lindsay, D., & Garvey, G. (2021). Wellbeing of indigenous peoples in Canada, Aotearoa (New Zealand) the United States: A systematic review. *International Journal of Environmental Research and Public Health*, 18(11). MDPI AG. https://doi.org/10.3390/ijerph18115832

Gartner, W. B. (2001). Is there an elephant in entrepreneurship? Blind assumptions in theory development. *Entrepreneurship Theory & Practice*, 25(4), 27–38.

Gopinath, C. (1998). Alternative approaches to indigenous management in India. *Management International Review*, 38, 257–275.

Heidegger, M. (1962). *Being and time*. Harper & Row.

Holland, T. (2012, August 28). *Islam: The untold story*. Channel 4/YouTube. https://www.youtube.com/watch?v=j9S_xbjIRgE

Jack, G., Westwood, R., Srinivas, N., & Sardar, Z. (2011). Deepening, broadening and re-asserting a postcolonial interrogative space in organization studies. *Organization*, 18(3), 275–302. https://doi.org/10.1177/1350508411398996

Kao, R. W. Y. (2007). *Stewardship-based economics*. World Scientific.

Kemple, T. M., & Mawani, R. (2009). The sociological imagination and its imperial shadows. *Theory, Culture & Society*, 26(7–8), 228–249. https://doi.org/10.1177/0263276409349283

Kimmerer, R. W. (2013). *Braiding Sweetgrass: Indigenous wisdom, scientific knowledge, and the teaching of plants*. Milkweed.

Louie, C. (2021). *Rez Rules: My indictment of Canada's and America's systematic racism against Indigenous peoples*. McClelland & Stewart.

Mann, C. (2005). *1491: New revelations of the Americas before Columbus*. Knopf.

Manuel, G., & Posluns, M. (1974). *The fourth world: An Indian reality*. Collier-MacMillan Canada Ltd.

*Map of Indigenous Australia*. (2022, October 11). AIATSIS. https://aiatsis.gov.au/explore/map-indigenous-australia

Marika, R. (1999). Milthun latju wanga romgu Yolngu: Valuing Yolngu knowledge in education systems. *Ngoonjook: A Journal of Australian Indigenous Issues, 16*, 107–129.

Martin, K., & Mirraboopa, B. (2003). Ways of knowing, being, and doing: A theoretical framework and methods for Indigenous and Indigenist re-search. *Journal of Australian Studies, 27*, 203–314.

Maxwell, K., Awatere, S., Ratana, K., Davies, K., & Taiapa, C. (2020). He waka eke noa/we are all in the same boat: A framework for co-governance from Aotearoa New Zealand. *Marine Policy, 121*. https://doi.org/10.1016/j.marpol.2020.104213

Moosavi, L. (2020). The decolonial bandwagon and the dangers of intellectual decolonisation. *International Review of Sociology, 30*(2), 1–23.

Nadasdy, P. (1999). The politics of TEK: Power and the "integration" of knowledge. *Arctic Anthropology, 36*, 1–18.

Onondaga Nation. (n.d.). *Two Row Wampum – Gaswêñdah*. Retrieved November 27, 2023, from https://www.onondaganation.org/culture/wampum/two-row-wampum-belt-guswenta/

Osmund, M. W., & Thorn, B. (1993). Feminist theories: The social construction of gender in families and society. In P. Boss, W. Doherty, R. LaRossa, & W. S. Schumm (Eds.), *Sourcebook of family theories and methods* (pp. 591–623). Plenum.

Parmenter, J. (2013). The Meaning of Kaswentha and the Two Row Wampum Belt in Haudenosaunee (Iroquois) History: Can indigenous oral tradition be reconciled with the documentary record? *Journal of Early American History, 3*(1), 82–109. https://doi.org/10.1163/18770703-00301005

Peredo, A. M., Anderson, R. B., Galbraith, C. S., Honig, B., & Dana, L. (2004). Towards a theory of indigenous entrepreneurship. *International Journal of Entrepreneurship and Small Business, 1*(1/2), 1–20. https://doi.org/10.1504/IJESB.2004.005374

Pimbott, K. (2020). Decolonising the university: The origins and meaning of a movement. *The Political Quarterly, 91*(1), 210–216.

Reid, A. J., Eckert, L. E., Lane, J. F., Young, N., Hinch, S. G., Darimont, C. T., Cooke, S. J., Ban, N. C., & Marshall, A. (2021). "Two-Eyed Seeing": An Indigenous framework to transform fisheries research and management. *Fish and Fisheries, 22*(2), 243–261. https://doi.org/10.1111/faf.12516

Said, E. W. (1994). *Culture and imperialism*. First Vintage.

Sillitoe, P., Dixon, P., & Barr, J. (2010). *Indigenous knowledge inquiries: A methodologies manual for development*. Practical Action.

Sinclair, M. (2019, March 7). *TRC Mini Documentary - Senator Murray Sinclair on Reconciliation*. National Centre for Truth and Reconciliation. https://www.youtube.com/watch?v=wjx2zDvyzs U&list=PLGESnaOwwVdClaC5BPUZBde6zOl27j944&index=6&t=55s

Sontag, R. (1962). Reviewed work: The origins of the Second World War by AJP Taylor. *The American Historical Review, 67*(4), 992–994.

Southam, T. (2021). PORTFOLIO: Academics as allies and accomplices: Practices for decolonized solidarity. *Anthropology & Aging, 42*(2), 150–165. https://doi.org/10.5195/aa.2021.366.

Srinivas, N. (2012). Epistemic and performative quests for authentic management in India. *Organization, 19*(2), 145–158. https://doi.org/10.1177/1350508411429398

Stewart, C. (2004). Changing patterns of native American trade in the middle Atlantic region and Chesapeake watershed: A world systems perspective. *North American Archaeologist, 25*(4). https://doi.org/10.2190/4URN-W222-2PC3-D1DP

TRC. (2015). *What we have learned: Principles of truth and reconciliation*.

Tuhiwai Smith, L. (2008). *Decolonizing methodologies: Research and indigenous peoples*. Zed Books.

United Nations. (2007). *United Nations Declaration on the Rights of Indigenous Peoples*. United Nations.

Watson, H., The Yolngu community at Yirrkala, & Wade Chambers, D. (1989). *Exhibit 1 · Ganma: A confluence of rivers Singing the Land, Signing the Land*. Singing the Land, Signing the Land: A Portfolio of Exhibits. http://singing.indigenousknowledge.org/exhibit-1.html

Weigand, H., & Williams, T. (2024, June 17–20). *A two-eyed seeing reflection of allyship* [Conference Presentation]. Gender, Work and Organization 14th International Interdisciplinary Conference, Sydney, NS, Canada.

Whiteman, G., & Cooper, W. H. (2000). Ecological embeddedness. *Academy of Management Journal, 43*(6), 1265–1282.

Whitley, J., & Barbour, A. L. (2007). *Archaeologies of the Greek past: Herodotus*. Joukowsky Institute for Archaeology. https://www.brown.edu/Departments/Joukowsky_Institute/courses/greek-past/4694.html#:~:text=Herodotus%20is%20most%20well%20known,barbarians%20to%20receive%20their%20due

Willmott, H. (2008). For informed pluralism, broad relevance and critical reflexivity. In D. Barry & H. Nansen (Eds.), *The SAGE handbook of new approaches to management and organization* (pp. 82–83). SAGE Publications.

Wilmer, F. (1993). *The indigenous voice in world politics*. Sage.

# GRAND CHALLENGES, DECOLONIALITY AND MANAGEMENT SCHOLARSHIP

Jess Auerbach Jahajeeah[a], Ali Aslan Gümüsay[b,c], Esther Salvi[d], Georg von Richthofen[c] and Lehlohonolo Kekana[a]

[a]University of Cape Town, South Africa
[b]LMU Munich, Germany
[c]Humboldt Institute for Internet & Society Berlin, Germany
[d]International Institute for Management Development, Switzerland

## ABSTRACT

*Societal grand challenges are global, yet management scholarship is dominated by the minority world. Tackling grand challenges requires changing – and decolonizing – our scholarship. In this article, we highlight four approaches toward inclusive research partnerships that are collaborative across the minority and majority world: we suggest a movement from* ignorance *through* awareness *and* integration, *and finally toward* elevation, *and present illustrative examples from three practical cases moving in this direction. We conclude by discussing challenges and pathways toward a decolonial management scholarship that engages inclusively with societal grand challenges.*

**Keywords:** Decoloniality; grand challenges; minority and majority worlds; research partnerships; management scholarship

Decolonizing Management and Organization Studies: Why, How, and What
Research in the Sociology of Organizations, Volume 93, 85–102
ISSN: 0733-558X/doi:10.1108/S0733-558X20250000093006

# INTRODUCTION

The world faces grand challenges induced by climate change, conflict, digitalization, shifting demographics, and other factors. Only 15% of the UN Sustainable
Development Goals (SDGs) are on track (UN, 2023). There has been significant
research in the field of management scholarship to understand and overcome
these societal grand challenges (Ferraro et al., 2015; George et al., 2016; Gümüsay
et al., 2022). Given that grand challenges are global (Gümüsay et al., 2022), they
must be globally and collaboratively tackled.

To achieve this, it is crucial for management scholarship to reflect on its axi-
ology, ontology, epistemology, and resulting language. Debated terms such as
*Global North* and *Global South* or *developing* and *developed* countries increase
epistemic barriers in management scholarship, hampering widely inclusive
approaches toward understanding, theorizing, and collaboratively shaping more
sustainable futures (Gümüsay & Reinecke, 2022, 2024; Muñoz & Dimov, 2023).
An alternative to the inaccurate and value-laden geography-related designations
of Global North and Global South (Makoni, 2023; Trisos et al., 2021) was provided by Shahidul Alam (2008) in the 1990s when he introduced the language of
*majority worlds* and *minority worlds* – which we adopt here.

In this article, we ask: *how can we decolonize management and organization
studies to conduct inclusive global scholarship that enables more impactful research
into tackling grand challenges?* We argue that employing decolonial approaches to
knowledge production regarding grand challenges has powerful potential. Done
carefully, it will both widen the scope of available theory and enable scholars
within management to be more inclusive, have a greater impact, and engage in
more ethical knowledge production processes across the world. Here, "we" refers
to the five authors. We acknowledge the complexity of positionality statements
and the danger of fixing authors in particular categories; nonetheless, they serve
to delineate the scope and limits of individual and collective expertise (Dixit,
2023; Martin et al., 2022; Savolainen et al., 2023; Trisos et al., 2021). Of the five
authors, three were trained in the minority world and work at institutions in
Europe. Two are based in the majority world, one having completed her training
in the minority world before returning home. The fifth has undertaken all of his
intellectual training in South Africa. Collectively, we represent diversity in terms
of gender, race/ethnicity, generation, spiritual belief, and socio-economic status.

After reviewing the relevant literature, we parse four approaches toward
grand challenges in management scholarship. Those move from (i) *ignorance* (the
situation whereby minority world scholars in management studies are usually
either ignorant of or actively ignore the reality of the majority of the world);
to (ii) *awareness* – the recognition of local perspectives and worldviews and
appreciation of local expertise (frequently, however, accompanied by extractive research practices); moving to (iii) *integration*, whereby the majority world
is an integrated but unequal partner to theorization undertaken by, in, and for
the minority world; and finally (iv) *elevation*, as a fundamental change in power
dynamics and scholarly practice that values and fosters local expertise. The fourth
approach manifests as a change in existing power dynamics. It holds the potential

to enable management scholars from both the majority and the minority worlds to jointly set agendas in research, teaching, and publication and to more effectively tackle the societal grand challenges of our era.

After explaining these four approaches, we articulate a dynamic perspective that highlights how to enable more inclusive management scholarship to tackle grand challenges. We demonstrate that addressing global challenges in a meaningful way requires what Aboderin and her colleagues call a "fundamental rebalancing [of] positions in the worldwide scientific effort" (2023, p. 2), including management scholarship. We believe the discipline could make practice-based changes that would enable profound shifts toward inclusion and equity, going beyond surface-level diversity efforts and adding richness and depth to available knowledge structures. While these processes are complex, we suggest they are valuable and necessary if we wish to progress as a scholarly field.

## THEORETICAL ORIENTATION

To develop a path toward producing more decolonial and impactful management scholarship, we draw on the literature on grand challenges in management and organization studies.

Serious social, economic, and political concerns remain in our globalized world. Overall, management and organization studies refer to these concerns as grand challenges – the "specific critical barrier(s) that, if removed, would help solve an important societal problem with a high likelihood of global impact through widespread implementation" (Grand Challenges Canada, 2011, p. iv). Grand challenges are complex, uncertain, and evaluative (Ferraro et al., 2015), requiring coordinated, collaborative, and collective effort that must overcome both systemic and interpersonal barriers. Management scholarship has developed significant research avenues relating to grand challenges (Ferraro et al., 2015; George et al., 2016; Gümüsay et al., 2022), and journals have started steering toward impact-oriented publications aimed at fostering positive change (Chen et al., 2022; Colquitt & George, 2011; Markman et al., 2019). At the same time, some authors have begun to highlight the need for deeper changes in management scholarship (Abdelnour, 2022; Bainazarov et al., 2022; Nkomo, 2011; Özkazanç-Pan, 2008; Zanoni & Mir, 2022) to better comprehend the mechanisms through which grand challenges arise, manifest, and expand, and how they could potentially be overcome. Drawing on these conversations, we distill two main opportunities to support the development of more impactful and decolonial management scholarship: *embracing decolonial perspectives* and *revisiting scholarship practices*.

### *Embracing Decolonial Perspectives*

Recent management and organization studies have called for research that embraces more decolonial perspectives (Banerjee, 2022; Boussebaa, 2023; Bruton et al., 2022) and goes beyond research extraction approaches (Bothello

& Bonfim, 2023; Wickert et al., 2024). These approaches help overcome Western-based theorizing and biases, producing more inclusive management scholarship – instrumental in deepening our understanding of societal grand challenges. For instance, the *Journal of Management Studies* has recently announced a special issue that features decoloniality as a way to recalibrate entrepreneurship research (George et al., 2023). Several sessions on the importance of decoloniality have been scheduled in recent and future management conferences.

Embracing decolonial perspectives also requires more inclusive language. Management studies have employed a number of terminologies to explore organizational phenomena spanning global regions and geographies (developing vs developed countries, Global South vs Global North, emerging vs emerged economies). Nevertheless, these terms do not carefully capture the distinctive local realities. A more inclusive language would help direct attention to global and local cues associated with societal grand challenges (Bansal et al., 2018). Here, we introduce the terms *majority world* and *minority world* into management and organization studies.

Majority world refers to those who live in the majority of the world's territory, influenced by shared conditions of economic precarity and social vulnerability. These conditions are historically based and perpetuated by global systems that do not enable the equal flourishing of humanity. Minority world describes the inhabitants of countries that have high levels of wealth, global political influence, and currency power. These have historically been referred to in management scholarship as "the Global North." Narratives and theories developed in minority-world contexts often purport to have global relevance and application, although in many cases they do not apply accurately to the majority of the world.

*Revisiting Scholarship Practices*

Tackling grand challenges requires collaboration across the majority and minority worlds, with careful attention to power dynamics. Often, what is called collaboration on paper is not in fact collaborative, but reflects structures that are often so deeply internalized by all parties that they are not questioned. They reflect a knowledge production system that developed partially by means of land and human resource appropriation, alongside systematic efforts made within the minority world to justify the ideological efforts of colonial powers to diminish indigenous institutions and promote inequalities (Lewis, 1973; Mafeje, 1986, 1998; Nyamnjoh, 2012).

Knowledge contestation continues in the contemporary academy. Within its varied spaces, scholars on editorial boards, hiring committees, and evaluation panels may not be fully aware of the cultural and historical specificity of management scholarship as a whole, upholding and reinforcing particular normative expectations in their everyday decision-making processes. These decisions include defining appropriate research questions, theory, language, and style of presentation and are usually (in)formed by the institutionalized training of authors. For example, there is a tendency to privilege knowledge that is written, produced through measurement, and/or published in minority-world peer-reviewed jour-nals over other kinds of knowledge (Darian-Smith, 2016).

Attending to the boundary-making and exclusionary practices of management scholarship is not meant to point fingers or condemn. Rather, we wish to highlight that this constitution is a matter of choice, and different choices can be made.

As a result of profound shifts in global power dynamics in the 20th century, knowledge structures have progressively been reconstituted – particularly in the minority world (Green, 2021). Critical self-examination on the part of those embedded in knowledge systems has led to several academic generations call-ing for the decolonization of disciplinary curricula (Nyamjoh, 2019). These movements have been amplified by broader societal and technological changes that have quickly enabled the globalization of discourses. The US-originated #BlackLivesMatter movement is one example; it has been argued that it drew energy from student-led interventions at the University of Cape Town in 2015 under the banner of #RhodesMustFall (Lange, 2019; Mamdani, 1998; Qambela, 2015).

Next, we critically illustrate the growing strength of interventions toward decolonial initiatives within management scholarship in both the majority and minority worlds and provide an overview from exclusive toward more inclusive approaches to tackle grand challenges.

# FOUR APPROACHES FROM EXCLUSIVE TO INCLUSIVE RESEARCH PARTNERSHIPS TO TACKLE GRAND CHALLENGES

Grand challenges are global. Scholarly engagement needs to be global, too. To develop impactful solutions, we require research partnerships between the major-ity and minority world. However, not all types of research partnerships are equally suitable for delivering the insights and solutions needed to tackle grand chal-lenges. Here, we outline four approaches. These approaches emerge as outcomes of our critical reflection on practices gathered from management scholarship in which majority world scholars play increasing roles in shaping and contributing to the fulfillment of research agendas. We consider each approach from the per-spectives of scholars in both the minority and the majority world, highlighting that such shifts require a change in the way scholars think and operate globally. The four approaches are illustrated in Fig. 1. In reality, these four approaches are not fixed and may overlap. For simplicity, we present them as abstract, ideal types, reporting their main features and expected impact on grand challenges.

## *Ignorance*

Research partnerships between minority and majority world scholars are still often characterized by *ignorance*. Despite access to globalized news sources, peo-ple are shaped by their local realities and the ability to access informed news or scholarship. We understand ignorance as manifesting through the following four

| | Ignorance | Awareness | Integration | Elevation |
|---|---|---|---|---|
| Local expertise | Lack of development of local and historical experts and expertise | Identification of local expertise, frequently accompanied with extractive approaches | Deep incorporation of local expertise | Enhanced local expertise to achieve full attribution, recognition and data control |
| Perspectives | No or little consideration for alternative perspectives | Recognition of perspectives of "others", different from "own" knowledge | Inclusive consideration of multiple perspectives throughout the entire research journey | Embeddedness of the entire research journey in multiple perspectives, esp. through epistemic humility |
| Resource allocation | Lack of commitment in terms of long-term relationships of care and/or investments in infrastructure | Unequal resource allocation | Balanced resource allocation, including long term data ownership | Equitable resource allocation enabled by capacity building of professions |
| Balance of partnership | No meaningful partnerships | Unequal partnerships | Integrated and balanced partnerships | Decolonized, inclusive partnerships |
| Research output on grand challenges | Deficient, biased, imposed, and colonized | Deficient and biased | Holistic and inclusive | Holistic, inclusive, and decolonized |

*Fig. 1.* Four Approaches Toward More Inclusive Research Partnerships to Tackle Grand Challenges.

characteristics: (1) lack of development of local and historical experts and expertise; (2) no or little consideration for alternative perspectives; (3) lack of commitment to long-term relationships of care and/or investments and infrastructure; (4) lack of meaningful partnerships. In many instances, ignorance – rather than expertise – is the starting point of global research partnerships.

While grand challenges are global, we witness most research on the topic stemming from the minority world, often ignoring local specificities and ground realities elsewhere (Wickert et al., 2024). Ignorance is accompanied by a lack of meaningful local partnerships and very confined research outputs on grand challenges. In part, ignorance is driven by cost-efficiency principles, as meaningful partnerships may require substantial investments of time and financial resources. A lack of partnerships can allow researchers to move faster in the publication process and theorize grand challenges. However, they rarely acknowledge the local challenges faced on the ground.

At present, scholars in the majority world can rarely afford to be equally ignorant of the minority. What happens at the Academy of Management's annual meeting has an impact beyond the US and Europe, and the conventions and expectations of US/EU academia have largely been uncritically exported. Majority-world scholars are often not aware of the socio-cultural specificities that comprise such institutions. For example, tenure-committee expectations in the US impact the entire management field because they indirectly influence how a large number of well-resourced actors in the field behave. Scholars in other regions then get caught up in these behaviors. Therefore, the socio-cultural specificity of minority-world knowledge structures needs to be better documented and explicitly taught. This shift will enable majority-world individuals to approach management from a perspective of difference rather than inferiority. In turn, this will enable more meaningful and inclusive approaches to tackling grand challenges.

To overcome ignorance, the socio-cultural specificities of both majority- and minority-world knowledge structures need to be better documented, made easily accessible, and taught as part of the management curriculum around the globe. The cultural, social, and economic specificities of majority world contexts (e.g., the famous slogan, "Africa is Not a Country") need to be reinforced at all stages of the research preparation process (Gümüsay & Amis, 2020). This will provide scholars with greater awareness of their own specificity instead of taking their knowledge practices as an unexamined global norm.

### Awareness

*Awareness* is the second approach along the journey toward inclusive research partnerships in tackling grand challenges. Although still limited, it represents an improvement over ignorance. The main characteristics of awareness in management scholarship are: (1) identification of local expertise; (2) recognition of "others'" perspectives different from "own" knowledge; (3) unequal resource allocation; (4) unequal partnerships.

Awareness is an improvement on ignorance as it acknowledges the existence of "others" – local actors and their specific perspectives and worldviews. Nevertheless, it is often still unequal; this cascades into a number of counterproductive consequences that hamper inclusive approaches to research partnerships and the production of meaningful research to tackle grand challenges. For example, awareness is often combined with data appropriation that does not provide those who obtained it with data ownership rights (Ramanathan et al., 2022), or using "others'" perspectives to confirm "own" knowledge.

Most theorizing in management scholarship has taken place in the minority world, and when the majority world has been involved as part of research partnerships, it has usually been in the role of data collector or data provider to fit minority-world theorizing (Ramanathan et al., 2022). Research partners are recognized to a greater or lesser extent depending on the particularities of a project, but partners in the majority world are rarely able to shape research questions, co-author arguments, or build theoretical applications that reflect majority world priorities. Scholars in the majority world are often complicit in the unequal extraction of data. Extraction characterizes the majority of contemporary data collection approaches. This results in unequal partnerships and contestation over ownership, control of the narrative, and the right to contest published findings.

It is essential that majority-world scholars prevent these imbalanced partnerships and extractive practices. They should do this by ensuring that data management systems exist in their local contexts and by requiring scholars who wish to collaborate to aspire to do so on equal intellectual terms. This is difficult; in resource-scarce environments, the funds offered by scholars from wealthy institutions in exchange for data are often of significant value. This is particularly true when the data being explored is not a priority in local realities. Despite this, managing collaborations so that they are what Aboderin and colleagues refer to as "transformational" (2023) is fundamental for inclusive, global management scholarship.

*Integration*

To overcome extractive management scholarship and develop more holistic approaches to tackle grand challenges, researchers in both majority and minority world spaces need to be integrated at all stages of the research process. *Integration* means including all parties in research partnerships by providing fair and equitable rights and obligations according to specific contributions. We have identified the following characteristics of an integrative approach to research partnerships in management scholarship: (1) deep incorporation of local expertise; (2) inclusive consideration of multiple perspectives throughout the entire research journey, including the formulation of research questions, research design, analysis, and publication; (3) balanced resource allocation, including long term data ownership; (4) integrated and balanced partnerships. An integrative approach to management scholarship also entails careful and transparent decisions as to who has what rights to data and the post-project rights to analyze gathered data.

The assertion of scholarly rights and obligations toward research is essential. For scholars based in majority world contexts to feel comfortable asserting such rights and obligations, attention must be given to internalized feelings of inferiority, as described by theorists such as Franz Fanon (1952) and Steve Bantu Biko (1981). When scholars have been educated in parameters that reinforce scarcity, it is often difficult to respond as equals to scholars from minority countries who have seemingly unlimited confidence and resources. This is compounded by weak institutional checks and balances (that often make it difficult for resources to be equitably distributed within localized universities), rigidity in minority world research frameworks (Makoni, 2023), and/or legal structures that may not have the capacity to ethically review all foreign research undertaken in a country. As part of scholarly assertion, scholars in the global majority must build reliable systems of evaluation and control so that no individual has to confront the force of "the West" (or increasingly "the East") alone. This is essential for enabling inclusive and holistic engagements with grand challenges that are not dominated by minority world perspectives.

*Elevation*

*Elevation* refers to an approach in which previously marginalized voices find space and amplify themselves within management scholarship. The four main characteristics of elevation are: (1) enhanced local expertise to achieve full attribution, recognition, and data control; (2) embeddedness of the entire research journey in multiple perspectives, especially through epistemic humility – the recognition of the limits to one's knowledge (which is valuable to *all* scholars); (3) equitable resource allocation enabled by capacity building of professions that carry out translation and storytelling in all relevant contexts; (4) decolonized, inclusive partnerships. Elevation represents the best-suited approach to overcoming ethnocentric management scholarship production and fostering meaningful theoretical approaches to tackle grand challenges inclusively.

Currently, researchers in the majority world are very rarely elevated for their role in international research partnerships. We believe more diverse promotion criteria are needed so that there are incentives and appraisal for engagement with international partners and societal impact of their scholarship. Recognizing that most human systems place great emphasis on prestige, new prestige markers need to be developed throughout the knowledge production environment. For example, new prestige markers could consider the extent to which positive societal impact and solutions to grand challenges are co-created.

Elevated approaches can be formed to give appropriate recognition to research partnerships that are ethically and equitably undertaken and that contribute to the resolution of grand challenges. New institutional processes need to be developed to support such elevation.

# MOVING TOWARD INCLUSIVE RESEARCH PARTNERSHIPS TO TACKLE GRAND CHALLENGES: A DYNAMIC PERSPECTIVE

We presented four approaches toward more inclusivity in research partnerships to foster decolonized approaches in tackling grand challenges in theory and practice. Next, we move from a static description of the four approaches toward a dynamic perspective on how to move from one approach to the next. We begin by describing the transition from *ignorance* to *awareness*, then we move from *awareness* to *integration*, and finally, we highlight best practices to move from *integration* to *elevation*. We provide evidence of these transitions in action using illustrative examples derived from our own experiences as scholars working on three projects fostering partnerships between the majority and minority worlds.

The *Sustainability, Entrepreneurship, and Global Digital Transformation (SET) research project* was implemented by two of us. We had received a research grant from the German Development Cooperation on behalf of the Federal Ministry of Economic Cooperation and Development that involved carrying out research and knowledge exchange activities in Benin, Ghana, Indonesia, Kenya, Kosovo, Marocco, Mexico, and Vietnam. The overall goal was to collaborate with researchers, practitioners, and policymakers in these countries to build application-oriented expertise, identify best practices, and develop concrete recommendations on issues related to sustainability, entrepreneurship, and digitalization. For instance, in Ghana and Kenya, our activities focused on improving conditions for online gig workers. In Benin, Mexico, Indonesia, and Vietnam, our activities were centered on promoting sustainable entrepreneurship and digital solutions in response to grand challenges such as maintaining biodiversity and mitigating climate change (von Richthofen & Gümüsay, 2023).

The second project, *the TUM SEED Center*, focused on fostering academic exchange around sustainable energy, entrepreneurship, and development; this was in relation to SDG 7, established by the UN General Assembly to tackle the grand challenge of our time related to "access to reliable, sustainable and modern energy for all." Approximately one billion people – or 14% of the world's population – currently lack access to electricity (International Energy Agency, 2017). While progress in electrification has been made since 2000, hundreds of millions of people still lack access to affordable energy. To tackle this grand challenge, we require decolonized and collaborative approaches involving actors from both the majority and minority worlds. We illustrate the case of the TUM Sustainable Energies, Entrepreneurship, and Development (SEED) Center, which was established in 2020 as an academic exchange center involving nine partner universities in Ethiopia, Germany, Ghana, India, Indonesia, Kenya, Namibia, Peru, and Uganda.

Lastly, we turn to the University of Cape Town and investigate the *Case Writing Centre*, a South African solution to the challenge of global imagination pertaining to Africa. Complex and varied, the African continent presents many challenges for businesses (Asongu & Odhiambo, 2020), including infrastructure gaps, debilitated economies, skilled labor gaps, climate change, weak governance, and poor leadership. These challenges create various obstacles for business and stifle the implementation of sustainable development policies (Asongu & Odhiambo, 2020). Management studies have made significant advances in contributing to our understanding of how industries and organizations respond to such challenges. However, this research has mostly produced insights from the minority world, with few examples from the majority world (Dang et al., 2020). In 2017, the University of Cape Town (UCT), the Graduate School of Business (GSB), and the Harvard Business School Alumni Africa collaborated to set up a Case Writing Centre at UCT to expose the practical realities and local nuances of doing business in African and emerging markets. This was achieved through the creation of local teaching cases derived from profiling leading businesses and start-ups in Africa.

Drawing on these three projects – the *SET research project, TUM SEED Center,* and the *UCT Case Writing Centre* – we provide cross-case examples to illustrate and reflect on current practices in moving toward inclusive research partnerships to tackle grand challenges. The choices made with these three projects reflect our own authorial proclivities and positionalities – something we again embrace and aim to bring to the fore.

### From Ignorance to Awareness

The first transition toward inclusive research partnerships to tackle grand challenges involves shifting from ignorance toward increasing awareness of local problems, expertise, and perspectives.

The SET research project embodied this transition in the initial stages of the collaborative endeavors between majority and minority world scholars. Several activities were designed to connect with experts from majority world countries to better understand their experiences and perspectives, including multi-stakeholder dialogues. The minority world research team also attended multiple events to connect with experts and learn about country-level discourses on issues such as AI, gig work, and green technologies. Thanks to these efforts, the minority world scholars became more aware of their own knowledge gaps in particular sectors and the challenges of fieldwork and accurate representation. The team, therefore, decided to allocate the planned study on sustainable digital entrepreneurship to a West African researcher (which relates to the third transition, explained below), who possessed knowledge of both the entrepreneurship literature and the contextual realities of local entrepreneurs.

The TUM SEED Center tackles the energy grand challenge. Majority-world partners have been included since before the project was funded. The center has enabled the electrification of eight rural villages within eight countries in the majority world, fostered teaching and research exchange activities between the minority and majority world, and has been active in the development of a decolonized research agenda at the intersection of sustainable energies, entrepreneurship, and grand challenges. The TUM SEED Center represents an exemplary case of what appears to be a successful process toward inclusive research partnerships, where actors from both the majority and the minority world collaborate to increase access to affordable and clean energy. Nevertheless, the journey began by moving from ignorance to awareness.

Minority world scholars had established the center to tackle SDG 7 and access to electricity, but it soon became evident that they were ignoring the true challenges on the ground. To build more inclusive scholarship and solutions to grand challenges, minority world scholars had to "unlearn" what they knew about the local challenges and build new awareness. The center has since established multiple forums for public dialogue to raise awareness, which is instrumental in building infrastructure and promoting academic exchange, teaching activities, research projects, and co-authorship. At the beginning of the project, the TUM SEED Center initiated a number of round tables to understand how to better co-develop systems embedded in local realities to enable sustainable energy access in rural villages (where access to electricity was previously not available). In this process, each of the eight partner universities in the majority world took leadership and responsibilities, ran a study of eligible sites, and selected a village that was most suitable for electrification. The rural specificities of each of the selected sites were evaluated by the majority world project leaders and different infrastructure was built according to local needs.

The UCT Case Writing Centre provides further examples of how important it is to move from ignorance to awareness. While grand challenges manifest globally, many of their roots can be found in local realities and need to be understood within their unique local context. Although lessons can be drawn from other parts of the world outside of Africa, there is no guarantee that these lessons will be relevant in addressing local African challenges as the reality in Africa may differ from elsewhere (Michalopoulos & Papaioannou, 2015; Zoogah et al., 2015). This demonstrates the need for research to draw attention to African realities and complexities (George et al., 2016; Hamann et al., 2020). This can be achieved through the development of theoretical or case-based literature from an emerging context, as well as translating insights from this research into the learning environment of universities and business schools. These attempts can result in initiatives to reform the curriculum in business schools and demands for broader changes in their scope and focus. The Case Writing Centre at UCT represents a new platform that allows scholars to become aware of African challenges and best practices by using teaching cases that draw attention to real-life examples. By providing these cases as teaching materials and promoting them as a research strategy, they provide a link between theory and practice centered on local realities.

*From Awareness to Integration*

Moving from ignorance to awareness is the first step in the journey to tackling grand challenges more inclusively. The second step involves moving from awareness toward becoming integrative of local problems, expertise, and perspectives. We illustrate this second transition using examples taken from our three cases.

The SET research project offers concrete examples of moving from awareness to integration in research partnerships to tackle grand challenges. The project involved the organization of two research sprints, one intended to understand and improve the working conditions in Ghana's gig economy, the other to foster entrepreneurial initiatives around the adoption of green technologies in Vietnam. Research sprints bring together a group of interdisciplinary and international researchers to develop actionable knowledge for local policymakers over several weeks or months.

The research sprints enabled the researchers in the minority world to integrate a wider variety of researchers who may go unheard in more traditional research collaborations (e.g., journal article projects), including junior scholars from the majority world. The shorter time frame of the research sprint further provided some predictability about the time allocation for the research; this was essential as researchers in majority world countries such as Ghana and Vietnam may face more challenging working conditions (e.g., time constraints) than researchers in the minority world.

Despite these benefits, the minority world scholars also realized that being in charge of both organizing the sprint and being responsible for the success of the overall project created challenges for equitable participation. Participants from the majority world frequently sought guidance from the organizers on matters ranging from framing the research question to the presentation of the findings. This possibly led to some biases and unintended imposition on the methodology and perspective applied by majority world researchers to illuminate local issues and approaches toward grand challenges. One way to address this issue could entail having an academic institution from the majority world serve as organizer of the sprint, who could then, in turn, involve researchers from the minority world as they see fit (von Richthofen & Gümüsay, 2023). This would also necessitate the institution from the majority world taking charge of where and how money is spent.

Similarly, the TUM SEED Center moved from awareness to integration by providing over 100 mobility grants per year for students, researchers, and practitioners from both the majority and the minority world to enhance integrative academic exchange on diverse topics of interest, such as informal entrepreneurship (Salvi et al., 2023). Each year, an in-person symposium is organized by one of the partner universities to enable community-building, networking, and the development of an integrative research strategy. A delegation of students, project leaders, researchers, and professors from each partner country participates in each symposium. Travel, accommodation, and conference participation are fully funded by the TUM SEED Center. A number of teaching activities are also jointly developed each year by academic staff from the majority and minority world. Students from the majority and minority world are involved in these activities.

Finally, The UCT Case Writing Centre moved from awareness toward integration by developing teaching cases through a collaborative and integrative effort between faculty, researchers, post-graduate students, and business partners to conduct rigorous research on diverse organizations. The unique teaching cases produced in these collaborations represent a form of integrative teaching material for business school classrooms that allows a worldwide audience to engage with the local realities and complexities of African businesses, leadership, and innovation.

### From Integration to Elevation

The examples above represent good practices for moving from awareness toward integration. Nevertheless, it is possible to go even further. Below, we provide illustrative examples from our cases to showcase how relevant it is to move from integration to elevation.

As a best practice example of the move from integration to elevation, the SET research project features the commissioning of studies to majority world scholars. In Kenya, the SET project study on the gig economy was conducted by two African researchers, one of whom was based in Nairobi (Kwanya & Wakunuma, 2023). The European team focused on providing infrastructure and support (such as proofreading, design, publication, and knowledge dissemination). The majority world researchers were responsible for both collecting and analyzing the data and remained in charge of data and intellectual property; moreover, they received full credit for their work as sole authors of the study. To move toward even higher degrees of elevation, an alternative approach could be for the studies to be commissioned by scholars in the majority world, who would then involve majority world scholars in the research process.

Finally, we highlight that co-organizing research sprints (see section on the transition from awareness to integration) can sometimes create platforms for building decolonized and true partnerships between majority and minority world researchers, who can jointly engage in the development of more cohesive research to tackle grand challenges. However, several challenges continue to inhibit such collaborations – most notably incentives. From the perspective of minority world scholars, the exercise was time-consuming, and they did not have as much space to focus on writing and publishing academic articles. Academic institutions and hiring committees in the minority world do not give sufficient credit for such endeavors, focusing primarily on the number of publications in top-tier journals. Therefore, our profession needs to change to incentivize similar activities. In some cases, scholars from the majority world will require additional funding, teaching relief, or administrative support for such activities so that they can afford to engage collaboratively in tackling grand challenges with minority world scholars rather than focusing on teaching and other paid activities.

To move from integration to elevation, the TUM SEED Center provided eight long-term research scholarships for PhD students from the majority world. The scholarship holders have the responsibility to jointly develop their research projects with actors from both the majority and minority world. Workshops are organized to enhance the joint formulation of research questions, the co-development of research designs, and engaged and collaborative approaches to data collection and analysis. Scholars from the majority and minority worlds are also supported in submitting joint articles to international conferences and journals.

The UCT Case Writing Centre moved from integration to elevation as it provided a platform for the joint investment by UCT GSB and Harvard Business School Alumni Africa – an example of a collaborative effort involving actors from both the majority world and the minority world (or as is the case for African Harvard alumni, scholars whose identity is in some way mixed). It is reflective of a somewhat decolonized collaborative approach where actors in the majority world have autonomy and ownership of narratives and means of production. The UCT Case Writing Centre calls for the understanding of African challenges from a localized context, developing elevated solutions that speak to the global discourse. Moreover, this is done in a manner that invites the rest of the world to engage in local phenomena and mechanisms from an African perspective, using African-originating solutions to tackle global challenges.

# DISCUSSION: CHALLENGES AND PATHWAYS FORWARD

We have provided illustrative examples from three cases to reflect current practices in moving toward inclusive research partnerships to tackle grand challenges. These examples illustrate some of the changes we believe are needed in scholarship across multiple scales – from the individual scholar, over the field of management, and across the broader structure of global higher education.

Firstly, the TUM SEED Center and SET project are both illustrative of the many instances when researchers in the minority world are shifting the status quo. Though far from perfect, these two projects take very seriously the need to change existing power paradigms in the interests of work that has a high impact outside of the Euro-American academy (and where much of the data is generated). Both projects have engaged majority-world actors throughout the entire research process. Authorship of publication has largely been allocated to those responsible for working with the data, and co-creation of research outputs and practical interventions have been prioritized. In this way, integration and elevation have been fostered within the two projects.

Though largely successful in terms of sustainable partnerships, what has been more challenging is the amount of work that this has required from minority world scholars that is not institutionally recognized as "counting" toward job stability, promotion, and prestige. In these instances, the work itself should not have to change, but rather the organizational structures that determine career recognition and progression. While documents such as the African "Charter for Transformative Research Collaborations" (Association of African Universities, 2023) or the Swiss "Guide for Transboundary Research Partnerships" (Swiss Academy of Sciences, 2019) acknowledge the challenges of this work and suggest steps forward, ensuring these steps are taken remains challenging in practice. An important enabler would be to provide recognition for the elevation of new perspectives, mentorship, teamwork, and co-authorship that transforms the current status quo of individualized academic competition.

UCT's Case Writing Centre is an important African source for information about Africa. We do not suggest that being in or from a place should automatically signify control over dominant narratives, but we *do* recognize that embedded relationships, commitments, and nuanced understanding informed by lived experience are important for adequate depth of work. Unfortunately, current structures often mean that "experts" are recognized less for their relationships with the spaces of data generation than for their location within prestigious departments in the minority world. While publication platforms do matter, these are unlikely to address global challenges in a meaningful way without serious work on assessment metrics, algorithmic bias, and publication credit.

A number of challenges that have surfaced from a colonial approach to management scholarship remain (Trisos et al., 2021). In the following, we briefly note the global and discipline-wide strategic challenges that shape management scholarship, identify stakeholders, and point to potential ways forward. Scholars from diverse geographies and lifeworlds are increasingly connected (Ramanathan et al., 2022), united by algorithms and structures of knowledge that determine digital results, rank business schools, enable journal impact, and determine how expertise is evaluated. Though these algorithms and structures largely originate in the minority world, they impact and significantly shape the boundaries, content, and reach of particular ideas. Given our position as management scholars, we believe that it is important to draw attention to and shift this dynamic at all levels of research projects and academic dialogue.

Meaningful changes in this domain require a rethinking and shifting of how research is conducted (Wickert et al., 2024). These changes have to be made in full consideration of the incentives and deterrents that direct the behavior of scholars in both the minority and majority world (Jansen, 2019). These include financial considerations, gendered responsibilities, promotion requirements, teaching obligations, and attention to relative passport and currency power. On the latter, we note that scholars with passports from minority countries generally have ease of global access supported by strong currencies that enable global travel (Doyle, 2005).

By contrast, scholars from the majority world, even if well-paid and highly respected in their home countries, often cannot travel with ease due to restrictive visa policies and relative currency weakness. This has obvious implications for whose voices are heard and in which form, and for who is able to do research in which country. It is difficult to imagine a group of researchers from Nigeria spending three months in Switzerland doing an analysis of the unique culture of the Swiss banking sector, yet Swiss researchers going to Nigeria to study the informal economy is widely accepted. This is because of the underlying and largely unquestioned structures of power in management scholarship.

Too often, the only way scholars in the majority world can gain legitimacy and visibility to the minority is to have qualifications and/or affiliations with minority-world institutions. Inevitably, this lessens the time and attention they can provide to engaging with complex challenges at home. In addition, topics like diversity, equity, inclusion, and innovation are dominated by theorizing from the minority world (George et al., 2016), where they are often treated as optional. For many scholars based in majority-world contexts, however, terms such as "diversity" often have very different points of reference, and "innovation" might be a question of daily necessity.

# CONCLUSION

Grand challenges are global, yet management scholarship is currently minority-world dominated. To tackle grand challenges requires adjusting – and decolonizing – our scholarship so that we are able to provide deeper insights and action at a "glocal" level. In this article, we highlighted four approaches, from exclusive to inclusive research partnerships, to tackle grand challenges: ignorance, awareness, integration, and elevation. Through three illustrative cases, we showed that the four approaches are not static but dynamic and presented evidence of how it is possible to develop more holistic, inclusive, and decolonized research outputs on grand challenges.

# REFERENCES

Abdelnour, S. (2022). What decolonizing is *Not*. *M@n@gement*, *25*(4), 81–82.

Aboderin, I. A. G., Fuh, D., Gebremariam, E. B., & Segalo, P. (2023). Beyond 'equitable partnerships': The imperative of transformative research collaborations with Africa. *Global Social Challenges Journal*, *2*(2), 212–228.

Alam, S. (2008). Majority world: Challenging the West's rhetoric of democracy. *Amerasia Journal*, *34*(1), 88–98.

Asongu, S. A., & Odhiambo, N. M. (2020). Challenges of doing business in Africa: A systematic review. Contemporary Issues and Prospects in Business Development in Africa, 105–114.

Association of African Universities. (2023). *African research universities, African academy of science, CODESRIA, & International network for higher education in Africa*. Africa Charter for Transformative Research Collaborations. https://parc.bristol.ac.uk/africa-charter/

Bainazarov, T., Gilzene, A. A., Kim, T., López, G. R., Louis, L., Oh, S., & Taylor, E. K. (2022). Toward decolonizing our scholarship and discourses: Lessons from the special issue on decoloniality for EAQ. *Educational Administration Quarterly*, *58*(5), 810–829. https://doi.org/10.1177/0013161X221136729

Banerjee, S. B. (2022). Decolonizing management theory: A critical perspective. *Journal of Management Studies*, *59*(4), 1074–1087.

Bansal, P., Kim, A., & Wood, M. (2018). Hidden in plain sight: The importance of scale on organizational attention to issues. *Academy of Management Review*, *43*(2), 217–241.

Biko, S. (1981). I write what I like. *Ufahamu: A Journal of African Studies*, *11*(1).

Bothello, J., & Bonfim, L. (2023). Marginalized communities and the problem of research extraction. *Journal of Management Studies, 62*(1), 526–532.

Boussebaa, M. (2023). Decolonizing international business. *Critical Perspectives on International Business*, *19*(4), 550–565.

Bruton, G. D., Zahra, S. A., Van de Ven, A. H., & Hitt, M. A. (2022). Indigenous theory uses, abuses, and future. *Journal of Management Studies*, *59*(4), 1057–1073.

Chen, S., Sharma, G., & Muñoz, P. (2022). In pursuit of impact: From research questions to problem formulation in entrepreneurship research. *Entrepreneurship Theory and Practice*, *47*(2), 232–264.

Colquitt, J. A., & George, G. (2011). From the editors: Publishing in AMJ—Part 1: Topic choice. *AMJ*, *54*, 432–435. https://doi.org/10.5465/amj.2011.61965960

Dang, Q. T., Jasovska, P., & Rammal, H. G. (2020). International business-government relations: The risk management strategies of MNEs in emerging economies. *Journal of World Business*, *55*(1), 101042.

Darian-Smith, E. (2016). Mismeasuring humanity: Examining indicators through a critical global studies perspective. *New Global Studies*, *10*(1), 73–99.

Dixit, A. (2023). Caste(d) knowledges: (Self)-problematising epistemic impunity and caste-privilege in academia. *Organization*, *0*(0). https://doi.org/10.1177/13505084231204102

Doyle, T. (2005). *Environmental movements in minority and majority worlds: A global perspective*. Rutgers University Press.

Fanon, F. (1952). *Black skin, white masks*. Grove Press.

Ferraro, F., Etzion, D., & Gehman, J. (2015). Tackling grand challenges pragmatically: Robust action revisited. *Organization Studies*, *36*(3), 363–390. https://doi.org/10.1177/0170840614563742

George, G., Corbishley, C., Khayesi, J. N. O., Haas, M. R., & Tihanyi, L. (2016). Bringing Africa in: Promising directions for management research. *Academy of Management Journal*, *59*(2), 377–393.

George, G., Haugh, H., Muñoz, P., Nason, R., & Welter, F. (2023). *Call for papers, Journal of Management Science: Recalibrating entrepreneurship research*. Retrieved April 20, 2024, from https://onlinelibrary.wiley.com/pb-assets/assets/14676486/JMS%20CfP%20SI-RCER%20October%202022-1667404599160.pdf

George, G., Howard-Grenville, J., Joshi, A., & Tihanyi, L. (2016). Understanding and tackling societal grand challenges through management research. *AMJ*, *59*, 1880–1895. https://doi.org/10.5465/amj.2016.4007

Grand Challenges Canada. (2011). *The grand challenges approach*. McLaughlin-Rotman Centre for Global Health. Retrieved April 20, 2024, from https://www.grandchallenges.ca/wp-content/uploads/2017/11/thegrandchallengesapproach.pdf

Green, L. (2021). *Rock water life: Ecology and humanities for a decolonial South Africa*. Duke University Press.

Gümüsay, A. A., & Amis, J. M. (2020). Contextual expertise and the development of organization and management theory. *European Management Review*, *18*, 9–24.

Gümüsay, A. A., Marti, E., Trittin-Ulbrich, H., & Wickert, C. (Eds.). (2022). *Organizing for societal grand challenges*. Research in the Sociology of Organizations (Vol. 79). Emerald Publishing Limited.

Gümüsay, A. A., & Reinecke, J. (2022). Researching for desirable futures: From real utopias to imagining alternatives. *Journal of Management Studies*, *59*, 236–242.

Gümüsay, A. A., & Reinecke, J. (2024). Imagining desirable futures: A call for prospective theorizing with speculative rigour. *Organization Theory*, *5*(1), 1–23.

Hamann, R., Luiz, J., Ramaboa, K., Khan, F., Dhlamini, X., & Nilsson, W. (2020). Neither colony nor enclave: Calling for dialogical contextualism in management and organization studies. *Organization Theory*, *1*(1). https://doi.org/10.1177/2631787719879705

International Energy Agency. (2017). *Energy access outlook 2017, IEA, Paris*. Retrieved April 20, 2024, from https://www.iea.org/reports/energy-access-outlook-2017

Jansen, J. (2019). *Decolonization in universities: The politics of knowledge*. Wits University Press.

Kwanya, T., & Wakunuma, K. (2023). Regulation of digital platforms for a socially-just gig economy in Kenya. *HIIG Impact Publication Series*. https://doi.org/10.5281/zenodo.7588795

Lewis, D. (1973). Anthropology and colonialism. *Current Anthropology*, *14*(5), 581–602.

Mafeje, A. (1986). South Africa: The dynamics of a beleaguered state. *African Journal of Political Economy*, *1*(1), 95–119.

Mafeje, A. (1998). Anthropology and independent Africans: Suicide or end of an era? *African Sociological Review*, *2*(1), 1–43.

Makoni, M. (2023). African researchers work is being overlooked: Here's how to change that' *Nature*. Retrieved April 20, 2024, from https://www.nature.com/articles/d41586-023-03322-w

Mamdani, M. (1998). When does a citizen become a Native? Reflections on the colonial roots of citizenship in Equatorial and South Africa. *New Series 208*. David Philip.

Markman, G. D., Waldron, T. L., Gianiodis, P. T., & Espina, M. I. (2019). E pluribus unum: Impact entrepreneurship as a solution to grand challenges. *Academy of Management Perspectives*, *33*, 371–382.

Martin, J., Desing, R., & Borrego, M. (2022). Positionality statements are just the tip of the iceberg: Moving towards a reflexive process. *Journal of Women and Minorities in Sciences and Engineering*, *28*(4), v–vii.

Michalopoulos, S., & Papaioannou, E. (2015). On the ethnic origins of African development: Chiefs and precolonial political centralization. *Academy of Management Perspectives, 29*(1), 32–71.

Muñoz, P., & Dimov, D. (2023). Facing the future through entrepreneurship theory: A prospective inquiry framework. *Journal of Business Venturing, 38*, art. 106303.

Nkomo, S. M. (2011). A postcolonial and anti-colonial reading of 'African' leadership and management in organization studies: Tensions, contradictions and possibilities. *Organization, 18*(3), 365–386. https://doi.org/10.1177/1350508411398731

Nyamnjoh, F.B. (2012). Potted plants in greenhouses: A critical reflection on the resilience of colonial education in Africa. *Journal of Asian and African Studies, 47*(2), 129–154.

Nyamnjoh, F. B. (2019). Decolonizing the university in Africa. In *Oxford research encyclopedia of politics.*

Özkazanç-Pan, B. (2008). International management research meets "the rest of the world". *Academy of Management Review, 33*(4), 964–974.

Qambela, G. (2015). A new tower of strength, or of ivory? *Mail & Guardian.* Retrieved April 20, 2024, from https://mg.co.za/article/2015-04-10-a-new-tower-of-strength-or-of-ivory

Ramanathan, N., Fruchterman, J., Fowler, A., & Carotti-Sha, G. (2022). Decolonize data. *Stanford Social Innovation Review, 20*(2), 59–60.

Salvi, E., Belz, F.-M., & Bacq, S. (2023). Informal entrepreneurship: An integrative review and future research agenda. *Entrepreneurship Theory and Practice, 47*(2), 265–303. https://doi.org/10.1177/10422587221115365

Savolainen, J., Casey, P. J., McBrayer, J. P., & Schwerdtle, P. N. (2023). Positionality and its problems: Questioning the value of reflexivity statements in research. *Perspectives on Psychological Science, 18*(6), 1331–1338. https://doi.org/10.1177/17456916221144988

Swiss Academy of Sciences. (2019). *A guide for transboundary research partnerships* (3rd ed.).

Trisos, C., Auerbach, J., & Katti, M. (2021). Decoloniality and anti-oppressive practices for a more ethical ecology. *Nature, Ecology and Evolution.* https://dx.doi.org/10.1038/s41559-021-01460-w

von Richthofen, G., & Gümüsay, A. A. (2023). Impact without imposition: What role for Northern academics in the Global South? *Stanford Social Innovation Review.*

Warwick & Stellenbosch (2023). *North-South dialogue on practice based approaches to management in Africa.* Retrieved April 20, 2024, from https://warwick.ac.uk/fac/soc/wbs/research/ikon/north-south-dialogue/

Wickert, C., Potočnik, K., Prashantham, S., Shi, W., & Snihur, Y. (2024). Embracing non-Western contexts in management scholarship. *Journal of Management Studies.*

Zanoni, P., & Mir, R. (2022). COVID-19: Interrogating the capitalist organization of the economy and society through the pandemic. *Organization, 29*(3), 369–378. https://doi.org/10.1177/13505084221090633

Zoogah, D. B., Peng, M. W., & Woldu, H. (2015). Institutions, resources, and organizational effectiveness in Africa. *Academy of Management Perspectives, 29*(1), 7–31.

# SECTION III

# HOW CAN WE DECOLONIZE MANAGEMENT AND ORGANIZATION STUDIES?

# REDUCING EPISTEMIC VIOLENCE IN THE PURSUIT OF ORGANIZATION STUDIES THROUGH REFLECTIVE PRAXIS: SOME REFLECTIONS

Snehanjali Chrispal

*Monash University, Australia*

## ABSTRACT

*We, as researchers trained in Western paradigms, are at risk of perpetrating epistemic violence on those often silenced and marginalized. By engaging in reflexive praxis, I draw on anecdotes from my time in the field researching the marginalization and violence perpetrated on women in India to explain how I was at risk of being complicit in this perpetration while trying to comply with research standards from the Global North. I trace my journey by addressing these risks that include the ensuring of safe spaces, silencing through anonymity, following interview protocols and procedures, and the translation of interviews. Finally, I end with a call for scholars to include the knowledge of those often silenced and marginalized within broader discourses of Academia.*

**Keywords:** Decolonization; epistemic violence; ethics; reflexivity; subaltern

Decolonizing Management and Organization Studies: Why, How, and What
Research in the Sociology of Organizations, Volume 93, 105–118
ISSN: 0733-558X/doi:10.1108/S0733-558X20250000093007

# INTRODUCTION

શું આપણે ભાગ્યે જ સાંભળેલા લોકોના અવાજો સાંભળીએ છીએ?
પરંતુ, જો આપણે તેમ કરીએ તો પણ તેમના વતી બોલનાર આપણે કોણ છીએ?
અમે તેમની દુર્દશા, ત્યાં મૌન અને હંસિા વશિ લખીએ છીએ,
તેમ છતાં, આપણે આમાં સંડોવાયેલા છીએ, જેમ આપણે ભૂલીએ છીએ,
અને જ્ઞાનની શોધમાં, તેમના અવાજોનું ખોટું અર્થઘટન કરે છે.
આપણે બોલનાર કોણ?
જ્યારે તેઓ ઇચ્છે છે કે તેઓ બોલે, અને સાંભળવામાં આવે.

क्या हम उन लोगों की आवाज़ सुन रहे हैं जन्हिें शायद ही कभी सुना जाता है?
लेकनि, अगर हम ऐसा करते भी हैं, तो हम उनकी ओर से बोलने वाले कौन होते हैं?
हम उनकी दुर्दशा, वहां की चुप्पी और हंसिा के बारे में लखिते हैं,
फरि भी, हम इनमें भागीदार हैं, क्योंकि हम भूल जाते हैं,
और ज़्ञान की खोज में, उनकी आवाज़ों की गलत व्याख्या करते हैं।
हम बोलने वाले कौन होते हैं?
जब वे केवल बोलना और सुना जाना चाहते हैं।

Are we listening to the voices of those rarely heard?
But, even if we do, who are we to speak on their behalf?
We write about their plight, their silencing, and violence,
Yet, we are complicit in these, as we forget,
And misinterpret their voices, in the pursuit of knowledge.
Who are we to speak?
When all they want is to speak, and to be heard.

I wrote the poem above in three languages. The language in which "stories" were told to me (Gujarati), the language that I was fluent in (Hindi), and then the language in which I have to write for the readers of this paper, English (a language that was also acquired by the Indian elites during the colonization of India to maintain and increase their status, Brass, 2004). I begin this paper with a disclaimer that in using the English language, I am complicit in the "loss of subjectivity incurred through the loss of language" and, to some extent, complicit in the silencing of voices (Dar, 2018, p. 570). By acquiring the English language, Indian elites maintained and increased their status, particularly during its colonization (Brass, 2004).

The poem is symbolic of the tensions I faced as a researcher, seeking to do justice to the voices of the oppressed, yet constantly finding myself trying to interpret and make sense of these voices using dominant theory and practices in line with the expectations of Western Academia. I draw on Spivak's (1988) "epistemic violence" to question whether this mirrors a bigger problem in organizational studies "of looking the other way to avoid uncomfortable truths" (Chrispal et al., 2021, p. 1502). As a management and organization studies' scholar, the questions I framed in this poem repeatedly push me to reflect on my complicity in silencing the voices of the Other.

Scholars within MOS have called for an interrogation of hegemonic epistemic traditions and the need for researchers to consider alternative knowledges (Khan & Naguib, 2019; Manning, 2018; Mir & Mir, 2013). However, as researchers, we are all embedded within an "Academic institution," a "global knowledge regime that governs the production, distribution, and consumption of research" (Khan & Naguib, 2019, p. 90). As we engage in knowledge production, we do so within the constraints of this institution. Papers need to be written in a particular way. Knowledge that doesn't fit within our understanding or within the Western programmatic approaches is deemed unusable or irrelevant. Methodologies that are outside of the conventional are doubted for rigor and applicability.

The Academy has often been charged with perpetuating "Western intellectual superiority" and at times, it is used to reject and renounce alternative knowledges (Smith, 2012). It has also become increasingly difficult for researchers to justify the critical need for knowledge produced outside of the West within the broader area of "world knowledge" and that it can contribute to present-day scholarship. Therefore, it is important for us, as researchers, to pay heed to epistemic and ontological colonization that push marginalized peoples to the peripheries and see their lives as not worthy of consideration (Santos, 2015).

For my study, I traced the lived experiences of women in Gujarat, India, who faced gendered violence and yet were able to craft different lives and disrupt a cycle of violence with the help and guidance of a community organization. I also traced the networks of powerful agents that the organization tied with to provide these women with the resources and tools to resist and escape their oppression. While following the narratives and journeys of these women, I often had to reconcile my own interpretations, the perspectives and interpretations of the elites I interviewed, and the alternative realities that were being experienced by these women. These women and their lived experiences, however, are situated outside of dominant Western knowledge and discourses, yet also influenced by it, including the language (Manning, 2018), which made their narratives and voices susceptible to being silenced and misinterpreted by me.

Drawing on my own experiences in the research field in India, I provide in this paper insights into the ways I was complicit in certain ways of being and researching, which could silence and denigrate marginalized others. What this paper attempts to do is to engage in a decolonial praxis to make restitutions to try to help to heal the "colonial wound." By engaging in "critical dialogue between diverse epistemic, ethical and political projects," I wanted to move toward a pluriversality of knowledge rather than falling prey to the myth of the universal truth (Grosfoguel, 2007, p. 212).

## EPISTEMIC VIOLENCE

Epistemic violence, coined by Spivak (1988) in her seminal essay "Can the Subaltern Speak?," refers to the silencing of the historically marginalized Others in the name of research and theory. She criticizes theory coming from the West and the ways they seek to engage the subaltern and calls for an "attribution of subjectivity" to these voices (De Schryver, 2021, p. 100). Knowledge has mostly been produced in and for the West; the lived realities of the "Other" are often subdued, ignored, or considered irrelevant (Dar & Cooke, 2008; Prasad, 2003).

The epistemic violence of Western knowledge plaguing our approaches to studying organizations and practices in the Global South is heightened by comparisons of how they differ from or parallel the West (Girei, 2017). Coloniality of power moves beyond the physical domination and exploitation associated with colonial domination and crosses into the realm of epistemological domination. It privileges the knowledge from the West and deems it all-encompassing, the universal truth (Escobar, 2004; Taylor, 2012). Mignolo (2007) contends that emancipation can only be realized by embracing a different epistemology that is derived from those knowledges silenced by colonial domination. This existing knowledge is not completely displaced by a frontier chartered into unknown territory.

Yet, in order for decolonization of knowledge to occur, it requires "border thinking," "the epistemology of the exteriority; that is, of the outside created from the inside" (Mignolo & Tlostanova, 2006, p. 206). It is a careful consideration of the different forms of knowing that stem from the embodied experiences and remnants of colonization (Icaza Garza, 2017; Yousfi, 2021).

It is where two distinct knowledges can meet and can move and merge while retaining their elemental characteristics (Mignolo & Tlostanova, 2006).

Hence, when researching in contexts where people were once colonized, it is critical to acknowledge the intellectual and epistemological ramifications that have often been excluded from Western scholarship (Gandhi, 1998). This exclusion is also evident in organizational studies, where theorizations and assumptions concerning the Global South are often Western-centric (Jack et al., 2011; Srinivas, 2013).

Any academic stream in pursuit of exposing the complex conception of the subaltern needs to understand the historically influenced relationships of dominance and subordination (Gandhi, 1998). Therefore, as researchers, we need to engage with these differences and find a middle-ground – a space where we are able to understand and produce knowledge that is true to the "Other" and where they are not exploited or "used" for the sake of reinforcing, legitimizing and even at times, questioning Western thought. It also requires us researchers to "be subject to scrutiny of self-problematizing" in the process of generating knowledge; a recognition that the self is made up of "uncontested 'truths' and the attendant effects that this has on the knowledges that one produces" (Dixit, 2023, pp. 3, 7). Often using Western discourses and frameworks, we assume that the phenomenon we observe should unfold in a certain way or ignore that which doesn't "fit." This assumption neglects the experiences of actors and unique structural arrangements that exist in contexts other than the West, which may actually reproduce epistemological domination and violence on part of these scholars (Spivak, 1988). Without this consideration, we may be blinded by our own conceptual baggage and assumptions that promote a "Western way" of seeing, being, and doing. We, as researchers, may neglect the diverse voices, lived experiences, and knowledges of those from the Global South – the historically and currently colonized, the oppressed, and the "subaltern" subjects. If our research does not account for these voices, our analyses and interpretations may be erroneously focused on the acting and reacting rather than on the relationships and affect that are significant in these contexts. Therefore, in my quest for multiple truths and realities undergirding the efforts to challenge gendered violence in India, I needed to minimize these acts of epistemic violence and help coalesce epistemic, political, and ethical considerations in this context.

## EPISTEMIC VIOLENCE WHEN COMPLYING WITH RESEARCH STANDARDS

Before I share a few anecdotes of my experience in the field, I want to begin by acknowledging my positionality and the burden it carries as a researcher trying to understand the lived experiences of the marginalized and oppressed in the Global South. I come from a lower-middle-class Indian family. However, I was afforded privilege through my education in an international school in India and my higher education in the US and then Australia. I also acknowledge the oppression and subjugation my parents and their ancestors experienced through colonization and other forms of oppression. While growing up in India, I often rebelled against my traditional Indian values and felt camaraderie with the "modern" and the "West." After returning to India in my 20s, I began to embrace and sought to reacquaint myself with my roots and my Indian culture. I do not claim I am from the communities I research, though I know some contextual insight. Moreover, I had to learn and open myself to the diverse voices I was exposed to and the alternative knowledges being produced.

Before entering the field for research, we need to fulfill the ethics requirements within the University to not only protect our participants but the researcher as well. However, these ethics protocols are designed in the Global North, forsaking the realities in the Global South. I agree that these processes are set up to ensure that harm is not done. However, some of these processes may unintentionally hinder the relationships between the researcher and participant if not navigated delicately.

In this research context, cultural offense and power imbalances could have impeded the understanding and interpretations of the lived experiences of the women. The ethical requirements for conducting research in Gujarat, India, go beyond the researcher's ethical commitment to principles of volunteerism, informed consent, non-exploitation, confidentiality, and so forth. Here, it relates to having regard for the participants' safety and well-being and respect for culture, tradition, and community. Scholars who conducted research in Gujarat (e.g., Limjerwala's, 2018 research on sexual violence, Vissandjée et al.'s (2002) focus group research) suggest that researchers need to spend time gathering support from the community in which the project will take place. This is especially true in village settings, where people might be distrustful of outsiders. Therefore, it is expected that researchers spend time preparing and planning in order to facilitate acceptance in the villages and by the participant communities.

### Ensuring Safe Spaces

As part of the university's ethics requirements, we had put some protocols in place to reduce any risk or threat to participants' safety. We had decided, before entering the field, that the participants would be interviewed at a location convenient for them and where they would feel safe and comfortable, a third location, e.g., in the Western context, this would be another location that is away from the organization. However, in the field, the reality was quite different. The beneficiaries wanted to conduct the interviews in the organization itself. For them, the organization was not just a crutch to help them, but rather, they saw it as a *Kutumb*, a family. *Ba*, the founder, and her daughter, the *Farishta*, are like the grandmother and sister who will always be there waiting with arms wide open. During my time in the organization, I saw how people of all ages would enter the organization like it was their home – to talk, have some *chai (tea)*, or, for many of the children, a safe place to study (an escape from the violence at home but also the riots in the community between religious groups). As when I first began, *Ba* had said:

"આ એક સમુદાય સંસ્થા છે. તે એક આશ્વાસનનું સ્થાન છે. જ્યાં મહિલાઓ અને બાળકો રમખાણોની હિંસા અને ઘરના જુલમથી બચવા આવી શકે છે."

"This is a community organization. It was a place of solace where women and children could come to escape the violence of the riots and the oppression at home."

Doing research in the Global South can often mean steering away from Western considerations of ethics. Decolonial research requires establishing trusting relationships between the researcher and participants. Those who were once colonized are often wary of those who don't seem like they belong to the community. I was an outsider, in a sense, and so I still needed to build the trust of the participants, and that meant allowing them to use a space that enabled dialogic and relational interactions (Kovach, 2015).

For example, there was an interview where a woman (a "beneficiary") brought along her husband for the interview but also wanted Ba and Ba's daughter. If this interview were conducted in the West, and with the consideration of Western ethics, the interview would need to be conducted only with the woman. But, here, it was the woman's decision, and part of the empowerment, that she wanted him to share his side of the story, as well. As I found, in many of my interviews, the safe space for dialogue was constructed when others were also present, whom the women trusted. Community was important to these women, who felt isolated when they were in the cycle of violence but now felt redemption from it and wanted the presence of safe relationships in their lives. This sense of community is important because the knowledge generated is not obtained for the interests of a sole individual, the researcher, but constructed and developed for the interest and benefit of the whole group (Goduka, 2012).

As researchers, we have the power to disseminate the knowledge and how that knowledge is presented. Decolonizing research requires relinquishing our own power and privilege and positioning the community in such a way where respect is earned and reciprocity and relationality are at the center (Smith, 2012). In relinquishing this power and privilege, decolonizing methodologies require us as researchers to be aware of the space around us while conducting research and respond through instinct and refer back to the contextual intelligence they gained previously. For instance, being brought up in India and watching others (we didn't practice this at home), I learned that touching someone's feet and taking a blessing is seen as a sign of respect and is mostly done by younger individuals. However, let me state here that this framing of touching feet as a mark of respect for elders is again the framing given by legitimators. For example, no one touches the feet of an old Dalit[1] sweeping streets or cleaning toilets. In reality, it is touching the feet of those in positions of power/authority. During one interview, for instance, the participant, who was significantly older than me, touched my feet before the interview. If I had not known the custom, I would have been placed in a position of power and privilege. Instead, I touched the participant's feet and sat on the floor next to her to conduct the interview. It is these subtle and often missed gestures that researchers need to acquaint themselves with to conduct research in such contexts. Moreover, when I spent a day with young Dalit girls during a workshop conducted by the organization, I made sure I sat on the floor with them and held hands as we gathered in a circle. These were girls who, seen as impure because of their caste, lived at the peripheries of the village, and were not allowed to interact with the other castes.

### Silencing Through Anonymity

While this was a context where it was probably necessary to anonymize my participants' names and identities to ensure their safety, in making that decision, through informed consent, I stripped them of power to make that decision for themselves. In other words, the subaltern didn't have a say in whether their real names and identities could be revealed in the research. Stories often lose their power and legitimacy when the storytellers are stripped of their decision to be identified by the researcher (Chilisa, 2019). The participants in my research didn't want pseudonyms to replace their names; this was their way of being recognized and professing their identity. They were individuals beyond being a mother, a wife, a daughter, or a victim. These women were owners of their lives, not defined by just their relationships with others. In anonymizing their names, I am complying with the institutional ethical norms of anonymity yet complicit in silencing marginalized voices and identities. And, moreover may even have stripped "epistemic agency" from my participants, rejecting them as co-producers of knowledge (Nduna et al., 2022, p. 2). However, what is needed is a dialogue between the researcher and participants to design ethical strategies to overcome risks of identification and anonymization (Svalastog & Eriksson, 2010).

### Following Interview Protocols

Epistemic violence also occurs by inhibiting the ways in which knowledge is shared and the use of research and methodological tools that restrict the voices of the subaltern. Often, as a researcher, you enter the field with methodological approaches and strategies that are taught to you in University subjects or by reading prior research that have utilized them. These are most often situated in the West, conducted by Western academics, or even when conducted by those outside of the West, or in research settings in the Global South, they are still influenced by these. However, prepared tools, like interview questions, seemed to inhibit knowledge production. Smith (2012) says that "most of the 'traditional' disciplines are grounded in cultural worldviews which are either antagonistic to other belief systems or have no methodology for dealing with other knowledge systems" (p. 65). For instance, I went into the research setting with a defined interview protocol, but I found that I elicited short responses without much elaboration. These were women who were stigmatized, confined to particular social boundaries, and unable to speak. I was reinforcing this confinement to those very same boundaries. The interview questions establish a power relationship, one that asks the questions and one that has to reply. In this way, the interviewer can direct the conversation and restrict what the responder says. So, I stopped asking questions and allowed them to speak and share their stories and narratives as they would with a "sister." I found that letting them do so answered the questions I had. If I didn't understand something, I would engage in dialogue with them, saying it back to them so I was sure that what they said was interpreted correctly.

When I interviewed the first of the beneficiaries, I was prepared with my list of questions that would help me understand their experiences and the organization's role in their lives. However, as I conducted the first couple of "interviews" (henceforth, I will use conversation instead of interview), I realized just how restricted and uncomfortable I made my participants feel. We were in a small room with a table, and I sat across from them and the translator. In trying to ensure that every question was answered, I was trying to extract the answers from the participants rather than allowing them to tell their stories.

We moved to a bigger room, where there was lots of natural light. I moved the chairs into a circle, and then I sat on the chair with my legs crossed.[2] The very first question I asked my participant was whether "आप ठीक है?" or "are you comfortable?." And she did the same, crossed her legs, and sat on the chair. After I received her oral consent, the words flew out of her mouth as she narrated her story of pain, of the recognition of her suffering, and then her strength and fight to just live.

Interestingly enough, in India, people like to engage in prolonged discussions in informal settings, and that is what I tried to create, even during my conversations. There were times I had these conversations outside on "*chatais*" (jute cots) or sitting on the floor in the living room. I tried to make the participants feel as relaxed as they could so it really didn't feel like an interview. These are almost like, as some scholars describe, "collaborative storying" (Bishop, 1999) or "yarning" (Bessarab & Ng'Andu, 2010), and in some instances, like when I was interviewing women counselors at a government agency, "sharing circles" (where groups can share their experiences) (Chilisa, 2019).

These "conversations" metamorphosized into transformational sessions of storytelling while I just listened and sometimes probed to understand a nuance of a word, phrase, or situation. Storytelling is found at the crux of Indigenous ontology and epistemology, which is profoundly linked to 'relational ways of knowing' (Datta, 2018; Hart, 2010). Storytelling, for the marginalized, is a tool to voice their lived experiential knowledge, constructing both story and reality. It is a way that the oppressed can break their silence and put forth the social conditions and tools needed for social change; thus, it allows for the empowerment of both the storyteller and the listener (Rodriguez, 2010). On a similar trajectory, Indian women who face violence (not to generalize because Indian women have different experiences across caste, class, region, etc.) share similar fates, and the "assertion of their subjectivity as creators and interpreters of texts is a political act" (Lawrence, 1995; Rodriguez, 2010, p. 494).

In another instance, when we went to the Sakhi Center, a place in the hospital where vulnerable women can seek help and receive medical treatment, the employees didn't want to be interviewed separately but as a group. For them, it was a chance to heal and dialogue. As one of them said in the language Hindi:

"हम हिंसा का सामना करने वाली बहुत सी महिलाओं की मदद करते हैं, लेकिन कोई भी हमारे मानसिक स्वास्थ्य के बारे में नहीं पूछता है। हमें उदासीन रहना होगा और भावनाओं को अपने काम में हस्तक्षेप नहीं करने देना होगा। वह कैसे संभव है? आप यहां हमारे अनुभवों को सुनने और हमारी निराशाओं और पराजयों को सुनने के लिए आए हैं।"

"We help so many women who face violence, but no one asks about our mental health. We have to remain emotionless and not let emotions interfere in our work. How is that possible? You have come here to hear our experiences and listen to us voice our frustrations and defeats."

The head of the center, in one of the informal interactions, started to cry as she told me of how she used to be a lawyer and at one point, had to fight a case against a man who had raped a girl with a disability who became pregnant. She didn't sleep for nights on end, and her fight within the justice system was so emotionally taxing that she decided to quit law. Colonizers and the colonized have accepted and legitimized a hyper-rational and hypermasculine discourse over time. Emotions are also intimately connected with power, where "local moral orders" or "feeling rules" shape "emotional regimes" of who gets to feel and express what (Ling, 2014, p. 582). Therefore, decolonial research seeks to acknowledge the emotions that "transgress cultures and reconstitute politics within and across bordered worlds" and "convey traditions, philosophies, and worldviews" (Ling, 2014, p. 582).

In line with this, researchers need to listen affectively, "which not only calls for eyes and ears to be opened but also hearts and minds" (Thambinathan & Kinsella, 2021, p. 4). By listening affectively, researchers can create spaces for becoming. These are spaces that hold the researcher accountable and enable growth (McDermott, 2013). If we as researchers can engage in affective dialogue, it will allow us to be open to transformation and the processes that are involved in the transformation (McDermott, 2013). Therefore, "listening is not a biological capacity but rather an emotional relationship between people and requires trust" (Cahill, 2007, p. 279).

*Translating Interviews*

To ease the data collection process, and even though I was fluent in one of the languages, Hindi, and I understood Gujarati (the local language) and Saurastra (Gujarati dialect) only a little, I needed a translator and transcriber, who were well-versed with the local languages and dialects. I would often be the pillion rider on the translator Meena's scooter to interview different participants, including the beneficiaries, government officers, and police agencies. During our time together, she would tell me about life in the community and the culture and helped me understand multiple interpretations of certain words and their nuances, placing them in the context of the stories being told to me. Although I understood their language, I was not an expert, and so being able to construct spaces for participants to be able to "capture linguistic nuances through their own language" was important in producing authentic knowledge and reclaiming alternative knowledges (Huff et al., 2020, p. 6).

These spaces need to be constructed to ensure that even words that were translated during the actual interviews were correctly interpreted during the transcription process. This is because, for some scholars like Vázquez (2011), translation is erasure. It is a "rhetoric of modernity" seeking to serve the imperial discourse, framing meanings, people, and practices into something comprehensible and within the control of those who have power (Mignolo, 2005, p. 144). Translation can often deem invisible everything that does not fit the "parameters of legibility" within its "epistemic territory" (Vázquez, 2011, p. 28). This complicity in erasure was exemplified in my pursuit of translating the voices that I encountered in different languages, where certain terms were manipulated to "fit" the understanding of the audience. For instance, an upper-caste leader said in Gujarati:

"અમારા સમાજમાં મહિલાઓનું સ્થાન ઉચ્ચ છે. અમારા માટે ઘર એક મંદિર છે. પુરૂષો બહાર કામ કરે છે. મહિલાઓ ઘરની સંભાળ રાખે છે."

This was originally translated and transcribed as:

"People consider home as a sacred place in our community. Men are generally out of the house earning. It is the women who handle the domestic chores and manage the household. They are considered as a goddess."

But re-checking with the cultural broker, the translation was:

"Women have a high position in our community. For us the house is a temple. Men work outside. Women take care of the household."

The first translation was made by a Hindu male linguistic specialist who also knows the local language, where his socialization may have played a role in the words he used to translate. This translation is also influenced by the discourse related to women in Hinduism as goddesses, as the violence I was studying showed. In other words, we need to think about whether translations actually do justice by stripping away the overall context in which those words are spoken. Although the overarching meanings of the two translations are similar, it is the nuance in the words used that reinforced the "epistemic territory." Meanings of words like "*mandir*," which was translated as "sacred place," but actually meant "temple," or the word for "*ucch sthaan*" was translated as "goddess" instead of "high status." These translations were made to show familiarity and resonance with the audience or to portray a rosy picture of the lives of women to the colonial world through terms like "goddess," rather than emphasizing the other aspects in the same quote that gendered norms are sustained, where men are the "breadwinners" and women are relegated to the house.

While the above omissions and replacement of words are examples of translation as erasure, for some scholars, however, translation can also be an "in-between space of multiplicities, exchanges, renegotiations and discontinuities that disturb linear flows and unsettle monological colonial truth" (Manning, 2018, p. 316). In addition, it can be a practice of "plurality" where translation is not used to delineate "epistemic territories" but used as "common ground" to resist hegemonic knowledge systems and promote spaces of dialogue amongst cultures (Santos et al., 2007; Vázquez, 2011, p. 41). The understanding of the language is imperative as it "shapes the construction of knowledge and the ways in which it is shared" (Huff et al., 2020, p. 3), while also acting as a medium by which varying worldviews are expressed (Kovach, 2015).

Even during the process of interpretation and analysis, I would repeatedly go back to what was said and looked into multiple meanings words would have. In addition, many words that were used challenged the "oppressive grammars of power" and some of those words were even "displaced and re-signified" within the broader discourse of gendered violence (Vázquez, 2011, p. 41). The Western human rights discourse, for example, frames the United Nations and NGOs from the West, as "saviors" who redeem women and children from the "tyrannies of the (third world) state, tradition and culture" (Chowdhury, 2011, p. xvii; Mutua, 2001). However, these organizations have been criticized for only spending a short time in the Global South and leaving a temporary band-aid of relief for many of these women and children who face continued violence. However, the community organization I studied refers to itself as "kutumb" or family, which suggests a sense of constancy and relationality, therefore creating spaces for translation that disrupt these hegemonic discourses.

## KEY TAKEAWAYS

To summarize, I provide a few key reflections from my research journey. The first is to ensure and create safe spaces for your participants. The word "safe" is conditional on a participant, i.e., what makes them feel safe in the context, and how do we create spaces that allow them to freely voice their stories? This also means taking measures to ensure that they are able to speak to us "eye to eye." In other words, to the best of our ability as researchers, we need to mitigate the power imbalances between our participants and us. Second is the issue pertaining to ethics, where we are expected to anonymize and maintain the confidentiality of those who are telling their stories. However, "they" may not want to be anonymized; they may want to be heard, and being able to take ownership of their stories is one of doing it. Third, in the pursuit of following interview protocols and procedures, we may not be able to fully access the stories and voices of those from the margins. Being able to familiarize ourselves with the context and creating spaces where the participants are able to open up, dialogue, and share their emotions without hesitating is critical to accessing their voices. Lastly, in order to authentically translate and interpret their voices, we, as researchers, need to scrutinize who translates and how it is interpreted and continuously engage the marginalized in checking whether the translation and interpretations are correct. While these are my overall reflections, they may or may not necessarily apply to research conducted in other contexts, and it is the responsibility of the researcher to engage in reflective praxis to open themselves to alternative ways of being and doing research to access and authentically interpret the voices of those from the Global South. It is also the responsibility of the researcher to dedicate significant time to socialize and understand the context before doing fieldwork.

This is in no way a how-to manual on how to avoid the perpetration of epistemic violence when researching the subaltern in the Global South. Rather, these are my reflections from the field and the ways that I engaged in reflective praxis to try to avoid being complicit in acts of perpetrating epistemic violence. There are still some unanswered questions that future research can draw attention to. What measures can be adopted to enhance such a reflective process on the part of the researchers, e.g., poetry, art, etc.? How can we ensure that the measures we take won't perpetrate epistemic violence? How can we reconcile ethics protocols in the West with other ways of being and doing research in the Global South, particularly when we are embedded in the ways of doing research in the West and in academic institutions that require certain protocols to be followed?

## A CALL

I end with a call for scholars to engage with those voices that are often silenced and to include their knowledge within the broader discourses of Academia. As organizational scholars, we enter the field with research tools that help us make sense of what we are seeing. However, these may actually impede authentic knowledge production. Therefore, I hope more scholars will be "critically disruptive" in their research and reflect on the risks of perpetrating epistemic violence, especially when conducting research in the Global South. Furthermore, researchers need to be bold and welcome alternative theories and methodologies that may not "fit" within hegemonic ways of thinking and doing organizational and management studies.

## NOTES

1. In the Indian caste system, Dalits are the low castes, seen as "untouchable" and subjected to occupations like street sweepers, cleaners, and sanitation workers.
2. In India, sitting cross-legged is seen as a way to relax the mind and improve familial bonding and relationships.

## ACKNOWLEDGMENTS

The author would like to thank Susan Ainsworth, Vanessa Pouthier, Hari Bapuji, and Vivek Soundararajan, as well as the participants in the Decolonizing Management and Organization Studies Workshop on the 19th of March 2024, for their guidance and comments on earlier versions of the paper. The author would also like to thank Emamdeen Fohim for his editorial guidance, and the anonymous reviewer for their valuable feedback on the manuscript.

# REFERENCES

Bessarab, D., & Ng'Andu, B. (2010). Yarning about yarning as a legitimate method in Indigenous research. *International Journal of Critical Indigenous Studies, 3*(1), 37–50.

Bishop, R. (1999, June 15–22). *Collaborative storytelling: Meeting indigenous peoples' desires for self-determination in research* [Conference presentation]. World Indigenous People's Conference, Albuquerque, NM.

Brass, P. (2004). Elite interests, popular passions, and social power in the language politics of India. *Ethnic and Racial Studies, 27*(3), 353–375.

Cahill, C. (2007). The personal is political: Developing new subjectivities through participatory action research. *Gender, Place and Culture, 14*(3), 267–292.

Chilisa, B. (2019). *Indigenous research methodologies*. Sage Publications.

Chowdhury, E. H. (2011). *Transnationalism reversed: Women organizing against gendered violence in Bangladesh*. State University of New York Press.

Chrispal, S., Bapuji, H., & Zietsma, C. (2021). Caste and organization studies: Our silence makes us complicit. *Organization Studies, 42*(9), 1501–1515.

Dar, S. (2018). De-colonizing the boundary-object. *Organization Studies, 39*(4), 565–584.

Dar, S., & Cooke, B. (Eds.). (2008). *The new development management: Critiquing the dual modernization*. Bloomsbury Publishing.

Datta, R. (2018). Traditional storytelling: An effective Indigenous research methodology and its implications for environmental research. *AlterNative: An International Journal of Indigenous Peoples, 14*(1), 35–44.

De Schryver, C. (2021). Deconstruction and epistemic violence. *The Southern Journal of Philosophy, 59*(2), 100–121.

Dixit, A. (2023). Caste (d) knowledges:(Self)-problematising epistemic impunity and caste-privilege in academia. *Organization*. https://doi.org/10.1177/13505084231204102

Escobar, A. (2004). Beyond the Third World: Imperial globality, global coloniality and anti-globalisation social movements. *Third World Quarterly, 25*(1), 207–230.

Gandhi, L. (1998). *A critical introduction to postcolonial theory*. Columbia University Press.

Girei, E. (2017). Decolonising management knowledge: A reflexive journey as practitioner and researcher in Uganda. *Management Learning, 48*(4), 453–470.

Goduka, N. (2012). Re-discovering indigenous knowledge-ulwazi lwemveli for strengthening sustainable livelihood opportunities within rural contexts in the eastern cape province. *Indilinga African Journal of Indigenous Knowledge Systems, 11*(1), 1–19.

Grosfoguel, R. (2007). The epistemic decolonial turn: Beyond political-economy paradigms. *Cultural Studies, 21*(2–3), 211–223.

Hart, M. A. (2010). Indigenous worldviews, knowledge, and research: The development of an indigenous research paradigm. *Journal of Indigenous Social Development, 1*(1), 1–18.

Huff, S., Rudman, D. L., Magalhães, L., Lawson, E., & Kanyamala, M. (2020). Enacting a critical decolonizing ethnographic approach in occupation-based research. *Journal of Occupational Science*, 1–15.

Icaza Garza, R. (2017). *Decolonial feminism and global politics: Border thinking and vulnerability as a knowing otherwise*.

Jack, G., Westwood, R., Srinivas, N., & Sardar, Z. (2011). Deepening, broadening and re-asserting a postcolonial interrogative space in organization studies. *Organization, 18*(3), 275–302.

Khan, F. R., & Naguib, R. (2019). Epistemic healing: A critical ethical response to epistemic violence in business ethics. *Journal of Business Ethics, 156*, 89–104.

Kovach, M. (2015). Emerging from the margins: Indigenous methodologies. *Research as Resistance: Revisiting Critical, Indigenous, and Anti-Oppressive Approaches, 2*, 43–64.

Lawrence, C. (1995) The word and the river: Pedagogy as scholarship as struggle. In K. Crenshaw, N. Gotanda, G. Peller, & K. Thomas (Eds.), *Critical race theory: The key writings that formed the movement* (pp. 336–351). The New Press.

Limjerwala, S. (2018). *Conducting research on sexual violence in Gujarat, India: An argument in favor of ethnography*. SAGE Publications Ltd.

Ling, L. H. (2014). Decolonizing the international: Towards multiple emotional worlds. *International Theory, 6*(3), 579–583.

Manning, J. (2018). Becoming a decolonial feminist ethnographer: Addressing the complexities of positionality and representation. *Management Learning*, *49*(3), 311–326.

McDermott, M. (2013). Mo(ve)ments of affect: Towards an embodied pedagogy for anti-racism education. In G. J. S. Dei & M. McDermott (Eds.), *Politics of anti-racism education: In search of strategies for transformative learning* (pp. 211–226). Springer.

Mignolo, W. D. (2005). *The idea of Latin America*. Blackwell Publishing.

Mignolo, W. D. (2007). Delinking: The rhetoric of modernity, the logic of coloniality and the grammar of de-coloniality. *Cultural Studies*, *21*(2–3), 449–514.

Mignolo, W. D., & Tlostanova, M. V. (2006). Theorizing from the borders: Shifting to geo-and body-politics of knowledge. *European Journal of Social Theory*, *9*(2), 205–221.

Mir, R., & Mir, A. (2013). The colony writes back: Organization as an early champion of non-Western organizational theory. *Organization*, *20*(1), 91–101.

Mutua, M. (2001). Human rights international NGOs: A critical evaluation. In J. Claude & E. Welch (Eds.), *NGOs and human rights: Promise and performance* (pp. 151–166). University of Pennsylvania Press.

Nduna, M., Mayisela, S., Balton, S., Gobodo-Madikizela, P., Kheswa, J. G., Khumalo, I. P., & Tabane, C. (2022). Research site anonymity in context. *Journal of Empirical Research on Human Research Ethics*, *17*(5), 554–564.

Prasad, A. (2003). *Postcolonial theory and organizational analysis: A critical engagement*. Springer.

Rodriguez, D. (2010). Storytelling in the field: Race, method, and the empowerment of Latina college students. *Cultural Studies? Critical Methodologies*, *10*(6), 491–507.

Santos, B. S. (2015). *Epistemologies of the South: Justice against epistemicide*. Routledge.

Santos, B. D. S., Nunes, J. A., & Meneses, M. P. (2007). Opening up the canon of knowledge and recognition of difference. In B. de Sousa Santos (Ed.), *Another knowledge is possible: Beyond Northern Epistemologies* (pp. XIX–LXII). Verso.

Smith, L. T. (2012) *Decolonizing methodologies: Research and indigenous peoples*. Zed Books.

Spivak, G. C. (1988). Can the subaltern speak? In R. Morris (Ed.), *Can the subaltern speak? Reflections on the history of an idea* (pp. 21–78). Columbia University Press.

Srinivas, N. (2013). Could a subaltern manage? Identity work and habitus in a colonial workplace. *Organization Studies*, *34*(11), 1655–1674.

Svalastog, A. L., & Eriksson, S. (2010). You can use my name; you don't have to steal my story–a critique of anonymity in indigenous studies. *Developing World Bioethics*, *10*(2), 104–110.

Taylor, L. (2012). Decolonizing international relations: Perspectives from Latin America. *International Studies Review*, *14*(3), 386–400.

Thambinathan, V., & Kinsella, E. A. (2021). Decolonizing methodologies in qualitative research: Creating spaces for transformative praxis. *International Journal of Qualitative Methods*, *20*, 16094069211014766.

Vázquez, R. (2011). Translation as erasure: Thoughts on modernity's epistemic violence. *Journal of Historical Sociology*, *24*(1), 27–44.

Vissandjée, B., Abdool, S. N., & Dupéré, S. (2002). Focus groups in rural Gujarat, India: A modified approach. *Qualitative Health Research*, *12*(6), 826–843.

Yousfi, H. (2021). Decolonizing Arab organizational knowledge: "Fahlawa" as a research practice. *Organization*, *28*(5), 836–856.

# ACCESS TO THE LOCAL LIVED EXPERIENCES: A PHENOMENOLOGICAL APPROACH TO DECOLONIZE MANAGEMENT AND ORGANIZATION STUDIES

Tadashi Uda

*Hokkaido University, Japan*

## ABSTRACT

*The purpose of this paper is to present a phenomenological approach as a meaningful way to decolonize management studies. We first review the decolonization literature and point out the lack of methodological discussion about it. Next, we show the basic perspective and a specific procedure of a phenomenological approach. We then discuss the limitations of the dominant positivism-based approach and the possibilities of the phenomenological approach by illustrating the phenomenon of the workplace in Japan, which was one of the first countries in the world to experience the colonization of MOS, while at the same time retaining its traditional culture and institutions.*

**Keywords:** Decolonization; epistemology; first-person perspective; lived experiences; management and organization studies; phenomenology

Decolonizing Management and Organization Studies: Why, How, and What
Research in the Sociology of Organizations, Volume 93, 119–135
ISSN: 0733-558X/doi:10.1108/S0733-558X20250000093008

# INTRODUCTION

The purpose of this paper is to present a phenomenological approach as one way to decolonize management and organization studies (MOS).

Decolonizing MOS means critically examining the dominant Western model or Eurocentrism in management studies (Banerjee, 2022; Girei, 2017; Jammulamadaka et al., 2021; Tourish, 2019) and presenting its ontological, epistemological, theoretical, and methodological alternatives (Banerjee, 2022; Jammulamadaka et al., 2021). Such debates have been particularly active since the 2000s (Jammulamadaka et al., 2021), and studies are accumulating that seek to understand a pluralistic world based on indigenous epistemologies rather than universal knowledge (Banerjee, 2022; Yousfi, 2021). For example, we can identify research practices that focus on indigenous perceptions and practices (Girei, 2017), social conflicts between colonization-based urban planning and local populations (Toivonen & Seremani, 2021), using interpretive approaches (Weber, 2004) and ethnographic methods. However, discussions of MOS decolonization tend to be biased toward theoretical considerations (Girei, 2017; Tourish, 2019), and in particular, there is a lack of discussion of methodological tools that are elaborately tuned to better understand indigenous management phenomena (Yousfi, 2021).

Therefore, this paper discusses the possibility of a phenomenological approach as one way to decolonize MOS. Phenomenology is a philosophical approach that seeks to understand the comprehensive experience of a phenomenon from the perspective of a party rather than an observer, i.e., from a first-person perspective (Gallagher & Zahavi, 2008; Goulding, 2005; Neubauer et al., 2019; Sanders, 1982). We present an example of the perspective and basic procedure of a phenomenological approach that differs from a natural scientific approach. We then illustrate how such an approach can help to better decipher lived experiences of local management phenomena. Specifically, we will focus on the phenomenon of "*sasshi*" found in Japanese workplaces and social relations. *Sasshi* is the act with the intentions of the other party (Aida, 1972; Enomoto, 2017). Specific examples include inferring the other person's intentions, expectations, and desires from ambiguous or polysemous words, carefully observing a situation, and fulfilling the other person's needs before he or she asks for something in words.

We then draw future prospects of this theme. Although the phenomenological approach can be said to be useful as a method for decolonizing MOS, it is also fraught with problems that cannot be overlooked. In particular, as phenomenology branches out in detail, there is a need for methodological development by clarifying the connection between the philosophical foundations on which a study relies and the appropriate methodological procedures (Gill, 2014; Lopez & Willis, 2004; Neubauer et al., 2019). Moreover, rather than criticizing and avoiding positivist approaches out of hand, it is also theoretically and practically relevant to ask how phenomenological approaches can contribute to the healthy development of the dominant Western model (Gallagher & Zahavi, 2008; Taguchi, 2014).

## EXPLORING THE ALTERNATIVES:
## DECOLONIZATION OF MOS

Decolonization of MOS means critically examining the Anglo-American-centered intellectual domination and creating more locally rooted and meaningful knowledge (Girei, 2017; Jammulamadaka et al., 2021; Mbembe, 2016; Scobie et al., 2021; Yousfi, 2021). Such debates have occurred since the late 1980s, began to gain prominence in the mid-2000s, and have been actively developed since the 2010s (Jammulamadaka et al., 2021; Scobie et al., 2021; Tourish, 2019). These studies rely on post-colonial geography, critical development studies, and critical management studies (Girei, 2017), but not necessarily in a unified direction (Jammulamadaka et al., 2021).

However, a common thread in the debate on the decolonization of MOS is to literally move away from the colonization of MOS. The reason why such an effort is considered important is that the colonization of MOS has resulted in the under-recognition (or invisibilization) or tacit disdain of Indigenous knowledge in local non-Western regions (Banerjee & Arjaliès, 2021), and it has not contributed to the meaningful development of MOS. Colonization, although various definitions exist, implies that management knowledge conforms to Western (especially Anglo-American-centric) theoretical assumptions (Girei, 2017). Behind this lies a historical structure in which the West is the cradle of modernity, and they have normalized knowledge as a theoretical subject. This means that the Western hegemony system has been established and strengthened in the production and utilization of management knowledge (Jammulamadaka et al., 2021; Scobie et al., 2021).

Here, we briefly summarize the characteristics of knowledge that underpin the colonization of MOS from ontological, epistemological, and methodological perspectives. First, ontologically, it is based on objectivism or foundationalism (Banerjee, 2022; Marsh et al., 2018; Nomura, 2017). As a result, an object is seen to exist in the same way (i.e., objectively) as anyone sees it if observed correctly, and our knowledge is seen to be founded on such unshakable truths. Second, epistemologically, it is based on positivism (Banerjee, 2022; Grey, 2010). Therefore, we take the position that, for management phenomena as for natural phenomena, it is possible to propose some rules or laws after testing theoretical hypotheses and clarifying causal relationships. Finally, in terms of methodology or research methods, quantitative methods are emphasized, and there is a strong need to carry out rigorous data collection and analysis (Tsui, 2018).

It is emphasized that in order to decolonize MOS, it is first necessary to acknowledge the current state of colonization and to start by questioning the assumptions of MOS, namely the ontological and epistemological assumptions (Banerjee, 2022). In fact, criticism has long been levied against dualism (Higaki, 2022; Omori, [1976] 2015), the foundation of ontology and epistemology based on Western philosophy, such as man and nature, consciousness and body, as well as hypothesis testing and causal inference based on the objectivism and positivism (Banerjee & Arjaliès; Jammulamadaka et al., 2021). This is because knowledge cannot be separated from the circumstances and historical context, including the beliefs and assumptions of the researcher in which it is produced (Banerjee, 2022; Morgan & Smircich, 1980; Yousfi, 2021).

Therefore, we need to pay attention to the social, political, economic, cultural, and historical context and strive to generate knowledge rooted in the epistemology of each local population rather than the universal knowledge pursued by the dominant paradigm (Girei, 2017; Scobie et al., 2021; Yousfi, 2021). It is argued that doing so will shed light on local knowledge, encourage the deciphering of a pluralistic world, and pave the way for theoretical development through a healthy cross-evaluation with colonization (Banerjee, 2022; Yousfi, 2021).

Based on the above beliefs, a gradual accumulation of studies that implement the decolonization of MOS is underway. For example, Girei (2017) reveals the process by which the author herself, a white Western woman, faced dilemmas with the perceptions and practices of people on the ground while working in organizational development for an NGO in Uganda and recursively generated management knowledge while reflecting on her own identity and position. Toivonen and Seremani (2021) show how management elites in public organizations in Cameroon, while facing resistance from the local population, skillfully legitimized urban planning based on Western management knowledge while also taking into account local circumstances. Moreover, Scobie et al. (2021) describe a case in which a doctoral student of Maori heritage and her supervisor collaborated on a project involving the tensions between decolonial research practice and the completion of a doctoral degree at the center of colonialism, a research university in the United Kingdom.

These and other studies aiming at decolonization practices have explained the need to draw on qualitative and interpretive methods rather than quantitative methods. Among them, the ethnographic approach is actively adopted because it is a "research practice" that could grasp a comprehensive understanding of the management phenomenon and its context, although we can find differences in the detailed procedures (Girei, 2017; Toivonen & Seremani, 2021; Yousfi, 2021).

However, it has been pointed out that existing studies on the decolonization of MOS are inclined to theoretical considerations, and studies based on qualitative methods as well as ethnographic approaches remain scarce (Girei, 2017; Tourish, 2019). Moreover, methodological considerations on how to decolonize MOS have not been sufficiently examined (Yousfi, 2021). For example, seeking ways to generate meaningful knowledge by capturing local management and organizational phenomena that are difficult to decipher adequately in the dominant Western-centered paradigm would contribute to the decolonization of MOS.

Therefore, this paper addresses a phenomenological approach as the alternative.

## APPRAISING A PHENOMENOLOGICAL APPROACH

### Focus of Phenomenology

Phenomenology is a new philosophical approach proposed by Husserl in the early 20th century (Gallagher & Zahavi, 2008; Gill, 2014; Moran, 2000; Neubauer et al., 2019). Specifically, phenomenology aims to understand the experience of a party about phenomena, that is, the lived experiences (how we experience the lived world we see, hear, and discuss in our daily lives) (Gallagher & Zahavi, 2008; Goulding, 2005; Neubauer et al., 2019; Sanders, 1982; Yoshikawa, 2017).

Here, phenomena are not the material properties of objects or the causal properties of objects that objective or empirical studies pursue, which are assumed to appear in the same way to everyone, but phenomena that appear and are experienced by the parties concerned. Moreover, a given object may appear in various modalities to the parties concerned. For example, one's supervisor's intention, as she perceives it at work, may appear to her as something that should be fulfilled with the highest priority, or it may appear to her as an opportunity to enhance her work reputation (Ohta, 2022), or it may appear to her as something that she should respond to discreetly and naturally so as not to give a bad impression to other colleagues. Thus, the appearance of the object for her depends on a variety of contexts, including the relationships with her superior and colleagues, the skills and experiences rooted in her own body, the evaluation system of the organization, and the norms of the workplace and the society surrounding it (Gallagher & Zahavi, 2008; Moran, 2000).

Therefore, the phenomenological approach seeks to faithfully describe the experiences as they appear, which are appearances of objects for parties involved embedded in various contexts: historical, social, cultural, institutional, spatial, material, and physical (Moran, 2000; Smith, 2016; Sokolowski, 2000).

Since Husserl, phenomenology has been developed by outstanding philosophers such as Heidegger, Merleau-Ponty, and Gadamer (Beck, 2021; Skea, 2016). However, it has been noted that there are various schools of phenomenology with different theoretical foundations (Gill, 2014; Lopez & Willis, 2004; Neubauer et al., 2019). Therefore, it is important to recognize that the phenomenological approach is not a single method but is diverse depending on the philosophical foundations relied upon (de Vaujany et al., 2023; Lopez & Willis, 2004; Moran, 2000).

We can identify several discussions that attempt to categorize the phenomenological approach, although they are still scarce (Gill, 2014; Neubauer et al., 2019). According to them, most phenomenologies can be broadly classified into descriptive phenomenology, relying on Husserl, and hermeneutic phenomenology, relying on Heidegger (Beck, 2021; Gill, 2014; Lopez & Willis, 2004; Neubauer et al., 2019).

Specifically, descriptive phenomenology focuses on the epistemological nature of an experience. That is, its approach seeks to explain the essence of what an experience is like (Gill, 2014; Neubauer et al., 2019). Hermeneutic phenomenology, on the other hand, focuses on the ontological nature of a party who experiences a given phenomenon. That is, its approach seeks to understand how a party exists in relation to its own lived world (Gill, 2014; Lopez & Willis, 2004; Neubauer et al., 2019). Each school of thought presents more detailed methodological procedures, which are applied in subsequent studies (Beck, 2021; Gill, 2014; Neubauer et al., 2019).

However, it has been pointed out that there is no agreement on the appropriate methodology for using the finely branched phenomenologies in descriptive and hermeneutic phenomenology, and no standard procedures have been established (Gill, 2014; Sanders, 1982; Skea, 2016). The purpose of this paper is not to discuss in detail the differences between the various phenomenological methods but to show the potential of the phenomenological approach as one way to decolonize MOS. Therefore, although the approach to be relied upon can be strictly different depending on what and how it is to be revealed (Lopez & Willis, 2004; Sanders, 1982), an example of the basic characteristics and procedures of the phenomenological approach is mentioned below.

*First-Person Perspective: Viewpoint of Phenomenological Approach*

Phenomenology approaches lived experiences from a first-person perspective (Goulding, 2005; Moran, 2000; Neubauer et al., 2019; Sanders, 1982; Yoshikawa, 2017; Zahavi, 2005). The first-person perspective is the perspective of the person involved. Specifically, an experience appears only as such to the party concerned, and it constitutes a certain whole as seen and perceived by him/her. (Yoshikawa, 2017). Thus, an experience and the knowledge based on it are rooted in the contextual appearances of things and events at "that time, place, and space" of the party involved.

On the other hand, studies that rely on the natural science approach, which is widely shared in contemporary MOS, are based on a third-person perspective (Gallagher & Zahavi, 2008; Rosa, 2023). That is, they adopt the theoretical assumption that the researcher can objectively observe a phenomenon from the perspective of an outsider rather than from that of the party involved. Phenomenologists have cast criticisms on such perspective (Gill, 2014; Moran, 2000), as Merleau-Ponty, for example, pointed out the naiveness and dishonesty (Merleau-Ponty, [1945] 1962). This is because the researcher's own first-person perspective is inevitably inherent in scientific practices. In other words, the researcher's own perception and orientation are not completely scientifically controlled. For example, when observing a phenomenon and interpreting its results, the researcher's own experience based on the first-person perspective influences them directly or indirectly, consciously or unconsciously. Thus, even if we attempt to observe a phenomenon objectively, we would not be able to perform so without the intervention of our own (ever-changing) point of view and experiences based on that viewpoint. Namely, we cannot continue to objectively observe a phenomenon at all times (Gallagher & Zahavi, 2008; Neubauer et al., 2019; Taguchi, 2014).

Here, based on phenomenology's criticism of the natural scientific approach, one might raise the opinion that a researcher who is not a party to the event may not be able to approach the experience of others. However, what the phenomenologist is emphasizing is not the inaccessibility of the experience of others due to the adoption of the first-person perspective but that every experience is based on the unique first-person perspective of the parties involved (including the researcher). Thus, they do not deny the possibility of an experience of a phenomenon from a first-person perspective other than that of the parties involved. Husserl, the founder of phenomenology, also recognized that there could be multiple first-person experiences of a phenomenon and regarded this as a problem to be considered (Yoshikawa, 2017). In phenomenology, the perspectives that "we," including the researcher, can draw upon for understanding the lived world are more precisely considered intersubjective ones that are grounded in multiple first-person perspectives (Gallagher & Zahavi, 2008).

## A Basic Procedure of Phenomenological Approach

Phenomenology is anti-naturalistic but not anti-scientific, and its approach is not haphazard (Gallagher & Zahavi, 2008; Taguchi, 2014). Although phenomenological approaches are diverse, we present the following four basic steps as an example when we specifically describe the lived experiences from a first-person perspective: suspension of natural attitude (epoché), phenomenological reduction, eidetic variation, and intersubjective corroboration (Gallagher & Zahavi, 2008). Other researchers have proposed similar procedures (e.g., Valera, 1996).

First, the natural attitude is the attitude we have when we are living naturally, and it is that we view the object or the living world as an objective entity (Sokolowski, 2000; Taguchi, 2014; Tani, 2002). Phenomenology initially calls for the suspension of this attitude to which we are prone, namely, withholding (as much as possible) from the application of our own beliefs about experience and of authoritative and justified theories (Gallagher & Zahavi, 2008).

Phenomenological reduction is a shift from a natural attitude to a phenomenological attitude and gives our attention to the mutual relationship between the appearance of the object and its experience for the parties concerned, which cannot be captured by the natural attitude (Sokolowski, 2000; Tani, 2002). In particular, the experiences that are significant to focus on here are those that are self-evident (Taguchi, 2014). This is because self-evident experiences are not focused on because they are self-evident, even though they are the basis or premise of experience.

We are engaged in goal-seeking activities on a daily basis. For example, when creating a document on a PC, our attention is focused on the letters, symbols, and charts on the display, the progress of the document, and the deadline for its creation. On the other hand, our experience of the physical actions we take when we type into our PCs and the artifacts and spaces that support those actions are non-thematic, i.e., they recede into the background. The reflective attitude and specific method of turning one's attention to structures of (basic) experience that are not captured in one's usual way of perception is not sufficiently emphasized in the ethnographic approach that is found, for example, in the decolonization-oriented research in management studies. Such an approach, which at first glance appears unnatural and circuitous, is one of the characteristics of phenomenology, unlike descriptions in psychology, anthropology, and other fields (Gallagher & Zahavi, 2008; Taguchi, 2014).

Eidetic variation is the exploration of the central nature of an object (Gallagher & Zahavi, 2008). That is, it is the process of identifying what makes an object what it is by eliminating non-essential features of the object. It should be noted that essence here does not mean the one and only invariant property but rather a common fundamental property that appears across phenomena, even if we change the aspect of an object in various ways (Gallagher & Zahavi, 2008; Taguchi, 2014).

Intersubjective corroboration is the intersubjective enhancement of the certainty of a phenomenological description by comparing it with the first-person perspective of others rather than by conducting the analysis alone (Gallagher & Zahavi, 2008). Husserl strongly insisted that phenomenology progresses through collaboration and that its results are fallible (Gallagher & Zahavi, 2008; Taguchi, 2014).

# ILLUSTRATING "*SASSHI*" IN THE WORKPLACE
## *What Is Sasshi?*

In light of the above discussion, this section illustrates two points. First, the knowledge about local management phenomena cannot be adequately understood as long as it is based on the ontological and epistemological assumptions assumed by the colonization. Second, the phenomenological approach presented in the previous section can be one way to capture such phenomena. Specifically, this paper will focus on the phenomenon of "*sasshi* (察し)" or "*sassuru* (察する)" (the verbal form of *sasshi*) in the workplace in Japan, where the author was born and raised.

The reasons to illuminate the phenomenon of management and organization in Japan are as follows. First, Japan was one of the first countries in the non-Western world to modernize under the influence of Western powers, and at the same time, it retains a culture, norms, and institutions that have taken an extremely long time to form, permeate, and transform under conditions of high ethnic homogeneity (Abegglen, 1958; Inagaki, 2007; Maruyama, 1961; Nakane, 1967; Sugayama, 2011; Suzuki, 2017). From the specific perspective of the emergence and development of management studies in Japan, Japan has also been an early and active adopter of management knowledge, especially from Germany and the United States (US), among Western countries. In fact, the world's first scholarly business management organization was established in Germany in 1924, but it may be surprising to learn that the Japan Academy of Business Administration was founded in 1926, ahead of the Academy of Management (founded in 1936) (Japan Academy of Business Administration, n.d.). Therefore, Japan was one of the earliest countries to experience the colonization of management studies. However, there have long been doubts and criticisms of management knowledge based on the colonization by researchers exploring management studies rooted in the Japanese context (Kagono, 1988; Nonaka, 1994; Nonaka & Takeuchi, 1995; Nonaka & Yamaguchi, 2019). Nevertheless, Japanese management scholars are now structurally more called upon to conform to the ontological and epistemological assumptions that underpin an intellectual hegemonic regime by the West that is growing stronger by the day (Asakawa, 2020; Numagami, 2000; Sato, 2022).

However, it should be noted here that Japan has not only been unilaterally influenced by Western society but has also developed into a major economic power and exported practical knowledge of science, technology, and management, such as production systems and quality control, that were developed independently in the historical context of Japan (Abegglen, 1973; Banerjee, 2022; Fujimoto, 1999; Schaede, 2020; Vogel, 1979). That is, it can be said that Japan, although in the non-Western world, is not only indirectly or partially involved in Western-led colonization but is also independently promoting the generalization of management knowledge. Thus, from the perspective of history, politics, economics, and culture, contemporary Japanese society is an extremely complex mixture of aspects that have been colonized by the West, aspects that have retained their local character, and hybridized aspects (Kato, 1974; Maraldo, 2020). Moreover, even now, there is ongoing tension, conflict, dialogue, and coordination between them. Based on these points, the organizational phenomenon in Japan is one of the significant subjects in discussing the decolonization of MOS.

The *sasshi* discussed in this paper is a deeply rooted phenomenon not only in contemporary organizations under such circumstances but also in society as a whole. While *sasshi* is sometimes taken to mean compassion in a broad sense, it is more specifically to act with the other person's intention in mind (Aida, 1972; Enomoto, 2017). For example, all of the following actions fall under the *sasshi*: taking in the other person's intentions even if they are not clearly communicated in words, adjusting one's own position, words, and actions while carefully observing the other person's behavior, taking the initiative to move before the other person's expectations and requests are communicated in words, and deciphering the meaning and intentions behind the other person's words.

In order to perform *sasshi*, or to *sassuru* something, we need to always perceive the situation and things from the other person's point of view, not our own. That is, we need to refrain from self-assertion (Aida, 1972). Certainly, for others, especially those from other countries or regions who have not internalized these values, it may be easier to express their own positions and opinions, and they may view such behavior as mutually beneficial because they can clearly share the issues. However, in light of traditional Japanese norms and virtues, such behavior is considered selfish and unseemly. In fact, according to an international comparative study, parents and preschool teachers in the US say that self-confidence is the most important thing that children learn at an early age. In Japan, on the other hand, confidence was only marginally mentioned; on the contrary, consideration, empathy, and sympathy for others were regarded as the most important (Enomoto, 2017; Tobin et al., 1989). Even if there is a gap between the other party's intentions and one's own intentions, one tries to guess the other party's response, emphasize commonalities, blur conflicts, and find a mutually acceptable point to reach a compromise (Enomoto, 2017). In fact, a person who can naturally or smoothly carry out attentiveness is evaluated as *"ki ga kiku* (気が利く) (witty) or *sasshi ga yoi* (察しが良い) (taking into account the intentions of the others well)" in social reference groups such as the family, kinship, school, and workplace, while a person who is unreserved and lacks humility is evaluated negatively (Enomoto, 2017; Katada, 2017).

It is said to be one of the characteristics of Japanese communication to refrain as much as possible from using words and statements that give priority to one's own intentions, such as asserting oneself or persuading others. (Aida, 1972).

### Polysemy and Contextuality of Sasshi

Based on the basic explanation of *sasshi*, we will focus on this phenomenon in organizations and workplaces.

First, imagine a certain situation. One day, you, a subordinate, are told by your boss, *"Asu wa yoroshiku* (明日はよろしく)". It is difficult to convey the meaning accurately when translating this message. Its nuance is similar to the statement, "I am counting on you to do a great job tomorrow," but it is more casual and not as explicit as the translated expression. How would you behave in this situation? Would you ask your boss what he meant by the ambiguous words? Unfortunately, this kind of behavior is not regarded as *sasshi ga yoi* (taking into account their intentions well). In the Japanese workplace, *sasshi* is one of the most important skills for organizational personnel, so much so that the ability to perform one's job is sometimes replaced by the ability to *sassuru* something to be done (Enomoto, 2017; Katada, 2017). As *sasshi* is to act with the other party's intentions in mind, you are implicitly expected to decipher as soon as possible the unspoken meaning of your supervisor's voice and carry it out even in the absence of explicit instructions from them (Ohta, 2021). For example, if you have an important meeting scheduled for tomorrow that your boss will also attend, you should decipher exactly what he/she wants you to do and make sure you do it. Those might be, for example, preparing materials, reporting key points in advance, reminding other prospective participants, arranging a debriefing or a reception after the meeting, and so on. You also need to guess whether the boss's implicit requests are one or several, whether they should be addressed now or not, whether you should share them with your colleagues or not, and so on, and to deal with them appropriately.

Let me give you another example. Let's assume that you are a newcomer who has just joined the company. One day, your supervisor told you to go home early today because you would not be able to go home on time sooner or later. However, all of your *senpai* (先輩) (senior or co-worker who has joined the company earlier than you) are working overtime. How would you behave? It would not be so recommended that you leave the office with impunity, thinking that since your work is done, it is only natural that you should go home without being told to do so by your supervisor. In order to be favorably evaluated by your boss (and others around you) as great *sasshi*, you need to more or less take into account his/her intentions in this situation as well. Specifically, the supervisor's intention may be an implicit instruction that "you should also stay behind and help with some tasks" since the rest of your colleagues are working overtime. Or it may be a pep talk, "Improve your task performance quickly so that you can be given more work to do". Or it may be a disappointment in you, saying that they are fed up with your work and want you to go home early because your presence in the office is demoralizing them. Of course, there are many other possibilities and examples of coping behaviors in response to the supervisor's intentions you decipher.

### Difficulty in Objectively Grasping Sasshi

Even from just two examples, one can imagine that individuals working in Japanese organizations are confronted with numerous situations that require them to *sassuru* (take into account the intentions of the other party) on a daily basis.

*Sasshi* in the workplace is deeply connected not only to the intentions of others but also to countless contexts, including their personality, mood, relationships with others, one's own background and position, responsibilities, motivation, abilities, the goals and size of the group to which one belongs, and recent group and organizational performance. That is, they do not exist as solid organizational or social entities but appear contextually and fluidly. Therefore, even if we identify a certain behavior of *sasshi* in isolation from its context, it is just a naive attitude or behavior and does not lead to meaningful knowledge about *sasshi* phenomena. Moreover, the success or failure of *sasshi* is basically a relational phenomenon determined not by oneself but by the other party, especially the superior who has authority in an organization (and in some cases, the surrounding people who read the behavior). For example, if a person attempts the same action multiple times as *sasshi* toward a supervisor, the supervisor may or may not recognize it as *sasshi*, depending on how well it is with his/her intentions. Furthermore, even if multiple subordinates practice the same action as *sasshi* toward a supervisor, the supervisor may or may not recognize it as *sasshi*, depending on how well it is with his/her intentions. That is, the exact same behavior may be evaluated favorably and appear as *sasshi*, or it may be evaluated negatively as insufficient consideration or misguided.

Since *sasshi* is a behavior that requires a certain degree of skill (Aida, 1972), it is not uncommon for the performer to misunderstand the intentions of the other party. In addition, the way the other party indicates his/her intention is not always the same. For example, it is easy to imagine that a supervisor may adjust his/her own behavior according to the intentions of his/her subordinates. When both parties carry out their own *sasshi*, the situation becomes increasingly complex, which is known as "*sasshiai* (acting with the intentions in mind each other)" (Enomoto, 2017). Moreover, *sasshi* can be elaborately concealed. For example, a supervisor may dare to hide the process in order to take credit for his/her subordinate's considerate behavior based on *sasshi* and its results. Furthermore, a subordinate, in order not to stand out too much from others (we have a well-known proverb, "deru kui wa utareru (出る杭は打たれる) (The stake that sticks out gets hammered in.)," may carry out his/her own *sasshi* as secretly as possible so as not to be identified.

From the above, it is not easy to observe and identify when and by whom, why and how the *sasshi* (or *sasshiai*) is done, and how it unfolds and ends. It is obviously not a consistent approach for an observer to try to objectively understand an extremely contextual, fluid, and relational phenomenon as the same phenomenon for everyone to see (Banerjee & Arjaliès, 2021; Inoue, 2007; Marsh et al., 2018; Nomura, 2017; Sato, 2001). Moreover, suppose that we rigorously measure certain attitudes and behaviors that are only labeled as *sasshi* divorced from context using a scale consisting of a limited number of items and infer causal relationships between them. It is difficult to say that the findings from such attempts will contribute much to the sound theoretical development of management studies as a whole, including studies based on the dominant paradigm (Banerjee, 2022; Jammulamadaka et al., 2021; Tourish, 2019; Yousfi, 2021).

*A Phenomenological Approach to Sasshi as the Lived Experiences*

On the other hand, if we follow the example of the phenomenological procedure, we can approach it as follows.

First, we are urged to refrain as much as possible from a natural attitude. That is, we should not see *sasshi* as an objective entity that is the same for everyone, based on a first-person perspective rather than the third-person perspective on which the natural scientific approach relies. We seek to explore the experience of *sasshi* in a workplace from the perspective of the parties involved rather than to draw on positivist-based theories and measures (Gallagher & Zahavi, 2008; Goulding, 2005; Neubauer et al., 2019).

The next step is to focus on the mutual relationship between the appearance of the object and its experience for the parties involved (phenomenological reduction). In particular, focusing on self-evident experiences will lead to an understanding of the basis of the experience of *sasshi* (Gallagher & Zahavi, 2008; Sanders, 1982; Taguchi, 2014). Specifically, in a series of process of *sasshi*, a person's own consciousness is directed toward understanding and fulfilling the intentions of the other party when carrying out *sasshi* in the workplace. However, the physical behavior and the material, spatial, and social experiences of the person or the other party in carrying out the *sasshi* are kept from his/her awareness. However, it is these experiences that can shape the foundation of *sasshi* (in contemporary organizations/workplaces), of which the parties involved may not even be aware. For example, we pay attention not only to the party's coping behavior in response to his/her supervisor's ambiguous "*Asu wa yoroshiku*," but also to the gestures of those involved in the process of that behavior, the relationships between the party and his/her organizations, supervisors, and colleagues, and the tools, techniques, values, and beliefs that support the party's behavior. As a result, we will be able to better understand the foundation and the entirety of the party's experience of *sasshi*. Moreover, interviews as well as observational research on the experience of *sasshi*, even for researchers unfamiliar with the Japanese workplace, will contribute to a more reliable understanding of the phenomenon as an experience based on his/her first-person perspective (Gallagher & Zahavi, 2008; Yoshikawa, 2017).

We will then explore the nature of the experience of *sasshi* (eidetic variation). Specifically, we will examine what and to what extent a *sasshi* must be trimmed before it ceases to be *sasshi* or identify common properties of *sasshi* that appear across diverse phenomena as a result of changing the aspect of *sasshi* in various ways. Because *sasshi* is interpersonal, it is essential to understand not only the experience of the subordinate who carries out the *sasshi*, but also at least the experience of the supervisor who is the object of the *sasshi*.

Finally, it is necessary to deepen our understanding of the experience of *sasshi* based on multiple first-person perspectives (intersubjective corroboration). For example, by comparing phenomenological analyses of *sasshi* among researchers with different attributes, we can expect to arrive at a more valid and reliable understanding of the phenomenon and a more sound presentation of knowledge (Gallagher & Zahavi, 2008; Taguchi, 2014; Tani, 2002). Table 1 contrastingly summarizes the characteristics of the natural scientific and phenomenological approaches referred to in this paper.

***Table 1.*** Comparison of Approaches.

| | Natural Scientific Approach | Phenomenological Approach |
| --- | --- | --- |
| Viewpoint | Third-person perspective | First-person perspective |
| Theoretical assumptions | Viewing the object or the living world as an objective entity (natural attitude) | Withholding from the application of our own beliefs about experience and of authoritative and justified theories (epoché) |
| Research focus | Object that can be not self-evident and newly explored and discovered | Basis of (self-evident) experience of how an object appears for the party involved (based on phenomenological reduction) |
| Object of understanding and explanation | Material and causal characteristics of an object that exist independently of our perceptions and beliefs | Essence of things, that is, common property that appears across phenomena (as a result of eidetic variation) |
| Verification of results | Results are verified to see if they can be replicated anytime, anywhere, using common measures and variables (replication) | Results are compared with phenomenological description based on the first-person perspective of others and intersubjectively discussed the certainty of them (intersubjective corroboration) |

# CONCLUSION: TOWARD THE PRODUCTION OF WHOLESOME MANAGEMENT KNOWLEDGE

This paper presents the phenomenological approach as one meaningful way to decolonize MOS. As a conclusion, the paper draws a future perspective by referring to the theoretical and methodological challenges to decolonize the management studies.

The following issues regarding the decolonization of MOS can be mentioned. First, it is necessary to avoid essentializing, privileging, and recolonizing the practice of decolonization and the knowledge generated. To do so, we need to be careful not to fall into naive rehashing of the findings of our great predecessors, being all about the dominant paradigm criticism, colonization of the project of decolonization, and essentialization of local knowledge (Banerjee & Arjaliès, 2021; Tourish, 2019). The next step is to build on research based on local ontologies and epistemologies. This is because, while oriented toward and practicing decolonization, there are scattered studies that are based on Western theoretical and ontological assumptions (Banerjee, 2022; Jammulamadaka et al., 2021). Furthermore, there is a need to decolonize methodologies as well as theories of management knowledge (Ingold, 2023; Scobie et al., 2021; Yousfi, 2021). Note that these are also deeply connected to the issues discussed below.

The phenomenological approach discussed in this paper has not only attracted attention in areas such as cognitive science, neuroscience, robotics, nursing, and caregiving but has also found significance as a useful method in management studies (de Vaujany et al., 2023; Gibson & Hanes, 2003; Gill, 2014; Holt & Sandberg, 2011; Kingma et al., 2018; Mingers, 2001; Taguchi, 2014; Tomkins & Eatough, 2013; Uda, 2021; vom Lehn, 2019). Underlying this is the insight and expectation that theoretical descriptions and explanations of comprehensive and contextual experiences of the lived world, which are different assumptions, perspectives, and attitudes from objectivist-based research, can provide a unique foundation for soundly complementing and developing the dominant knowledge (Sokolowski, 2000; Tsoukas, 2023). Research practices based on the dominant paradigm are not carried out in a vacuum (Gallagher & Zahavi, 2008; Moran, 2000; Tourish, 2019). A phenomenological approach would provide a perspective to better understand the process from the appearance of the object to "the constitution of objectivity for the parties involved." On the other hand, the fundamental question remains as to how and to what extent phenomenology and naturalistic research (in management studies) should be specifically integrated (Banerjee, 2022; Gallagher & Zahavi, 2008). Even the application of phenomenology to MOS is still insufficient, and its methodological procedures are finely branched. Therefore, sound comparisons and discussions among these studies are not easy (Gill, 2014; Lopez & Willis, 2004; Neubauer et al., 2019; Skea, 2016). Moreover, phenomenological descriptions based on local ontology and epistemology are also scarce (Banerjee & Arjaliès, 2021; Tourish, 2019; Uda, 2023; Uemura, 2023). Phenomenology is fallible, and therefore, it would be essential to examine the ways to make our ontology pluralize, refine the methodological procedures, and bridge with naturalistic research in order to produce meaningful contextualized knowledge.

# REFERENCES

Abegglen, J. C. (1958). *The Japanese factory: Aspects of its social organization*. Free Press.

Abegglen, J. C. (1973). *Management and worker: The Japanese solution*. Sophia University in cooperation with Kodansha International.

Aida, Y. (1972). *Nihonjin no ishiki kôzô: Fûdo, rekishi, shakai*. Kodansha.

Asakawa, K. (2020). Keiei kenkyû no kokusai hyôjunka jidai ni okeru shitsu no takai ronbun no jôken: Nihon kara no apurô-chi. In Y. Aoshima (Ed.). *Shitsu no takai kenkyû ronbun no kakikata: Tayô na ronja no shiten kara miete kuru jibun no ronbun no katachi*. Hakuto Shobo.

Banerjee, S. B. (2022). Decolonizing management theory: A critical perspective. *Journal of Management Studies, 59*(4), 1074–1087. https://doi.org/10.1111/joms.12756

Banerjee, S. B., & Arjaliès, D.-L. (2021). Celebrating the end of enlightenment: Organization theory in the age of the Anthropocene and Gaia (and why neither is the solution to our ecological crisis). *Organization Theory, 2*, 1–24. https://doi.org/10.1177/26317877211036714

Beck, C. T. (2021). *Introduction to phenomenology: Focus on methodology*. Sage.

de Vaujany, F.-X., Aroles, J., & Perézts, P. (2023). Phenomenologies and organization studies: Organizing through and beyond appearances. In F.-X. de Vaujany, J. Aroles, & M. Perézts (Eds.), *The Oxford handbook of phenomenologies and organization studies*. Oxford University Press. https://doi.org/10.1093/oxfordhb/9780192865755.013.2

Enomoto, H. (2017). *"Sontaku" no kôzô: Kûki o yomi sugiru buka sekinin o toranai jôshi*. Eastpress.

Fujimoto, T. (1999). *The Evolution of Manufacturing Systems at Toyota*. Oxford University Press.

Gallagher, S., & Zahavi, D. (2008). *The phenomenological mind: An introduction to philosophy of mind and cognitive science*. Routledge.

Gibson, S. K., & Hanes, L. A. (2003). The contribution of phenomenology to HRD research. *Human Resource Development Review, 2*(2), 181–205. https://doi.org/10.1177/1534484303002002005.

Gill, M. J. (2014). The possibilities of phenomenology for organizational research. *Organizational Research Methods, 17*(2), 118–137. https://journals.sagepub.com/doi/10.1177/1094428113518348

Girei, E. (2017). Decolonising management knowledge: A reflexive journey as practitioner and researcher in Uganda. *Management Learning, 48*(4), 453–470. https://doi.org/10.1177/1350507617697867

Goulding, C. (2005). Grounded theory, ethnography and phenomenology: A comparative analysis of three qualitative strategies for marketing research. *European Journal of Marketing, 39*(3/4), 294–308. https://doi.org/10.1108/03090560510581782

Grey, C. (2010). Organizing studies: Publications, politics and polemic. *Organization Studies, 31*(6), 677–694. https://doi.org/10.1177/0170840610372575

Higaki, T. (2022). *Nihon kindai shisôron: Gijutsu, kagaku, seimei*. Seidosha.

Holt, R., & Sandberg, J. (2011). Phenomenology and organization theory. In H. Tsoukas & R. Chia (Eds.), *Philosophy and organization theory* (*Research in the Sociology of Organizations*, Vol. 32). Emerald Group Publishing Limited. https://doi.org/10.1108/S0733-558X(2011)0000032010

Inagaki, H. (2007). *Kokka, kojin, shûkyô: Kingendai nihon no seishin*. Kodansha.

Ingold, T. (2023). Postscript: An anthropologist lands in phenomenology. In F.-X. de Vaujany, J. Aroles, & M. Perézts (Eds.), *The Oxford handbook of phenomenologies and organization studies*. Oxford University Press. https://doi.org/10.1093/oxfordhb/9780192865755.013.39

Inoue, T. (2007). *"Sekentei" no kôzô: Shakai shinrishi eno kokoromi*. Kodansha.

Jammulamadaka, N., Faria, A., Jack, G., & Ruggunan, S. (2021). Decolonising management and organizational knowledge (MOK): Praxistical theorising for potential worlds. *Organization, 28*(5), 717–740. https://doi.org/10.1177/13505084211020463

Japan Academy of Business Administration. (n.d.). *About us: Japan Academy of Business Administration*. Retrieved November, 24, 2023 from https://keiei-gakkai.jp/en/keieigakkai/

Kagono, T. (1988). *Soshiki ninshikiron: Kigyô ni okeru sôzô to kakushin no kenkyû*. Chikura shobo.

Katada, T. (2017). *Sontaku shakai Nippon*. KADOKAWA.

Kato, S. (1974). *Zasshu bunka*. Kodansha.

Kingma, S. F., Dale, K., & Wasserman, V. (2018). Introduction: Henri Lefebvre and organization studies. In S. F. Kingma, K. Dale, & V. Wasserman (Eds.), *Organizational space and beyond: The significance of Henri Lefebvre for organization studies* (pp. 1–24). Routledge.

Lopez, K. A., & Willis, D. G. (2004). Descriptive versus interpretive phenomenology: Their contributions to nursing knowledge. *Qualitative Health Research, 14*(5), 726–735. https://doi.org/10.1177/1049732304263638

Maraldo, J. C. (2020). The Japanese encounter with and appropriation of western philosophy. In B. W. Davis (Ed.), *The Oxford handbook of Japanese Philosophy*. Oxford University Press. https://doi.org/10.1093/oxfordhb/9780199945726.013.19

Marsh, D., Ercan, S. A., &, Furlong, P. (2018). A skin not a sweater: Ontology and epistemology in political science. In V. Lowndes, D. Marsh, & G. Stroker (Eds.), *Theory and methods in political science* (4th ed, pp. 177–198). Palgrave Macmillan.

Maruyama, M. (1961). *Nihon no shisô*. Iwanami Shoten.

Mbembe, A. J. (2016). Decolonizing the university: New directions. *Arts & Humanities in Higher Education, 15*(1), 29–45. https://doi.org/10.1177/1474022215618513

Merleau-Ponty, M. ([1945] 1962). *Phenomenology of perception* (*Phénoménologie de la perception*, trans. C. Smith). Routledge & Kegan Paul.

Mingers, J. (2001). Embodying information systems: The contribution of phenomenology. *Information and Organization, 11*(2), 103–128. https://doi.org/10.1016/S1471-7727(00)00005-1

Moran, D. (2000). *Introduction to phenomenology*. Routledge.

Morgan, G., & Smircich, L. (1980). The case for qualitative research. *Academy of Management Review, 5*(4), 491–500. https://doi.org/10.2307/257453

Nakane, C. (1967). *Tate shakai no ningen kankei: Tan'itsu shakai no riron*. Kodansha.

Neubauer, B. E., Witkop, C. T., & Varpio, L. (2019). How phenomenology can help us learn from the experiences of others. *Perspectives on Medical Education, 8*, 90–97. https://doi.org/10.1007/s40037-019-0509-2

Nomura, K. (2017). *Shakaikagaku no kangaekata: Ninshikiron, risâ-chi dezain, shuhô*. The University of Nagoya Press.

Nonaka, I. (1994). A dynamic theory of organizational knowledge creation. *Organization Science, 5*(1), 14–37. https://www.jstor.org/stable/2635068

Nonaka, I., & Takeuchi, H. (1995). *The Knowledge-creating company*. Oxford University Press.

Nonaka, I., & Yamaguchi, I. (2019). *Chokkan no keiei: Kyôkan no tetsugaku de yomi toku dôtai keieiron*. KADOKAWA.

Numagami, T. (2000). *Kôi no keieigaku: Keieigaku ni okeru ito sezaru kekka no tankyû*. Hakuto Shobo.

Ohta, H. (2021). *Dôchô atsuryoku no shôtai*. PHP Institute.

Ohta, H. (2022). *Nihonjin no shônin yokkyû: Terewâ-ku ga sarashita shinsô*. Shinchosha.

Omori, S. ([1976] 2015). *Mono to kokoro*. Chikuma Shobo.

Rosa, H. (2023). Preface. In F.-X. de Vaujany, J. Aroles, & M. Perézts (Eds.), *The Oxford handbook of phenomenology and organization studies*. Oxford University Press. https://doi.org/10.1093/oxfordhb/9780192865755.002.0004

Sanders, P. (1982). Phenomenology: A new way of viewing organizational research. *Academy of Management Review, 7*(3), 353–360. https://doi.org/10.2307/257327

Sato, I. (2022). Yakusha kaisetsu: Keieigaku no "futsugô na shinjitsu" to saisei eno michisuji. In D. Tourish (2019), *Keieigaku no kiki: Sajutsu, giman, muimi na kenkyû (Management studies in Crisis: Fraud, deception and meaningless research*, trans. Sato I.). Hakuto Shobo.

Sato, N. (2001). *"Seken" no genshôgaku*. Seikyusha.

Schaede, U. (2020). *The business reinvention of Japan: How to make sense of the new Japan and why it matters*. Stanford University Press.

Scobie, M., Lee, B., & Smyth, S. (2021). Braiding together student and supervisor aspirations in a struggle to decolonize. *Organization, 28*(5), 857–875. https://doi.org/10.1177/13505084211015370

Skea, D. (2016). Phenomenological enquiry and psychological research in caring and quality of life contexts: Acknowledging the invisible. *International Journal of Caring Sciences, 9*(3), 1134–1146.

Smith, J. (2016). *Experiencing Phenomenology: An introduction*. Routledge.

Sokolowski, R. (2000). *Introduction to phenomenology*. Cambridge University Press.

Sugayama, S. (2011). *"Shûsha" shakai no tanjô: Howaitokarâ- kara burû-karâ- e*. The University of Nagoya Press.

Suzuki, T. (2017). *Tozasareta gengo nihongo no sekai zôho shinpan*. Shinchosha.

Taguchi, S. (2014). *Genshôgaku to iu shikô: "Jimei na mono" no chi e*. Chikuma Shobo.

Tani, T. (2002). *Kore ga genshôgaku da*. Kodansha.

Tobin, J. J., Wu, D. Y. H., & Davidson, D. H. (1989). *Preschool in three cultures: Japan, China and the United States*. Yale University Press.

Toivonen, A., & Seremani, T. (2021). The enemy within: The legitimating role of local managerial elites in the global managerial colonization of the Global South. *Organization, 28*(5), 798–816. https://doi.org/10.1177/13505084211015373

Tomkins, L., & Eatough, V. (2013). The feel of experience: Phenomenological ideas for organizational research. *Qualitative Research in Organizations and Management, 8*(3), 258–275. https://doi.org/10.1108/QROM-04-2012-1060

Tourish, D. (2019). *Management studies in Crisis: Fraud, deception and meaningless research*. Cambridge University Press.

Tsoukas, H. (2023). Afterward: Why and how phenomenology matters to organizational research. In F.-X. de Vaujany, J. Aroles, & M. Perézts (Eds.), *The Oxford handbook of phenomenology and organization studies*. Oxford University Press. https://doi.org/10.1093/oxfordhb/9780192865755.013.38

Tsui, A. (2018). Ivory tower, value-free ideal, and responsible science. *Academy of Management Perspectives, 32*(4), 412–442. https://doi.org/10.5465/amp.2015.0167

Uda, T. (2021). Expressing experiences of coworking spaces: Insights from social media. In M. Orel, O. Dvouletý, & V. Ratten (Eds.), *The flexible workplace: Coworking and other modern workplace transformations*. Springer. https://doi.org/10.1007/978-3-030-62167-4_10

Uda, T. (2023). Producing the organizational space: Buddhist temples as co-working spaces. In F.-X. de Vaujany, J. Aroles, & M. Perézts (Eds.), *The Oxford handbook of phenomenology and organization studies*. Oxford University Press. https://doi.org/10.1093/oxfordhb/9780192865755.013.35

Uemura, G. (2023). Phenomenology in Japan: A brief history with a focus on its reception in applied areas. In F.-X. de Vaujany, J. Aroles, & M. Perézts (Eds.), *The Oxford handbook of phenomenology and organization studies*. Oxford University Press. https://doi.org/10.1093/oxfordhb/9780192865755.013.30

Valera, F. J. (1996). Neurophenomenology: A methodological remedy for the hard problem. *Journal of Consciousness Studies, 3*(4), 330–349.

Vogel, E. F. (1979). *Japan as number one: Lessons for America*. Harvard University Press.

vom Lehn, D. (2019). Phenomenology-based ethnography for management studies and organizational analysis. *British Journal of Management, 30*(1), 188–202. https://doi.org/10.1111/1467-8551.12309

Weber, R. (2004). Editor's comments: The rhetoric of positivism versus interpretivism: A personal view. *MIS Quarterly, 28*(1), iii–xii. https://doi.org/10.2307/25148621

Yoshikawa, T. (2017). Gendai genshôgaku towa nani ka. In G. Uemura, T. Yaegashi, & T. Yoshikawa (Eds.), *Gendai genshôgaku: Keiken kara hajimeru tetsugaku nyûmon*. Shinyosha.

Yousfi, H. (2021). Decolonizing Arab organizational knowledge: "Fahlawa" as a research practice. *Organization*, *28*(5), 836–856. https://doi.org/10.1177/13505084211015371

Zahavi, D. (2005). *Subjectivity and selfhood: Investigating the first-person perspective*. MIT Press.

# TAKING CONTEXT SERIOUSLY THROUGH A PHENOMENOLOGY OF PLACE: AN ILLUSTRATION OF HOME-BASED WORK

Bernadetta Aloina Ginting-Szczesny,
Carmelita Euline Ginting-Carlström,
Ewald Kibler and Myrto Chliova

*Aalto University School of Business, Finland*

## ABSTRACT

*Contextualization has received increased attention in organization and entrepreneurship studies, yet predominant assumptions remain of contexts as fixed and having objectivist effects on organizing and entrepreneurial activities, independent from local actors' perceptions. In this paper, we bring forward the phenomenology of place as a means to be reflexive about contexts and resist the epistemic coloniality in organization and entrepreneurship studies. Drawing on our work with home-based women entrepreneurs in rural Central Java, Indonesia, we illustrate how we can examine "home as a place" that is experienced and practiced, offering new insights that challenge dominant assumptions underlying the notion of home.*

**Keywords:** Context; entrepreneurship; home; home-based work; organizing; phenomenology; place

Decolonizing Management and Organization Studies: Why, How, and What
Research in the Sociology of Organizations, Volume 93, 137–153
ISSN: 0733-558X/doi:10.1108/S0733-558X20250000093009

# INTRODUCTION

Two world-views were in collision; and the poverty of white accounts of these canoe journeys
reflect the colonialists' blindness to the native sea. They didn't get it – couldn't grasp the fact
that for Indians the water was a place, and the great bulk of the land was undifferentiated
space. (Raban, 1999, p. 103)

The above excerpt from the book *Passage to Juneau* provocatively highlights the
profound divide in knowledge resulting from a colonial mindset regarding place.
The native Tlingits' deep connection to water as a meaningful place is lost on the
early European explorers' minds, which, driven by a capitalist and exploitative
view of natural resources, were more tuned toward land as a place. This excerpt
vividly illustrates the situated and subjective construction of place, in which the
meanings and experiences associated with a place are shaped by social, cultural,
and historical practices (Cresswell, 2004; Gieryn, 2000).

Later on in the book, the author reflects on these conflicting views and finds
himself wondering how the Tlingits could be ignorant of their land surroundings
(Raban, 1999). This exemplifies how perceived superiority of Western knowledge
erases and devalues local ways of existence and knowing, creating a profound rift
in contemporary knowledge. An emerging perspective within organization and
entrepreneurship scholarship seeks to address this problem through contextualization (Bruton et al., 2022; Johns, 2006, 2017; Welter, 2011; Welter et al., 2019),
notably by incorporating diverse and often unheard voices and perspectives when
conducting research in non-western contexts. Yet, as Banerjee (2022) points out,
our attempts for deeper contextualization fall short if "Western scholarship
[remains] the norm for assessing other knowledges" (p. 1079) as it can retain the
often taken-for-granted, positional superiority of Western knowledge and understandings of what "context" is (Mignolo, 2012; Said, 1993). Overcoming such
epistemic violence would require us to be "critically disruptive" in conducting
research, as Chrispal (2025) points out in this volume, and to welcome theories
and methodologies that do not necessarily fit the knowledge that predominates
organization and entrepreneurship scholarship.

In this paper, we demonstrate how incorporating "place" as an active concept
and dynamic ingredient can enhance the study of organizing and entrepreneurial
activities (Dacin et al., 2024; Kimmitt et al., 2024; Wright et al., 2022). We draw
on the phenomenology of place (Relph, 1976; Tuan, 1974) to develop a situated
approach to understanding these practices (Cartel et al., 2022). This approach
enables critical reflection on the multiplicity of interpretations of place (Dovey,
2016) and disrupts dominant, often simplified narratives (Jammulamadaka et al.,
2021). We advocate for appreciating place as experienced, dynamic, and socially
constructed rather than a fixed "context" (Dacin et al., 2024). Given the historical
grounding of organization and entrepreneurship studies in Western ideals (Bruton
et al., 2018; 2022; Jammulamadaka et al., 2021), a place-sensitive approach unveils
marginalized perspectives and resists the epistemic coloniality that prioritizes
Western knowledge in determining what is "interesting" and "worthy" of exploration (Weston & Imas, 2018). As James et al. (2025) critically argue, developing

a situated understanding of place based on local ways of knowing, being, and doing is key to decolonizing organization and entrepreneurship research.

Against this backdrop, we argue in this paper that approaching place as an experience and practice (Cartel et al., 2022) through the phenomenology of place perspective allows for more critical modes of contextualization, reflection, and theorization on local forms of engagement and lived experiences (Wright et al., 2023). We do so by drawing on our experiences of, and reflections around, our engagement with home-based women entrepreneurs in rural villages in Central Java, Indonesia.

## RESISTING COLONIZATION THROUGH THE PHENOMENOLOGY OF PLACE

The concept of place has gained significance in the field of organization and entrepreneurship studies, as it explores how the meanings attached to various places such as offices (e.g., Alexandersson & Kalonaityte, 2018) and communities (e.g., Cnossen, 2023) impact organizational actors (Kibler et al., 2015; Welter & Baker, 2021; Wright et al., 2022). There are multiple definitions and perspectives on place, which are rooted in disciplines such as human and cultural geography, sociology, and philosophies of meaning (see, for instance, Cresswell, 2004 or Gieryn, 2000 for a short review). In this discussion, we primarily take inspiration from the work by Cartel et al. (2022) and Dacin et al. (2024) and draw on the phenomenology of place (Relph, 1976).

Relph's (1976) approach emphasizes the embodied, experiential nature of place and the importance of understanding individuals' emotional connection to it. Place is defined here as "a unique location (either geographical or digital), endowed with material form (either crafted by nature or by humans) and a socially constructed set of meanings" (Cartel et al., 2022, p. 351). Place is, therefore, not just a physical context or object but rather a complex and dynamic interplay of meanings, emotions, and experiences closely tied to that specific location (Dacin et al., 2024). This is contrary to the view that place might be a static container, an existing and stable context "out there" and independent from the individual, with an "objective" effect on organizing and entrepreneurial actions (Johns, 2006, 2017). Such a static view has been increasingly criticized as it disregards the active role of individuals in making sense of their contexts and responding toward them (Welter, 2011). In this light, simply diversifying our research contexts to decolonize hegemonic theories is insufficient; it is also crucial to comprehend how various local actors develop specific meanings within and about a particular place (Mellor, 2022). As illustrated in the opening excerpt above, what may be a significant place for one group in terms of organizing might be deemed irrelevant or even disputed by others. It is crucial that we recognize the agency of individuals and groups in relation to places rather than treating them as passive victims of their surroundings (Dacin et al., 2024).

Adopting a phenomenological perspective on place prompts us to move beyond the stability of contexts and their effects, delving into the important question of "what makes a place a place?" (Cresswell, 2004, p. 27). Drawing on Cartel et al. (2022), we present two ontologies of place for place-sensitive research. The first is place as an experience, focusing on the "subjective and emotional attachment that people develop in relation to a place" (Cartel et al., 2022, p. 354). A sense of place develops through "every aspect of individuals' life experience" and "pervades everyday life and experience" (Rose, 1995, p. 88). The second ontology is placed as a practice, understanding that place is performed and produced by everyday activities (Cresswell, 2004). Research on place as practice focuses on the physical and social actions through which people shape a place, known as "place-making." These actions range from maintaining and preserving the existing meanings of a place through rituals and traditions (Dacin et al., 2010) to creating new meanings and identities by influencing its physical features and social interactions (Kibler & Muñoz, 2020).

In reference to the opening excerpt on the Tlingits and the colonialists on the sea, experience and practice in this context are multifaceted, encompassing sensory, emotional, intellectual, and even spiritual dimensions (Gilmore & Kenny, 2015). While the colonialists may undergo similar sensory experiences when engaging in the same activities as the Tlingits in the river, the more abstract aspects of their experience, including emotional, social, and psychological elements, may diverge due to their unique identities and sociohistorical backgrounds (Mohanty, 1988). Therefore, the same place can hold distinct meanings for different individuals, leading to contested interpretations (Dacin et al., 2024).

The challenge we face as organization and entrepreneurship scholars is to explore how we can effectively capture the experiences and practices related to the places that our respondents engage with. One of the critical issues in decolonializing organization and entrepreneurship studies is whether we, as scholars, should assume an "authoritative stance" when presenting the viewpoints of the respondents in our interpretative works (Alcoff, 1992). The Global North (colonialist) perspectives have historically dominated theory and praxis, establishing analytical categories and strategies that revolve around its own understandings (Banerjee, 2022; Jammulamadaka et al., 2021; Welter et al., 2017), which has often led to viewing those in the Global South as homogeneous. However, based on our experience examining home as a place with home-based self-employed workers in Indonesia, we have come to recognize that the issue is not only about us assuming authority over the data and interpretation (Alcoff, 1992; Mohanty, 1988) but also the quest for "objectivity" by maintaining a neutral stance in research. To avoid this pitfall, we argue for conscious subjectivity when approaching place as experience and practice, whereby researchers try to be continuously aware of their own identities and personal histories (Manning, 2018). This heightened awareness can be nurtured through ongoing and dialectical discussions, conducted both individually and collaboratively among co-authors (Mauthner & Doucet, 1998) to surface any tensions and disparities in the understanding of meanings, practices, and experiences related to place in our interactions with respondents and within the research team.

## THE SITUATED MEANING OF HOME AND HOME-BASED WORK: AN EMPIRICAL ILLUSTRATION

Home-based work can be broadly understood as "economic activity by members of households who produce within their place of residence commodities for exchange in the market" (Felstead & Jewson, 1999, p. 15). The recent COVID-19 pandemic has brought renewed attention to research on home-based work, as many individuals globally were required to transition from office spaces and other designated work areas to conduct their work from their homes. Two perspectives commonly arise when discussing home-based work: one that emphasizes the challenges stemming from a "context" with blurred boundaries between work and personal life (Delanoeije et al., 2019; Tietze & Musson, 2005) and another that views it as a liberating and empowering "context", offering opportunities to have the best of both worlds (Al-Dajani & Marlow, 2010; Kwaramba et al., 2012). These discussions often touch upon topics such as productivity (Kwaramba et al., 2012; Wang et al., 2021), work-life balance (Blyton et al., 2006; Gherardi, 2015), work-family interface (Hunter et al., 2019; Kreiner et al., 2009), physical space transformations (Goodwin et al., 2023; Halford, 2005), identity (Brocklehurst, 2001; Di Domenico, 2008), and well-being (Prugl & Tinker, 1997; Standen et al., 1999). Yet, a review of home-based work literature suggested that "home" is still primarily defined in terms of its physical space and structures (Tietze et al., 2009) as the alternative to office. What defines home as a place inscribed with personal meanings (Easthope, 2004; Wise, 2000) and sets it apart from other locations where work can be conducted remains an important question, especially for both contextualizing and understanding the unique experiences of home-based workers.

Several assumptions underlie existing literature on home-based work in organization and entrepreneurship studies that can benefit from greater scrutiny. First is the notion of home as a safe and perhaps neutral place. Indeed, early place scholars have often brought about home as the ideal place, associated with positive meanings, attachment, and a sense of belonging (Easthope, 2004; Relph, 1976; Tuan, 1974). However, feminist scholars have criticized such views and argued that home could also be a place of oppression and resistance (Boeri, 2018; Prentice, 2017; Prugl & Tinker, 1997). This is particularly relevant for women who often experience power asymmetry and are subordinated within their homes and who are traditionally the sole bearers of domestic and care work (Kwaramba et al., 2012; Morgan & Winkler, 2020).

Furthermore, the neutrality of home implies a clear distinction between work and non-work, with the home traditionally reserved for non-work activities. As a result, conducting work in one's home would be perceived as a violation of this sacred place. This and other binaries that prevail in discussions around home-based work (e.g., public/private, work/life, work/family) underscore separate yet interconnected domains within the home. Together with the notion of a standardized work schedule (e.g., 9-to-5 working hours), they are rooted in the Industrial Revolution and the emergence of industrial capitalism (Hardill & Green, 2003; Tietze & Musson, 2005). However, this model disregards the diversity of existing work schedules and operations. For instance, agricultural workers' schedules are shaped by seasons, weather conditions, and daily contingencies; informal businesses often operate according to irregular supply/demand and schedule. Despite this, the traditional model of work remains the benchmark against which work activities, including home-based work, are measured.

Moreover, there is a clear distinction between paid and unpaid work in the Global North literature based on the capitalist assumption that every activity has monetary value. Care work in households holds economic value for producing future labor power for capitalism (Bakker, 2007). However, this type of work is undervalued due to the pervasive gendered division of labor at home, causing women to persist in providing such work without compensation (Dowling, 2016). In the Global North, some degree of progress has been made toward the feminist agenda of compensating certain forms of care work, exemplified by initiatives like public childcare provision. This initiative facilitates women in selling their labor to the highest bidder, enabling them to participate in paid work either at home or outside, free from interruptions (Prugl & Tinker, 1997). However, the absence of childcare privilege in the Global South positions women as victims of asymmetrical power relations at home (Boeri, 2018; Morgan & Winkler, 2020), overshadowing the structural nature of the issue. This perception arises as women continue to provide unpaid social reproductive labor (Al-Dajani & Marlow, 2010; Kwaramba et al., 2012), acting as a barrier to their realization of their full productive potential.

These taken-for-granted assumptions could become problematic when taken at face value and applied to understanding home-based work in diverse contexts and cultures. They can inadvertently perpetuate Western-centric perspectives, neglecting the nuanced experiences and meanings of "home as a place." Furthermore, they fail to acknowledge the gendered nature of home and the power structures that exist in and around home. The sociocultural influences that shape the experience and practice of home and work are also disregarded. Rather than acknowledging the diversity of experiences and practices around home, there is an assumption of homogeneity where the home is depicted as neutral.

To illustrate and unpack the complexity of home as a place, we now turn toward the exploration of the lived experiences and practices of self-employed women engaged in home-based entrepreneurial work in rural Indonesia. Rather than a comprehensive decolonizing study, our aim is to offer a glimpse of how an approach informed by phenomenology of place can be applied to the concept of home and home-based work.

### *Research Context: Home and Home-Based Work in Rural Indonesia*

The interplay of religion, ethnicity, and social class shapes the economic involvement of women in Indonesia, setting this country apart from other Islamic contexts. Indonesia, with the world's largest Muslim population, is not an Islamic state; instead, it embraces Pancasila as its ideological foundation, which celebrates religious and cultural diversity within a democratic framework (Oktaviani et al., 2021). Adding to this rich tapestry, the Islamic teachings and perspectives on gender roles are diverse (Qibtiyah, 2018). The majority of Indonesian Muslims, including the women in this study, affiliate with moderate Islam. Moderate Islam approaches gender relationships within households as equal and complementary (Rinaldo, 2019). As demonstrated by Wahyuni and Wafiroh (2013), moderate Islamic teaching views men and women as equal in the eyes of God, but their distinct biological characteristics define their roles and responsibilities. Men are seen as leaders and providers, while women follow their husbands' leadership and oversee household and childcare duties. Importantly, these distinctions are not meant to imply one gender has more power than the other. Instead, they underscore the mutual responsibility of both parties to fulfill each other's roles in times of need. Hence, in the face of financial challenges, it is considered perfectly acceptable for women to engage in economic activities to support their husbands in providing for the family.

The dynamics of women's economic engagement also exhibit intriguing variations within the intricate social hierarchy of Javanese ethnicity. Studies by Brenner (1991) and Smith-Hefner (2007) demonstrate that historically, economic activities within the household have been prevalent among Javanese noblewomen but relatively absent among their counterparts from lower social strata. The Javanese upper-class women have been traditionally admired for being submissive and dependent on men. Even when some of them engage in crafting traditional batik within the confines of their homes, the selling of batik is typically delegated to someone else who takes their products to the market. On the other hand, these studies (Brenner, 1991; Smith-Hefner, 2007) document that Javanese women from the lower social class are esteemed for their productivity and financial independence. It is furthermore crucial to acknowledge that the colonial era played a significant role in influencing the circumstances of young, unmarried Javanese girls from all social classes. They were often confined to their homes until marriage, a practice intended to protect them from potential abuse and unwanted relations with Dutch colonialists (Suhandjati & Kusuma, 2018). However, following marriage, women from the lower social class actively engage in various economic pursuits in the marketplace (Smith-Hefner, 2007), further illustrating the complex interplay of class, tradition, and historical influences on women's economic roles in this region.

Thus, it comes as no surprise that a considerable number of lower-social-class Muslim Javanese women are actively engaged in economic endeavors in both the informal and formal sectors (Suhandjati & Kusuma, 2018). Some venture to larger cities and foreign countries, taking up roles as domestic laborers (i.e., maids, babysitters, nannies, and carers for the elderly or disabled) in pursuit of higher income to support their families. Nevertheless, a discernible trend has arisen where more women opt for home-based work. This trend can be partially attributed to national labor regulations that, regrettably, offer little support for women who aspire to maintain their presence in the job market following marriage and motherhood (Schaner & Das, 2016). Furthermore, people increasingly turn to religious teachings as guiding principles in determining one's roles and responsibilities (Rinaldo, 2008). As such, women who uphold moderate Islamic teachings tend to prioritize their roles as wives and mothers above all else, including economic pursuits, in an earnest effort to align their lives with their faith (Rinaldo, 2019; Sakai, 2019; Sakai & Fauzia, 2016). Adhering to these religious teachings shields them from societal stigmatization, but it prevents them from being perceived as disrespecting their husband by taking over his provider role and for neglecting their caretaking responsibilities (Parker & Creese, 2016; Rinaldo, 2019). Hence, home-based work emerges as a pragmatic solution for many lower social-class Javanese women. Working from home allows them to outwardly uphold the existing dynamics of marital relationships while discreetly engaging in economic activities that, though not entirely conforming to societal expectations, do not pose a substantial challenge to the established order (Ginting-Carlström & Chliova, 2022).

*Method*

Our data was generated as part of two research projects that have been carried out by the authors. The first and third authors have been involved in a study of around 31 self-employed women who had formerly worked as domestic laborers, with the aim of studying narrative identity construction. The second and fourth authors have studied 34 women micro-business owners in rural Islamic communities to understand power and discourse dynamics in entrepreneurship. Hence, the first and second author, who are both Indonesians, have interviewed collectively a total of 65 self-employed women whose micro-businesses involved one or more of the following: selling cooked food (32 women), groceries (14 women), clothes (7 women) and other household goods (5 women); providing services such as tailoring and laundry (6 women); and producing food and crafts (12 women). The interviews were focused on their stories and experiences as women entrepreneurs in rural Indonesia. While the projects were separate, both projects were undertaken in neighboring villages in the same region in Central Java. The demographic profile of these villages exhibits striking similarities, with the majority of the population identifying as Muslims of Javanese ethnicity. Additionally, a significant portion of the residents falls within the lower socioeconomic class, primarily attributable to the economic challenges stemming from the declining rural economy. Other than self-employment, formal work opportunities tend to lie beyond the village boundaries, often requiring migration to larger cities or even abroad.

The word home in Bahasa Indonesia is "rumah." While in the English language, there is a different word for the building one resides in ("house") and the more personal "home," in Bahasa Indonesia, the word *rumah* is used to refer to both. The word *rumah* is also used in relation to experiences and practices beyond the physical space of one's dwelling place. Beyond the differences in terms, we observe the diverse ways that we, as researchers, can understand home as experience and practice among women home-based workers. We found certain practices and experiences profoundly familiar, while others were more bewildering or unfamiliar. We, therefore, acknowledge that our preconceptions and personal history with home and work can affect our interpretation process, which prompted the more expanded reflection in this paper.

Each of the co-authors resided outside their home country for the duration of the study, having established permanent residence in a new country with their own multicultural families. Notably, the first and second authors, both Indonesian women, spent a significant portion of their formative years outside their home country, which has led to the development of a distinct cultural identity influenced by their cross-cultural upbringing. The third author, a man, and the fourth author, a woman, are of European origin and educational backgrounds. Due to our diverse backgrounds, the concept of "home" holds a multifaceted meaning for us. For all of us, "home" is primarily tied to people rather than a physical location or structure. In the past, it revolved around our parents and siblings, and now, it is linked to our nuclear family. Nevertheless, the house and the country where our parents once lived still evoke a strong sense of home, a place we yearn to return to. Our personal attachment to home, particularly the people within it, significantly influences our perspective on working from home. Having experienced the conventional office environment with set working hours, we recognize the importance of maintaining a separation between work and home, even when working from home. We have designated a specific office space within our homes and adhere to a work schedule, albeit with the flexibility to attend to domestic and caregiving responsibilities. However, we acknowledge the challenging nature of preserving clear boundaries between work and home as the two inevitably intersect. Based on this, we continuously acknowledge our own multifaceted and fluid understanding of home and home-based work as we delve into the two ontologies of place, that of experience and that of practice.

### Experiencing a Sense of Home

To delve deeper into the multiplicity of meanings around *rumah*, we revisited our interview transcripts to explore how our research participants constructed narratives surrounding their home. Recognizing that one's sense of home is intricately woven from personal experiences within and related to the home (Easthope, 2004; Hultin et al., 2022; Relph, 1976; Tuan, 1974), we aimed to uncover what *rumah* signifies for our participants. We delved into the aspects that contribute to their sense of belonging and attachment, or conversely, their sense of detachment from *rumah*. This encompassed a closer examination of what *rumah* represents to them, as well as what it does not. We probed into the tangible (e.g., material objects, household members) and intangible elements (e.g., relationships, emotions) that collectively shape their unique interpretation of *rumah*. To accomplish this, our approach involved an initial search for sentences containing the term "rumah." Furthermore, we paid attention to the word "pulang," which means "to go or return home." This word offers a poignant insight into their perception of where or what they identify as their return destination, thus revealing the essence of their concept of "home."

Drawing on the analysis, we observed diverse and fluid meanings surrounding *rumah* in this context. While the notion is used to refer to one's house or physical dwelling, *rumah* is also widely used to refer to one's village of origin, regardless of their physical location in the present. This double meaning is especially prevalent among women who have migrated to larger cities or abroad, who consider their *rumah* to be their home village even though they have lived away for a long period of time. Interestingly, we find that the women still consider their *rumah* to be their home village even when they are living with their husbands and, for some, with their young children in a different village or bigger cities. In other words, *rumah* is intertwined with the village where they were born or raised up in rather than where their nuclear family is located, as exemplified in Vignette 1 below:

---

**Vignette 1**. 40-year-old Wati (pseudonym) had her first work experience when she was 15, right after she graduated from middle school. She went to work as a maid in Jakarta for a year before quitting and going back (*pulang*) to her village. She was at home (*rumah*) for about five months when she got married, and afterwards she continues being at home (*rumah*). When her first child was one year old, they moved together with her husband to Jakarta. Her husband worked, but his income was not enough to cover their living expenses, so Wati went around the neighborhood selling homemade Javanese salad, all while carrying her child along with her. When her child was about to enter elementary school, Wati told her husband she was going to her home village (*rumah*) to stay there while taking care of their child. Upon her return, she was wondering what she would do at home (*rumah*), as it was impossible to work at a factory with her child being so young. She then worked as a tea harvester for a tea plantation in the village, which she considered as working from home (*kerja di rumah*). When she was pregnant with her second child, Wati quit her tea harvesting job because it would be difficult to look after her newborn. Meanwhile, her parents were too old to look after the baby, and her husband still worked outside of the village. Wati then decided to open a small food stall at home (*rumah*).

---

For many of the women, *rumah* also encompasses a feeling of safety and security. Like Wati, they would mention that despite the challenges of living in a rural village, such as limited income-generating opportunities and the lack of fulfilling activities, at least they are at home (*rumah*). The women strive to maintain this sense of safety and security by seeking or creating productive activities around the house. In Wati's case, even though her work in the tea plantation is situated outside her physical dwelling place and requires significant effort to reach, she still regards it as working from home due to her perception of the village as her *rumah*. The majority of the women, however, create productive activities within the bounds of their dwelling place by establishing businesses inside their houses.

Interestingly, the view of *rumah* being invaded or violated due to the work activities carried out in and around the place did not emerge in our interactions with the participants. Instead, the women often express concern about being idle at home as they feel the need to maximize use of their time at home, as Vignette 2 below shows:

---

**Vignette 2**. Sri (pseudonym), a mother of two, lovingly cares for her preschooler and middle-schooler. While tending to her children, she has a longstanding tradition of frying tea leaves alongside her widowed grandmother. They use tea leaves from their garden and sometimes acquire additional leaves from neighbors, later selling the tea to the village cooperative. Their two houses, attached to each other, serve as the heart of this endeavor, where they prepare the tea in the grandmother's kitchen. Her widowed sister occasionally watches over the younger child. Meals are shared with her husband and elder child, showing self-sufficiency in preparing their own food when she has not cooked. In the evening, after prayers, Sri serves her family tea, signaling the end of her workday. However, she often finds herself with idle time, her children being well-behaved. This idle time troubles her, and she desires to make better use of it. Her husband suggested opening a market stall, but she hesitated due to their young child. Instead, she launched a home-based online snack business. She produces, packages, and personally delivers the snacks to customers. Sri strives to maintain a balance between her roles as a wife, parent, and worker through effective time management. She is ready to pause work whenever her child needs her, ensuring that both responsibilities are met.

The desire to "do something" was still prevalent despite the time and energy they already spent on caring responsibilities and, as in Sri's case, existing business activities. Rather than home being a place where one can relax and unwind, it is viewed as a place to be industrious and useful. With work being the solution for optimizing their time use at home, the women do not view income-generating work and care work as contradictory or mutually exclusive. The women's view toward working at home, therefore, suggests that work is not an infringement on the sanctity of the home (Methot & LePine, 2016).

### Making and Shaping a Home

One's experiences and engagement with home as a place are deeply intertwined – our sense of home informs how we enact it, and in turn, our physical and social engagement with home as a place shape the meanings we construct around it (Cartel et al., 2022). In the present section, our focus shifts from understanding the multiplicity of meanings around the notion of *rumah* to exploring how home-based women entrepreneurs in our research context create, maintain, and/or disrupt the meanings of *rumah* through mundane, everyday actions and interactions (Hultin et al., 2022). We, therefore, went back to our interview materials and focused on the narrations of their daily activities in and around *rumah*, paying attention to how they engage with and shape the physical and social aspects of their homes.

We observed several similarities across the everyday activities of the women in our context. We offer a glimpse of a typical day through Vignette 3 below, which describes the activities of Retno (pseudonym), who produces an array of traditional Indonesian cakes:

**Vignette 3.** Retno's day starts early, waking up at 4 am to prepare the dough and ingredients for traditional cakes. At dawn, Retno does the Fajr prayer, and afterward, she starts steaming the cakes and frying the spring rolls. Her oldest child would be awake by then and help Retno before going to school. The food for sale will be ready at around 6 am, they just need to be packed. Retno's younger child usually wakes up around that time and she would ask Retno to bathe and dress her. The oldest one can already do things themself, but the youngest still needs help. Retno would comb her youngest child's hair, veil her with hijab, and prepare her bag for school. Then, she packs the food to sell while waiting for school time. After dropping off her youngest at elementary school – the eldest goes by themself as they're in middle school – Retno returns home around 7 am to pick up the packed food and take it to the store. Once done, she heads back home to prepare food for the family before prepping for the next day: she cuts the vegetables for filling the spring rolls, prepares brownies – it depends on what she plans to sell. She then fries the vegetables and filling for the spring rolls at night. Still, she cannot prepare everything in advance as some ingredients are better prepared fresh in the morning than keeping it in the fridge overnight.

The above vignette exemplifies what is common across the practices, namely that there is an absence of a clear spatial divide between work and non-work areas within their *rumah*. In the case of Retno, her kitchen serves as a space for both domestic cooking for her family and for food preparation for sale. This blurring of boundaries between work and non-work areas reflects the interconnectedness of domestic and economic activities in her daily routine. This common space also allows her to transition seamlessly between different roles: from being a mother to a cook to a businesswoman. Boundaries between these roles remain porous and are enacted in a continuous flow. The involvement of children and, at times, husbands in the business operations also occurs organically, and it becomes part of the family's routine.

Another interesting finding is how religion shapes the concept of time and, consequently, influences the daily operations in and around *rumah*. This is further exemplified in the following Vignette 4 about Yuni:

---

**Vignette 4**. Yuni wakes up at three in the morning, and the first thing she does is, of course, pray. At around 3.30 am, she starts her work in the kitchen until it is time to prepare her child for school. By 8 am, she has finished bathing her child and they go to school together. While Yuni's husband leaves for work around 8.30 am, their child is at school until 10, so Yuni takes care of the house during this time: cooking, cleaning, doing the dishes, sweeping the floor – but sometimes all of this is done after her child returns from school. Around Dhuhr (midday prayer time), her husband returns home. *Alhamdulillah* [praise be to God], everything is taken care of by then, and Yuni takes care of her husband, prepares his meal, and then rests until late afternoon. Then Yuni fries the food that her husband will later sell around the neighborhood. Once the food for selling is ready, Yuni takes her child to the *mushola* [prayer hall] for Quran lessons. They do the Maghrib (after sunset) prayer at the *mushola*, and the child continues with learning to read the Quran until it is time for Isha (nighttime) prayer. Yuni then takes her child home before shopping for groceries. Later, she starts preparing the ingredients for the next day, so in the morning, she only needs to put them together and cook. Yuni and her husband are planning to enroll their child in a school that goes until late afternoon, which includes basic education and Quranic studies. Maybe then Yuni will have more time to work on her business, as her child will return home later in the day.

---

Yuni's daily routine illustrates the interplay between work, care responsibilities, and the observance of Islamic religious practices. As shown in Vignettes 2, 3, and 4, there are two ways in which the women refer to time: the normal 12-hour time and the Islamic prayer time (i.e., Fajr, Dhuhr, Maghrib, Isha), which is determined by the position of the sun. As illustrated by Yuni (Vignette 4), 12-hour time is used for formal activities outside of the house that do not directly involve them, such as time-related to the husband's work and the children's school. In contrast, they synchronize their personal activities with Islamic prayer times. The standardized "9-to-5 work schedule" therefore does not apply to these women, not simply because of juggling between work and domestic responsibilities (Hilbrecht et al., 2008), but because of aligning their daily schedules with religious obligations. This demonstrates how the local cultural and religious understanding of temporality shapes how *rumah* is enacted in everyday life.

## DISCUSSION AND REFLECTION

In this paper, we have argued that there are taken-for-granted assumptions around context that need to be further problematized to foster decolonial thinking in organization and entrepreneurship studies. This becomes particularly important as the interest in diversifying research sites and examining "underexplored" contexts in the Global South is growing (Bruton et al., 2018, 2022) and because the promise of expanding existing knowledge will not be accomplished unless we can really shed some of the dominant assumptions in our research (Banerjee, 2022; Jammulamadaka et al., 2021; Welter, 2011). To counter prevailing views of contexts as pre-existing and static, we have proposed a phenomenology of place (Relph, 1976), which values reflexive, pluralist, and intersubjective understandings of place. By regarding place as both an experience and a practice, researchers are able to delve even deeper into the complex and dynamic meanings individuals construct in and around places, as well as the myriad ways they create, maintain, and/or disrupt place in their everyday lives (Cartel et al., 2022; Dacin et al., 2024). This approach shifts the focus away from an authoritative stance (Alcoff, 1992) and toward experienced and grounded understandings of "contexts" in organization and entrepreneurship studies (James et al., 2025; Weston & Imas, 2018).

Through the empirical example of "home as a place" for home-based women entrepreneurs in rural Indonesia, we illustrate how the phenomenology of place can be used as a methodological approach for resisting colonialization. By unpacking the experiences and practices around *rumah*, we shed light on the multifaceted nature of home and home-based work and offer several insights that inform existing literature on these concepts in organization and entrepreneurship studies. Our examples illustrate that the work-family distinction, often referenced in numerous studies on home-based work (Boeri, 2018; Hunter et al., 2019; Kreiner et al., 2009; Morgan & Winkler, 2020), where work and family are portrayed as contradictory or opposing, might be irrelevant in many sociocultural contexts. We demonstrate this, particularly in relation to the dynamics of home-based entrepreneurial work (Wainwright & Kibler, 2014), a topic that remains underresearched in the field of entrepreneurship. While we could reduce "place" to mere "context" in our theorizing, we argue that these examples actually confirm prior research on the blurring of work and family in home-based work, perpetuating dichotomies such as work-life balance (Blyton et al., 2006; Gherardi, 2015) and the work-family interface (Boeri, 2018; Hunter et al., 2019; Kreiner et al., 2009; Morgan & Winkler, 2020). However, a place-sensitive approach encourages us to view home beyond its role as a mere dwelling place, instead considering it as an experience and a practice (Cartel et al., 2022).

If we are to be sensitive to the phenomenology of place, then we must question whether the typical emphasis on work versus family, even when blurred, truly captures the essence of home-based work in this particular sociocultural context. The expansion of boundaries implies that more social relationships are at play within a "home," including the often-cited marital and parent-child relationships (Gherardi, 2015; Hunter et al., 2019; Kreiner et al., 2009), but also encompassing extended family and members of the community. Home is, therefore, a place where multiple roles intersect and are performed. In our research context, these roles go beyond traditional labels such as wife, mother, or worker to include identities as active community members and devout Muslims. This expanded understanding of home-based work challenges dominant Western notions of work versus family, highlighting the importance of cultural, social, and religious contexts in shaping the experiences and practices of home-based work.

In closing, we want to share our critical reflections on the entire research journey and our efforts to bring a decolonial perspective into organization and entrepreneurship studies through a phenomenology of place. It is important to note that our intent to decolonize mainstream ideas about home and home-based work emerged *after* we had completed the data collection phase. We recognize that this sequence is far from ideal, as decolonial thinking should ideally be woven throughout the research process (Weston & Imas, 2018). This means involving local stakeholders in shaping data collection methodologies and co-creating knowledge in the interpretation phase (Manning, 2018; Mellor, 2022). Unfortunately, we were unable to do this. However, it is worth highlighting that many researchers face similar challenges. Whether it is a gradual realization of the need to decolonize our perspectives or the practical limitations, such as funding, community accessibility, or personal mobility, these challenges can sometimes hinder the full application of decolonial research methods.

In light of this, we believe that it is crucial to create space not only for research that fully embraces decolonial research design (Chrispal, 2025; Manning, 2018; Mellor, 2022; Weston & Imas, 2018) but also for research that operates within traditional research designs yet applies decolonial interpretations and frameworks. This is precisely what we have aimed to illustrate in this paper as we analyzed data generated through conventional qualitative interviews and thereafter used a combination of a place-sensitive approach and reflective, conscious subjectivity during the interpretation and theorizing phase. This approach has allowed us to perceive home-based work in new and insightful ways. We have witnessed how our understanding has evolved from our initial analysis to the present, enabling us to better contextualize our findings and develop new insights.

# REFERENCES

Alcoff, L. (1992). The problem of speaking for others. *Cultural Critique, 20*, 5–32.

Al-Dajani, H., & Marlow, S. (2010). Impact of women's home-based enterprise on family dynamics: Evidence from Jordan. *International Small Business Journal, 28*(5), 470–486.

Alexandersson, A., & Kalonaityte, V. (2018). Playing to dissent: The aesthetics and politics of playful office design. *Organization Studies, 39*(2–3), 297–317.

Bakker, I. (2007). Social reproduction and the constitution of a gendered political economy. *New Political Economy, 12*(4), 541–556.

Banerjee, S. B. (2022). Decolonizing management theory: A critical perspective. *Journal of Management Studies, 59*(4), 1074–1087.

Blyton, P., Blunsdon, B., Reed, K., & Dastmalchian, A. (Eds.). (2006). *Work-life integration: International perspectives on the balancing of multiple roles*. Palgrave Macmillan.

Boeri, N. (2018). Challenging the gendered entrepreneurial subject: Gender, development, and the informal economy in India. *Gender & Society, 32*(2), 157–179.

Brenner, S. A. (1991). Competing hierarchies: Javanese merchants and the Priyayi elite in Solo, Central Java. *Indonesia, 52*, 55–83.

Brocklehurst, M. (2001). Power, identity and new technology homework: Implications for 'New Forms' of organizing. *Organization Studies*, *22*(3), 445–466.

Bruton, G. D., Zahra, S. A., & Cai, L. (2018). Examining entrepreneurship through indigenous lenses. *Entrepreneurship Theory and Practice*, *42*(3), 351–361.

Bruton, G. D., Zahra, S. A., Van de Ven, A. H., & Hitt, M. A. (2022). Indigenous theory uses, abuses, and future. *Journal of Management Studies*, *59*(4), 1057–1073.

Cartel, M., Kibler, E., & Dacin, M. T. (2022). Unpacking "sense of place" and "place-making" in organization studies: A toolkit for place-sensitive research. *The Journal of Applied Behavioral Science*, *58*(2), 350–363.

Chrispal, S. (2025). Reducing epistemic violence in the pursuit of organization studies through reflective praxis: Some reflections. In E. Fohim (Ed.), *Decolonizing management and organization studies: Why, how, and what (Research in the Sociology of Organizations)* (pp. 105–118). Emerald Group Publishing Limited.

Cnossen, B. (2023). Tuning into things: Sensing the role of place in an emerging alternative urban community. In F.-X. de Vaujany, J. Aroles, & M. Pérezts (Eds.), *The Oxford handbook of phenomenologies and organization studies* (pp. 508–521). Oxford University Press.

Cresswell, T. (2004). *Place: A short introduction*. Blackwell Publishing.

Dacin, M. T., Munir, K., & Tracey, P. (2010). Formal dining at Cambridge Colleges: Linking ritual performance and institutional maintenance. *Academy of Management Journal*, *53*(6), 1393–1418.

Dacin, M. T., Zilber, T., Cartel, M., & Kibler, E. (2024). Navigating place: Extending perspectives on place in organization studies. *Organization Studies*, *45*(8), 1191–1212.

Delanoeije, J., Verbruggen, M., & Germeys, L. (2019). Boundary role transitions: A day-to-day approach to explain the effects of home-based telework on work-to-home conflict and home-to-work conflict. *Human Relations*, *72*(12), 1843–1868.

Di Domenico, M. (2008). 'I'm Not Just a Housewife': Gendered roles and identities in the home-based hospitality enterprise. *Gender, Work & Organization*, *15*(4), 313–332.

Dovey, K. (2016). Place as multiplicity. In R. Freestone & E. Liu (Eds.), *Place and placelessness revisited* (pp. 257–268). Routledge.

Dowling, E. (2016). Valorised but not valued? Affective remuneration, social reproduction and feminist politics beyond the crisis. *British Politics*, *11*(4), 452–468.

Easthope, H. (2004). A place called home. *Housing, Theory and Society*, *21*(3), 128–138.

Felstead, A., & Jewson, N. (1999). *In work, at home: Towards an understanding of homeworking*. Routledge.

Gherardi, S. (2015). Authoring the female entrepreneur while talking the discourse of work–family life balance. *International Small Business Journal*, *33*(6), 649–666.

Gieryn, T. F. (2000). A space for place in sociology. *Annual Review of Sociology*, *26*, 463–496.

Gilmore, S., & Kenny, K. (2015). Work-worlds colliding: Self-reflexivity, power and emotion in organizational ethnography. *Human Relations*, *68*(1), 55–78.

Ginting-Carlström, C. E., & Chliova, M. (2022). A discourse of virtue: How poor women entrepreneurs justify their activities in the context of moderate Islam. *Entrepreneurship & Regional Development*, 1–25.

Goodwin, B., Webber, N., Baker, T., & Bartos, A. E. (2023). Working from home: Negotiations of domestic functionality and aesthetics. *International Journal of Housing Policy*, *23*(1), 47–69.

Halford, S. (2005). Hybrid workspace: Re-spatialisations of work, organisation and management. *New Technology, Work and Employment*, *20*(1), 19–33.

Hardill, I., & Green, A. (2003). Remote working – Altering the spatial contours of work and home in the new economy. *New Technology, Work and Employment*, *18*(3), 212–222.

Hilbrecht, M., Shaw, S. M., Johnson, L. C., & Andrey, J. (2008). 'I'm home for the kids': Contradictory implications for work–life balance of teleworking mothers. *Gender, Work & Organization*, *15*(5), 454–476.

Hultin, L., Introna, L. D., Göransson, M. B., & Mähring, M. (2022). Precarity, hospitality, and the becoming of a subject that matters: A study of Syrian refugees in Lebanese tented settlements. *Organization Studies*, *43*(5), 669–697.

Hunter, E. M., Clark, M. A., & Carlson, D. S. (2019). Violating work-family boundaries: Reactions to interruptions at work and home. *Journal of Management*, *45*(3), 1284–1308.

James, A. E., Salamzadeh, A., & Dana, L.-P. (2025). Decolonizing entrepreneurship: Time to open both eyes. In E. Fohim (Ed.), *Decolonizing management and organization studies: Why, how, and what (Research in the Sociology of Organizations)* (pp. 65–82). Emerald Group Publishing Limited.

Jammulamadaka, N., Faria, A., Jack, G., & Ruggunan, S. (2021). Decolonising management and organisational knowledge (MOK): Praxistical theorising for potential worlds. *Organization*, *28*(5), 717–740.

Johns, G. (2006). The essential impact of context on organizational behavior. *Academy of Management Review*, *31*(2), 386–408.

Johns, G. (2017). Reflections on the 2016 Decade Award: Incorporating context in organizational research. *Academy of Management Review*, *42*(4), 577–595.

Kibler, E., Fink, M., Lang, R., & Muñoz, P. (2015). Place attachment and social legitimacy: Revisiting the sustainable entrepreneurship journey. *Journal of Business Venturing Insights*, *3*, 24–29.

Kibler, E., & Muñoz, P. (2020). What do we talk about when we talk about community? *Academy of Management Discoveries*, *6*(4), 721–725.

Kimmitt, J., Kibler, E., Schildt, H., & Oinas, P. (2024). Place in entrepreneurial storytelling: A study of cultural entrepreneurship in a deprived context. *Journal of Management Studies*, *61*(3), 1036–1073.

Kreiner, G. E., Hollensbe, E. C., & Sheep, M. L. (2009). Balancing borders and bridges: Negotiating the work-home interface via boundary work tactics. *Academy of Management Journal*, *52*(4), 704–730.

Kwaramba, H. M., Lovett, J. C., Louw, L., & Chipumuro, J. (2012). Emotional confidence levels and success of tourism development for poverty reduction: The South African Kwam eMakana home-stay project. *Tourism Management*, *33*(4), 885–894.

Manning, J. (2018). Becoming a decolonial feminist ethnographer: Addressing the complexities of positionality and representation. *Management Learning*, *49*(3), 311–326.

Mauthner, N., & Doucet, A. (1998). Reflections on a voice-centred relational method: Analysing maternal and domestic voices. In J. Ribbens & R. Edwards (Eds.), *Feminist dilemmas in qualitative research* (pp. 119–146). Sage.

Mellor, K. (2022). Developing a decolonial gaze: Articulating research/er positionality and relationship to colonial power. *Access: Critical Explorations of Equity in Higher Education*, *10*(1), 26–41.

Methot, J. R., & LePine, J. A. (2016). Too close for comfort? Investigating the nature and functioning of work and non-work role segmentation preferences. *Journal of Business and Psychology*, *31*(1), 103–123.

Mignolo, W. (2012). *Local histories/global designs: Coloniality, subaltern knowledges, and border thinking*. Princeton University Press.

Mohanty, C. T. (1988). Under Western eyes: Feminist scholarship and colonial discourses. *Feminist Review*, *30*, 61–88.

Morgan, M. S., & Winkler, R. L. (2020). The third shift? Gender and empowerment in a women's ecotourism cooperative. *Rural Sociology*, *85*(1), 137–164.

Oktaviani, F. H., McKenna, B., & Fitzsimmons, T. (2021). Trapped within ideological wars: Femininities in a Muslim society and the contest of women as leaders. *Gender, Work & Organization*, *28*(3), 1152–1176.

Parker, L., & Creese, H. (2016). The stigmatisation of widows and divorcees (janda) in Indonesian society. *Indonesia and the Malay World*, *44*(128), 1–6.

Prentice, R. (2017). Microenterprise development, industrial labour and the seductions of precarity. *Critique of Anthropology*, *37*(2), 201–222.

Prugl, E., & Tinker, I. (1997). Microentrepreneurs and homeworkers: Convergent categories. *World Development*, *25*(9), 1471–1482.

Qibtiyah, A. (2018). Mapping of Muslims' understandings on gender issues in Islam at six universities in Yogyakarta, Indonesia. Al-Jami'ah. *Journal of Islamic Studies*, *56*(2), 305–340.

Raban, J. (1999). *Passage to Juneau: A sea and its meanings*. Pantheon Books.

Relph, E. (1976). *Place and placelessness*. Pion.

Rinaldo, R. (2008). Muslim women, middle class habitus, and modernity in Indonesia. *Contemporary Islam*, *2*(1), 23–39.

Rinaldo, R. (2019). Obedience and authority among Muslim couples: Negotiating gendered religious scripts in contemporary Indonesia. *Sociology of Religion: A Quarterly Review*, *80*(3), 323–349.

Rose, G. (1995). Place and identity: A sense of place. In D. Massey & P. Jess (Eds.), *A place in the world?: Places, cultures and globalization* (pp. 87–132). Oxford University Press.

Said, E. (1993). *Culture and imperialism*. Knopf.

Sakai, M. (2019). Embracing Islam, work and family: Women's economic empowerment in Islamising Indonesia. *Intersections: Gender and Sexuality in Asia and the Pacific, 43*. http://intersections. anu.edu.au/issue43/sakai2.html

Sakai, M., & Fauzia, A. (2016). Performing Muslim womanhood: Muslim business women moderating Islamic practices in contemporary Indonesia. *Islam and Christian–Muslim Relations, 27*(3), 229–249.

Schaner, S., & Das, S. (2016). *Female labor force participation in Asia: Indonesia country study*. ADB Economics Working Paper Series. Asian Development Bank.

Smith-Hefner, N. J. (2007). Javanese women and the veil in Post-Soeharto Indonesia. *Journal of Asian Studies, 66*(2), 389–420.

Standen, P., Daniels, K., & Lamond, D. (1999). The home as a workplace: Work–family interaction and psychological well-being in telework. *Journal of Occupational Health Psychology, 4*(4), 368–381.

Suhandjati, S., & Kusuma, H. H. (2018). Reinterpretation of women's domestic roles: Saleh Darat's thought on strengthening women's roles in Indonesia. *Journal of Indonesian Islam, 12*(2), 195–218.

Tietze, S., & Musson, G. (2005). Recasting the home-work relationship: A case of mutual adjustment? *Organization Studies, 26*(9), 1331–1352.

Tietze, S., Musson, G., & Scurry, T. (2009). Homebased work: A review of research into themes, directions and implications. *Personnel Review, 38*(6), 585–604.

Tuan, Y.-F. (1974). *Topophilia: A study of environmental perceptions, attitudes, and values*. Prentice Hall.

Wahyuni, S., & Wafiroh, H. (2013). *Perempuan Di Mata NU: Bahtsul Masa'il NU Tentang Perempuan Dari Masa Ke Masa*. Gapura Publishing.

Wainwright, T., & Kibler, E. (2014). Beyond financialization: Older entrepreneurship and retirement planning. *Journal of Economic Geography, 14*(4), 849–864.

Wang, B., Liu, Y., Qian, J., & Parker, S. K. (2021). Achieving effective remote working during the COVID-19 pandemic: A work design perspective. *Applied Psychology, 70*(1), 16–59.

Welter, F. (2011). Contextualizing entrepreneurship – Conceptual challenges and ways forward. *Entrepreneurship Theory and Practice, 35*(1), 165–184.

Welter, F., & Baker, T. (2021). Moving contexts onto new roads: Clues from other disciplines. *Entrepreneurship Theory and Practice, 45*(5), 1154–1175.

Welter, F., Baker, T., Audretsch, D. B., & Gartner, W. B. (2017). Everyday entrepreneurship – A call for entrepreneurship research to embrace entrepreneurial diversity. *Entrepreneurship Theory and Practice, 41*(3), 311–321.

Welter, F., Baker, T., & Wirsching, K. (2019). Three waves and counting: The rising tide of contextualization in entrepreneurship research. *Small Business Economics, 52*(2), 319–330.

Weston, A., & Imas, J. M. (2018). *Resisting colonization in business and management studies: From postcolonialism to decolonization* (pp. 119–137). Sage.

Wise, J. M. (2000). Home: Territory and identity. *Cultural Studies, 14*(2), 295–310.

Wright, A. L., Irving, G., Zafar, A., & Reay, T. (2022). The role of space and place in organizational and institutional change: A systematic review of the literature. *Journal of Management Studies*.

Wright, A. L., Kent, D., Hällgren, M., & Rouleau, L. (2023). Theorizing as mode of engagement in and through extreme contexts research. *Organization Theory, 4*(4), 26317877231217310.

# SECTION IV

# WHAT ASPECTS OF MANAGEMENT AND ORGANIZATION STUDIES SHOULD BE DECOLONIZED?

# MĀTAURANGA MĀORI: A CASE OF INCORPORATING INDIGENOUS MĀORI KNOWLEDGE IN A BUSINESS SCHOOL MINOR

Ella Henry

*Auckland University of Technology, New Zealand*

## ABSTRACT

*This paper offers the case of Auckland University of Technology, which developed a Māori Indigenous Business Minor in the Business School as a means of introducing traditional Māori knowledge into the curriculum. We offer this as an example of a strategy that contributes to decolonizing business and management studies. This is achieved through a complementary combination of factors, including strategic academic leadership, the engagement of specialized Māori Indigenous expertise, and the development of curriculum in consultation with target communities, to ensure the program validates Māori language and culture, enhances mātauranga, and supports aspirations for social change to address intergenerational disadvantage.*

**Keywords:** Decolonization; Indigenous peoples; Māori; traditional knowledge; business school

Decolonizing Management and Organization Studies: Why, How, and What
Research in the Sociology of Organizations, Volume 93, 157–172

ISSN: 0733-558X/doi:10.1108/S0733-558X20250000093010

# INTRODUCTION

This case draws on an initiative created by Auckland University of Technology, an option for Māori Indigenous studies within the Bachelor of Business Studies. This program, comprising four undergraduate courses, entitled the Māori Indigenous Business Minor, is available to all students enrolled in any undergraduate degrees across the university and to the general public wishing to undertake Māori business studies. This program contributes to decolonizing the business school curriculum by introducing traditional Māori knowledge (mātauranga) and incorporating traditional pedagogy (akonga) to challenge the over-arching hegemony of mainstream business school content and approaches.

The literature locates the drive for indigenizing management studies within a wider call for decolonization of business schools, so poignantly defined in the Keelie Manifesto, "Decolonization involves identifying colonial systems, structures, and relationships and working to challenge those systems" (Union & Keele Student, 2018, p. 97). The Manifesto argues that colonization has led to a Western-centric knowledge perspective, neglecting Indigenous forms of knowledge.

Analysis of the contextual issues that underpin aspirations for decolonizing business schools in Aotearoa, New Zealand, must begin with an understanding of Māori, the Indigenous people. This begins with an overview of Māori society and the negative experience of colonization, which are reflected in other settler states (Cornell, 2015). Some impacts have been ameliorated in Aotearoa through the revitalization of Māori language and culture in the latter part of the 20th century (Walker, 1990). This renaissance provided the impetus for increased respect for and acknowledgment of traditional knowledge (mātauranga), introducing that knowledge into education curricula. Another contextual factor relates to the individual engaged in developing and delivering the program, a Māori Indigenous woman who has researched and taught Māori development and business for over thirty years, alongside extensive community work, for, with, and by tribes and Māori enterprise around the country.

The case study provides insights into the development of this program, exploring the factors and processes that shaped the program, its contents, and teaching style, evolving out of a broader agenda to address grievances and compensate for losses and damage done due to colonization. These factors may also be replicated by other BIPOC (Black, Indigenous, People of Color) communities engaged in strategies for social change and social justice, working in and with business schools to decolonize business and management.

## DECOLONIZING THE CURRICULUM: INCORPORATING MĀORI KNOWLEDGE INTO HIGHER EDUCATION

The Open University (2019, p. 3) in the UK devoted an entire publication to this topic, stating from the outset that,

> A curriculum provides a way of identifying the knowledge we value. It structures the ways in which we are taught to think and talk about the world... Decolonizing learning prompts us to consider everything we study from new perspectives.

On that point, Charles refers to decolonizing the curriculum as a phenomenon "of high currency in higher education in the UK. [where it] has been in currency since at least 2011. with its quest for non-Eurocentric paradigms" (Charles,
2019, p. 1). Naude discusses the ways that the Ubuntu culture offers an example
for decolonizing Western knowledge based on their traditional values and ethics. He proposes this as an attempt to frame business ethics that are drawn from
an alternative, non-Western theoretical framework. On this point, he states that
"Eurocentrism is replaced by Afro-centrism. Mbembe... explains decolonization
exactly as such a process of decentring" (Naude, 2019, p. 32).

Also coming from a distinctive, non-Western position, Jammulamadaka et al.
(2021) contribute to our understanding of ongoing efforts to decolonize what they
term Management and Organizational Knowledge (MOK). Jammulamadaka
et al. (2021, p. 719) state that,

> Decolonial thought and practice inspired by anticolonial movements... However, decolonising
> is not a term which is necessarily used by those engaged in such struggles, such as Indigenous
> Peoples, landless farmers, workers or those who may already propose, enact and embody alter-
> native and/or disruptive practices of their own.

They propose an alternative epistemology of love, respect, life, caring, and
connection as a foundation for decolonizing knowledge, histories, peoples, and
societies. They write of a decolonizing workshop in Africa, where the participants
taught the workshop organizers and each other the "most valuable lessons in the
importance of decolonial praxis and affective engagement with epistemologies of
love, hope and solidarity for decolonizing MOK beyond formal theory" (2019,
p. 728).

Another decolonization writer in business studies, Banerjee (2016), asks what
a decolonial research agenda for management and organization studies might
entail, stating it must begin with a critical analysis of the colonial dimensions
inherent in the theories that are the foundations of business studies. For Banerjee,
the focus must be on a decolonization agenda for the whole world, for those people
who are more likely to suffer the negative consequences of violence perpetuated
by governments and the market. He refers to countries in Asia and Africa that are
purportedly post-colonial because they have undergone a form of independence
but are too often ruled by democratically elected governments that perpetuate the
practices of the previous colonial rulers. On this point, Banerjee (2022a, p. 290)
writes of settler colonies in the Americas, Australia, and New Zealand, where
"Indigenous peoples who had survived genocide, forms of apartheid, and assimilation became interpellated into the modern democratic nation-state as second-
class citizens in their own land."

Continuing in this vein, Banerjee refers to Indigenous views of land as being
predicated on deep relationships with and connection to the physical environment. He notes a key feature of settler colonialism has been the transformation of
property rights and land ownership, which he refers to as "a process that involved
profound epistemic, ontological, cosmological violence" (Banerjee, 2022a,
p. 291). Not only has land and the economic foundations of Indigenous peoples
been systematically expropriated, but it has occurred alongside the diminution of

culture, language, identity, and knowledge systems. Banerjee decries the lack of awareness of these historical facts when discussing business studies and curricula and the ways that the epistemic power of the dominant culture encourages the ethnocentric view that the dominant culture is universal. She states that "Culture as a body of knowledge is also a form of discursive power because it reproduces knowledge through practices that are made possible by the structural assumptions of that knowledge" (Banerjee, 2022b, p. 1075). Thus, she notes, the theories of the "Global North" become inculcated by the "Global South," whilst the producers of those theories of, or from, dominant cultures may ignore insights and critiques that emerge as part of the postcolonial discourse.

One of few papers by Māori around decolonizing business studies comes from Love and Hall (2022, p. 202), who focus on decolonizing the marketing academy, starting from the premise that,

> the marketing discipline and its institutions has no choice but to face up to its embeddedness in social issues it is therefore important and timely to consider how marketing in colonial states – in which indigenous lands were/are appropriated, cultures systematically discriminated against, and identities, language and generations stolen – acknowledges its past and confront its future.

They call for greater incorporation of Indigenous knowledge and worldviews. They also call for universities and business schools that are sited on Indigenous lands to do more than "opening a meeting with greetings or formal introductions... they become little more than indigenous tokenism unless they are part of a wider journey of change and understanding" (Love & Hall, 2022, p. 202).

Māori scholars have also focused on decolonization as part of an ongoing process for addressing power imbalances and associated hierarchies of knowledge "that require critical self-reflection from those teaching in business schools today... As educators, if we are to take decolonizing seriously, we must create space for Indigenous Peoples to reconnect and engage with their own knowledge systems and ways of knowing" (Woods et al., 2022, p. 82). They conclude that indigenizing the academy and its classrooms converts them into sacred sites where Indigenous and non-Indigenous peoples share experiences and explore new decolonized models of learning and understanding "in a spirit of hope, love and shared community" (Woods et al., 2022, p. 85).

This newfound site of decolonization privileges Indigenous voices and knowledge, thus allowing students to "express an indigenous spirit, experience or world view that honours their experience and understanding" (Woods et al., 2022, p. 94). Thus, colonization as a process of disconnection and dislocation is transformed by the process of Indigenous decolonization to one of heart-felt connection. This brief review of the small but growing field of interest in decolonizing business and management studies from an Indigenous perspective has thrown up issues that inform the analysis of the case study presented below. We know that colonization, as a process, emerged out of the imperial agendas of the Global North over hundreds of years. Many of the peoples that have been colonized are leading the move for decolonization as a part of the redress for past injustices and to restore their traditional cultures, values, and knowledge systems. Universities have an important role to play in decolonization as arbiters and instruments of knowledge production. One such case, from AUT, offers an insight into the rationale and process underpinning the introduction of Māori content into the mainstream business curriculum. However, the case study is prefaced with a discussion of the historical context.

## HISTORY FROM AN INDIGENOUS PERSPECTIVE: MĀORI CULTURE AND SOCIETY

Māori discovered Aotearoa, as part of the Austronesian Diaspora (Chambers & Edinur, 2015; Soares et al., 2011) who traversed and populated the South Pacific for thousands of years. We begin by recognizing that "Polynesian peoples of the Pacific Ocean" is itself a colonial construct. However, for the purposes of brevity, these terms are applied to the analysis of the culture and history of the Māori people.

Archaeological and linguistic evidence points to seafaring voyagers originating from Taiwan some 4,000 years ago who first ventured into the South Pacific approximately three thousand years ago. The Austronesian language group is found from Taiwan, throughout Southeast Asia, into the Pacific, and as far afield as Madagascar in the Indian Ocean (Soares et al., 2011). This suggests these people were curious, risk-taking, and entrepreneurial, who saw the ocean and its horizon as a challenge to be met rather than a harbinger of doom.

The earliest arrivals to Fiji are estimated at 3,000 years ago, and to Aotearoa around 1,000 years ago. These hardy voyagers crossed the most expansive ocean on the planet, using knowledge of astronomy, winds, weather, and the migratory patterns of birds and sea life to navigate. This knowledge was passed on through oral traditions, without recourse to written texts or mathematical equations, aboard sturdy outrigger canoes (Irwin & Flay, 2015). Alongside a common language, Lapita pottery, named after the village in New Caledonia, can be found throughout Melanesia, Samoa, Fiji, and Tonga (McNiven et al., 2011). These Lapita patterns are remarkably similar to those that continue to be seen across all Māori art forms.

The exact date of arrival by Māori to Aotearoa is unknown and not relevant to this case. Tribal groups were often named for the waka-canoe upon which they arrived, and these continue to underpin the whakapapa/genealogy that links contemporary Māori to tribal homelands, eponymous ancestors, and voyaging waka. Though Māori brought with them an existing language and culture, over the centuries, both these were adapted to the new environment (Wilson, 2013).

Traditional society was founded on a political economy, which Mauss (1990) describes as one of gift exchange and reciprocity. More recent work from Henare (2022) has given us greater insight into that economy. Henare (2001) found that the ancient Māori cosmology determined economic and social relations, identifying cultural concepts that bound traditional society together through shared values and ethics, handed down from generation to generation, as a moral and social code. At the heart of the belief system is the critical importance of kinship and community, solidarity, spirituality, and genealogical connection to the metaphysical, as well as the responsibilities of stewardship for all that is precious. These ancestral linkages to the gods, from whom humanity originated, and the intrinsic sacredness of all things animate and inanimate, are at the core of this belief system. Thus, if all things are sacred and all things are connected, then one's relationship with them must be underpinned by obligations of respect and care (Henare, 2001).

Kaupapa Māori is a term used by Māori to describe these values and beliefs (that which is *tika*, or true) and the associated social practices and protocols (*tikanga*) that maintain social cohesion. For example, the importance of collective identity is exemplified by *whanaungatanga*, which means kinship, and is practiced as a set of tikanga protocols to enhance relationships. The recitation of genealogy, or whakapapa, articulates connection to human ancestors, but also the lands, mountains, rivers, and sea to which one is related through ancestral ties (Henare, 2001).

The interdependence between and among all living things is expressed as *kōtahitanga*, which means solidarity and which is manifest in *tikanga* to enhance unity and solidarity. This can be seen in the protocols around welcome (*pōwhiri*), farewell (*poroporoaki*), and death (*tangi*) because solidarity with and connection to ancestors transcends death. This intimate relationship with the spiritual realm is reflected in *wairuatanga*, spirituality, and spiritual practice. This is expressed in a wide range of *tikanga*, including *karakia* (prayer or communion) and acknowledgment of *wāhi tapu* (spiritually significant and sacred places). These and other similar values (*tika*) and protocols (*tikanga*), shaped Māori beliefs and behavior in traditional society and continue to resonate in contemporary society (Henare, 2001).

From this cosmology originates the political economy, which Henare describes as an "economy of affection." Within this economy, one affects and is affected by all things corporeal and spiritual. These "affects" determine one's sense of place, identity, ownership and kinship bonds. The "economy of affection" is in opposition to the "economy of exploitation" that informs contemporary Western capitalist society, which was introduced as part of the colonial process (Henare, 2022).

However, much of traditional society and knowledge was systematically unraveled when the country was formally annexed by the British on February 6th, 1840. A gathering of Chiefs signed Te Tiriti o Waitangi with William Hobson, representing the British Crown (Walker, 1990). The Treaty came about after seventy years of mutually beneficial interaction and trade with Europeans since the arrival of Captain Cook in 1769. It also followed the signing of Te Wakaputanga (Declaration of Independence), which declared the country a sovereign nation in 1835. This document clearly enunciated the sovereignty of the Māori Chiefs as a confederation, who together ruled the nation-state of Nu Tirani, the name given to the islands after a visit by Abel Tasman in 1640. The declaration and the Māori flag were recognized by the British Parliament in 1836, thereby ensuring Māori vessels would receive protection from the Royal Navy when trading in international waters (Henry, 2012).

Since Cook's arrival, trade had become increasingly important to Māori. Petrie (2013) noted significant trade to Australia and farther afield from the 1820s, carried by Māori-owned ships, delivering goods manufactured in Aotearoa. This trade spawned a rise in the migration of European traders, seafarers, and early settlers, whose behavior in the coastal towns of the north sparked concerns from local chiefs (Orange, 2015). Thus, in 1840, a delegation arrived from Britain seeking a treaty with the natives (Henry, 2012).

Different versions of the Treaty traveled the country. However, there were significant differences between the English and te reo versions. In te reo, the first clause gives kawanatanga (the right to govern their lands) to the British Queen. The second clause ensures the Queen will protect the chiefs in the exercise of their chieftainship and all the things Māori consider tāonga, or precious; in return, Māori give the Crown rights of pre-emption over land sales. The third clause confers the rights of British citizenship on all Māori. The English version varied significantly. This ceded absolute sovereignty, as opposed to the right to govern, to the British Crown (Orange, 2015). These different versions of the Treaty have caused enormous conflict between Māori and, first, the British and then settler governments (after the New Zealand Constitution Act of 1852 came into being, giving parliamentary rights to the settler government). The conflict resulted in open warfare from the 1850s, which in turn resulted in large tracts of Māori land being confiscated by the Crown for the ever-insatiable needs of new settlers (Belich, 2002).

Between 1840 and 1900, Māori went from being chiefs of their own lands, owning 60 million acres to less than 6 million, and that was reduced to less than 3 million by the middle of the 20th century. Alongside this loss of land, a raft of legislation was enacted that destroyed Māori sovereignty, decimated the Māori economy, and reduced Māori people to poverty and alienation in their own country (King, 2003). This tragic tale of colonization has been replicated in other settler countries. However, the Māori have maintained a population and level of political participation that has ensured some protection from the worst excesses of colonial rule. By the 1960s, a significant proportion of Māori relocated to cities as part of an urban drift toward work in the Post-War industrial boom. Alongside this urban drift, a growing number of younger folk exploited opportunities for higher education. They were exposed to the truth of a history that had been anonymized by the notion of racial harmony perpetuated in the myths of the colonizer, emerging out of sanitized histories from the late 19th century. Thus, was borne a generation of activism, culminating in what is now referred to as the Māori Renaissance since the 1970s (Walker, 1990). Protests and political lobbying in that decade saw the creation of the Waitangi Tribunal, "a commission of inquiry to make recommendations on claims brought by Māori relating to Crown actions which breach the promises made in the Treaty of Waitangi" (Waitangi Tribunal, n.d.).

For the first ten years of its existence, the Waitangi Tribunal could only look at contemporary grievances, but the 1984 Labor Government extended that authority, giving the Tribunal "retrospective power to investigate claims from the date of the signing of the Treaty of Waitangi in 1840" (Derby, 2012). However, the Tribunal can only make non-binding recommendations, so the government is not required to accept these judgments. Since 1985, more than 2000 claims have been lodged, citing grievances including invasion, massacre, deception, expropriation, and inaction on the part of the Crown, resulting in the loss of land, life, and cultural well-being for the tribes (Durie, 1998). The Office of Treaty Settlements, which sits under the Ministry of Justice, is charged with negotiating the settlement of these claims. Whilst some of the larger claims incorporate many tribes and thousands of acres of land (Kawharu, 1998; Orange, 2015), there are still over a thousand claims to be heard in the 2020s.

These Treaty settlements have resulted in the growth of tribal wealth, with the Māori economy estimated to be worth around $70 billion in 2022. It has been recognized that tribal investment strategies differ in many ways from traditional Western models and more frequently mirror traditional Māori values of shared, inter-generation wealth, kinship, and connection (Henry & Poyser, 2022). This economic change has occurred besides the ongoing revitalization of the Māori language and culture. Whilst te reo was expected to die out (Benton, 1989) and was actively legislated against (Ka'ai-Mahuta, 2011), the birth of Māori-language nests (kōhanga reo) in the 1980s has seen the language come from the brink of extinction (King, 2001), to an increasingly valuable cultural artifact for more than just Māori New Zealanders (O'Toole, 2020). The resurgence of economic and political strength and the growing uptake of te reo Māori by the wider population has seen an increased focus on a better understanding of Māori people, culture, and history in education, with proposed curriculum changes, to teach "an authentic history of Aotearoa New Zealand" (Jones, 2022). This has flowed on to tertiary education, with growing calls from Māori scholars to ensure mātauranga is being offered across a range of courses and programmes (Jones et al., 2020; Ruru & Nikora, 2021; Stewart, 2022).

Thus, Kaupapa Māori, embracing traditional beliefs whilst incorporating contemporary resistance strategies that embody the drive for "*tino rangatiratanga*," self-determination and empowerment for Māori people, as opposed to the subjugation wrought by the colonial experience, has been growing in interest since the late 20th century. Since then, there has been a proliferation of educational programs founded on mātauranga Māori, ancient and contemporary Māori knowledge. This is happening alongside growing calls around the world for decolonization of education in general and business education in particular.

## ETHNOGRAPHY: A PERSONAL HISTORY

Hammersley (2017) refers to ethnography as a naturalistic study that captures social meaning and involves the researcher as a participant. Thus, I write as an active participant in the development of this case, with a distinct history and connection to the Kaupapa Māori agenda. I began my academic career later than usual. In 1986, a Māori woman, who had left school aged 15 and enrolled at 31, a single parent, the first in her family to attend university, hailing from tribes in the rural north, but brought to the city as a child in 1960, by parents hoping to escape grinding poverty, only to be caught in the struggling working class of the Māori urban drift.

I knew very little of the acrimonious and traumatic history of my people and my country when I first entered university, having been raised on the myth of racial harmony in this country (Mikaere, 2004). The history of the worst excesses of colonization was not something I was taught. As I have learned the truth of our colonial past over the last forty years, I moved from rage to recognition that changing the system from the inside is as important as rallying against it from the outside.

Over the last 35 years, I have devoted my career to researching and teaching Māori history and culture, particularly within the business school. For my MPhil thesis, I focused on Māori women and leadership. At that time, I was employed by the University of Auckland to investigate a potential course in Māori business. In 1991, this was unheard of, but for six months, I canvassed widely, calling on a wide range of Māori leaders in community and business. My recommendations were to create a separate program rather than adding one course to the existing BCom electives. When I presented the findings to the faculty, the response was underwhelming until the visionary Dean of Commerce, Professor Alistair McCormack, declared his absolute support for the idea. Thus, in 1993, the Postgraduate Diploma in Business (Māori Development) was offered. I taught on the Diploma while completing my Master's (Henry, 1995) until leaving that university in 2001, but I remain immensely proud of its success and longevity. It was the first of its kind in Aotearoa and continues to be offered and held in high regard (Ratana, 2023).

However, by 2001, I felt the need to be more immersed in Māori education, so I took the position of Head of the School of Māori Education at UNITEC for two years until returning to my homelands, taking up a role as negotiator for the Treaty Claim taken by my tribe. The call of the city remained strong, as it provided better educational opportunities for my young family, and I returned to Auckland to take on a role as a television presenter for a show on the newly minted Māori Television Service in 2004, set up as a Treaty partnership between Māori and Government, part of settlement for the Māori Broadcasting Claim (Henry, 2012; Smith, 2016). This continued for three years, cementing my interest in Māori screen production. When the show was canceled in 2007, I returned to academia, to the Faculty of Māori Development, where I completed a PhD in 2012, focusing on Māori entrepreneurship in screen production (Henry, 2012).

Along the way, I have been actively involved in research and work with tribal and business groups, acting as chief negotiator for the Treaty Claim (WAI116) on behalf of my tribe, finally concluding that role when we settled a claim lodged in 1987, finally culminating in 2017. Throughout my academic career, my research and publications have encompassed a wide range of topics related to Māori development, including leadership, management, governance, entrepreneurship, careers, culture and society, gender and politics, and Kaupapa Māori Research, a research paradigm founded on Māori culture, values and aspirations (Henry & Foley, 2018). Alongside my research and teaching, I remain actively involved in Māori development, I have been instrumental in setting up a community organization in Māori media and screen production (Henry & Wikaire, 2013). It is this overarching commitment and passion that drives my work, incorporating traditional knowledge into contemporary learning and applying that philosophy as a strategy for the decolonization of the business school at AUT.

## DECOLONIZING THE CURRICULUM: THE MĀORI INDIGENOUS BUSINESS MINOR

Four Māori Indigenous Business courses are offered as an elective Minor at AUT, the newest university in the country, opening in 2000. It was initially Auckland Technical School, formed in 1895, then became Auckland Technical College in 1906. It is in close proximity to the University of Auckland. These two institutions have served the city of Auckland for over one hundred years. Writing in 2013, Wilson compared AUT and UOA, stating,

> AUT, the country's newest university and right over the road from UOA, is a pretty interesting place. While Auckland [university] works on its elite model and tries to reduce its student numbers, AUT… is the fastest-growing university in the country.

AUT is also known as Te Wānanga Aronui o Tāmaki Makaurau.[1] The bestowing of Māori-language identities to New Zealand enterprises is recognized and increasingly common. According to Stock (2021), "adopting a te reo name could send a message to the community that an organisation had a willingness to serve the whole community" but he warns that it also it "had to be accompanied with action. Organisations had to ask themselves what they were going to do to better ground themselves in Aotearoa and represent the whole community." Thus, all of the universities and polytechnics in the country have a Māori language name alongside their English-language one. These naming conventions attest to a social climate where te reo, once banned from use in educational environments, is now more commonly used, not only as a language of delivery but as a meaningful way to identify organizations and their aspirations. The Higher Education Times states that, "AUT creates graduates who are world ready, not just career ready…. AUT is proudly and uniquely Kiwi with a firmly global perspective" (THE, 2023). Furthermore, the core values of AUT are expressed as aroha, pono, tika, which are glossed as integrity, respect, and compassion, "at the heart of everything we do" (AUT website).

The AUT Business Faculty incorporates the schools of business, economics, and law. It is within in this setting that the Māori Indigenous Business courses began being developed. This began with the appointment of a new role, the Director of Māori Advancement, through secondment of a senior Māori scholar from the Faculty of Māori Indigenous Development in 2019. I accepted the offer of secondment, open to coming back into a business school.

Early in 2020, before the world was struck by the global pandemic, the AUT Business School employed the highest number of Māori scholars in business, and I was excited to join them. These scholars, 10 in number, were located across the faculty in management, marketing, entrepreneurship, finance, and law. They were complemented by research and teaching assistants and two professional staff. Taken together, we comprised a cohort of 15. Therefore, as the newly appointed Director of Māori Advancement, I moved into an existing community of Māori scholars, who were only infrequently brought together as Māori. This was the first such role in the Business School, though other Faculties at AUT have Māori scholars in equally senior roles. It was assumed that new innovations around support for Māori staff and students and curricula development would flow from my appointment.

In 2020, I developed a Māori advancement strategy, adopted by the faculty despite the impacts of COVID-19, which cut a swathe through New Zealand, with devastating and life-threatening impacts for many. However, the country was amongst the first to take a hard line on shutting down and closing borders as a means of protecting the population. The exclusion of international students has proven to have a devastating impact on all New Zealand universities, which has resulted in painful financial recovery strategies. For AUT, it has meant laying off hundreds of staff (Hendry-Tennant, 2022), which has caused deep distress for many across the institution. It slowed the development of Māori advancement strategies, though others have managed to reach fruition:

- Piki Ake Kaipakihi Māori: The Māori Advancement Strategy, adopted by the Faculty in early 2020, which includes the Tuakana (big sister) – Teina (little sister) peer tutoring program for Māori students across BEL, based on Māori protocols of mentoring and support;
- The Māori Caucus, a committee of all Māori staff, academic and professional, in the Faculty, who meet regularly to plan activities and receive support;
- Creation of a website to promote and celebrate the achievements of Māori in the faculty (www.pakm.aut.ac.nz)
- Development of curriculum focusing on Māori knowledge, which eventuated in the Māori Indigenous Business Minor.

The Māori "Minor," a suite of courses available as electives, was developed with the approval of the Faculty Executive and through collaboration with the Māori Caucus to ensure the subjects would be founded on Māori knowledge and values and taught by Māori academics. The process began in 2020, but formal accreditation was not completed until late 2022. The Minor comprises the following courses and academic staff and includes their tribal affiliation:

- FINA504: Introductory Financial Management for Māori Business, taught by Professor Aaron Gilbert (Tainui), HOD Finance;
- MGMT604: Māori Indigenous Management & Marketing, to be taught by Dr Nimbus Staniland (Ngāti Awa, Ngāi Tūhoe) from Management (who left late in 2023), and Dr Megan Phillips (Ngāti Hape) from Marketing (who went on maternity leave in 2024;
- ENTR601: Māori Indigenous Entrepreneurship & Social Innovation, taught by Ella Henry;
- BUSS730: A Māori Indigenous Business Project, in which students would undertake individual research and/or practical projects relevant to their area of business interest. I coordinate the course, and, where appropriate, organize supervisors from amongst the other Māori scholars in the Faculty.

The courses are delivered in wānanga, day-long workshops that immerse the students in a cooperative learning environment. In the Māori world, a wānanga fosters networking, collaboration (whanaungatanga), and group decision-making, thereby reflecting a Māori pedagogy. The courses are taught on weekends so that the wānanga do not interfere with the students' existing lecture schedule. It also facilitates the enrollment of students who are not currently engaged in an AUT course of study. Consultation with the Māori business community found that this program would be attractive to those currently working in or with Māori organizations and who wanted to deepen their understanding of the field.

Whilst these plans are laudable, there has been no budget set aside for marketing the program externally, so enrollments to date have relied on internal communications to existing students. The first cohort of students joined the program in March 2023, the beginning of Semester One. The course being taught was Māori Indigenous Entrepreneurship & Social Innovation. The plans to offer the Introductory Financial Management for Māori Business course were postponed because of a lack of enrollments. In all fourteen students enrolled. Of those, only seven were Māori, and all but one of the others were from a range of BIPoC (Black, Indigenous, People of Color) ethnic groups. During introductions, it was found that the non-Māori had enrolled in this course out of interest and because they wanted to study something that was not necessarily Western or Eurocentric. There was one non-Māori New Zealander of European descent (known as Pākehā in Aotearoa) who enrolled out of interest in the topic. The course progressed well, and 80% of students passed, with three dropping out for a variety of reasons, including work commitments and health issues. In Semester 1, 2024, the entrepreneurship course attracted 17 students, again only half being Māori students. The Management and Finance papers have smaller enrollments of those who completed the entrepreneurship course in 2023 and want to finish their Minor to complete their degrees in 2024.

Overall, these are disappointing results for the Minor, and there will need to be an extensive review, perhaps amendments to the courses and the content, as well as availability of teaching staff. Whilst this adds additional pressure, the Māori indigenous Business Minor continues to be extolled as an example of the commitment of the Business School to Māori knowledge and business, particularly for international accreditations, such as EQUIS.

Time will tell if the reduced staffing, and lack of a concerted marketing strategy, will continue to impact the program and its ultimate sustainability. There will need to be in-depth reflection and planning, and a bringing together of resources, human and intellectual, from senior executives in the Faculty to Māori academic staff delivering these courses, as critical components to support and build the program moving forward. What has started out with great bravura is encountering issues that will impact its future sustainability, including adequate Māori staffing, commitment to marketing, and decreasing numbers of domestic students enrolling in universities around the country (Gerritsen, 2024).

## CONCLUSION

According to Banerjee (2020), decolonizing the business school and its curricula is more than merely ticking a few boxes to show respect for diversity; it must involve what he calls concrete actions, and he offers the following strategies:

- Including theory and case studies that amplify the voices that have been left out of business and management teaching and research;
- Changing hiring and promotion practices to address the underrepresentation of BIPoC;
- Supporting and engaging with communities of BIPoC who are already doing decolonizing work in or with business schools.

Drawing on the above criteria, based on this case study, we can attest that the Māori Indigenous Business Minor offered by Auckland University of Technology is a genuine effort to include a Māori voice in business studies and the teaching of management subjects and research. Furthermore, it has involved bringing into the Faculty a Māori scholar who has published extensively in the fields of Māori and Indigenous business, management, and decolonization. This appointment is at a senior level, with a broad brief to support the Faculty, to better reflect the values of AUT values, tika, pono, and aroha, as well as to advise on and deliver curricula that are more meaningful for, by, and with Māori. This has involved engaging with the Māori community, inside and outside the university, in the development of the Minor. This was to be the first step in a process that would see the courses become a stand-alone Certificate in Māori Business. Adding a dissertation or extended research project could see the creation of a Diploma in Māori Business, both of which could be offered to non-traditional university students, e.g., Māori leaders, elders, or those involved in community development, with no previous tertiary studies. Those plans must be put on hold as the future sustainability of the Minor is assessed within a broader context. After the elections in 2023, a new right-wing government is fostering a political environment that is not so supportive of Māori language or programmes (Craymer, 2023).

Other challenges include the AUT Financial Recovery Plan, initiated in 2022, resulting in more than one hundred job losses in 2023. This was a traumatic process for many, no doubt leading to stress and demotivation. In turn, this may have been the reason why a number of Māori resigned from the Business School in 2023, with numbers halving in that year. Furthermore, the lack of a cohesive marketing strategy and associated resources may be the reason that enrollments were lower than expected. Taken together, these issues can be overcome with continued support and resources from the senior executive team in the Business School. It is hoped by all involved with the Office of Māori Advancement in the Business School at Auckland University of Technology that the steps toward developing more Māori knowledge curriculum, programs, and research will continue to make a significant contribution to decolonizing the school and the university.

The key lessons taken from this case are that if:

- There is a commitment to decolonization from senior management in the university;
- Indigenous scholars are recruited and adequately supported to develop and deliver decolonized curricula;
- There is a critical mass of Indigenous scholars across the faculty to facilitate the delivery of decolonized curricula;
- There is an appetite for learning about, incorporating, and acknowledging Indigenous history, culture, and knowledge in the wider society.
- There is a political environment that supports Māori initiatives.

Then, decolonization of the curriculum and the faculty delivering such curriculum might flourish.

In the context of Aotearoa, New Zealand, that means that greater awareness of traditional and contemporary Indigenous knowledge, mātauranga Māori, will continue to be incorporated into the mainstream business curriculum, thereby contributing to the further decolonization of the business school and its curricula. However, in Aotearoa, the wider political context has changed significantly since late 2023, with the election of a coalition government, which has, in its first few months, enacted policies that some have argued are anti-Māori (Watson, 2023). These include dissolving the Māori Health Authority, rolling back the use of the Māori language, and ending the country's limit on tobacco sales (despite high Māori lung cancer rates). Thus, positive affirmations from universities may not be enough to countervail an aggressively anti-Māori government. Only time will tell if these positive changes, for the greater incorporation of Māori knowledge and greater respect for Māori ways of knowing, being, and doing business and management, will continue to flourish.

# NOTE

1. Te Wānanga Aronui, literally means university of higher learning, Tāmaki Makaurau is the traditional Māori name for Auckland

# REFERENCES

AUT website. (n.d.). *Our values: working at AUT*. https://www.aut.ac.nz/about/careers-at-aut/working-at-aut/what-its-like-to-work-at-aut/our-values-working-at-aut

Banerjee, B. (2020, July 13). Beyond name changes and pulling down statues – how to decolonise business schools. *The Conversation*. https://theconversation.com/beyond-name-changes-and-pulling-down-statues-how-to-decolonise-business-schools-142394

Banerjee, M. (2016). Decolonization and subaltern sovereignty: India and the Tokyo trial. In *War crimes trials in the wake of decolonization and cold war in Asia, 1945-1956: Justice in Time of Turmoil* (pp. 69–91).

Banerjee, S. (2022a). Decolonizing deliberative democracy: Perspectives from below. *Journal of Business Ethics*, *181*(2), 283–299.

Banerjee, S. (2022b). Decolonizing management theory: A critical perspective. *Journal of Management Studies*, *59*(4), 1074–1087.

Belich, J. (2002). *Making peoples: A history of the New Zealanders from Polynesian settlement to the end of the nineteenth century*. University of Hawaii Press.

Benton, N. (1989). Education, language decline and language revitalisation: The case of Maori in New Zealand. *Language and Education*, *3*(2), 65–82.

Chambers, G. K., & Edinur, H. A. (2015). The Austronesian diaspora: A synthetic total evidence model. *Global Journal of Anthropology Research*, *2*(2), 53–65.

Charles, E. (2019). Decolonizing the curriculum. *Insights*, *32*(24), 1–7. https://doi.org/10.1629/uksg.475

Cornell, S. (2015). Processes of native nationhood: The indigenous politics of self-government. *The International Indigenous Policy Journal*, *6*(4).

Craymer, L. (2023, December 11). New Zealand's swing right on Maori issues reveals new fault lines. *Reuters*. https://www.reuters.com/world/asia-pacific/new-zealands-swing-right-maori-issues-reveals-new-fault-lines-2023-12-10/

Derby, M. (2012). Te Rōpū Whakamana i te Tiriti o Waitangi. Te Ara Encyclopedia New Zealand. https://teara.govt.nz/en/waitangi-tribunal-te-ropu-whakamana/print#:~:text=The%20 1984%20Labour%20government%20significantly, Tiriti%20o%20Waitangi%20in%201840

Durie, M. H. (1998). *Te Mana, Te Kāwanatanga: the politics of self determination*. Oxford University Press.

Gerritsen, J. (2024, February 12). Universities positive about enrolments after tough financial year. *RNZ News.* https://www.rnz.co.nz/news/national/508922/universities-positive-about-enrolments-after-tough-financial-year

Hammersley, M. (2017). Research ethics. *Research Methods and Methodologies in Education,* 57–67.

Henare, M. (2001). Tapu, mana, mauri, hau, wairua: A Maori philosophy of vitalism and cosmos. In C. Spiller & R. Wolfgramm (Eds.), *Indigenous traditions and ecology: The interbeing of cosmology and community* (pp. 197–221). Information Age Publishing.

Henare, M. (2022). *He Whenua Rangatira: a mana Māori history of the early-mid nineteenth century.* University of Auckland Research in Anthropology and Linguistics electronic series (RALe).

Hendry-Tennant, I. (2022, September 5). Auckland University of Technology laying off hundreds of staff due to lack of students. *Newshub online.* https://www.newshub.co.nz/home/new-zealand/2022/09/auckland-university-of-technology-laying-off-hundreds-of-staff-due-to-lack-of-students.html

Henry, E. (1995). Rangatira Wahine: Maori women and management. [Unpublished MPhil thesis, University of Auckland].

Henry, E. (2012). *Te Wairua Auaha: emancipatory Māori entrepreneurship in screen production* [Doctoral dissertation, Auckland University of Technology].

Henry, E., & Foley, D. (2018). Indigenous research: Ontologies, axiologies, epistemologies and methodologies. In R. Bendl, L. Booysen, & J. Pringle (Eds.), *Handbook of research methods on diversity management, equality and inclusion at work* (pp. 212–227). Edward Elgar.

Henry, E., & Poyser, A. (2022). Indigenous history, culture and values as investment philosophy: Lessons from the New Zealand Māori. *Journal of Sustainable Finance & Investment,* 1–13.

Henry, E., & Wikaire, M. (2013). *The Brown Book: Protocols for working with Māori in the screen industry.* Ngā Aho Whakaari. https://www.nzfilm.co.nz/resources/brown-book

Irwin, G., & Flay, R. G. (2015). Pacific colonisation and canoe performance: Experiments in the science of sailing. *The Journal of the Polynesian Society, 124*(4), 419–443.

Jammulamadaka, N., Faria, A., Jack, G., & Ruggunan, S. (2021). Decolonising management and organisational knowledge (MOK): Praxistical theorising for potential worlds. *Organization, 28*(5), 717–740.

Jones, D., Hikuroa, D., Gregory, E., & Ihaka-McLeod, H. (2020). Weaving mātauranga into environmental decision-making. *New Zealand Science Review, 76*(1–2), 49–54.

Jones, K. (2022, October 7). *New curriculum aims for authentic history of Aotearoa New Zealand.* Stuff online. https://www.stuff.co.nz/national/education/130075111/new-curriculum-aims-for-authentic-history-of-aotearoa-new-zealand

Ka'ai-Mahuta, R. (2011). The impact of colonisation on te reo Māori: A critical review of the State education system. *Te Kaharoa, 4*(1).

Kawharu, M. (1998). *Dimensions of kaitiakitanga: an investigation of a customary Maori principle of resource management* [Doctoral dissertation, University of Oxford].

King, J. (2001). Te Kohanga Reo: Maori Language Revitalization. In *The green book of language revitalization in practice* (pp. 119–131). Brill.

King, M. (2003). *The penguin history of New Zealand.* Penguin Random House New Zealand Limited.

Love, T. R., & Hall, C. M. (2022). Decolonising the marketing academy: An indigenous Māori perspective on engagement, methodologies and practices. *Australasian Marketing Journal, 30*(3), 202–208.

Mauss, M. (1990) *The exchange of gifts.* (Translated by W.D. Halls, with Fore- word by Mary Douglas.) Routledge.

McNiven, I. J., David, B., Richards, T., Aplin, K., Asmussen, B., Mialanes, J., & Ulm, S. (2011). New direction in human colonisation of the Pacific: Lapita settlement of south coast New Guinea. *Australian Archaeology, 72*(1), 1–6.

Mikaere, A. (2004). Are we all New Zealanders now? A Māori response to the Pakeha quest for indigeneity. *Red and Green, 4,* 33–45.

Naude, P. (2019). Decolonising knowledge: Can Ubuntu ethics save us from coloniality? *Journal of Business Ethics, 159*(1), 23–37.

O'Toole, M. (2020). Responsibility, language movement, and social transformation: The shifting value of te reo for non-Māori in Aotearoa New Zealand. In L. Siragusa & J. Ferguson (Eds.), *Responsibility and language practices in place* (Vol. 5, pp. 195–212). Studja Fennica Anthropologica.

Open University. (2019). *"The Innovating Pedagogy 2019 Exploring new forms of teaching, learning and assessment, to guide educators and policy makers,"* Open University Report. https://iet.open. ac.uk/file/innovating-pedagogy-2019.pdf

Orange, C. (2015). *The treaty of Waitangi.* Bridget Williams Books.

Petrie, H. (2013). *Chiefs of industry: Maori tribal enterprise in early colonial New Zealand.* Auckland University Press.

Ratana, L. (2023, June 28). The course fostering a new generation of Māori leaders. *The Spinoff.* https://thespinoff.co.nz/partner/28-06-2023/the-course-fostering-a-new-generation-of-maori-business-leaders?itm_source=spinoff-homepage-layouts&itm_medium=card-1

Ruru, J., & Nikora, L. W. (2021). *Ngā Kete Mātauranga. Māori scholars at the research interface.* Otago University Press.

Smith, J. (2016). *Maori Television: The first ten years.* Auckland University Press.

Soares, P., Rito, T., Trejaut, J., Mormina, M., Hill, C., Tinkler-Hundal, E., & Richards, M. B. (2011). Ancient voyaging and Polynesian origins. *The American Journal of Human Genetics, 88*(2), 239–247.

Stewart, G. T. (2022). Mātauranga Māori: A philosophy from Aotearoa. *Journal of the Royal Society of New Zealand, 52*(1), 18–24.

Stock, R. (2021, September 15). Government and business leaders explain their organisations' te reo Māori names. *Stuff news online.* https://www.stuff.co.nz/business/126337832/government-and-business-leaders-explain-their-organisations-te-reo-mori-names

THE. (2023). Auckland University of Technology. *Time Higher Education website.* https://www. timeshighereducation.com/world-university-rankings/auckland-university-technology

Union, Keele Student. (2018). Why is my curriculum so white? *Journal of Global Faultlines, 5*(1–2), 100–101. https://www.keele.ac.uk/equalitydiversity/equalityframeworksandactivities/equality-awardsandreports/equalityawards/raccequalitycharter/keeledecolonisingthecurriculumnetwork/

Waitangi Tribunal. (n.d.). Tribunal website. https://www.waitangitribunal.govt.nz/

Walker, R. (1990). *Ka whawhai tonu mātou: Struggle without end.* Penguin Books.

Watson, A. (2023, December 17). Weeks-old government dubded 'anti-Māori' as culture wars rage in New Zealand. *CNN World News.* https://edition.cnn.com/2023/12/17/world/new-zealand-nationals-luxon-maori-intl-hnk/index.html#:~:text=Under%20Luxon%2C%20the%20government%20is,of%20smoking%20among%20their%20people

Wilson, S. (2013). The Best Universities in New Zealand: What to Know Before You Choose. *Metro Magazine* online. https://www.metromag.co.nz/society/society-schools/the-best-universities-in-new-zealand-what-to-know-before-you-choose

Woods, C., Dell, K., & Carroll, B. (2022). Decolonizing the business school: Reconstructing the entrepreneurship classroom through Indigenizing pedagogy and learning. *Academy of Management Learning & Education, 21*(1), 82–100.

# DECOLONIZING THROUGH VIRTUAL EXCHANGES? REFLECTIONS ON AN EDUCATIONAL EXPERIMENT BETWEEN BOTSWANA AND SWITZERLAND

Michael Asiedu[a], Dorothy Mpabanga[b], Claus D. Jacobs[c] and Mogopodi Lekorwe[b]

[a]University of St.Gallen, Switzerland
[b]University of Botswana, Botswana
[c]University of Bern, Switzerland

## ABSTRACT

*In response to calls to decolonize universities in general, decolonizing individual programs, curricula, and courses is a small but important piece to the jigsaw. Intercultural exchange – in person or virtual – contributes to this at the level of students' experience and interactions for that matter. Increased digitalization around the globe has made digitally enabled virtual exchange (VE) courses affordable. Acknowledging that technology and digitalization in general and VE courses are no panacea to colonialism overall, such joint projects contribute incrementally and over time to bridging the gap between student populations and faculty. We reflect on one such VE course on Public*

Decolonizing Management and Organization Studies: Why, How, and What
Research in the Sociology of Organizations, Volume 93, 173–189
ISSN: 0733-558X/doi:10.1108/S0733-558X20250000093011

*Administration Reforms between the Universities of Bern (UniBe) and Botswana (UB). We reveal actionable insights through an Ubuntu analytical lens and offer critical reflections that revolve around the design, content, and structure of this VE course.*

**Keywords:** Decolonizing; management studies; organizational studies; public administration; virtual exchange course

## INTRODUCTION

Evidenced by the syllabus of any **MBA** or **MPA** program in the Global North and South alike, the conventionalized management curriculum has failed to account for, let alone to include, voices of previously (and currently) colonized people. This is even more disturbing as a significant number of multinational organizations draw on these people in terms of racialized precarious, low-pay, low-skill work (Barthold, 2020). The knowledge for conventionalized management teaching is mainly authored in and authorized by international publishers based in the United States and Europe.

As an emancipatory program, decolonization aims at identifying vestiges of colonial histories embedded in socio-political circles as well as at challenging and orchestrating corresponding reforms (Nayar, 2010; Young, 2016). In terms of management education, decolonizing should center on a pedagogy of multiplicity in terms of a plurality of perspectives, worldviews, ontologies, epistemologies, and methodologies (Allen, 2023; Banerjee, 2022; Banerjee & Berrier-Lucas, 2022; Bhambra et al., 2018, p. 2; Everett, 2023).

Within the broad endeavor to decolonize universities in general, decolonizing individual programs, curricula, and courses is a small but important piece to the jigsaw. Intercultural exchange – in person or virtual – contributes to this at the level of students' experience and interactions for that matter. In view of the increasing digitalization around the globe, digitally enabled VE courses have become affordable. Acknowledging that technology and digitalization in general and VE courses are no panacea to colonialism overall, such joint projects contribute incrementally and over time to bridging the gap between student populations and faculty.

In this paper, we critically reflect on a VE course between UniBe and Botswana UB to explore whether and how such courses can play their role in decolonizing management studies. Importantly, we ground our critical reflection deliberately in Ubuntu philosophy, an integral, emancipatory, non-Western paradigm to broaden and enhance the hermeneutic apparatus of our field. While we did not mobilize Ubuntu principles in the design and delivery of this course, they served us very well in critically reflecting on the structure, process, and practices of the course and, moreover, to better understand whether and how such a VE might contribute to the decolonization of management education.

# DECOLONIZING MANAGEMENT EDUCATION

*Decolonization: Perspectives, Practices, and Domains*

Definitions, aims, and strategies of decolonization abound (e.g., Bhambra, 2014), whereby two important perspectives can be distinguished. Whereas a formal perspective focuses primarily on legal and governmental independence and sovereignty, a more encompassing view refers to the reversal of all European imperial expansive ramifications (Mignolo, 2007; Quijano, 2000). In terms of the former, decolonization is referred to as a process where legally dependent territories gained their constitutional independence and joined the international relations state of play as sovereign states. Thus, countries proudly hoisted their own flags, created national anthems, and joined the United Nations as full-fledged members (Collins, 2016). As this formal conceptualization restricts itself to political and constitutional dimensions, it avoids decolonization's transformative process through economic, social, and cultural repercussions in former colonies (Bhambra, 2014). In terms of the latter, decolonization encompasses the reversal of European imperial expansion with all political, economic, social, cultural, and linguistic ramifications (Von Bismarck, 2012).

While approving of the principle that a formerly colonized territory can be ridden off every remnant of its colonial past, rarely is there a clean slate (Bhambra, 2014; Collins, 2016). But then it becomes important to view decolonizing in terms of objects (what gets decolonized?) and subjects (who gets decolonized?) (Wenzel, 2017). While the former question demonstrates the unfinishedness of decolonization, the latter question refers to the political aspirations of a people to be free and run their own affairs. However, decolonization is – be it confronting elements of colonialism in society, calling for overhauling of entire systems such as penal codes, the language of instruction, requesting the return of cultural artifacts – a complex spectrum ranging from calls for entire overhaul of systems to calls for incremental transformation of systems (Eckhardt et al., 2022; Ehrmann, 2022).

Practices of decolonization have been examined in three broad domains, namely international (governmental & non-governmental) organizations, social movements, and academia (Mallard et al., 2021). In international governmental & non-governmental organizations, professionals of global health, humanitarian aid, and development have actively been reconsidering their work practices between practitioners from the Global North and those from the Global South (Kickbusch et al., 2021). Secondly, social movements (including "Black Lives Matter," "Why is my curriculum so white?," or "Rhodes Must Fall") have all questioned the social practices impregnated by the legacy of colonialism in Western societies where colonial artifacts are still visible and operating as manifest for instance in street names, statues, or museum artifacts (Bhambra et al., 2018; Chowdhury, 2021).

Thirdly, academia has also begun to scrutinize its colonial roots and sediments, which are still at play to this day. It has witnessed scholars calling within many disciplines to reflect on their teaching philosophy, research methodology, and epistemology (Kessi et al., 2021; Mbembe, 2016; Mintz, 2021; Yousfi, 2021). In a similar vein, scholars have begun confronting and addressing the colonial origins of their fields

(Conrad, 2016; Joo & Kim, 2017; Le Grange et al., 2020; Stanek, 2019). As Mbembe (2016) concludes so compellingly in this regard, no professional, school administrator, scholar, or student can afford to disentangle from decolonizing.

## Decolonizing Academia

Yet, the decolonization of academia has been subject to a lively debate. While some scholars argue it is a matter of historical narrative, epistemological (De Sousa, 2015; Matasci, 2022; Lazem et al., 2022; Connell, 2018) exclusion, language, and social equity, other scholars view it as concerning border-thinking, counter-story telling, and territory reclaiming (Kester, 2019; Mackinlay & Barney, 2014; Zavala, 2016).

The parallel evolution and institutionalization of the contemporary university weaponized epistemologies in shaping a narrative of Western civilizational and racial superiority that induced a marginalization, if not near erasure, of non-Western traditions and world views – often referred to as "epistemicide" (Mignolo, 2017; Santos, 2014). Over time, this development resulted in a dependence by non-Western countries on neo-colonialism as well as in a dominance of Western educational approaches, practices, and institutions (Esteban, 2020).

Overall, the fundamental critique of Westo-centric education has been that it has been perpetuating hegemony and reinforcing a Eurocentric worldview, thereby not just defining and determining epistemologies but, moreover, also economic, political, and social spheres (Escobar, 1995; Said, 1983, 1993). Westo-centric, enlightenment-informed epistemological traditions restrict, at least, scholarly efforts to interrogate and comprehend the phenomena and experiences of non-Western peoples in their own right and in their own epistemologies (Adefila et al., 2022; Fougère & Moulettes 2007).

Decolonizing education, therefore, demands the conscious, critical recognition of a historically specific set of colonial power relations ingrained in our academic institutions, relations, and processes today (Mignolo, 2007; Picower, 2009). Faul (2021) identifies five closely related arenas in this regard, namely teaching, research, institutions, estates, and reparations. Institutions, estates, and reparations have already seen notable attempts, such as Harvard University's appointment of its first black president, Claudine Gay. Equally, faculty composition becomes increasingly diversified to reflect present realities, and scholarships and grants are being made accessible to people who would have traditionally been left out (Faul, 2021). Importantly, decolonization should not be confused with the integration or inclusion of epistemic accomplishments of non-white, non-Western cultures. Enhancing academia to advance social justice, embrace critical methodologies, or implement more student-centered pedagogies are adjacent but distinct political projects to decolonization (Arshad et al., 2021; Shahjahan et al., 2022).

Countering Westo-centric hegemony and epistemic dominance, a decolonized academia allows for a multiplicity and plurality of perspectives, worldviews, ontologies, epistemologies, and methodologies (Bhambra et al., 2018, p. 2; Kothiyal et al., 2018).

## Decolonizing Management Education

Within the broad program of decolonizing academia, decolonizing the field of management education is a tall order in its own right. Pivotal educational institutions (including universities and faculty), teaching, and learning approaches have become objects of decolonization (Grosfoguel, 2011; Mbembe, 2015, 2016; Nyamnjoh, 2021). With academics from the Global South paving the way, universities around the globe have experienced a wide array of decolonizing approaches (Jammulammadaka et al., 2021; Mbembe, 2016; Mignolo & Walsh, 2018) aiming at disentangling colonialism in its structural, racial, and epistemic manifestations (Santos, 2014).

As a discipline, management (including public management) has not been an exception to such normalization (Dadze-Arthur, 2022). Hence, the onus is on Western business and government schools to contribute to the broader aim of decolonizing (Jack et al., 2011; Prasad, 2012; Seremani & Clegg, 2016). For instance, colonial bureaucracy and public administration focused not only on managerial efficiency but also on a calculated repression of colonial subjects (Akinwale & Jude, 2014; Berda, 2022).

Countering the dominant discourse, Prasad (2012, 2003) and Jammulammadaka et al. (2021) have actively introduced postcolonial perspectives on management. Specifically, they refer to decolonizing as a radical praxis of "(un) doing academia" that transforms individuals and the ways to comprehend, study, and practice management studies (Jammalumadaka et al., 2021).

Thus, decolonizing academia necessitates substantive changes. More often than not, sustainable change starts small and on the periphery of an institution. In the case of universities, one niche to experiment with decolonial learning consists of student exchange initiatives.

## *Decolonizing Through VE Courses?*

Decolonizing course practice is a humble, practical niche for experimenting with novel learning formats (Morreira et al., 2021). Student exchange programs are very effective in sensitizing students to different cultures, worldviews, and ethics (Thomas, 2005). However, such exchange programs are often very expensive and not affordable for a significant majority of global students. Thus, the concept and practice of VE courses have gained traction in universities (O'Dowd, 2021).

Emergent research on VE education demonstrates its potential contribution to the decolonization project (Aatkar, 2020). These courses are suggested to invite and enable intercultural dialogue by facilitating meaningful interactions between students from diverse cultural backgrounds that challenge stereotypes and foster mutual understanding and respect. Moreover, they provide an empowering discursive arena for marginalized communities to share their perspectives and experiences (Abuzaid, 2019). Also, they allow for challenging dominant narratives and contribute to the construction of more inclusive educational spaces. VE rely on equitable learning environments where all participants feel valued and respected, regardless of their cultural background or socio-economic status. Overall, these VE courses enhance intercultural competence and improve students' ability to navigate diverse cultural contexts. (Aatkar, 2020; Abuzaid, 2019).

Importantly, VE initiatives must be mindful of technological barriers, cultural differences and unequal access to resources, but moreover, of colonial legacies and epistemic injustices that may shape relationships between participating universities. As structural inequalities influence VE partnerships, an ethos of mutual respect, reciprocity, and knowledge sharing is advised (Adam, 2021; Robinson et al., 2015).

In light of the above, this paper seeks to critically reflect on how VE might contribute to decolonizing management education.

## OUR REFLECTIVE LENS: THE UBUNTU PARADIGM

At the heart of decolonizing education is the creation of a physical and intellectual space in which everyone feels safe, valued, and respected and is, therefore, able to learn effectively (Bhambra et al., 2018). Specifically, a decolonizing learning environment allows for dialogue, awareness of colonial power dynamics and legacy, as well as for a pluralism of voices and perspectives. A compelling concept and exemplar of such a pedagogy of multiplicity consist of a decolonizing curriculum based on and informed by the integral ethical paradigm of Ubuntu.

Ubuntu, a cosmology deeply rooted in African philosophy, embodies interconnectedness, community, and mutual support (Taylor, 2014). Derived from various African languages, it signifies "humanity towards others" or "I am because we are." In a synoptic review of different philosophical strands, Hailey (2008) highlights Ubuntu as a moral framework, emphasizing the significance of relationships and communal harmony in African societies. On the same note, Konadu-Osei et al. (2023) delve into the historical and cultural significance of Ubuntu, tracing its origins to indigenous African societies and its integration into various aspects of life, including governance, conflict resolution, and societal organization.

This integration reflects Ubuntu's role as a guiding principle for fostering cohesion and collective well-being. Discussing how Ubuntu might inform global management, Lutz (2009) investigates Ubuntu's philosophical dimensions, highlighting its contrast with individualistic Western ideologies. Ubuntu emphasizes the interconnectedness of humanity and the importance of shared humanity, promoting a holistic worldview that prioritizes collective welfare over individual interests.

In summary, Ubuntu represents much more than a mere philosophical concept; it embodies a way of life, a social cosmology of sorts characterized by compassion, communal solidarity, and respect for others (Taylor, 2014). Its principles offer valuable insights into fostering harmonious relationships, promoting social cohesion, and addressing collective challenges in diverse cultural contexts. While Naude (2019) points to the risk of an overly simplistic transfer and application of Ubuntu to other contexts and rather calls for acknowledging its complexities and limitations, he also recognizes its potential as a framework for promoting social justice, reconciliation, and ethical conduct.

Specifically concerned with discussing the usefulness of Ubuntu in the context of decolonizing education, Dennis et al. (2018) emphasize its potential for informing, if not reshaping, pedagogical approaches. She foregrounds the importance of relationships and mutual dependence among people as well as to their environment; the pertinence of a communal ethic, wherein the well-being of the community takes precedence over individual interests; the importance of empathy and compassion toward others as well as the respect for diversity in perspectives, experiences, and identities within the community.

By incorporating Ubuntu values into pedagogical interventions, educators can create learning environments that nurture empathy, foster collaboration, and empower learners to become active participants in building a more just and equitable society. Very usefully, Dennis et al. (2018, 200pp.) integrate these overarching norms and values into four didactical principles as follows.

## Relational Accountability

This principle underscores the interconnectedness of all elements within the curriculum, acknowledging their accountability to both human and non-human entities. It goes beyond human-centric perspectives to recognize the importance of ecological, cultural, and spiritual dimensions. For instance, a science curriculum might integrate indigenous ecological knowledge alongside conventional scientific concepts, acknowledging the interconnectedness between humans and the natural world.

## Respectful Representation

In line with decolonizing education, this principle emphasizes the importance of creating inclusive spaces within the curriculum where the voices, perspectives, and knowledges of indigenous peoples are respected and valued. It involves incorporating indigenous narratives, histories, and ways of knowing into the curriculum, challenging Eurocentric biases and stereotypes, and promoting cultural authenticity and dignity.

## Reciprocal Appropriation

This principle acknowledges that knowledge production is not a one-way process but rather a reciprocal exchange between universities and communities. It recognizes that communities contribute valuable insights, experiences, and expertise to the educational process and should, therefore, benefit from the outcomes of knowledge production. This might involve collaborative research projects, community-engaged learning initiatives, or knowledge-sharing platforms that facilitate mutual learning and empowerment.

## Rights and Regulation

This principle advocates for ethical frameworks that recognize the rights of indigenous communities over their knowledge systems and cultural heritage. It emphasizes the importance of respecting intellectual property rights, traditional knowledge systems, and cultural protocols. Educational institutions should adopt policies and practices that ensure indigenous communities have ownership, control, and decision-making power over how their knowledge is used, disseminated, and preserved.

By integrating these principles into educational practices, institutions and faculty can move toward more inclusive, equitable, and socially just approaches to teaching and learning. This not only enriches the educational experience for all learners but also contributes to the revitalization and empowerment of Indigenous communities and knowledge systems. As an integral, emancipatory paradigm, we draw on Ubuntu as our analytical lens and conceptual framework to critically reflect on our educational experiment in the next section and, moreover, whether and how a VE seminar might contribute to management education.

## THE EXPERIMENT: VE COURSE

In this section, we briefly outline the VE course thereby focusing mainly on design, content, and struture of the course. The course, a 7-week VE, Masters-level course called "Public Sector Management, Reforms, and Innovation – Comparing the Botswana and Swiss Contexts" (see Fig. 1) was held in the Fall semester 2023 designed for eight students and four members of faculty from both UniBe and UB.

### Designing the VE

Based on initial personal contacts between two academics from UniBe and UB, the idea of a collaborative exchange emerged and was subsequenetly formalized in a *memorandum of understanding (MoU)* in 2022. Aligned with the mission and strategy of both universities, the MoU included joint activities in terms of

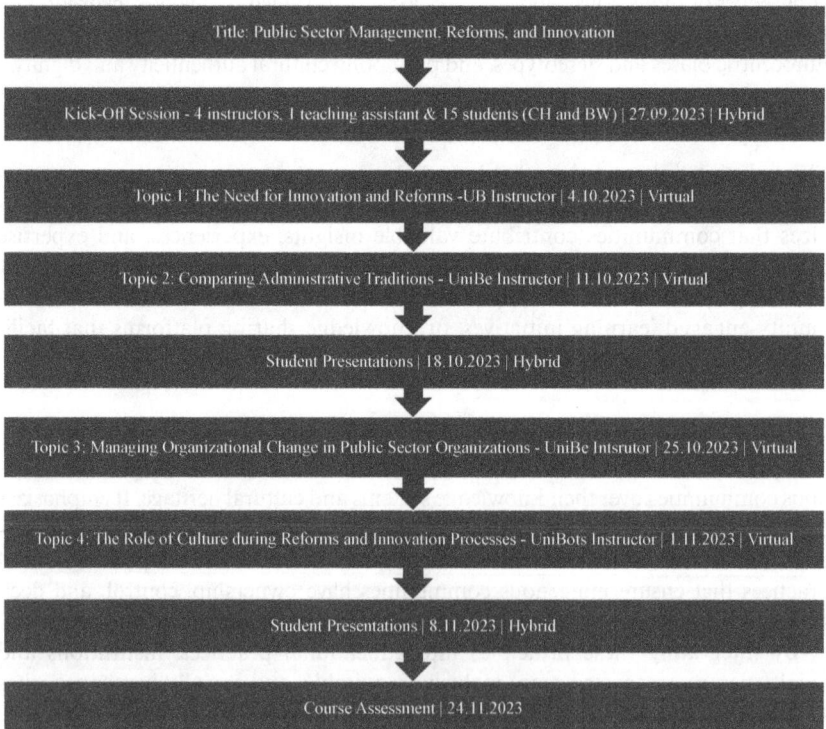

Title: Public Sector Management, Reforms, and Innovation

Kick-Off Session - 4 instructors, 1 teaching assistant & 15 students (CH and BW) | 27.09.2023 | Hybrid

Topic 1: The Need for Innovation and Reforms -UB Instructor | 4.10.2023 | Virtual

Topic 2: Comparing Administrative Traditions - UniBe Instructor | 11.10.2023 | Virtual

Student Presentations | 18.10.2023 | Hybrid

Topic 3: Managing Organizational Change in Public Sector Organizations - UniBe Intsrutor | 25.10.2023 | Virtual

Topic 4: The Role of Culture during Reforms and Innovation Processes - UniBots Instructor | 1.11.2023 | Virtual

Student Presentations | 8.11.2023 | Hybrid

Course Assessment | 24.11.2023

*Fig. 1.* Outline of the VE Course.

research, teaching and staff/student exchanges. Legal offices in both universities ensured all due diligence and all necessary *formal requirements* were met.

As semester calendars between the two universities are not synchronized, we pragmatically settled to consider the VE as a dedicated course for each university. While the teaching period in UniBe's Fall 2023 semester ran from September 18, 2023 to December 22, 2023 (formal end January 31, 2024; UB's Semester Two (2) teaching ran from July 31, 2023 to November 10, 2023 with the exam period ending on November 24, 2023. Given these constraints, we pragmatically focused on the overlap of 8 weeks in both university calendars.

In terms of the *design and delivery* of the course, we agreed on equality in the number of faculty members on the design committee as well as in the number of participating students. For virtual student breakout groups to co-create and co-own their own spaces, we also ensured parity from both universities. Furthermore, four sessions consisted in lectures, delivered by two members of each faculty.

The physicality-virtuality aspects of space and place were also of concern in our planning. Overall, a virtual, i.e., video-conferencing technology-enabled endeavor using virtual whiteboards (Fig. 2), we deliberately held three hybrid sessions at each university in which students and instructors were in the same lecture room. As shown in Fig. 3, the paradoxical experience of space in terms of being (partially) physically together while being (partially) distanced created a shared sense of commonality and difference at the same time.

### Delivering and Experiencing the Course: Content and Process of Learning

As both Master's programs are dedicated to public administration and management in their specific countries, *reforming and innovating in the public sector* were deemed pertinent challenges in both contexts and, moreover, very amenable for comparison.

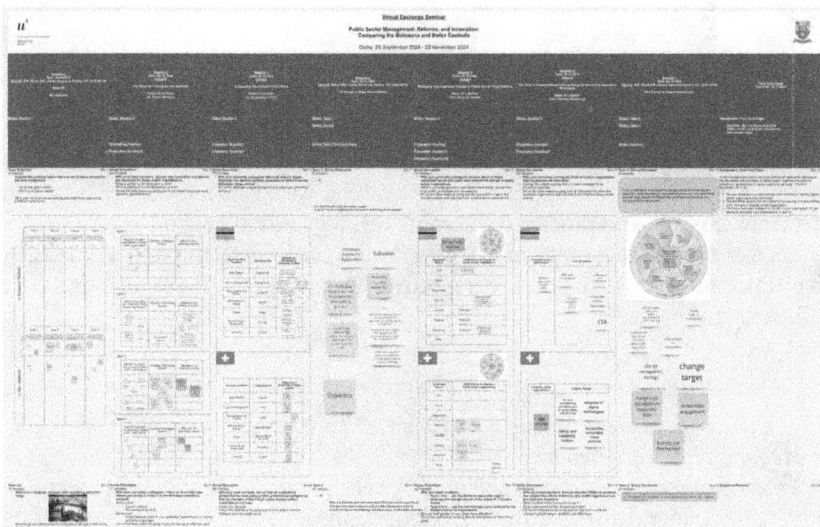

*Fig. 2.* Screenshot of Fully Accessible Virtual White Board.

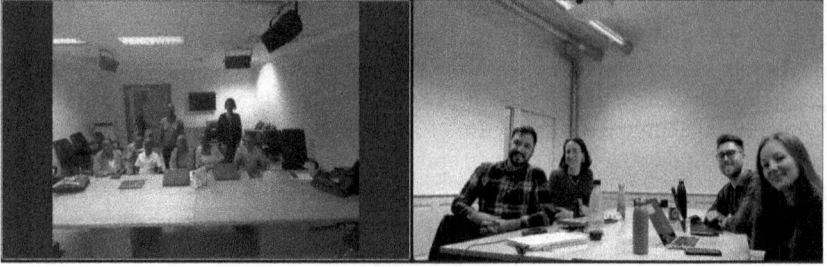

*Fig. 3.*    Screenshot from Hybrid Sessions.

Within the broad topic of reforms and innovation, we assigned four specific topic areas (see Fig. 1) and alternated in their delivery: "need for reform and innovation" as well as "the role of culture in reform and innovation" (UB) "comparison of administrative traditions" as well as "change in public sector organizations" (UniBe).

In terms of the learning process, the course drew on lectures, group work, and presentations, as well as plenary discussions. We thereby offered equal airtime and respectful listening as guiding principles of our virtual interactions. Also, we aimed to make sure that different perspectives and voices were invited and heard. By welcoming a multiplicity of voices, we aimed to avoid a one-sided, authoritative voice or perspective as to how public administration is to be learned. Moreover, we recognized our own implicitness within the structures of conventionalized public management studies and, therefore, invited authentic, comparative narratives by students and instructors alike of public administration knowledge in the two countries.

Whether and how our design and delivery of this VE course might have allowed for decolonizing moments in the learning process is subject to our critical reflection in the following section.

# CRITICAL REFLECTION

Undoubtedly and as evidenced by the evaluation form, students have appreciated this learning experience. However, student satisfaction is not the main concern of this paper. Rather and in a reflexive gesture, we wish to critically reflect on structure, content and process of learning through a decolonizing lens.

As to structure these reflections, we draw on the aforementioned four normative trajectories of an Ubuntu perspective (Dennis et al., 2018) and frame the following questions:

## *Relational Accountability*

*To What Extent Had the Course Been Connected in a Co-Relation of Accountability to Humans and Non-Humans?*

In terms of relational accountability and given the topical orientation of the course, non-human, natural aspects had been backgrounded. For instance, deliberate efforts were made to formalize the partnership between the two universities; the embodiment of this is found in an MoU between the two universities. Essentially grounded interconnectedness is both for the implementation of this VE course and other future endeavors. Again, although not explicitly stated, the idea of creating public value was preeminent in regard to the United Nations (UN) Sustainable Development Goal (SDG) 4 and the African Union (AU) Agenda 2063, which aims to push the frontiers of quality education and make it accessible to all.

However, the fundamental, if not foundational, premise of the course was the *relevance of equality and the importance of relationships*. Meeting each other on equal footing was at the center of the ethos with which the design committee planned the course.

Issues of social cohesion, equal student participation, discussion of course content, addressing challenges in course delivery and cultural diversity, as well as country-specific/contextual issues, were given utmost relevance in fashioning a common footing. Yet, there were limitations and blind spots in the relational realm, especially in the incorporation of indigenous knowledge. Again, implicit cultural assumptions that had not been problematized (e.g., how do you address a professor in the plenary).

However, technological constraints may crop up (e.g., the differences in internet connectivity, data bandwidths, etc.). were duly acknowledged and accommodated; for instance, UB had onsite IT assistance throughout the virtual sessions for scenarios such as connectivity issues, technicalities pertaining to logins/logons, etc.

## Respectful Representation

*To What Extent Has the Course Created Space for Different Voices and Knowledge?*
In terms of respectful representation, the core materials of the course drew very much on Western concepts (e.g., reform, innovation, change, culture). In this regard, the representation was very much informed by Westo-centric concepts and frameworks. However, we deliberately designed for and invited different voices and knowledges as we probed into comparing the institutional and cultural specifics of each country, for instance, on histories behind State-Owned Enterprises.

Thus, country-specific, comparative case studies were explored, discussed, and then presented in the plenary in cross-country student teams – within which the different voices and perspectives were expressed. This was achieved by creating inclusive spaces where all students from both universities were given an opportunity to participate in class, voice their ideas and opinions, and share their knowledge through group discussions and presentations.

## Reciprocal Appropriation

*To What Extent Have the Benefits of Knowledge Been Shared by Both the Universities and Communities?*
Appropriation in the strict sense had not been at play in this context. However, there was a lot of complementarity in terms of both communities benefiting from the exchange of knowledge and expertise through knowledge-sharing platforms

like MiroBoard (see Fig. 2), WhatsApp, and Zoom, a sort of technological bridge building. Yet the reciprocity dimension raises the crucial question of whether the knowledge used, applied, and gained in this course would be used outside and beyond the immediate context of the university.

### Rights and Regulation

*To What Extent Has the Course Recognized Ownership of Knowledge from Non-Western Origins?*

As per the above, the course concepts and reading operated mainly, if not exclusively, on Westo-centric materials. However, the key to recognizing alternative knowledge and their equal relevance to learning was introduced via the constant comparison between the Swiss and the Botswanan context. Ethical frameworks that recognized the rights of lecturers and students were observed during the module planning, delivery, and post-course evaluation phases.

For example, course delivery and assessment protocols were discussed, both countries' cultural issues were discussed and addressed, and lecturers and students were given an opportunity to prepare for the introduction and induction sessions so that they learn about each other's culture and country-specific contextual factors/issues. Again, operational details such as issues of time management in the two countries, how to address each other during sessions, what to discuss on social media platforms like WhatsApp, and what to post on the Miro Board were ironed out during the preparation phase. These were mainly aimed at setting up and establishing a code of conduct for lecturers and students as well as between the two universities.

This short reflection on the course in light of the ideas and ideals of an Ubuntu curriculum demonstrates how far the course was in the design and delivery of such a Ubuntu perspective. Despite the positives, in relation to the course content, this should have been the time when we could have, as course designers, challenged and explored why Western ideologies are not that effective in transforming the management of organizations in developing countries and explored when/where indigenous management principles have worked in Botswana, Switzerland or in other African or developing country contexts.

Oftentimes, we make progress not by providing answers but by raising and entertaining challenging questions. In this case, the design and delivery of the course are not an answer to colonization, but our ubuntu-based reflection raises important questions for us and other designers of learning how to advance in decolonizing learning through these incremental yet reflexive learning and reflection processes that we will make advances in decolonizing learning.

## DISCUSSION

In this brief essay, we set out to offer the case of a jointly designed and delivered VE course of two Master-level public management and administration programs in Botswana and Switzerland as a foil to critically reflect on its potential and limitations to decolonize management learning. Of course, it would be injudicious to oversell the merits of a VE course in its contribution to decolonizing MOS. However, it would equally be a mistake to overlook its potential, for instance, in creating episte-mological third spaces where conversations between the West and "non-West" and their ways of knowing could be nurtured (Seremani & Bazana, 2025).

As the decolonization project aims at contesting entrenched epistemological imbalances, it is crucial to offer psychologically and culturally "safe spaces" in which difficult conversations can take place. In that sense, this VE course is, for participants and faculty alike, a starting point in tackling such epistemic imbalances. It forms part of a gradual yet ever-evolving decolonizing set of activities. Acknowledging that there is no neutral space (e.g., the bandwidth in the north is higher), the physi-cal and relational aspects of virtuality (e.g., participants' images are all the same size) allow for contouring a third space. Virtual, in essence, ushers participants into a third dimension where, having circumvented attendant technological challenges, they meet together in one place as a whole/unit, although physically miles apart.

Exchanges – virtual or not – invite you to reconsider long-held, taken-for-granted assumptions. Comparisons in content or semester calendars are, therefore, very form-ative for designers and participants alike. The structure and content of the course allowed faculty from across the geopolitical divide to not only design a course but also to find synergies on what is relevant for both parties, on approaches, style, methods of assessment, joint student endeavors, etc. For many of the students, too, it was the first of such exchanges to be in a space where experiences across geographical divides could not only be shared but also learned, with their pres-ence not only seen but felt and varying experiences treated as valid.

Given the almost commoditized ubiquity of virtual technologies and acknowl-edging the remaining colonial challenges, we should engage more in such VE as the benefits seem to outweigh the risks or disadvantages. This is not to relegate in-person exchanges to the background. They matter and are weightier in terms of lived expo-sure and contextualization regarding cultural and structural developments. Such in-person exchanges would allow faculty and students alike an experience of Botswana and Switzerland that no however sophisticated technology can offer. When you con-sider all the logistics involved, it's almost impossible to pursue decolonizing endeav-ors all the time through traditional means such as in-person approaches.

When we imagine the grand task of decolonizing, scholars should not seek to exclusively uncover unadulterated precolonial perspectives of the Global South and the various ways theories and approaches in MOS could have been deliv-ered had there been no colonialism (Seremani & Clegg, 2016). Instead, what we acknowledge is that colonialism has impacted reality both in the Global North and South in profound and irreversible ways (Bhabha, 1994; Hamann et al., 2020). Essentially, innovative ways should be found to shine a light on this hybrid-ity, a claim to which we argue a VE course might contribute.

VE courses do come with important limitations, one of which is the difficulty in recognizing cultural cues. Acknowledging the cultural protocols of a place is difficult over an online platform. Therefore, given the objective of embracing diverse cultural backgrounds, it is important to acknowledge that what is consid-ered appropriate may vary. For instance, in terms of salutations, it is imperative to ascertain the appropriate form of address for a professor, whether it should be on the basis of first name or last name. Another illustration is the manner of participation in seminars, whether silence should be interpreted as concern or tacit approval of the lecture's progression. It is vital for designers and students to be cognizant of the fact that educational settings, including virtual ones, have the potential to function as sites of power, privilege, hierarchy, inclusion, exclusion, and implicit norms regarding appropriate forms of argumentation and behavior. These dynamics may give rise to certain cultural presumptions (Mintz, 2021).

All in all, while a VE has legitimate limitations compared to, for example, a face-to-face exchange, it does offer valid potential in terms of cost reduction, and it provides a "pseudo-neutral space" in which the difficult work of decolonization can begin to be not only imagined but discussed among faculty and students alike. However, its significant contribution lies in the practicality it brings.

Irrespective of how the four principles of the Ubuntu framework were incorporated into the planning and design of this VE, no single course or an eight-week VE course will do justice in decolonizing management studies or even an entire university or respective faculties. However, decolonizing does not only concern itself with the macro structures but also the micro- essentially the act of *doing decolonization*. This is where we find the most strength in terms of what our VE was able to achieve: enhancing plurality in curriculum development and delivery, student empowerment, diversity and inclusiveness, social justice and equality in teaching and learning, small yet vital and incremental facets of the decolonizing agenda.

While far from a perfect contribution to the decolonization project, the VE course had a dual effect: it was a micro-contribution of doing decolonization and, at the same time, has raised important questions for faculty and participants. We hope that our essay invites others to join the quest!

## REFERENCES

Aatkar, S. (2020). VE as a decolonizing practice: Challenging hierarchies and centering marginalized voices. *Journal of Intercultural Education*, *31*(4), 419–434.

Abuzaid, M. (2019). Decolonizing higher education through VE: Amplifying marginalized voices. *Higher Education Research & Development*, *38*(5), 1085–1100.

Adam, T. (2021). Decolonizing VE: Toward critical engagements with power and solidarity. *International Journal of VE and Blended Learning*, *2*(1), 34–48.

Adefila, A., Teixeira, V. R., Morini, L., Garcia, T. L. M., Delboni, F. G. Z. M. T., Spolander, G. & Khalil-Babatunde, M. (2022). Higher education decolonisation: #Whose voices and their geographical locations? *Globalisation, Societies and Education*, *20*(3), 262–276. https://doi.org/ 10.1080/14767724.2021.1887724

Akinwale, A., & Jude, E. (2014, May 30). A historical and comparative analysis of colonial and post colonial bureaucracy in Nigeria. *Journal of Public Administration and Governance*, *4*(2), 1. https://doi.org/10.5296/jpag.v4i2.5602.

Allen, S. (2023). *The University of Sheffield Decolonizing Management Knowledge and Education: Emerging themes in public debate and developing understanding of reflexive discomfort*. The University of Sheffield. Organization Studies. https://www.sheffield.ac.uk/organization-studies/ research/research-projects/decolonizing-management-knowledge-and-education

Arshad, M., Dada, R., Elliott, C., Kalinowska, I., Khan, M., Lipinski, R., Vassanth, V., Bhandal, J., de Quinto Schneider, M., Georgis, I., & Shilston, F. (2021). Diversity or decolonization? Searching for the tools to dismantle the "master's house". *London Review of Education*, *19*(1), 1–18. https://doi.org/10.14324/lre.19.1.19

Banerjee, S. B. (2022). Decolonizing management theory: A critical perspective. *Journal of Management Studies*, *59*(4), 1074–1087. https://doi.org/10.1111/joms.12756

Banerjee, S. B., & Berrier-Lucas, C. (2022). Foreword decolonizing the business schools: A journey on paths less traveled. *Revue de l'Organisation Responsable, 17*(2). Hal-04135235.

Barthold, C. (2020). *Decolonising the idea of culture in management studies.* Open Learn. The Open University. https://www.open.edu/openlearn/money-business/decolonising-the-idea-culture-management-studies

Berda, Y. (2022). *Colonial bureaucracy and contemporary citizenship: Legacies of race and emergency in the Former British Empire.* Cambridge University Press.

Bhabha, H. K. (1994). *The location of culture.* Routledge.

Bhambra, K. G. (2014). Postcolonial and decolonial dialogues. *Postcolonial Studies, 17*(2), 115–121. https://doi.org/10.1080/13688790.2014.966414

Bhambra, G. K., Gebrial, D., & Nişancıoğlu, K. (2018). *Decolonising the university.* Pluto Press.

Chowdhury, R. (2021). From black pain to rhodes must fall: A rejectionist perspective. *Journal of Business Ethics, 170*, 287–311. https://doi.org/10.1007/s10551-019-04350-1

Collins, M. (2016). Decolonization. In J. Mackenzie (Ed.), *The Encyclopedia of Empire: Volume 2* (pp. 1–15). Wiley-Blackwell.

Connell, R. (2018). Decolonizing sociology. *Contemporary Sociology, 47*(4), 399–407. https://doi.org/10.1177/0094306118779811

Conrad, S. (2016). *What is global history?* Princeton University Press.

Dadze-Arthur, A. (2022). Democracy, governance, and participation: Epistemic colonialism in public administration and management courses. In K. Bottom, J. Diamond, P. Dunning, I. Elliot (Eds.), *Handbook of teaching public adminstration.*

De Sousa, S. B. (2015). Decolonising the university: The challenge of deep cognitive justice. Cambridge Univerdsity Press.

Dennis, A. C. (2018). *Decolonising education: A pedagogic intervention in Bhambra et al. (2018). Decolonizing the University* (pp. 190–207). https://library.oapen.org/bitstream/handle/20.500.12657/25936/1004145.pdf?sequence=1

Eckhardt, G. M., Belk, R., Bradford, T. W., Dobscha, S., Ger, G., & Varman, R. (2022). Decolonizing marketing. *Consumption Markets & Culture, 25*(2), 176–186. https://doi.org/10.1080/10253866.2021.1996734

Ehrmann, J. (2022). Within, beyond or against the canon: What does it mean to decolonize social and political theory? *Journal of Classical Sociology, 22*(4), 388–395. https://doi.org/10.1177/1468795X221106631

Escobar, A. (1995). *Encountering development: The making and unmaking of the third world* (2nd ed.). Princeton University Press.

Esteban, L. S. (2020). *Postcolonial public administration: A critical discourse analysis.* [University of Central Florida. Electronic Theses and Dissertations 128]. http://library.ucf.edu/

Everett, S. (2023). *Decolonizing the Business School Curriculum.* AACSB. https://www.aacsb.edu/insights/articles/2023/02/decolonizing-the-business-school-curriculum

Faul, V. M. (2021). *Decolonizing education. Global Changes. Decolonization* (p. 10). https://globalchallenges.ch/issue/10/decolonising-education/#_ednref5

Fougère, M., & Moulettes, A. (2007). The construction of the modern west and the backward rest: Studying the discourse of Hofstede's culture's consequences. *Journal of Multicultural Discourses, 2*(1), 1–19. https://doi.org/10.2167/md051.0

Grosfoguel, R. (2011). Decolonizing post-colonial studies and paradigms of political-economy: Transmodernity, decolonial thinking, and global coloniality. *Transmodernity: Journal of Peripheral Cultural Production of the Luso-Hispanic World, 1*(1). http://dx.doi.org/10.5070/T411000004. https://escholarship.org/uc/item/21k6t3fq

Hailey, J. (2008). *Ubuntu: A literature review. Document* (pp. 1–26). Tutu Foundation.

Hamann, R., Luiz, J., Ramaboa, K., Khan, F., Dhlamini, X., & Nilsson, W. (2020). Neither colony nor enclave: Calling for dialogical contextualism in management and organization studies. *Organization Theory, 1*(1), 2631787719879705.

Jack, G., Westwood, R., Srinivas, N., & Sardar, Z. (2011). Deepening, broadening and re-asserting a postcolonial interrogative space in organization studies. *Organization, 18*(3), 275–302. https://doi.org/10.1177/1350508411398996

Jammulammadaka, N., Faria, A., Jack, G., & Ruggunan, S. (2021). Decolonising management and organisational knowledge (MOK): Praxistical theorising for potential worlds. Special Issue: Decolonising Management and Organisational Knowledge. *Organization, 28*(5), 717–740.

Joo, J. H., & Kim, Y. C. (2017). Key themes in post-colonial curriculum studies. *Journal of Curriculum Studies, 35*(4), 231–257.

Kessi, S., Marks, Z., & Ramugondo, E. (2021). Decolonizing knowledge within and beyond the classroom. *Critical African Studies, 13*(1), 19. https://doi.org/10.1080/21681392.2021.1920749

Kester, K. (2019). Reproducing peace? A CRT analysis of whiteness in the Decolonizing Higher Education curriculum and teaching at a university of the UN. *Teaching in Higher Education, 24*(2), 212–230.

Kickbusch, I., Nikogosian, H., Kazatchkine, M., Kökèny, M. (2021). *A guide to global health diplomacy*. Global Health Centre. Graduate Institute of Geneva. https://www.graduateinstitute.ch/sites/internet/files/2021-02/GHC-Guide.pdf

Konadu-Osei, O. A., Boroş, S., & Bosch, A. (2023). Methodological decolonisation and local epistemologies in business ethics research. *Journal of Business Ethics, 186*(1), 1–12.

Kothiyal, N., Bell, E., & Clarke, C. (2018). Moving beyond mimicry: Developing hybrid spaces in Indian business schools. *Academy of Management Learning & Education, 17*(2), 137–154.

Lazem, S., Giglitto, D., Nkwo, M. S., Mithoko, H., Upani, J., & Peters, A. (2022). Challenges and paradoxes in decolonising HCI: A critical discussion. *Computer Supported Cooperative Work, 31*, 159–196. https://doi.org/10.1007/s10606-021-09398-0

Le Grange, L., Du Preez, P. Ramrathan, L., & Blignaut, S. (2020). Decolonising the university curriculum or decolonial-washing? A multiple case study. *Journal of Education, 80*, 25–48. http://dx.doi.org/10.17159/2520-9868/i80a02

Lutz, D. W. (2009). African Ubuntu philosophy and global management. *Journal of business ethics, 84*(Suppl 3), 313–328.

Mackinlay, E., & Barney, K. (2014). Unknown and unknowing possibilities: Transformative learning, social justice, and decolonizing pedagogy in indigenous Australian studies. *Journal of Transformative Education, 12*(1), 54–73.

Mallard, G., Eggel, D., & Galvin, M. (2021). *Decolonization: The many facets of an ongoing struggle. Global challenges*. Graduate Institute of Geneva. Issue No. 10. https://globalchallenges.ch/issue/10/decolonisation-the-many-facets-of-an-ongoing-struggle/

Matasci, D. (2022). Decolonizing education: Historical perspectives and contemporary challenges. *African Studies Review, 65*(3), 761–770. https://doi.org/10.1017/asr.2022.71

Mbembe, A. J. (2016). Decolonizing the university: New directions. *Arts & Humanities in Higher Education, 15*(1), 29–45.

Mbembe, A. (2015). "Mbembe, Achille. 2015. "Decolonizing Knowledge and the Question of the Archive." Africa is a Country.", contributed by Angela Okune (2018). Platform for Experimental Collaborative Ethnography. https://worldpece.org/content/mbembe-achille-2015-%E2%80%9Cdecolonizing-knowledge-and-question-archive%E2%80%9D-africa-country

Mignolo, D. W. (2017). Coloniality is far from over, and so must be decoloniality. Afterall. *Journal of Art, Context and Enquiry, 43*, 38–45.

Mignolo, W. (2007). Delinking: The rhetoric of modernity, the logic of coloniality, and the grammar of decoloniality. *Cultural Studies, 21*(2), 449–514.

Mignolo, W. D., & Walsh, C. E. (2018). *On decoloniality: Concepts, analytics, praxis*. Duke University Press.

Mintz, S. (2021). Decolonizing the academy. *Inside Higher Ed.* https://www.insidehighered.com/blogs/higher-ed-gamma/decolonizing-academy

Morreira, S., Luckett, K., Kumalo, S. H., & Ramgotra, M. (Eds.). (2021). *Decolonising curricula and pedagogy in higher education: Bringing decolonial theory into contact with teaching practice*. Routledge.

Naude, P. (2019). Decolonising knowledge: Can Ubuntu ethics save us from coloniality?. *Journal of Business Ethics, 159*(1), 23–37.

Nayar, P. K. (2010). *Postcolonialism: A guide for the perplexed*. Continuum International Publishing Group.

Nyamnjoh, F. B. (2021). *Decolonizing The University in Africa*. Oxford University Press. https://doi.org/10.1093/acrefore/9780190228637.013.717

O'Dowd, R. (2021). What do students learn in VE? A qualitative content analysis of learning outcomes across multiple exchanges. *International Journal of Educational Research, 109*, 101804.

Prasad, A. (Ed.) (2003). *Postcolonial theory and organizational analysis.* A critical reader. Palgrave.

Picower, B. (2009). The unexamined whiteness of teaching: How white teachers maintain and enact dominant racial ideologies. *Race, Ethnicity, and Education, 12*(2), 197–215.

Prasad, A. (2012). *Against the grain: Advances in postcolonial organization studies.* Copehagen Business School Press.

Quijano, A. (2000). Coloniality of power and Eurocentrism in Latin America. *International Sociology, 15*(2), 215–232.

Robinson, L., Cotten, S. R., Ono, H., Quan-Haase, A., Mesch, G., Chen, W., & Stern, M. J. (2015). Digital inequalities and why they matter. *Information, Communication & Society, 18*(5), 569–582. https://doi.org/10.1080/1369118X.2015.1012532

Said, W. E. (1983). *The world, the text and the critic.* Harvard University Press.

Said, W. E. (1993). *Culture and imperialism.* Vintage Books. A Division of Random House.

Santos, B. D. S. (2014). *Epistemologies of the south: Justice against epistemicide* (1st ed.). Routledge. https://doi.org/10.4324/9781315634876

Seremani, T. W., & Clegg, S. (2016). Postcolonialism, organization, and management theory: The role of "epis- temological third spaces." *Journal of Management Inquiry, 25*(2), 171–183.

Seremani, T., & Bazana, S. (2025). In Emamdeen Fohim (Ed.), *Decolonizing management and organization studies: Why, how, and what (Research in the Sociology of Organizations)* (pp. 23–36). Emerald Group Publishing Limited.

Shahjahan, R. A., Estera, A. L., Surla, K. L., & Edwards, K. T. (2022). "Decolonizing" curriculum and pedagogy: A comparative review across disciplines and global higher education contexts. *Review of Educational Research, 92*(1), 73–113. https://doi.org/10.3102/00346543211042423

Stanek, M. B. (2019). Decolonial education and geography: Beyond the 2017 Royal Geographical Society with the Institute of British Geographers Annual Conference. *Geography Compass, 13*(12), 1–13.

Taylor, D. F. (2014). Defining ubuntu for business ethics –A deontological approach. *South African Journal of Philosophy, 33*(3), 331–345.

Thomas, A. (2005). Long-term effects of international student exchange programs. In *Culture and human development* (pp. 274–290). Psychology Press.

Von Bismarck, H. (2012). *Defining decolonization. Essay for The British Scholar Society.* http://british-scholar.org/publications/2012/12/27/defining-decolonization/

Wenzel, J. (2017). Decolonization. In I. Szeman, S. Blacker, & J. Sully (Eds.), *A companion to critical and cultural theory.* https://doi.org/10.1002/9781118472262.ch28

Young, R. (2016). *Postcolonialism: An historical introduction.* John Wiley & Sons.

Yousfi, H. (2021). Decolonizing Arab organizational knowledge: "Fahlawa" as a Research Practice. *Organization, 28*(5), 836–856. https://doi.org/10.1177/13505084211015371

Zavala, M. (2016). Decolonial methodologies in education. In M. A. Peters (Ed.), *Encyclopedia of educational philosophy and theory* (pp. 1–6). Springer.

# THE ROLE OF *AFRICA JOURNAL OF MANAGEMENT* IN DECOLONIZING MANAGEMENT AND ORGANIZATION STUDIES

Baniyelme D. Zoogah[a], Stella M. Nkomo[b] and Moses N. Kiggundu[c]

[a] *McMaster University, Canada*
[b] *University of Pretoria, South Africa*
[c] *Carleton University, Canada*

## ABSTRACT

*In this paper, we discuss the role of journals in decolonizing management and organization knowledge. We illustrate that role by using the Africa Journal of Management (AJOM), a publication of the Africa Academy of Management (AFAM). AJOM was deemed critical to decolonizing knowledge about and in Africa, the context where the colonial enterprise wreaked havoc on all sectors of African societies, from political structures, commerce, and culture to knowledge production. In describing the genesis and goals of AJOM, as well as the successes, limitations, and challenges of a journal dedicated to management and organization science, we contribute to epistemic decolonization.*

**Keywords:** Africa Academy of Management; *Africa Journal of Management*; decolonization; epistemic decolonization; knowledge production

Decolonizing Management and Organization Studies: Why, How, and What
Research in the Sociology of Organizations, Volume 93, 191–207
ISSN: 0733-558X/doi:10.1108/S0733-558X20250000093012

# INTRODUCTION

The management and organization science (MOS) literature is focused on the "decolonial turn" where scholars contend that "taking colonialism seriously as a context is not only about acknowledging culturally different ways of knowing, but also about recognizing and undoing the authority of the West" to determine what happens around the world epistemologically (Greedharry et al., 2020, p. 13). It is based on the recognition that MOS has colonial foundations in "old-fashioned and frequently Eurocentric, scholarly concerns and/or approaches to social scientific inquiry" (Prasad, 2012, p. 14).

Colonialism sought to entrench Eurocentric domination of the economy, culture, subjectivity, and knowledge in colonized nations (e.g., Mbembe, 2001; Mudimbe, 1988; Said, 1979). Although formal colonialism is past, its legacies persist. Postcolonial scholar Gayatri Spivak (1988, p. 80) introduced the concept of epistemic violence to capture the ways in which colonizers distorted, excluded, and subjugated the perceptions and world views of the colonized. Some MOS scholars have demonstrated the contemporary manifestations of epistemic violence by documenting the effects of colonization on knowledge production and dissemination of research from the "Global South."[1] For example, scholars have pointed to the minuscule presence of research from the "Global South" in mainstream management journals (e.g., Alcadipani et al., 2012; Barros & Alcadipani, 2023; Hamann et al., 2020; Zoogah & Nkomo, 2013) and the challenges academics encounter in writing in another language and for a different audience (e.g., Barros & Alcadipani, 2023). There are studies that focus specifically on the subjugation of management knowledge in Africa (e.g., Mbalyohere et al., 2018; Nkomo, 2011; Zoogah & Nkomo, 2013). The latter work documents the general absence of Africa in MOS and the negative ways in which it is represented when included.

The growing critique of hegemonic knowledge production has given way to increasing attention to how to decolonize MOS knowledge. As a result, research in international business (Boussebaa, 2023), diversity (Yountae, 2020), organizational behavior (Nkomo, 2021), and ethics (Dunford, 2017) are increasingly advocating for decolonizing mainstream epistemology. Even though these scholarly initiatives are laudable, the implementation of decolonization of knowledge seems to be missing (Banerjee, 2022; Jammulamadaka et al., 2021). Specifically, knowledge dissemination mechanisms such as journals tend to be ignored in the advocacy for decolonization of MOS epistemology. Journals are mediums by which knowledge is published, and they can play a critical role in decolonization of knowledge. To ignore them, therefore, is to exclude a major instrument of decolonization.

In this paper, we demonstrate how the AJOM engaged in decolonization of knowledge. As a publication of the Africa Academy of Management, AJOM was deemed critical to decolonizing knowledge about and in Africa, the context where the colonial enterprise wreaked havoc on all sectors of African societies from political structures, commerce, and culture to knowledge production (Rodney, 2018; Zoogah, 2021). Not only was the lingua franca of African societies changed, but also traditional educational and knowledge systems were displaced and entangled in Western systems. In describing the genesis and goals of AJOM, we contribute to epistemic decolonization. We provide one way of "doing management research differently and adding new and unique layers to the current understanding of management and organizations" (Prasad, 2012, p. 14).

Specifically, we describe the strategy of AJOM as *pluriversal collaboration*. This strategy recognizes the call from decolonial scholars for pluriversal rather than universal knowledge creation and dissemination (de Sousa Santos, 2015; Escobar, 2020). We embrace Escobar's (2020) assertion that the realities of the world are always plural and constantly in the making. If managing and organizing take diverse forms in diverse locations, then knowledge creation requires multivocal representations and engagement across historical epistemological divisions and practices of domination.

Pluriversal collaboration, as a strategy, created an intellectual space for knowledge exchange and co-learning among African and non-African scholars as well as between academics and practitioners. AFAM's goal for the journal was not just to disrupt epistemic exclusion but to imagine a different, sustainable way of resurfacing African management scholarship. We discuss the processes and practices of AJOM that were used to implement pluriversal collaboration. Reflecting on Spivak's profound question, "Can the subaltern speak unproblematically?" and recognizing journals are embedded within a large ecosystem with many actors and conventions, we describe the successes as well as the limitations and challenges of a journal dedicated to MOS in Africa.

## THEORY: EPISTEMIC PLURALISM

At the center of the decolonial initiative is the argument that other voices are excluded from the conversation on knowledge generation and dissemination. In other words, it advocates for pluralism in MOS epistemology. Pluralism in MOS has been growing since the beginning of the 21st century as manifested in journals such as the *Academy of Management Review*, Volume 24, No. 4 on change and pluralism; the *Academy of Management Journal*, Volume 57, No. 2 on relational pluralism; and the *Administration & Society*, Volume 47, No. 9 on value pluralism) and by specific scholars such as Denis et al. (2007), Lewis (2000), and Zoogah (2021).

A review of the literature suggests that Pluralism theory permeates the social sciences (Connolly, 2017). It contends that many actors or conditions influence politics (Moore, 2010) and business (Spender, 1998). Pluralism is either endogenously induced (i.e., originating from within the organization) or exogenously induced (originating from without, from the broader environment). Endogenously induced pluralism is characterized here by "multiple objectives, diffuse power, and knowledge-based work processes" (Denis et al., 2007, p. 180) and focuses on impacts on organizations' processes, systems, and structures (Denis et al., 2007). Exogenously induced pluralism centers on institutional logics and how the broader social context affects organizational dynamics.

Recently, Zoogah (2021, p. 382) used the latter to

> trace the historical trajectory of MO education from the traditional era, wherein ancient civilizations, empires, and kingdoms rife with commerce, education, and epistemologies were displaced, during the modern era, by colonialism and European domination, which contributed to the adoption and focus on Western education (management practice and knowledge systems).

He argued that the extant MOS in Africa results from the "multiplicity of power, multiplicity of logics, and multiplicity of preferences" (Zoogah, 2021, p. 382). To balance the epistemic tilt, he proposed a "reconfiguration of MO education based on greater societal embeddedness and…integration of formal, nonformal, and informal education – consistent with the traditional principles and values of Africa on business conduct and education."

Pluralism theory also has relevance to journals. First, there are multiple journals that are categorized as either Western or non-Western, top-tier or lower-ranked, theoretical or empirical. Not only do they have different objectives, but their power also seems to be diffused regarding what they reject or accept, which suggests that they determine the knowledge that is disseminated. To the extent that the owners are biased against a particular epistemological source or content, the journals are unlikely to endorse its acceptance. The pervasiveness of this bias resulted in the characterization of MOS as a parochial dinosaur (Boyacigiller & Adler, 1991) and contributed to the increasing demands for decolonization of MOS.

In actualizing our decision to launch AJOM as a journal dedicated to MOS in and about Africa, our strategy of pluriversal collaboration was emergent rather than predetermined. There were three major forces that moved us toward this strategy. First, the general absence of Africa in MOS knowledge was a reality that had to be changed. Second, scholars who joined AFAM were not only from Africa but also from other parts of the globe. Lastly, the challenges organizations in Africa faced required knowledge that informed practice and education. We therefore wedded pluralism theory with elements of decolonial thinking, which is a way of dismantling the hegemony of Western ways of knowing and thinking (de Sousa Santos, 2015; Escobar, 2020). A pluriversal approach to decolonization underscores not only the idea that the realities of the world are diverse but also it allows for the resuscitation of knowledge contributions by formerly colonized nations and communities. Furthermore, pluriversal knowledge creation and dissemination inherently requires collaboration across and between diverse locations, epistemologies, and actors.

## ROLE OF JOURNALS AND DECOLONIZATION OF KNOWLEDGE

Journals are the primary mechanisms of knowledge dissemination. As a result, they play a significant role in epistemic decolonization, defined as "the redemption of worldviews and theories and ways of knowing that are not rooted in, nor oriented around Euro-American theory" (Haraway, 1988, p. 582). Given that decolonization has structural, epistemic, personal, and relational dimensions

(Kessi et al., 2020), journals have a unique role to engage in decolonial work by ensuring that all attempts at knowing and articulating reality are grounded in the particular social and political contexts (Boidin et al., 2012; Haraway, 1988) despite the subjectivity, situatedness, and positionality attributes of the journals' agents.

This can be achieved in three ways. First, journals must be "wrecking balls" in the sense that they are ready to dismantle the traditional hegemonic structures associated with epistemic colonization. That role requires courage and moral fortitude. Second, they should be equalizers regarding representation. By that, we mean they must be inclusive of everyone, both the powerful and the less powerful. Lastly, they must empower all constituents. By empowerment, we mean ensuring that the less privileged and minorities have as much access to knowledge disseminated via their channels as those most privileged or the majority. Before we discuss how AJOM fulfills these roles, we provide a summary of the history of the Africa Academy of Management (AFAM).[2]

## HISTORY OF THE AFRICA ACADEMY OF MANAGEMENT (AFAM)

The formation of the Africa Academy of Management resulted from a series of personal, theoretical, and epistemological struggles whose deep roots sprung from the colonization of Africa but more so from immediate challenges. In 2005, the first author of this paper was seeking identification with scholarship about management in Africa. Although he found two academic associations that focused on Africa, the International Academy of African Business and Development (IAABD) and the African Association for Public Administration and Management (AAPAM), their focus was not management. Turning to the Academy of Management (AOM), the premier association for academics in the field of management, he learned Africans constituted less than .01% of its 19,000+ members (Nkomo et al., 2015).

Becoming aware of associations from India and Latin America who were affiliates of AOM, he decided to organize a caucus meeting at its 2008 annual meeting to find others interested in management *in* and *about* Africa. He joined forces with another early career scholar, Moses Acquaah, to co-chair the session. The attendance at the session attracted others with a similar interest in management in Africa. At the second successful caucus at the 2009 AOM annual meeting, attendees decided to become a formal association. Participants nominated an executive committee with an initial responsibility to prepare by-laws.

AFAM adopted the following inaugural mission:

"To foster the general advancement of knowledge and scholarship in the theory and practice of management among African scholars and/or academics interested in management and organization issues in Africa. Africa is defined broadly to include all of Africa and individuals of African descent in the Diaspora (i.e., Caribbean, South America, Europe, Asia, Oceania, Middle East, and North America)" and "to perform and support educational activities that contribute to intellectual and operational leadership in the field of management within the African context." (Africa Academy of Management, 2022)

There was a great deal of discussion about identifying the best activities and programs for AFAM's mission. Previous studies of the reasons for low research productivity of African academics pointed to several structural (i.e., inadequate research infrastructure from libraries to funding and an approach to doctoral education based on the class British apprentice model) and individual level factors (i.e., lack of research skills and access to senior scholars) (Dietz et al., 2006; Habib & Morrow, 2006; Ngobeni, 2010; Sawyerr, 2004).

AFAM decided to focus on two activities that were core to its mission: capacity building targeted at doctoral students and early career academics and organizing biennial conferences on the African continent. AFAM initiated faculty development workshops facilitated by senior academics from Africa and the Diaspora as its main intervention for capacity building on the continent. The primary goal of the workshops was to impart skills to strengthen research capacity for building local knowledge. They were also designed to help African academics engage in what decolonial scholar Walter Mignolo refers to as epistemic disobedience – disrupting Western MOS by inserting local knowledge into extant knowledge that would challenge the boundaries of what is known about a phenomenon (Nkomo, 2017). This form of scholarly writing forces the contextualization demanded of scholars from the rest of the world back to those demanding it (Keet, 2014). The workshops also provided an opportunity for community building as participants had a week for deep engagement with fellow scholars on the continent.

During the 14 years of its existence, AFAM has attracted a strong membership base, became an independent affiliate of AOM, introduced a Fellowship Programme, and launched its own journal which is the focus of this paper.

# ROLE OF AJOM

The AJOM was conceived to fulfill the roles discussed previously. At the Second Biennial Conference of AFAM in 2014 in Gaborone, Botswana, the first on the continent, the Executive team announced the appointment of the Founding Editor of the Journal after having selected the publisher, Routledge of Taylor and Francis Publishing. That year marked the inception of AJOM. The selection of Botswana, one of the best-governed postcolonial states in Africa, signaled the focus on the best of Africa and pointed to the drive for "Africanization" of management scholarship.

The mission, objectives, and aspirations of AJOM were spelled out in the first issue by the Founding Editor and the Senior Associate Editor (see Kiggundu & Lamont, *Introduction to the Africa Journal of Management: The Journey Begins.* AJOM Volume 1 March 2015:1–3). They stated briefly: (1) The launch of a top-tier management journal devoted to the African context as had been spelled out by AFAM and other management scholars; (2) The high-quality research was intended to benefit businesses and governments in Africa, leading to improvement in the social economics of countries and people of Africa; (3) Building quality research capacity to build and strengthen African universities, especially business schools; (4) Advancing management education and practice in Africa, (5) Bringing together "Western management" scholars interested in knowing more about the idiosyncrasies and challenges of business and management in Africa and management scholars and students whose research was very African contextualized trying to solve "big societal problems" such as HIV, poverty, corruption, etc. (6) Creation of AJOM as a "big, inclusive tent or platform for dialogue among various constituencies; and (7) Bringing together Africa and the rest of the world on topics of global significance (e.g., climate change, Covid-19, security, etc.). In other words, AJOM was created to promote traditional/Indigenous (African) sustainable knowledge systems and practices: knowledge development, creation, application, problem-solving, sharing, dissemination, and contribution to human progress.

The first issues of the journal provide evidence of illustrations of the inclusive, African, and global publication. AJOM promotes collaboration and teamwork among its contributors (editors, authors, reviewers, etc.). It is committed to bringing scholars, professionals, practitioners, students, donors, government officials, and informed citizens together to work collaboratively to advance management scholarship and bring it home to benefit all. The editors understood that due in part to the colonial legacy, both management and the continent are highly differentiated and needed integration to serve the common good. As a result, the journal took the position that decolonization does not mean total rejection of existing concepts or practices of MOS developed elsewhere but that what is needed is contextualization and local validation. They reasoned that if you want to decolonize a discipline, you must localize the way it conducts its scholarship: theory development, testing, dissemination, teaching, and practice. The editors envisioned that as a top-tier journal, AJOM would be the place to go for scholarly materials on MOS by Africans and for Africa. This would be a significant step toward decolonization of MOS. AJOM was, therefore, to be both rigorous and relevant. Both rigor and relevance contribute to decolonization because they are not mutually exclusive.

AJOM seeks to legitimize native scholarships cognizant of the challenges involved in understanding and undertaking the publication value chain: activities, skills, institutional support, etc., needed to publish, democratize, and decolonize a regional top-tier journal in MOS. The editors realized, more now than before, that building capacity (leadership, editorial, review, professional, ethics, etc.) for a top-tier regional MOS print journal would take time, patience, resources, and planning. Previous scholars and practitioners had already raised concerns about MOS Western theories and practices. For example, Dia (1996) pointed out the disconnect between Western institutions and African realities. Yet, little progress had been made. The legacy of colonialism at various levels of society made progress impossible. Given that AJOM was founded on the principles that MOS conforms with the values, norms, and practices of "good conduct" as recognized and institutionalized in society, tendencies of colonialism, in whatever form, do not seem acceptable.

## AJOM TOOLS OF DECOLONIZATION

How does AJOM engage in epistemic decolonization through its strategy of pluriversal collaboration? First, AJOM attracts leading management scholars outside Africa (e.g., the Academy of Management, editors of other journals, Presidents of International forums, etc.). This approach shows the attraction of the journal with Western management scholars and suggests that decolonization is not isolated but a collaborative effort with scholars both in and outside Africa. Second, to ensure the effectiveness of the initiative, the editors got advice and support from Editors of regional and other established MOS journals, pointing out opportunities but mostly challenges of a new regional print journal in a world rapidly moving digital. They had many hurdles to overcome, including what they and their constituencies meant by "Africa." Third, print, digitization, and Special Issues were all designed to spread the word using methods of dissemination more widely and making management knowledge more pluralistic and democratic. AJOM publishes foundational management knowledge covering a wide range of topics as a starting point and to lay the foundation for localization and eventual decolonization. Foundation knowledge provides the building blocks for localization. Fourth, the editors invited and challenged the African junior scholars and graduate students, especially women, to use AJOM as a platform for advancing and localizing management scholarship. This has paid off, as some of these are now serving in AJOM leadership roles and championing management scholarships in Africa and beyond.

To concretize these logics, the editors initiated some mechanisms that have the potential of influencing diverse and wider readership consistent with the pluriversal collaboration. The first was *AJOM Special Issues and Inclusiveness*. AJOM publishes special issues as part of the design to grow and localize (Africanize) the journal, enrich and promote participation (e.g., DEI), and set the stage for MOS decolonization. The second is *AJOM Structure and Inclusion*. The journal designed its structure to be inclusive. First, the board has diverse representations: "The AJOM editorial board is composed of some of the most prominent and respected scholars in management research in the world." In addition to benefiting from their wise counsel, we wanted to ensure that Africa and African management scholarship are connected, not disconnected. We made sure to include prominent African scholars on the board. Second, the Editorial Review Board was deliberately designed for inclusion and to help with a developmental review process. The AJOM original editorial review board was made up of ninety top scholars from sixty-nine universities in twenty-two countries, representing all continents. Both the Advisory and editorial review boards served to support and promote AJOM's mission and objectives. The Africanization contributes to the decolonization of MOS.

Third, AJOM has three portfolios that are structured to allow for epistemic diversity. There is academic research targeting scholars. AJOM Research attracts high-quality research articles, which is expected of a top-tier scholarly journal. There is also dialogue for exchange between practitioners and scholars. AJOM Dialogue is a forum for discussing or commenting on previously published articles. The third, AJOM Insight, is directed at practitioners and policy constituents. It is a one-way forum or commentary, grounded in contextualized research on the unique challenges in particular countries or settings about issues that can inform the global academic community about the African context. In presenting the AJOM structure, it was stated, "We view this as a multi-directional conversation, analogous to giving voice to the "tribe" with the intent of encouraging richer discussions of our research and theories" (AJOM, Volume 1 March 2015).

The first issue of *AJOM ( Vol. 1, #1 )*, published in March 2015, provides some clues on epistemic pluralism and pluriversal collaboration. A closer look at the structure and contents of the Issue, which came out on time, illustrates the broader directions and aspirations of the journal, including Africanization (contents, contributors), gender diversification and inclusion, institutions, theory, practice, multi-disciplinarity (Papadopoulos & Hamzaoui-Essoussi, 2015, pp. 54–77), and global reach and connectivity (Jackson, 2015, pp. 78–88). For example, Linah K. Mohohlo (2015, pp. 89–93), an accomplished African public sector administrator and first female governor of an African National Central Bank, gave the keynote address and spoke quite eloquently about the role management can and needs to play in the sustainable development of Africa and Africans. She observed that "there is, therefore, a need to investigate how best management theory, research, and practice (emphasis as in original), can sustain African development...to ensure that the continent's natural resources are harnessed productively to sustain socio-economic growth and improve people's well-being" (p. 89). She added that the "research findings should be widely disseminated for the benefit of domestic policymakers and private business."

Decolonization requires wide dissemination to various local constituencies with the capacity to understand and apply knowledge. This would contribute to the decolonization of MOS theory and practice. In addition, she called on management scholars to integrate MOS in the African "socio-cultural heritage and social mores/customs" (p. 90). She gave the example of Kgotla, a system of governance in Botswana whereby a village assembly limits the power of the village elders by providing opportunities for all members of the community to participate in decision-making. It is rooted in Botswana's traditional social philosophy, which, among other things, expresses that "aggression is best expressed through dialogue than spear." This is the art of leadership through dialogue. AJOM continues to be a forum for other African traditional social and cultural philosophies relevant to MOS. Consistent with that view, Zoogah (2020) leveraged the ancient Egyptian philosophy of Maat, which enjoined companionship or *shemsw* to propose companionate leadership. Knowledge-based on traditional principles, philosophies, and practices is a necessary step for decolonization. The editors broadened the dialogue by asking three African scholars from various parts of the continent to provide commentaries on the governor's thoughts (also see Beugre, 2015).

The journal has been strategic in its decolonial goal of pluriversal collaboration. The strategy recognizes the importance of epistemic pluralism and the dangers of implicit bias of characterizing MOS as a "parochial dinosaur." As a result, it advocates for pluriversal, rather than universal, knowledge creation, validation, and dissemination. No methods of inquiry are privileged over others, and no single worldview of truth is allowed to dominate over others. In addition, the strategy recognizes and accepts diverse ways of being and doing while emphasizing the dynamic interactions of humans/societies/communities in various parts of the world. The strategy starts from the premise of interconnections, multipolarity, non-Eurocentrism, and ontological pluralism (collaboration), recognizing that wisdom, knowledge, truths, etc., are not "out there" but co-generated, maintained, and propagated, and shared as a collective process. In that regard, it rejects a "one world- world view." (Trownsell et al., 2022). In other words, it set out to accept different ontological understandings to forge a pluriversal management research agenda. In so doing, it does not dismiss advocates of the one world view or those who treat Africa as a junior partner in advancing management scholarship (Kiggundu, 2013). Rather, the idea is to invite them to join the conversation and make the tent bigger and better. AJOM advances the view of a multiple world, with different participants and contributions equal in status. That is because every process of knowledge creation, dissemination and knowing is necessarily a collective process involving humans from diverse backgrounds.

Besides, the locus of the journal – Africa – suggests that AJOM recognized that non-Eurocentric voices have been historically excluded, ignored, marginalized, disallowed, colonized, and given no space to contribute to the advancement of management scholarship. For that reason, the strategy sets out to change this by developing a structure, editorial management team, advisory board, editorial review board, and ad hoc reviewers, the composition of which is global and designed for the implementation of the pluriversal collaboration strategy. The journal's original structure laid the foundation and established the institutional infrastructure for worldwide collaboration.

> The editorial review board is a bit larger and more diverse than most new journals to accommodate the three-part structure of the journal, but it is equally impressive, consisting of over 90 top scholars from 69 universities and 22 countries, all committed to making the journal a quality outlet from the start. (Kiggundu & Lamont, 2015, p. 2)

It was also intended to give voice to and strengthen scholarly networks between those on the ground and those from the diaspora (Kiggundu & Lamont, 2015, p. 2). With regards to different Management Scholarship for and on Africa, the journal's strategy was based on the realization that scholars, especially Africanists, were demanding a different perspective of management scholarship for and on Africa…different from the discovery and conceptualization of Africa by Western institutions "that decide and expect power by knowing what is best for Africa" (Jackson, 2015, p. 78; see also Blunt, AJOM, 2023).

A recent 10-year bibliometric analysis of the journal provides additional support of the journal's contributions to pluriversal collaboration and decolonization of management scholarship (Galdino & Lawong, 2024). The authors note that

> this 10-year bibliometric review of AJOM highlights key accomplishments of the journal, such as SCOPUS accreditation and a category 2 ranking by the Academic Journal Guide. Also noteworthy is AJOM's wider reach and accessibility to readers via inclusion in the Emerging Sources Citation Index of WoSc. (2024, p. 12)

This speaks to wider acceptance by different audiences, accreditation, inclusion in leading research databases, facilitating pluriversal collaboration. Further, the authors observe a wider definition of management (MOS) as evident in the journal. The pluriversalism is also manifested in the total submissions: 219 documents, 146 research articles, 26 dialogues/insights/essays, 13 managers' stories, 13 editorials, and 9 papers related to AFAM. It reflects growth, given that in 2015, the total submissions were only 57 but increased to about 250–300 in 2023. Additional evidence of improvement is indicated by the acceptance rate, which decreased from 44% in 2015 to 6% in 2023. It reflects a rate comparable to top-tier journals.

The analysis also showed that the double-blind review process, which is developmental, seeks to bring the reviewer and author(s) closer in a scholarly and personal manner to facilitate intimate interaction that brings the author's work closer to publication (for application of the developmental review process see Nsakanda, 2021). This approach may have helped the increased high downloads that quintupled from 7,000 (2015) to 37,523 (2023). This strategy also likely helped the journal receive SCOPUS accreditation after only three years of publication and a Category 2 ranking on the Academic Journal Guide.[3] That is relatively fast, considering that longer established journals did not achieve that rank with the same speed. Since 2019, AJOM was also included in the Web of Science Emerging Sources Citation Index. From Volume 3, AJOM can be searched via WoSc. That qualified it as an impact factor. These achievements point to the effectiveness of AJOM's pluriversal collaboration strategy, as such achievements would not be possible without collaboration with scholars of diverse backgrounds, institutions, countries, and sub-disciplines.

Consistent with AJOM's strategy as a top-tier journal to advance management scholarship to benefit all of Africa, the journal gives voice and space for African management scholars to join the conversation as equal partners, as evidenced by the citations in the bibliometric analysis. The bibliometric analysis identified the topmost cited Google Scholar of AJOM publications. They note that Google Scholar represents a community of scholars dedicated to the advancement of management (MOS), and Google citations indicate AJOM's membership and association with this community. The topmost cited papers represent a wide range of different topics (e.g., strategy, entrepreneurship, regionalism, entrepreneurs/innovation/women, context, etc.), Africa and non-Africa-based scholars, sectors (e.g., informal, mining, agribusiness, telecommunications, banking). Total citation is an important indicator of impact research because high-impact research contributes to recognition, empowerment, and collaboration.

The studies reported in AJOM also provide insights into the importance and uniqueness of the African context and provide a clear picture of how the context can inform management scholarship. The bibliometric analysis listed the following as the most cited journals among AJOM publications: *Academy of Management Review* (AMR), *Academy of Management Journal* (AMJ), and *Strategic Management Journal* (SMJ). These are top-tier publications, putting AJOM in a "good" scholarly company. The authors' affiliations also indicate the pluriversal strategy. The study reports that AJOM authors came from 37 countries, all 5 continents, and a wide range of universities. This speaks to a more pluriversal collaboration and building a global scholarly community dedicated to advancing management scholarship for and about Africa. No breakdown of gender or domicile, but AJOM has always given priority to female and junior scholars, especially those based in Africa. The journal also covers a broad array of topics over the ten-year period. They include Africa, context, entrepreneurship, innovation, females, institutions, COVID-19, Sub-Saharan Africa, informal sector management/research/education, case studies, performance, challenges, opportunities, etc. The study showed that AJOM started out with more descriptive and case studies but has increasingly published more empirical and quantitative studies.... targeting more diverse audiences. They add that "AJOM has established a solid reputation as a top-tier journal publishing original, rigorous, and relevant research on management theory, education, policy, practice, and service in the context of Africa" (Galdino & Lawong, 2024, p. 12).

In line with the strategy, a fellowship was established: AJOM Junior Faculty Fellowship. The Junior Fellowship was established to promote more rigorous scholarship and collaboration for search in Africa. The aim was to create opportunities for resources, mentorship, and training for Africa-based scholars to grow their research skillset, knowledge, ethics, and networking as they worked on research aimed at publication in AJOM or similar journals. This allowed inter-institutional collaboration with mentors in North America and Europe (Kiggundu & Lamont, 2021; Namada et al., 2019).

> As noted by Namada et al. (2019: 384), the Fellowship emanates from a mission to foster an inclusive, collaborative, and entrepreneurial learning community dedicated to sharing values, knowledge, and skills to prepare current and future business professionals to contribute successfully and responsibly in a global business environment.

In addition to the fellowship, AJOM publishes a supplement. As AJOM became more focused on higher quality theoretical and empirical publications, it became clear that there was also a growing need for publications focused more on more applied areas of management. AJOM needed to grow and was growing in other aspects but could not by itself serve emerging areas of interest. AJOM Supplement was established as a separate publication designed for more balance between research, theory, policy, practice, service, and education. It was aimed at attracting more diverse audiences and management sub-disciplines. AJOM Supplement was intended to create opportunities for collaboration between academics and practicing managers to merge theory and practice in a way that benefits both in different settings in Africa (Kiggundu & Lamont, 2021; Nsakanda, 2021). The purpose of the supplement is to encourage "participations among scholars and professional management associations, thinktanks, institutes, schools, specialized agencies, etc. to work on areas of common interest related to the advancement of management scholarship and Africa's changing needs and realities" (Kiggundu & Lamont, 2021, p. 2). The "inaugural AJOM Supplement is the result of collaborative partnership between academics from different parts of the globe, academics and practicing professionals, executives, and professional associations" (2021, p. 3).

In support of the Supplement as a Tool of Collaboration between academics and professionals and among academics from various parts of the world, Nsakanda (based in Canada, originally from DRC) wrote:

> The African Operations Management Conference (AOMC) is an initiative of the University of South Africa's Department of Operations Management. It aims to bring together researchers and practitioners from academia, industry, and governments across the African continent and beyond to engage in a fruitful exchange of ideas to advance the broad field of Operations Management as one of the major veins to achieve economic growth in Africa. The biennial conference enables participants to share cutting-edge knowledge, develop inter-institutional research collaborations, and foster networking and information sharing. (Nsakanda, 2021, p. 9)

In making the link between academia and professional practice, he describes all African organizations: "The Africa Automation Fair (AAF) is Africa's largest showcase of industrial automation and smart control technologies...." This invites operations management scholars to engage in research that advances the practice in the field while explicitly considering the context, particularly of Africa in the 4IR era.

Lastly, the journal promotes technical writing, networking, and ethical scholarly conduct in much the same ways as in AFAM's PDWs where participants are admonished to avoid predatory journals/publications.

In summary, AJOM has deliberately sought to decolonize knowledge using diverse mechanisms including multiple structures, engagement of constituents, and platforms of knowledge. These efforts have been fruitful with regards to knowledge generation and distribution. Of course, success has not been without challenges which we talk about next.

## CHALLENGES AND LIMITATIONS

In the efforts to decolonize knowledge, AJOM experienced challenges that might be summarized in Spivak's intriguing question – "Can the subaltern speak?". In other words, can knowledge of, from, and about that which has been silenced solve the deep hegemony of Western epistemology and knowledge production? First, decolonization requires a concerted effort of a critical mass of citizens (champions, leaders, followers, scholars, managers, etc.), working together to repatriate (bring home) the discipline and its knowledge, indigenization of institutions, values, and practices. Mobilization of these diverse constituents has not been easy. While some outrightly refused to participate in the AJOM initiative, others half-heartedly agreed but did not optimize their engagement. Second, the medium of communication – English – is not native to Africa. As a result, decolonization is unlikely to be successful if the medium of knowledge generation and distribution is colonial. Native language is critical for decolonization. Language and literacy are important. Mandela is reported to have said, "If you talk to a man in a language he understands, that goes to his head. If you talk to him in his native language, that goes to his heart. Likewise, if people listen to one another in their native language, the understandings, feelings, and sentiments are intrinsic or Indigenous, and for that matter, real. AJOM, as an English publication, has had limited success covering other African regions and cultures (e.g., "Francophone" countries).

Overcoming the language issue is not an easy task, given the heterogeneity of the continent. Third, decolonization runs into problems related to the legacy of colonialism as it exists in society, government, and the economy today. Decolonization is a long and protracted multidimensional process of political, social, economic, and cultural transformation supported by corresponding institutions, values, principles, and practices. Therefore, the wide ecosystem must align with and support all efforts of decolonization. It is not a stroke of the pen. Fourth, decolonization requires democracy. The system must be democratized and humanized to be inclusive. Fifth, disciplines such as MOS do not exist in a vacuum but are interdependent with others. As a result, effective decolonization of MOS must involve the decolonization of interdependent disciplines. In other words, the ecosystem of MOS must engage in epistemic decolonization. Some political economists, for example, argue that management exists to serve the interests of capital and colonialism. This makes it more challenging for management to localize and decolonize. Blunt et al. write, "Management education in Africa is complicit because it contributes to the manufacture of consent" for Africa as the victim of "capitalist rampage" (Blunt et al., AJOM, March 2023, p. 1). One manifestation of this is the pursuit of "global statuses" by many universities in Africa, which results in academics being incentivized to publish in mainstream international journals with the highest rankings. The problem, of course, is that the top-ranked journals in MOS are primarily European- and USA-based. AJOM needs a critical mass of capable and dedicated supporters. This is still a work in progress because individual motivations and institutional incentives do not always align with the journal's mission and objectives.

Related to the above challenge is the fact that colonialism, wherever it exists, is hard to dig out: it has deep, pervasive, insidious, multilayered, and multidimensional aspects that seem entrenched. A scholarly regional journal like AJOM may be necessary but not necessarily sufficient for total decolonization. What is needed is a combination of different tools, strategies, and interventions at various levels to bring about lasting decolonization. Added to this is the fact that respect for the region in which the journal is sourced is now disrespected (Armah, 2018; Soyinka, 2012). In other words, it lacks the attractive mechanism necessary to mobilize constituents. This is compounded by the fact that AJOM is a new regional top-tier journal that, as a start-up, faces developmental and institutional challenges that limit its ability to decolonize as quickly and totally as would be necessary. Previous scholars and practitioners already raised concerns about Western theories of MOS compared to African realities and practices. For example, Dia (1996) recognized the disconnect between Western and African institutions and called for reconciling indigenous and transplanted institutions. Along with this is the challenge that faith or religion has something to do with decolonization. Nations and societies that are founded on foreign creeds (e.g., Christianity, Islam, etc.) may be less able to decolonize because of the linkages to the allochthonous sources than those founded on indigenous religions.

## CONCLUSION

In this paper, we discuss how AJOM, a publication of AFAM, engages in the decolonization of epistemology through a strategy of pluriversal collaboration. The paper also shares the broader context within which the journal was launched. Given that journals are major instruments of knowledge dissemination, the extent to which they facilitate decolonization is likely to influence the decolonial initiative in MOS. The strategy, structures, mechanisms, and processes are based on the pluriversal orientation because of the belief that knowledge from Africa is as important and meaningful as that from other places. In so doing, it seeks to minimize the excessive dependence on foreign, particularly Western, epistemologies. Yet, AJOM as a tool for decolonizing management knowledge must be understood within a broader ecosystem comprised of many layers and components. Nevertheless, moving toward epistemic pluralism in understanding management and organizations in Africa is an ongoing project.

## NOTES

1. We place this term in single quotation marks to indicate its contested meaning and that not all countries located geographically in the Southern Hemisphere would be considered marginalized or excluded from the hegemony of Eurocentric knowledge (e.g., Australia).
2. For the full history of AFAM see: Nkomo, S. M., Zoogah, D., & Acquaah, M. (2015). Why Africa journal of management and why now? *Africa Journal of Management, 1*(1), 4–26.
3. https://charteredabs.org/academic-journal-guide

## REFERENCES

Africa Academy of Management. (2022). *Governance (By-Laws). Unpublished document.*

Alcadipani, R., Khan, F. R., Gantman, E., & Nkomo, S. (2012). Southern voices management and organization knowledge. *Organization, 19*(2), 131–143.

Armah, A. K. (2018). *Wat nt shemsw: Myth, history, philosophy, and literature. The African record.* Per Ankh: The African Publishing Cooperative.

Banerjee, S. B. (2022). Decolonizing management theory: A critical perspective. *Journal of Management Studies, 59*(4), 1074–1087.

Barros, A., & Alcadipani, R. (2023). Decolonizing journals in management and organizations? Epistemological colonial encounters and the double translation. *Management Learning, 54*(4), 576–586.

Beugre, C. D. (2015). The challenge of management scholarship in Africa. *AJOM,* (1), 94–98.

Blunt, P. Escobar, C., & Missos, V. (2023). The political economy of bilateral aid: African development and the manufacture of consent. *Africa Journal of Management, 9*(1), 1–19.

Boidin, C., Cohen, J., & Grosfoguel, R. (2012). Introduction: From university to pluriversity: A decolonial approach to the present crisis of western universities. *Human Architecture: Journal of the Sociology of Self-Knowledge, 10*(1), 1.

Boussebaa, M. (2023). *Decolonizing international business.* Critical Perspectives on International Business.

Boyacigiller, N. A., & Adler, N. J. (1991). The parochial dinosaur: Organizational science in a global context. *Academy of management Review, 16*(2), 262–290.

Connolly, W. E. (2017). *Facing the planetary: Entangled humanism and the politics of swarming.* Duke University Press.

de Sousa Santos, B. (2015). *Epistemologies of the South: Justice against epistemicide.* Routledge.

Denis, J. L., Langley, A., & Rouleau, L. (2007). Strategizing in pluralistic contexts: Rethinking theoretical frames. *Human relations*, 60(1), 179–215.

Dia, M. (1996). *Africa's Management in the 1990s and beyond*. The World Bank.

Dietz, A. J., Jansen, J. D., & Wadee, A. A. 2006. *Effective PhD supervision and mentorship: A workbook based on experiences from South Africa and the Netherlands*. Rozenbeg Publishers and Pretoria: Unisa Press.

Dunford, R. (2017). Toward a decolonial global ethics. *Journal of Global Ethics*, 13(3), 380–397.

Escobar, A. (2020). *Pluriversal politics: The real and the possible*. Duke University Press.

Galdino, K. M., & Lawong, D. (2024). 10 Years of the Africa Journal of Management: A bibliometric analysis. *Africa Journal of Managements*, 10(1), 6–23.

Greedharry, M., Ahonen, P., & Tienari, J. (2020). Colonialism as context in diversity research. In S. N. Just, A. Risberg, & F. Villeseche (Eds.), *The Routledge companion to organizational diversity research methods* (pp. 13–23). Routledge.

Habib, A., & Morrow, S. (2006). Research, research productivity and the state in the South Africa. *Transformation: Critical Perspectives on Southern Africa*, 62(1), 9–29.

Hamann, R., Luiz, J., Ramaboa, K., Khan, F., Dhlamini, X., & Nilsson, W. (2020). Neither colony nor enclave: Calling for dialogical contextualism in management and organization studies. *Organization Theory*, 1(1), 2631787719879705.

Haraway, D. (1988). Situated knowledges: The science question in feminism as a site of discourse on the privilege of partial perspective. *Feminist Studies*, 14(3), 575–599.

Jackson, T. (2015). Management studies from Africa: A cross-cultural critique. *Africa Journal of Management*, 1(1), 78–88. https://doi.org/10.1080/23322373.2015.994425

Jammulamadaka, N., Faria, A., Jack, G., & Ruggunan, S. (2021). Decolonising management and organisational knowledge (MOK): Praxistical theorising for potential worlds. *Organization*, 28(5), 717–740.

Keet, A. (2014). Epistemic 'othering' and the decolonisation of knowledge. *Africa Insight*, 44(1), 23–35.

Kessi, S., Marks, Z., & Ramugondo, E. (2020). Decolonizing African Studies. *Critical African Studies*, 12(3), 271–282.

Kiggundu, M. N. (2013). Personal reflections on African management: Looking in, looking out and looking ahead. *African Journal of Economic and Management Studies*, 177–200. https://doi.org/10.1108/AJEMS-Feb-2012-0008.

Kiggundu, M., & Lamont, B. (2015). Introduction to the Africa Journal of Management: The journey begins. *AJOM*, 1–3.

Kiggundu, M. N., & Lamont, B. (2021). Introduction to the Africa Journal of Management Supplement: The journey continues. *Africa Journal of Management Supplement*, 7, 1–5. https://doi.org/10.1080/233322373.2021.1935792

Lewis, M. W. (2000). Exploring paradox: Toward a more comprehensive guide. *Academy of Management Review*, 25(4), 760–776.

Mbalyohere, C., Onaji-Benson, T., & Daniel, G. O. (2018). Navigating institutional differences in Africa: Moving beyond the institutional voids' perspective. *AIB Insights*, 18(4), 15–19.

Mbembe, A. (2001). *On the Postcolony*. University of California Press.

Mohohlo, L. K. (2015, March). Africa Academy of Management 2nd Biannual Conference at the University of Botswana, Gaborone "Sustainable development in Africa through Management Theory, Research and Practice" Official Opening. *AJOM*, 1, 89–93.

Moore, M. R. (2010). Articulating A Politics Of (Multiple) Identities1: LGBT Sexuality and Inclusion in Black Community Life. *Du Bois Review: Social Science Research on Race*, 7(2), 315–334.

Mudimbe, V. Y. (1988). *The invention of Africa: Gnosis, philosophy, and the order of knowledge*. Indiana University Press.

Namada, J. M., Brunt, C., & Knapp, J. (2019). A reflective note: AJOM Augural Junior Faculty Fellowship. *Africa Journal of Management*, 5(4), 382–400. https://doi.org/10.1080/23322373.2019.1676102

Ngobeni, S. (2010). *Scholarly publishing in Africa: Opportunities and impediments*. Africa Institute of South Africa.

Nkomo, S. M. (2011). A postcolonial and anti-colonial reading of 'African' leadership and management in organization studies: Tensions, contradictions and possibilities. *Organization*, 18(3), 365–386.

Nkomo, S. M., Zoogah, D., & Acquaah, M. (2015). Why Africa journal of management and why now? *Africa Journal of Management, 1*(1), 4–26.

Nkomo, S. M. (2017). Time to look in the mirror: Producing management theory and knowledge for Africa. *Africa Journal of Management, 3*(1), 7–16.

Nkomo, S. M. (2021). Reflections on the continuing denial of the centrality of "race" in management and organization studies. *Equality, Diversity and Inclusion: An International Journal, 40*(2), 212–224.

Nsakanda, A. L. (2021). Introduction to the Supplement: Advancing the practice of operations management and innovation to drive Africa forward in the era of the Fourth Industrial Revolution (4IR). *Africa Journal of Management Supplement, 7*(S1), 6–16.

Papadopoulos, N., & Hamzaoui-Essoussi, L. (2015, March). Place images and national branding in the African Context: Challenges, opportunities, and questions for policy and research. *AJOM, 1*, 54–77.

Prasad, A. (Ed.). (2012). *Against the grain: Advances in postcolonial organization studies* (Vol. 28). Copenhagen Business School Press DK.

Rodney, W. (2018). *How Europe underdeveloped Africa*. Verso.

Said, E. W. (1979). *Orientalism*. Vintage.

Sawyerr, A. (2004). African universities and the challenge of research capacity development. *Journal of Higher Education in Africa/Revue de l'enseignement supérieur en Afrique, 2*(1), 213–242.

Soyinka, W. (2012). *Of Africa*. Yale University Press.

Spender, J. C. (1998). Pluralist epistemology and the knowledge-based theory of the firm. *Organization, 5*(2), 233–256.

Spivak, G. (1988). Can the subaltern speak? In C. Nelson & L. Grossberg (Eds.), *Marxism and the interpretation of culture* (pp. 271–316). University of Illinois Press. https://doi.org/10.1007/978-1-349-19059-1

Spivak, G. (1998). Can the subaltern speak? In C. Nelson & L. Grossberg (Eds.), *Marxism and the interpretation of culture*. University of Illinois Press.

Trownsell, T., Chadha, N., & Shannia, G. (2022, September). Introduction to the Special Issue: Pluriversal relationality. *Review of International Studies, 48*(5), 29.

Yountae, A. (2020). A decolonial theory of religion: Race, coloniality, and secularity in the Americas. *Journal of the American Academy of Religion, 88*(4), 947–980.

Zoogah, B. D. (2020). Companionate leadership: A shemswian perspective. *Africa Journal of Management, 6*(3), 214–247.

Zoogah, B. D. (2021). Historicizing management and organization in Africa. *Academy of Management Learning & Education, 20*(3), 382–406.

Zoogah, D., & Nkomo, S. M. (2013). Management research in Africa: Past, present and future possibilities. In T. Lituchy, B. J. Punnett, & B. Puplampu (Eds.), *Management in Africa: Macro and micro perspectives* (pp. 9–31). Routledge.

# CURATING *OPEN* ACADEMIC FORA

Anupama Kondayya[a], Emamdeen Fohim[b] and Markus A. Höllerer[c]

[a]*Indian Institute of Management Calcutta, India*
[b]*University of Bern, Switzerland*
[c]*UNSW Sydney, Australia*

## ABSTRACT

*Recently, there have been urgent calls to decolonize the discipline of Management and Organization Studies (MOS). Arguably serving as field-configuring events, academic conferences have an important role to play in this endeavor. Contemporary conferencing has been called out for its predominantly Western institutional arrangements and praxis that hark back to colonialism and disproportionately disadvantage scholars from the Global South. In this paper, we draw on non-Western perspectives on scholarly dialogue and exchange to distill shared principles into a purposefully open-ended framework that might serve to scrutinize and reimagine current institutional arrangements of conferencing. Envisaging scholarly dialogue and exchange in such a way informs Bhabha's "third space" with the potential to invite the MOS community to collectively reflect on (and act upon) creating alternative and truly open academic fora for the years to come.*

**Keywords:** Academia; conferencing; forum; holistic scholarship; non-western philosophies; scholarly dialogue; scholarly exchange

Decolonizing Management and Organization Studies: Why, How, and What
Research in the Sociology of Organizations, Volume 93, 209–226
ISSN: 0733-558X/doi:10.1108/S0733-558X20250000093013

# INTRODUCTION

Decolonizing Management and Organization Studies (MOS) has emerged as an important stream in recent literature (for instance, Allen & Girei, 2024; Jammulamadaka et al., 2021; Pal et al., 2022; Yousfi, 2021) that recognizes a strong Western-centric bias, which generates lopsided knowledge and theories incommensurate with other cultural contexts (Banerjee, 2022; Filatotchev et al., 2022) and urgently calls for engaging in alternative "forms of theorizing" (Cornelissen et al., 2021) – including forms of theorizing rooted in Indigenous perspectives (Bothello et al., 2019; Bruton et al., 2022; Salmon et al., 2023). It requires going beyond just recognizing WEIRD bias[1] and undertaking serious "emancipatory" steps to recognize and address institutional factors hampering the heterogenization of knowledge creation (Banerjee, 2022; Cornelissen et al., 2021). Normalizing the inclusion of previously unheard voices in academia demands reflection and reconfiguration of the setup of scientific journals (Barros & Alcadipani, 2023; Zoogah et al., 2025), universities, especially business schools (Abdallah, 2024; Woods et al., 2022), or curricula and pedagogy (Allen & Girei, 2024; Jaya, 2001).

Such a reconfiguration necessitates paying attention to MOS workshops and conferences as potentially field-configuring events that can link individual action to field evolution (Lampel & Meyer, 2008) toward decolonizing our discipline (Etzion et al., 2022; Henderson & Burford, 2020; Höllerer & Geiger, 2022; King et al., 2023). On these lines, we look to MOS conferences and seek to "open up" academic fora. Contemporary academic conferences have been described as "neoliberal commodities" (Nicolson, 2017) and may be described as characterizing instrumentality and exclusion (Chatterjee, 2022; Owusu-Gyamfi, 2024). We wish to envision and advocate a move away from "instrumental scholarship" toward a more "holistic scholarship" that nurtures pluralism, community, and a developmental spirit (Robinson et al., 2022).

To do so, we start by highlighting a number of issues with current modes of Western-style academic conferencing before turning to, and critically reviewing, selected non-Western and arguably more Indigenous perspectives of learning and scholarship. We then derive a set of shared ideals to build what we dub a "6-R framework," centering around the principles of *Representation, Relationality, Responsibility, Reciprocity, Reflexivity, and Respect*, supported by an underlying shared rationale.

With our work, we aim to contribute to the conversation on decolonizing MOS in two major ways. First, we strive to concretize what Bhabha (1994) calls the "third space": a liminal, temporal, and transient space with transformative potential, where dominant and suppressed cultures and discourses can engage in unexpected ways, enabling new hybrid identities and futures to emerge (Tatham, 2023). In this sense, an *open* academic forum embracing the idea of a third space can give voice to previously marginalized actors and, therefore, provide the opportunity to contribute to decolonial endeavors (Seremani & Clegg, 2016). Second, we hope to encourage the academic community to find tangible ways and "practical solutions" (Seremani & Bazana, 2025) for decolonizing MOS by approaching the proposed 6-R framework not as *the* ideal solution but as a starting point for reimagining contemporary conferencing and reconfiguring traditional arrangements for inclusive academic fora.


## CONTEMPORARY ACADEMIC CONFERENCING

For more than 2,500 years, colloquia and conferences – in all their varying forms – have been central to the academic endeavor in civilizations across the world. The scholarly dialogue and exchange they foster are essential for researchers (Stanley, 1995) and their individual journeys through refining ongoing scholarly work, sharing and gaining information and insights (De Vries & Pieters, 2007), learning about new frontiers of knowledge, having intellectually stimulating discussions with peers (Henderson, 2015), and providing valuable opportunities for serendipity and collaboration that can lead to methodological advantages and promising research (Wang et al., 2017). When the 2012 *American Political Science Association's* Annual Meeting was canceled due to Hurricane Isaac, manuscripts scheduled for presentation there were cited less (De Leon & McQuillin, 2020). The COVID-19 pandemic similarly prevented informal, spontaneous encounters among colleagues as conferences went online and negatively affected knowledge dissemination (Hauss, 2021; Medina & Shrum, 2022). Evidently, scholarly dialogue and exchange are crucial in contemporary academia: what is discussed, amongst whom, and how at conferences defines research agenda, output, impact, and career trajectories.

MOS are no exception to this. On-site conferences remain popular despite increasing environmental concerns around global academic travel and hurdles to inclusive community building (Gill, 2021; Nevins et al., 2022; Poggioli & Hoffman, 2022; Reay, 2004). For instance, the annual meeting of the *Academy of Management* (AOM) reverted to its pre-pandemic attendance in 2023 with over 10,000 attendees (AOM, 2023). A significant number of scholars participate in annual gatherings of other scholarly associations such as the *European Group for Organizational Studies* (EGOS), the *European Academy of Management* (EURAM), the *Strategic Management Society* (SMS), the *Institute for Operations Research and Management Sciences* (INFORMS), the *Academy of International Business* (AIB), the *Association for Information Systems* (AIS), along with their regional affiliates. Besides some differences in modalities, most of them are relatively "closed" settings with specific, Western-centric institutional arrangements, often aligned with the norms of the AOM as the "gold standard" in the field.

We now proceed to elaborate on how institutional arrangements shape "mainstream" academic conferencing and influence *who* attends, *what* is done/privileged during a conference, *how* participants engage, and *why* participants attend conferences.


### Who?

The first aspect to consider about contemporary conferences is the "who" – who governs and who attends conferences.

In terms of the "governance" of conferences – that is, decisions about locations, organizers, format, rules of engagement, selection criteria for participants, and so on – the responsibility usually lies with boards and committees having officers elected by members of the scholarly associations legally and financially responsible for organizing the conference. Many of these associations originated and have the majority of their members in the Global North (although continental European scholars also bemoan the continued Anglo-American hegemony in many scholarly disciplines and fields), and despite some noteworthy attempts at inclusion and diversity (for instance, EGOS' inclusivity policy (*EGOS - Inclusivity Policy - European Group for Organizational Studies*, n.d.)), conferences cater to the "typical" attendee and "gate-keeping" tendencies remain. While some associations such as AIB and AIS have made efforts to democratize access by hosting conferences worldwide, including in the Global South, most conferences are consistently held in and scheduled according to academic calendars of North America and Europe, effectively signaling the target audience.

These decisions are crucial and dictate who is able to attend and benefit from conferences on a consistent basis. Statistics reveal the lack of diversity of participants at international conferences. For instance, 75% of the more than 8,000 attendees of the Annual Meeting of the AOM in 2022 belonged to North American and European universities, even as the conference theme talked about "Creating a Better World Together" (AOM Newsletter, August 24, 2022). This is a throwback to colonialism, with scholars from the Global South disproportionately experiencing inaccessible locations, humiliating visa regimes, and hefty costs of registration and travel (Chatterjee, 2022; Owusu-Gyamfi, 2024). The consequences are inconsistent attendance and a related Sisyphean relationship-building, minority status in a crowd of academic elites from the Global North deterring non-Western voices, and interrupted experience of belonging, all making conferences into "closed" arrangements. Indeed, mainstream conferences limit the inclusion of diverse voices (Ford & Harding, 2010).

Surprisingly, virtual and hybrid conferencing seems to have had little effect. To us, this points to a deeper set of hurdles that hamper participation in international conferences due to the signals communicated by conference agenda, norms, and praxis. Evidently, the potential answers here are all but simple.

### What?

Similarly, the "what" – the themes and research agenda – driving academic conferences in MOS are skewed by the demography of participants and governing bodies, even as they claim to cater to the *global* scientific community. Further, although regional scholarly associations increase accessibility for non-Western scholars in Africa, South America, or Asia, even their agenda aligns with the mainstream Western template. It comes as no surprise, then, that the discourse at contemporary MOS conferences remains rather narrow and too often uninspiring and misses the opportunity to engage with novel and innovative themes, topics, phenomena, and methodologies.

## *How?*

Another issue is "how" knowledge and research insights are currently exchanged at MOS conferences, with the norms of engagement dominated by Western standards.

Prestigious MOS conferences require research to be submitted in a standardized format, often influenced by templates of top Western journals, and regional affiliates follow suit. Thus, acceptance at conferences depends on understanding, internalizing, and reproducing Western standards of knowledge communication.

This is problematic, as Barros and Alcadipani (2023) elaborate: Based on their experience as Brazilian scholars, they share how epistemic coloniality poses a hurdle to acceptance in such arenas. Not only do they have to communicate their ideas in a foreign language but also in a certain style targeted at a mainly Western audience. This type of Anglicization or "Colonialingualism" is prevalent across the board (Boussebaa & Brown, 2017; Meighan, 2023). Implicit epistemological and ontological assumptions in MOS, often building on Enlightenment thoughts (Banerjee & Arjaliès, 2021) and limiting methodological approaches, further hamper non-Western insights from being shared at MOS conferences.

Even when accepted, non-Western scholars may be unable to fully participate in these fora. MOS conferences are characterized by Western and hypermasculine culture, discourse, and performativity (Mills, 2006), leading to low diversity and the experience of "stage fright" and "performance anxiety" for groups that do not share the praxis. Studies have shown that ethnic minority members experience less psychological safety if such issues are not actively tackled (Fujimoto & Presbitero, 2022).

Beyond the listed conference program, contemporary conferencing involves socializing and networking, the norms around which also reinforce Western cultural and social praxis and can lead to non-Western scholars experiencing heightened anxiety and low belonging. Lipton (2020) notes experiencing the pressure to conform in such spaces and missing the collegiality such encounters should provide. Not surprisingly, Nicolson (2017) labels today's academic conferences as "neoliberal commodities" where knowledge is created as a product and evaluated based on certain performance standards, such as journal rankings. Ford and Harding (2010) go so far as to describe conferences as a setting that fosters control over academics.

## *Why?*

Finally, the core motivations or "why" for scholars to attend conferences have shifted over the past decades; the rise of business schools, the broader "managerialization" of universities, and the performativity of a myriad of metrics on the individual and organizational level have contributed their fair share to this development. We want to be neither nostalgic nor naïve here. Substantial reputation and power games have always characterized modern academia. Yet, what arguably still used to be a contest of ideas in an intellectual arena has increasingly come to be shaped by the neoliberal rulebook, focused on gaining visibility and status, instrumental networking, and chasing future publications that help improve individual metrics and institutional rankings (Höllerer & Geiger, 2022). The development of a balanced body of relevant knowledge, the spirit of shared scholarship, and the joy of experiencing community have taken somewhat of a backseat with an increasingly capitalistic production paradigm percolating into academia.

### The Need for Reimagination

While mainstream conferences are but one – albeit central – mosaic stone toward decolonizing MOS (Nevins et al., 2022), the predominance of Western institutional arrangements in *global* scholarly debates and exchange is problematic for two reasons: it unfairly discriminates against scholars from the Global South, and it risks generating skewed and impractical insights incongruent with the diversity of the social world and global challenges due to the centrality of MOS conferences for setting the research agenda and output (Auerbach Jahajeeah et al., 2025).

In response, observers have called to "collectively work to create spaces where diversity and inclusion are the norm" (Rydstedt & Lachowsky, 2020, p. 202) by incorporating an ethic of interconnectedness and care, rethinking the prevalent hierarchical model to address power differentials and promote dialogic engagement (Bell & King, 2010), considering "partnerships with local associations to promote meetings and conferences between communities" (Barros & Alcadipani, 2023, p. 582), and even redesigning the physical environment and spaces at conferences to disrupt the status quo (Bell & King, 2010). The time is ripe to engage in decoloniality and proactively reimagine institutional arrangements, driving academic fora to provide space for diverse approaches to knowledge creation by looking beyond Western thought as the sole framework or source of knowledge (Mignolo & Walsh, 2018).

Some noteworthy attempts toward addressing the status quo are formats such as "Open Walked Event-Based Experimentations" (OWEE) (de Vaujany et al., 2018), "unconferences" (King et al., 2023; Owen, 2008), "slow conferencing" (Ruddick, 2019) and a "federated model of conferencing" (Etzion et al., 2022). Together, these efforts seek to counter hierarchy in academic exchange by promoting horizontal linkages to encourage the free flow of ideas among peers and improve solidarity, deepen engagement among participants, and better situate the conversation in its local context for better governance and solutions. While the issues at hand are multilayered and complex, these efforts are valuable in envisaging alternatives.

We intend to further these efforts and contribute toward decolonizing MOS (Banerjee, 2022) by transcending practices and focusing on foundational principles that may help transform academic exchange through "emancipatory" steps and inspired by the "third space" (Bhabha, 1994) since "knowledge production spaces have the potential to be sites of liberation from oppressive norms and practices, rather than sites of disenfranchisement for members of marginalized communities" (Rydstedt & Lachowsky, 2020, p. 202).

Overall, we hope to collectively address the question of *how to curate open academic fora by reimagining the institutional arrangements for scholarly dialogue and exchange.*

# INSPIRATION FROM INDIGENOUS PERSPECTIVES

In search of alternative principles of conferencing – beyond Western or Eurocentric perspectives – that could serve as the foundation of curating academic fora and facilitate reimagination, reconfiguration, and reconstitution of scholarly exchange, we turned to the "Others" and sought out diverse Indigenous perspectives on scholarship and learning in search of non-hegemonic conceptualizations of scholars and principles of scholarship. Here, we understand Indigenous as referring to knowledge and perspectives native or original to a particular region or area and developed in the civilizations and communities of that region or area. We turned to perspectives from communities in Africa, the First Nations of the American continents, Indian Hinduism and Buddhism, and Chinese Confucianism. None of these are monoliths, and their practical interpretations, coupled with colonial impositions, have resulted in deeply problematic societal institutions and inequalities such as gender, race, caste, class, and more in various parts of the world. However, we follow Shroff's (2011) lead and look for similarities at the level of perspectives to extract and translate their essence into guiding principles for our purpose. In the following sections, we present a summary of the principles of scholarship distilled from Indigenous perspectives to help reimagine academic fora.

## *Holistic Ontology*

In contrast with the Cartesian dualism of mind and body that makes the mind the central source and target of learning, Indigenous perspectives are rooted in a holistic and socio-ecological view of individuals as well as of education and scholarship, emphasizing the interconnectedness of mind, body, spirit, and environment such that education encompasses not only cognitive but also physical, emotional and spiritual development (Merriam & Kim, 2008; Reagan, 2005; Shroff, 2011; Walker, 2001). As an example, among Indigenous American peoples belonging to the Cree, Cherokee, Anishinaabeg, Navajo, Ojibwa, and other nations, the concept of the Medicine Wheel (or Sacred Circle or the Great Hoop of Life) symbolizes four components of a whole person and considers equal development of all four components necessary for achieving harmony – the ultimate aim of education (Merriam & Kim, 2008; Underwood, 2000), while Yoga and Buddhist thought in India hold enlightenment as the goal of education, to be attained by balancing mind, body and spirit (Merriam & Kim, 2008).

Further, the individual is interconnected with the community, an entity central to Indigenous perspectives: the community is both the facilitator and beneficiary of all learning and scholarship, with its issues and problems dictating the teleology of the scholarly endeavor (Merriam & Kim, 2008).

## *Intertwined Teleology: Individual and Community Development*

The above relational ontology of the individual manifests in education and scholarship, which have the intertwined goals of individual development and community benefit (Peters, 2019).

At the individual level, scholarship and the pursuit of knowledge are means for self-actualization, a goal that manifests in diverse ways across perspectives. The pursuit of knowledge serves self-realization in Confucianism and Indian Hindu philosophy (Merriam & Kim, 2008; Mookerji, 1944; Nanavati, 2022; Reagan, 2005; Thaker, 2007), the attainment of harmony through personal responsibility and efforts toward salvation in Indian Buddhist and Indigenous American perspectives (Cajete (Tewa), 2005; Reagan, 2005), and the strengthening of values and character across perspectives (A. S. Altekar, 1933; Mookerji, 1944; Moumouni, 1968; Reagan, 2005).

However, this individual development is not an end in itself but in service of the community. Indigenous African perspectives prioritize communal interests over the individual; in Indigenous American and Indigenous Australian perspectives, "love" for the people and the land fuels the pursuit of knowledge along with an aspiration to assimilate in society; and Confucianism and Indian Hindu perspectives value a harmonious society based on societal ideals and achieved through individual learning and scholarship (A. S. Altekar, 1933; Cajete (Tewa), 2005; Merriam & Kim, 2008; Merriam & Ntseane, 2008; Reagan, 2005). Thus, education and scholarship are structured by community problems and issues, and the effectiveness of these endeavors assessed by the efficacy of solutions provided to the community's problems (Merriam & Kim, 2008).

### Epistemological Diversity

Indigenous perspectives are also often characterized by epistemological diversity, allowing for a broader range of sources and forms of data to be considered valid for the generation of knowledge. Learning and scholarship are seen as lifelong processes that are naturalistic and intertwined with everyday praxis such that education is situated at the nexus of nature, community, life, and leisure (Cajete (Tewa), 2005; Cajete in Denzin et al., 2008; Merriam & Kim, 2008; Reagan, 2005). Observation, interaction, imitation, participation in the rites and rituals of the community, assimilation, and context-ed experience are key in this regard (Cajete in Denzin et al., 2008; Merriam & Kim, 2008; Reagan, 2005). Furthermore, the oral tradition and effective use of language are central to nearly all Indigenous perspectives (Reagan, 2005), leading to knowledge being embedded in, generated from, and transmitted through a myriad of narrative tools such as myths and mythology, legends, fables and storytelling, songs and dances, proverbs, metaphors, riddles, and even gossip as seen among the African Hausa, for example (Reagan, 2005).

### Engaged and Reciprocal Mentorship

The idea of a specialized and separate teacher with expertise and skills is alien to many Indigenous philosophical perspectives; instead, everyone, irrespective of age and stage of learning, has a responsibility bordering on obligation to share knowledge while continuing to learn (Merriam & Kim, 2008; Reagan, 2005). Among many First Nations, all adults, as well as older children, are meant to engage in teaching, while community elders pass on ritual and ceremonial knowledge and function as custodians of community wisdom, experience, and culture (Reagan, 2005). The idea of reciprocity concerning knowledge is embedded within Chinese, Indian Hindu, and Indian Buddhist perspectives, even if the role of a teacher is more formalized in practice (Merriam & Kim, 2008; Mookerji, 1944; Reagan, 2005). Similarly embedded is the idea of engaged learning.

### Inclusive Axiology

Finally, Indigenous perspectives of education and scholarship value equality, inclusion, and access but not necessarily along the same dimensions, resulting in concerning exclusions over time. For example, in ancient India, financial hurdles to scholarship were addressed with scholarships drawn from royal patronage but social structures evolved over time to institutionalize exclusions based on gender and caste (Nanavati, 2022). This makes it important to focus on the spirit rather than dimensions of inclusion for our purpose.

Confucianism deems everyone to be alike but differing owing to their experience. It considers education to be transformative, advocating for it to be available to all who stand to benefit from it (Reagan, 2005). The principles of Buddhist philosophy decried caste, descent, and status and advocated for recognizing competence such that ancient Buddhist educational centers admitted everyone and attracted students from across South-East Asia (Altekar, 1944; Merriam & Kim, 2008). The Aztecs ensured universal schooling regardless of gender and class, and at the end of formal education in the *cuicacalli*, made equivalent institutions available for males and females (Reagan, 2005). Furthermore, perspectives from African communities and the First Nations recognize and accommodate individual differences in the intellectual capacities of children while educating them without imposing normative standards (Reagan, 2005). Thus, the aim was to be meritocratic, accessible, and accommodative of individual differences in backgrounds and capacities.

The set of common characteristics that emerged across perspectives is preliminarily summarized in Table 1.

# A FRAMEWORK FOR REIMAGINING SCHOLARLY EXCHANGE

Inspired by the various Indigenous perspectives reviewed, we develop a set of principles addressing aspects of who, what, how, and why to serve as the basis for reimagining institutional arrangements for scholarly dialogue and exchange.

The core principle manifested across Indigenous perspectives, as seen in Table 1, is one of holism, relationality, or connectedness – the lack of a stark divide between the body-mind-spirit, individual and community, living and learning, mentor and mentee. We draw on these core principles and suggest that academic exchange and fora be reimagined to facilitate a move away from current paradigms of instrumental scholarship toward "holistic scholarship" (Robinson et al., 2022), marked by "pluralism, community building, nurturing,

***Table 1.*** Selected Principles of Holistic Scholarship Distilled from Non-Western/Indigenous Perspectives.

| Dimension of Scholarship | Essence from Perspectives Examined |
|---|---|
| *Ontology* | • Holistic, relational, and ecological |
| *Teleology* | • Dualistic concern with individual and community |
| | • Self-actualization of the individual leading to community development due to holism |
| | • Addressing the community's issues and problems |
| *Epistemology* | • Diverse |
| | • Rooted in practical experience |
| | • Intertwined with daily living and lived experience |
| | • Knowledge acquired and disseminated through oral tradition including myths and mythology, legends, fables, and storytelling, songs and dances, proverbs, metaphors, riddles, and even gossip |
| *Characterization of mentoring relationships* | • Some degree of reciprocity between mentor and mentee |
| | • Knowledge sharing as a responsibility and obligation |
| | • Importance of elders and knowledge custodians |
| *Axiology* | • Inclusive |
| | • Belief in similarity of potential across individuals |
| | • Access to learning irrespective of background |
| | • Recognition of individual differences when ensuring learning |

and developing of individuals and the field" (Robinson et al., 2022, p. 365). We propose a 6-R framework to this end, centering around the principles of *Representation, Relationality, Responsibility, Reciprocity, Reflexivity, and Respect*, supported by an underlying rationale. Together, they guide the vision for curating open academic fora toward enabling holistic scholarship:

> *Ensuring **representation** and development of diverse individual scholars using **relational** approaches and with **responsibility**, and by demonstrating **reciprocity**, **reflexivity**, and **respect** as a community in the process of scholarly development and knowledge production.*

The goal here is to facilitate the self-fulfillment of scholars by addressing problems identified collectively. We suggest moving away from an individualistic view of scholars, which leads us to look at a scholarly community as a constellation of individual "stars" and those who are best at connecting to each other through often imaginary and fungible ties. Instead, a relational (or ecological) view of the scholarly community may be adopted, where scholars and their work are interconnected and interrelated, and indeed, individual successes and failures impact the sustainability and credibility of the community. The development and fulfillment of a scholar in this paradigm is the community's responsibility, while it is the responsibility of the scholar to support the community by sharing knowledge. This view also involves transcending differences and dichotomies and enabling access, irrespective of background and financial capacity, to celebrate unique backgrounds and world views that can help address community problems in novel ways. The process is ongoing and lifelong, employs diverse epistemologies, and is characterized by reciprocity and sustained engagement between scholars simultaneously responsible for learning from and developing each other with reflexivity and respect.

## Representation

Open academic fora will foster inclusivity and representation by moving toward recognition of differences and of the inequity that these differences entail, along with relocating in time and space to enable equity.

*Representation with recognition.* Curating open academic fora must begin with addressing who attends and governs scholarly exchange and reconsidering what constitutes representation. This involves accounting for underrepresented institutions and countries, recognizing differences among participants of the field, recognizing how these differences derive from or perpetrate structural barriers such as income disparities, acknowledging that economic strength does not represent voice and worth, and finding ways to facilitate the congregation of diverse scholars and plural perspectives by addressing these realities.

Representation also needs to be ensured in the governance of open academic fora to ensure fair academic exchange. The Indigenous democratic system of *Kgotla* driven by principles of tolerance and freedom of expression may be pertinent here, with its roots in the principle of *Ubuntu* that emphasizes community and interconnectedness, its focus on equitable dialogue and discussion about any issues concerning the community, and everyone having the right to have their views heard (Molebatsi & Morobolo, 2021; Tlou & Tlou, 2021).

*Relocation in space and time.* The oppression and humiliation faced by scholars from most countries while trying to access Western geographies, along with the obliviousness of dominant groups to these problems, necessitate considering more accessible geographies that do not symbolize hegemonic ways of being. Further, deferring to North American and European academic calendars creates trade-offs for academics from "misaligned" contexts: between academic duties and academic exchange, between scholarly responsibilities and private life. This necessitates temporal reconsiderations for scholarly exchange to improve representation.

## Relationality and Responsibility

Relationality is central to moving away from existing arrangements and norms of scholarly exchange such that individual and community development are seen as interrelated and interdependent. In this paradigm, acquiring and sharing knowledge are considered responsibilities of individual scholars, while the community is responsible for developing individual scholars. The norms and activities in open academic fora may be organized around symbiotic individuals and community development focused on issues the community considers important.

*The individual as a collective responsibility.* Open academic fora will transcend dehumanized scholarship and be deeply concerned with the development and self-fulfillment of individual scholars at various stages of the academic journey. Such a forum would enable scholars to chart their own path, discover scholarly purpose, and experience belonging to better contribute to the community. The product and practice of scholarship will be intertwined. Furthermore, the product of scholarship may not be commoditized forms of knowledge, rather the individual scholar shaped by a community that cares.

*Issue focus.* The above community-supported individual development occurs through and toward addressing issues relevant to the community. It is pertinent here to consider how these issues may be identified. In the spirit of *Kgotla*, open academic fora may introduce mechanisms for the community to dialogue and build consensus on issues of interest, around which scholars congregate and generate solutions and draw upon plural perspectives through deliberation in issue-driven dialogue circles. The circle is "an ancient symbol that can offer new possibilities and hope across many cultures to those who are discouraged with their life" (Garner et al., 2011, p. 65). Everyone is equal in a circle, but it also acknowledges the knowledge and wisdom of those with more experience. Thus, the circle could inspire organizing knowledge exchange without hierarchy around challenges faced by society or scholars. Scholarly challenge circles could be proposed afresh by scholars based on the needs of the times and the context. Resorting to circles allows for flexibility and interdisciplinary engagements; topical circles may be merged in different ways to allow for generativity such that radical theoretical and practical insights may emerge. The effectiveness of solutions and, hence, the quality of knowledge is judged by its ability to address identified solutions.

*Inclusive epistemologies.* Open academic fora will encourage alternate ways of developing and disseminating knowledge by drawing upon broader sources and forms of knowledge, diverse methodologies and modes of engagement, and better integration with lived realities. The crux is a radical transformation regarding what is considered valid knowledge and valid ways of generating knowledge. Broadening the epistemological repertoire and embracing other ways of knowing (Thambinathan & Kinsella, 2021) seems imperative for generating solutions in a world rife with challenges. Further, refocusing is required to assess the worth of a contribution and consider scholarly contributions' ability to address problems identified by the community rather than commoditizing knowledge. The possibilities are rich here to promote knowledge creation by breaking away from set molds of knowledge dissemination and engaging in forms foreign to Western contexts to generate solutions.

### Reciprocity, Reflexivity, and Respect

The "how" of open academic fora concerns rules of engagement that imbibe reciprocity, reflexivity, and respect. Indigenous scholarly perspectives are characterized by a fluid boundary between mentors and mentees and a necessary reciprocity between them. Everyone teaches, and everyone learns from each other through praxis. Reciprocity is key to realizing an open academic forum. Again, we suggest resorting to the circle as an enabling form of more equal dialogue among participants. Furthermore, scholarly circles may be overseen by the equivalents of elders and custodians, driven by the spirit of tolerance and dialogue.

At the same time, it is important to remember that we are not entering or approaching new institutional arrangements tabula rasa but are pre-conditioned by existing forms of engagement. Thus, an important element of enabling reciprocity in open academic fora is reflexivity (Thambinathan & Kinsella, 2021). By reflecting on their positionality and being acutely aware of power dynamics that are embedded, entrenched, and internalized (Cajete in Denzin et al., 2008) and of how their worldview may have been shaped by dominant discourses (Thambinathan & Kinsella, 2021), scholars can aspire to create a space for more equal dialogue and voice for diverse participants. Dei's (2008, p. 8) notion of "epistemological equity" is essential here for facilitating conversations between plural perspectives with an awareness of the power-knowledge complex (Thambinathan & Kinsella, 2021). Rather than assuming that Western methodologies are the only valid ways of understanding reality, scholars reflect on their own assumptions and seek to engage with and integrate non-Western methodologies with respect (Simonds & Christopher, 2013), which is the third component of the rules of engagement in open academic fora. To go from representation to voice, scholars thus must demonstrate respect for perspectives and engage respectfully with not only open ears and eyes but also open hearts and minds (Delpit, 1988; Thambinathan & Kinsella, 2021). Listening affectively and actively is central to creating space for growth and becoming (McDermott, 2014).

Knowledge generation and problem-solving in this paradigm might employ various methodologies that communities devise to allow plural perspectives to converse with reciprocity, reflexivity, and respect. An example is Cajete's (in Denzin et al., 2008, p. 493) approach, which seeks to open up conversations between plural perspectives on science by demonstrating analogous approaches across Native American and Western thought to "illustrate that these principles are the result of the creative thought process and to establish this as a point of commonality between both cultural perspectives." The approach emulates real-world problem-solving that synthesizes collective learning to generate ideas and applies the best solution to problems identified in salient situations (Cajete in Denzin et al., 2008). Ultimately, "'Braiding Indigenous Science and Western Science' is a powerful metaphor used to symbolize and acknowledge that different ways of knowing can coexist; in this metaphor, each strand remains a separate entity, however all strands come together to form a whole (Snively & Williams, 2016)" (Thambinathan & Kinsella, 2021, p. 5).

## Rationale

Finally, we come to the why of the enterprise. Open academic fora seek to readjust the focus of scholarly exchange on scholarship, scholarly development, and scholarly community/camaraderie driven by the 6-Rs outlined in pursuit of holistic scholarship that embraces a non-individualistic relational view of scholars and knowledge, and fosters a true community that invests care in scholars and is enriched with scholarship in the process. As Thambinathan and Kinsella (2021) suggest, the key is to adopt a transformative praxis: theorizing based on issues deemed important by the community, aligned with the community's values, and enriching the community with individual capability and service.

## CONCLUDING REMARKS

This paper seeks to reimagine scholarly dialogue and exchange, focusing on academic conferencing (Etzion et al., 2022; Höllerer & Geiger, 2022) and believes that lasting change requires philosophical reconsiderations. We, thus, offer ontological, epistemological, teleological, and axiological principles through a 6-R framework to help reimagine MOS conferences. The aim is to reconfigure institutional arrangements toward dismantling colonizing influences, effecting inclusion, ensuring holistic scholarship, and promoting diversity in knowledge generation. With this, we aim to contribute to discussions on decolonizing MOS in two ways.

First, we look to the concept and possibilities of Bhabha's (1994) "third space," which is an "inherently productive" space marked by productive and disruptive tensions arising from ongoing contestations, negotiations, and transformations that result from "subversion, transgression and resistance" (Haig-Brown, 2021; Tatham, 2023, p. 4). It is characterized by hybridity, openness, and possibilities of new positions (Bhabha in Rutherford, 1990), and "displaces the histories that constitute it, and sets up new structures of authority, new political initiatives, which are inadequately understood through received wisdom" (Koliska & Roberts, 2021; Bhabha in Rutherford, 1990, p. 211). Following recent discussions on how epistemological third spaces can contribute to decolonizing MOS (Hamann et al., 2020; Kothiyal et al., 2018; Seremani & Clegg, 2016), we suggest seeing open academic fora as third spaces, wherein epistemological encounters between dominant perspectives and perspectives long suppressed can occur resulting in contestations, negotiations and transformations of conferencing. The disruptions and reconfigurations of structures in these spaces, which essentially are field-configuring events, shall allow new hybrid meanings and understandings to emerge and transform the larger field through individual realizations and actions.

Second, we offer the 6-R framework not as a fruit or end product but as a seed or starting point. We invite the academic community to make the framework their own, reflect on and extend the principles for reimagining contemporary conferencing, and adapt them in ways that speak to their context and community toward realizing the vision of open academic fora. In keeping with the spirit of the framework, we hope this will lead to a diversity of imaginaries and a myriad of "practical suggestions" (Seremani & Bazana, 2025) for decolonizing MOS and building momentum toward institutional change and inclusive academic fora.

## NOTE

1. WEIRD: the narrow research focus on and with actors from countries with a Western, Educated, Industrialized, Rich, and Democratic background (Henrich et al., 2010).

## REFERENCES

Academy of Management (AOM). (2023). Putting the Worker Front and Center. *AOM_CMS*. https://aom.org/events/annual-meeting/past-annual-meetings/2023-putting-the-worker-front-and-center

Abdallah, C. (2024). Against mastery: Epistemic decolonizing in the margins of the Business School. Management Learning.

Allen, S., & Girei, E. (2024). Developing decolonial reflexivity: Decolonizing management education by confronting White Skin, White Identities, and Whiteness. Academy of Management Learning & Education, *23*(2), 246–264. https://doi.org/10.5465/amle.2022.0387

Altekar, A. S. (1933). Ideals, merits and defects of Ancient Indian Educational System. *Annals of the Bhandarkar Oriental Research Institute, 15*(3/4), 137–158.

Altekar, A. S. (1944). *Education in Ancient India.* N. Kishore.

Auerbach Jahajeeah, J., Gümüsay, A. A., Salvi, E., von Richthofen, G., & Kekana, L. (2025). Grand challenges, decoloniality and management scholarship. In E. Fohim (Ed.), *Decolonizing management and organization studies: Why, how, and what ( Research in the Sociology of Organizations)* (pp. 83–101). Emerald Group Publishing Limited.

Banerjee, S. B. (2022). Decolonizing management theory: A critical perspective. *Journal of Management Studies, 59*(4), 1074–1087. https://doi.org/10.1111/joms.12756

Banerjee, S. B., & Arjaliès, D. (2021). Celebrating the end of enlightenment: Organization theory in the age of the Anthropocene and Gaia (and why neither is the solution to our ecological crisis). *Organization Theory, 2*(4), 263178772110367. https://doi.org/10.1177/26317877211036714

Barros, A., & Alcadipani, R. (2023). Decolonizing journals in management and organizations? Epistemological colonial encounters and the double translation. *Management Learning, 54*(4), 576–586. https://doi.org/10.1177/13505076221083204

Bell, E., & King, D. (2010). The elephant in the room: Critical management studies conferences as a site of body pedagogics. *Management Learning, 41*(4), 429–442. https://doi.org/10.1177/1350507609348851

Bhabha, H. K. (1994). *The location of culture.* Routledge.

Bothello, J., Nason, R. S., & Schnyder, G. (2019). Institutional voids and organization studies: Towards an epistemological rupture. *Organization Studies, 40*(10), 1499–1512. https://doi.org/10.1177/0170840618819037

Boussebaa, M., & Brown, A. D. (2017). Englishization, identity regulation and imperialism. *Organization Studies, 38*(1), 7–29. https://doi.org/10.1177/0170840616655494

Bruton, G. D., Zahra, S. A., Van De Ven, A. H., & Hitt, M. A. (2022). Indigenous theory uses, abuses, and future. *Journal of Management Studies, 59*(4), 1057–1073. https://doi.org/10.1111/joms.12755

Cajete (Tewa), G.A., (2005). American Indian epistemologies. *New Directions for Student Services, 2005*(109), 69–78. https://doi.org/10.1002/ss.155

Chatterjee, D. (2022, August 5). How international conferences fail scholars from the global South. *International Affairs Blog.* https://medium.com/international-affairs-blog/how-international-conferences-fail-scholars-from-the-global-south-fbde14e5d1f1

Cornelissen, J., Höllerer, M. A., & Seidl, D. (2021). What theory is and can be: Forms of theorizing in organizational scholarship. *Organization Theory, 2*(3), 263178772110203. https://doi.org/10.1177/26317877211020328

De Leon, F., & McQuillin, B. (2020). The role of conferences on the pathway to academic impact: Evidence from a natural experiment. *Journal of Human Resources, 55*(1), 164–193. https://doi.org/10.3368/jhr.55.1.1116-8387R

de Vaujany, F. X. et al. (2018). *Walking the Commons: Driftng Together in the City* [Doctoral dissertation, RGCS (Research Group on Collaborative Spaces)].

De Vries, B., & Pieters, J. (2007). Knowledge sharing at conferences. *Educational Research and Evaluation, 13*(3), 237–247. https://doi.org/10.1080/13803610701626168

Dei, G. J. S. (2008). Indigenous knowledge studies and the next generation: Pedagogical possibilites for anti-colonial education. *The Australian Journal of Indigenous Education, 37*(S1), 5–13. https://doi.org/10.1375/S1326011100000326

Delpit, L. (1988). The silenced dialogue: Power and pedagogy in educating other people's children. *Harvard Educational Review, 58*(3), 280–299. https://doi.org/10.17763/haer.58.3.c43481778r528qw4

Denzin, N., Lincoln, Y., & Smith, L. (2008). *Handbook of critical and indigenous methodologies.* SAGE Publications, Inc. https://doi.org/10.4135/9781483385686

*EGOS – Inclusivity Policy – European Group for Organizational Studies.* (n.d.). Retrieved June 12, 2024, from https://www.egos.org/egos/about_egos/egos_Inclusivity_Policy

Etzion, D, Gehman, J., & Davis, G. F. (2022). Reimagining academic conferences: Toward a federated model of conferencing. *Management Learning*, *53*(2), 350–362. https://doi.org/10.1177/
13505076211019529
Filatotchev, I., Ireland, R. D., & Stahl, G. K. (2022). Contextualizing management research: An open
systems perspective. *Journal of Management Studies*, *59*(4), 1036–1056. https://doi.org/10.1111/
joms.12754
Ford, J., & Harding, N. (2010). Get back into that kitchen, woman: Management conferences and
the making of the female professional worker. *Gender, Work & Organization*, *17*(5), 503–520.
https://doi.org/10.1111/j.1468-0432.2009.00476.x
Fujimoto, Y., & Presbitero, A. (2022). Culturally intelligent supervisors: Inclusion, intercultural cooperation, and psychological safety. *Applied Psychology*, *71*(2), 407–435. https://doi.org/10.1111/
apps.12326
Garner, H., Bruce, M. A., & Stellern, J. (2011). The goal wheel: Adapting navajo philosophy and the
medicine wheel to work with adolescents. *The Journal for Specialists in Group Work*, *36*(1),
62–77. https://doi.org/10.1080/01933922.2010.537735
Gill, M. J. (2021). High flying business schools: Working together to address the impact of management
education and research on climate change. *Journal of Management Studies*, *58*(2), 554–561.
https://doi.org/10.1111/joms.12575
Haig-Brown, C. (2021). Working a third space: Indigenous knowledge in the post/colonial univer-
sity. *Canadian Journal of Native Education*, *31*(1) (2008). https://doi.org/10.14288/CJNE.
V31I1.196454
Hamann, R., Luiz, J., Ramaboa, K., Khan, F., Dhlamini, X., & Nilsson, W. (2020). Neither colony
nor enclave: Calling for dialogical contextualism in management and organization studies.
*Organization Theory*, *1*(1), 263178771987970. https://doi.org/10.1177/2631787719879705
Hauss, K. (2021). What are the social and scientific benefits of participating at academic conferences?
Insights from a survey among doctoral students and postdocs in Germany. *Research Evaluation*,
*30*(1), 1–12. https://doi.org/10.1093/reseval/rvaa018
Henderson, E. F. (2015). Academic conferences: Representative and resistant sites for higher education
research. *Higher Education Research & Development*, *34*(5), 914–925. https://doi.org/10.1080/
07294360.2015.1011093
Henderson, E. F., & Burford, J. (2020). Thoughtful gatherings: Gendering conferences as spaces of
learning, knowledge production and community. *Gender and Education*, *32*(1), 1–10. https://doi.
org/10.1080/09540253.2019.1691718
Henrich, J., Heine, S. J., & Norenzayan, A. (2010). The weirdest people in the world? *Behavioral and
Brain Sciences*, *33*(2–3), 61–83. https://doi.org/10.1017/S0140525X0999152X
Höllerer, M. A., & Geiger, D. (2022). Academia in the post-pandemic world: Leapfrogging into
the Unknown – Tales from Organizing EGOS 2020. *Journal of Management Studies*, *59*(3),
843–850. https://doi.org/10.1111/joms.12704
Jammulamadaka, N., Faria, A., Jack, G., & Ruggunan, S. (2021). Decolonising management and
organisational knowledge (MOK): Praxistical theorising for potential worlds. *Organization*,
*28*(5), 717–740. https://doi.org/10.1177/13505084211020463
Jaya, P. S. (2001). Do We Really 'Know' and 'Profess'? Decolonizing management knowledge.
*Organization*, *8*(2), 227–233. https://doi.org/10.1177/1350508401082008
King, D., Griffin, M., & Bell, E. (2023). Inclusion and exclusion in management education and learn-
ing: A deliberative approach to conferences. *Academy of Management Learning & Education*,
*22*(1), 40–62. https://doi.org/10.5465/amle.2020.0089
Koliska, M., & Roberts, J. (2021). Space, place, and the self: Reimagining selfies as thirdspace. *Social
Media + Society*, *7*(2), 205630512110272. https://doi.org/10.1177/20563051211027213
Kothiyal, N., Bell, E., & Clarke, C. (2018). Moving beyond mimicry: Developing hybrid spaces in
Indian Business Schools. *Academy of Management Learning & Education*, *17*(2), 137–154.
https://doi.org/10.5465/amle.2015.0137
Lampel, J., & Meyer, A. D. (2008). Guest editors' introduction: Field-configuring events as structur-
ing mechanisms: How conferences, ceremonies, and trade shows constitute new technologies, industries, and markets. *Journal of Management Studies*, *45*(6), 1025–1035. https://doi.
org/10.1111/j.1467-6486.2008.00787.x

Lipton, B. (2020). Academic conferences: Collegiality and competition. In B. Lipton (Ed.), *Academic women in neoliberal times* (pp. 165–201). Springer International Publishing. https://doi.org/10.1007/978-3-030-45062-5_5

McDermott, M. (2014). Mo(ve)ments of Affect: Towards an Embodied Pedagogy for Anti-racism Education. In G. J. Sefa Dei & M. McDermott (Eds.), *Politics of anti-racism education: In search of strategies for transformative learning* (Vol. 27, pp. 211–226). Springer Netherlands. https://doi.org/10.1007/978-94-007-7627-2_15

Medina, L. R., & Shrum, W. (2022). Going virtual: Academic conferences in the age of COVID-19. *First Monday*. https://doi.org/10.5210/fm.v27i4.12571

Meighan, P. J. (2023). *Colonialingualism*: Colonial legacies, imperial mindsets, and inequitable practices in English language education. *Diaspora, Indigenous, and Minority Education, 17*(2), 146–155. https://doi.org/10.1080/15595692.2022.2082406

Merriam, S. B., & Kim, Y. S. (2008). Non-Western perspectives on learning and knowing. *New Directions for Adult and Continuing Education, 2008*(119), 71–81. https://doi.org/10.1002/ace.307

Merriam, S. B., & Ntseane, G. (2008). Transformational learning in Botswana: How culture shapes the process. *Adult Education Quarterly, 58*(3), 183–197. https://doi.org/10.1177/0741713608314087

Mignolo, W., & Walsh, C. E. (2018). *On decoloniality: Concepts, analytics, praxis*. Duke University Press.

Mills, S. (2006). Gender and performance anxiety at academic conferences. In J. Baxter (Ed.), *Speaking out* (pp. 61–80). Palgrave Macmillan UK. https://doi.org/10.1057/9780230522435_4

Molebatsi, C., & Morobolo, S. B. (2021). Reading the place and role of endogenous governance structures in modernist physical planning: The Case of the *Bogosi* and the *Kgotla* in Botswana. *African Studies, 80*(2), 134–152. https://doi.org/10.1080/00020184.2021.1937057

Mookerji, R. K. (1944). Glimpses of Education in Ancient India. *Annals of the Bhandarkar Oriental Research Institute, 25*(1/3), 63–81.

Moumouni, A. (1968). *Education in Africa*. Deutsch.

Nanavati, M. (2022, June 22). The Gurukul Tradition of Ancient India. *The Acropolitan Magazine*. https://theacropolitan.in/2022/06/22/the-gurukul-tradition-of-ancient-india/

Nevins, J., Allen, S., & Watson, M. (2022). A path to decolonization? Reducing air travel and resource consumption in higher education. *Travel Behaviour and Society, 26*, 231–239. https://doi.org/10.1016/j.tbs.2021.09.012

Nicolson, D. J. (2017). *Academic conferences as neoliberal commodities*. Springer International Publishing. https://doi.org/10.1007/978-3-319-49190-5

Owen, H. (2008). *Open space technology: A user's guide* (3rd ed., revised and expanded). Berrett-Koehler.

Owusu-Gyamfi, S. (2024). 'Exhausted and insulted': How harsh visa-application policies are hobbling global research. *Nature, 627*(8005), 705–705.

Pal, M., Kim, H., Harris, K. L., Long, Z., Linabary, J., Wilhoit L., Elizabeth, J., Peter, R., Gist-Mackey, A. N., McDonald, J., Nieto-Fernandez, B., Jiang, J., Misra, S., & Dempsey, S. E. (2022). Decolonizing organizational communication. *Management Communication Quarterly, 36*(3), 547–577. https://doi.org/10.1177/08933189221090255

Peters, M. A. (2019). Ancient centers of higher learning: A bias in the comparative history of the university? *Educational Philosophy and Theory, 51*(11), 1063–1072. https://doi.org/10.1080/00131857.2018.1553490

Poggioli, N. A., & Hoffman, A. J. (2022). Decarbonising academia's flyout culture. In K. Bjørkdahl & A. S. F. Duharte (Eds.), *Academic flying and the means of communication* (pp. 237–267). Springer Nature Singapore. https://doi.org/10.1007/978-981-16-4911-0_10

Reagan, T. G. (2005). *Non-Western educational traditions: Indigenous approaches to educational thought and practice* (3rd ed.). Lawrence Erlbaum.

Reay, D. S. (2004). New Directions: Flying in the face of the climate change convention. *Atmospheric Environment, 38*(5), 793–794. https://doi.org/10.1016/j.atmosenv.2003.10.026

Robinson, S., Contu, A., Elliott, C., Gagnon, S., Antonacopoulou, E., Bogolyubov, P., Crossan, M., Cunliffe, A., Elkjaer, B., Graça, M., Kars, S., Li, S., Lyles, M., Snell, R., St Amour, W., Stead, V., Thorpe, R., & Vera, D. (2022). In praise of holistic scholarship: A collective essay in memory of Mark Easterby-Smith. *Management Learning, 53*(2), 363–385. https://doi.org/10.1177/13505076211032207

Ruddick, S. (2019). Slow conferencing: A recipe for connection in troubled times. *ACME: An International Journal for Critical Geographies*, *18*(3), Article 3.

Rutherford, J. (Ed.). (1990). *Identity: Community, culture, difference*. Lawrence & Wishart.

Rydstedt, D., & Lachowsky, N. (2020). Sex research conferences as heterotopias: A queer crip theory perspective on universal design. *The Canadian Journal of Human Sexuality*, *29*(2), 197–204.

Salmon, E., Chavez R., J. F., & Murphy, M. (2023). New perspectives and critical insights from indigenous peoples' research: A systematic review of indigenous management and organization literature. *Academy of Management Annals*, *17*(2), 439–491. https://doi.org/10.5465/annals.2021.0132

Seremani, T., & Bazana, S. (2025). In Emamdeen Fohim (Ed.), *Decolonizing management and organization studies: Why, how, and what (Research in the Sociology of Organizations)* (pp. 23–36). Emerald Group Publishing Limited.

Seremani, T. W., & Clegg, S. (2016). Postcolonialism, organization, and management theory: The role of "Epistemological Third Spaces." *Journal of Management Inquiry*, *25*(2), 171–183. https://doi.org/10.1177/1056492615589973

Shroff, F. (2011). Chapter Three: We are all one: Holistic thought-forms within indigenous societies indigeneity and holism. *Counterpoints*, *379*, 53–67.

Simonds, V. W., & Christopher, S. (2013). Adapting western research methods to indigenous ways of knowing. *American Journal of Public Health*, *103*(12), 2185–2192. https://doi.org/10.2105/AJPH.2012.301157

Stanley, J. (1995). Pain(t) for healing: The academic conference and the classed/embodied self. In V. Walsh & L. Morley (Eds.), *Feminist academics: Creative agents for change* (pp. 169–182). Taylor & Francis.

Tatham, C. (2023). A systematic literature review of Third Space theory in research with children (aged 4-12) in multicultural educational settings. *Pedagogy, Culture & Society*, 1–20. https://doi.org/10.1080/14681366.2023.2283798

Thaker, S. N. (2007). Hinduism and learning. In S. B. Merriam (Ed.), *Non-Western perspectives on learning and knowing*. Krieger Pub. Co.

Thambinathan, V., & Kinsella, E. A. (2021). Decolonizing methodologies in qualitative research: Creating spaces for transformative praxis. *International Journal of Qualitative Methods*, *20*, 16094069211014766. https://doi.org/10.1177/16094069211014766

Tlou, J. S., & Tlou, J. S. (2021). *Ubuntu as Reflected in the Kgotla System of the Government in Botswana* (ubuntu-as-reflected-in-the-kgotla-system-of-the-government-in-botswana) [Chapter]. Https://Services.Igi-Global.Com/Resolvedoi/Resolve.Aspx?Doi=10.4018/978-1-7998-7947-3.Ch006; IGI Global. https://www.igi-global.com/gateway/chapter/www.igi-global.com/gateway/chapter/276723

Underwood, P. (2000). *The great hoop of life. Vol. 1: A traditional medicine wheel for enabling learning and for gathering wisdom*. A Tribe of Two Press.

Walker, P. (2001). Journeys around the medicine wheel: A story of indigenous research in a Western University. *The Australian Journal of Indigenous Education*, *29*(2), 18–21. https://doi.org/10.1017/S1326011100001356

Wang, W., Bai, X., Xia, F., Bekele, T. M., Su, X., & Tolba, A. (2017). From triadic closure to conference closure: The role of academic conferences in promoting scientific collaborations. *Scientometrics*, *113*, 177–193.

Woods, C., Dell, K., & Carroll, B. (2022). Decolonizing the business school: Reconstructing the entrepreneurship classroom through indigenizing pedagogy and learning. *Academy of Management Learning & Education*, *21*(1), 82–100.

Yousfi, H. (2021). International management, should we abandon the myth of cultural hybridity? A re-examination of the contribution of postcolonial and decolonial approaches. *M@n@gement*, *24*(1), 80–89.

Zoogah, B. D., Nkomo, S. M., & Kiggundu, M. N. (2025). The role of Africa Journal of Management in decolonizing management and organization studies. In E. Fohim (Ed.), *Decolonizing management and organization studies: Why, how, and what (Research in the Sociology of Organizations)* (pp. 191–207). Emerald Group Publishing Limited.

# SECTION V

# FURTHER EXPLORATIONS

# AT THE RISK OF NOT BEING DECOLONIAL ENOUGH

Luciano Barin Cruz[a], Charlene Zietsma[b],
Natalia Aguilar Delgado[a] and Sarah De Smet[c]

[a]HEC Montréal, Canada
[b]University of Michigan, USA
[c]Ghent University, Belgium

## ABSTRACT

*Market-based approaches feature development interventions designed to enable poor people in the Global South to benefit from markets. Decolonial approaches criticize these Western-based interventions in marginalized settings by challenging the implicit assumption that good intentions lead to good outcomes. Despite the many well-founded issues with market-based approaches, as researchers working in this field, we believe we have resources and a privileged platform to make a difference in shaping the ways these interventions take place. We propose a framework distinguishing different approaches to research on market-based interventions that build on two key practices: reflexivity and engagement with local actors. Particularly, we put forward the concept of* reflexive pragmatism, *which combines strong engagement with local actors and deep reflexivity to produce long-lasting impacts that meet the needs of the poor. Based on our own research experience and the papers in this volume, we suggest ideas for how researchers can consciously strive to decolonize*

Decolonizing Management and Organization Studies: Why, How, and What
Research in the Sociology of Organizations, Volume 93, 229–243
ISSN: 0733-558X/doi:10.1108/S0733-558X20250000093014

*market-based interventions while, at the same time, making their scholarly practices more impactful for communities.*

**Keywords:** Decolonization; local actor engagement; market-based approach; reflexivity; reflexive pragmatism

# INTRODUCTION

A burgeoning area of scholarship and practice focuses on market-based approaches to development, such as capacity building for entrepreneurship, value chain development, and provision of microfinance to enable poor people in the Global South to benefit from markets (Elliot et al., 2008; McMullen, 2011; Meyer-Stamer, 2006; van Wijk et al., 2020). Market mechanisms have been seen as promoting economic growth for all, including poor people (Brännvall, 2023; Gabre-Madhin & Nagarajan, 2004). One such mechanism, entrepreneurship, is seen as having enormous potential to eradicate poverty by remedying market failures and reforming or even revolutionizing markets (Sutter et al., 2019).

Yet a contrasting branch of literature on decolonization is particularly critical of market-based approaches. This critique focuses on unequal power relationships between development agencies and beneficiaries (Khan et al., 2007), and the use of Western approaches that do not center the voices of beneficiaries (Saldanha et al., 2022) and thus fail to consider local realities and needs (De Smet & Boroş, 2021). Furthermore, development organizations' evaluation of such approaches may be blind to systemic flaws (Mignolo & Escobar, 2010; Ramarajan & Reid, 2020): interveners may pick the easiest targets (Calás et al., 2009) or focus more on quantity (reaching as many people as possible) than quality (matching the needs of people) (De Smet & Boroş, 2021). Hence, critiques of Western-based interventions in marginalized settings in the Global South challenge the implicit assumption that good intentions lead to good outcomes (Khan et al., 2007).

Despite the many well-founded issues with the approach, we (two women from the West and a woman and a man from the Global South) want to avoid throwing the baby out with the bathwater: doing nothing to respond to crushing poverty and inequality is not acceptable either. As academics working with development organizations, we have resources and a privileged platform to make a difference. These privileges strengthen our moral obligation to contribute to poverty alleviation – yet we must also be critical of our own research practices. We can positively affect environments with good intentions (Wegener et al., 2024), but we must also be aware of the potential to cause unintentional harm (Chrispal, 2025).

We propose a framework distinguishing different approaches to research on market-based interventions that build on two key practices: reflexivity and engagement with local actors. Based on our own research and the papers in this Research in the Sociology of Organizations volume (Fohim, 2025), we suggest ways that researchers can consciously strive to decolonize market-based interventions to make their scholarly practices more impactful for communities. We argue that taking a *reflexive pragmatist* approach to intervention can be an avenue for impacting grand challenges that can respond to the needs of marginalized people while at the same time creating space for them to question the structures they are part of and their place within those structures.

## BETWEEN MARKET-BASED AND DECOLONIZING APPROACHES TO POVERTY ALLEVIATION

At first glance, the literatures on market-based and decolonizing approaches seem to have incongruent assumptions and characteristics. Many market-based approaches rely on entrepreneurship initiatives, seeing the promotion of micro-enterprise creation (McMullen, 2011) or entrepreneurial skills and methods development (Slade Shantz et al., 2024) in the Global South as a concrete way to generate local impact and empower those in marginalized conditions (Alvarez & Barney, 2013). On the other hand, literature on decolonization highlights the detrimental effects of international organizations' interventions on local beneficiaries, suggesting that many entrepreneurship initiatives risk doing more harm than good by simply reinforcing existing power structures and norms (Brännvall, 2023; Calás et al., 2009; Khan et al., 2007). As researchers of market-based approaches, we find this critique bears careful thought in several areas.

### Naïve Agentic Perspective

Market-based approaches often focus on changing the behavior of marginalized entrepreneurs, indirectly placing on them the responsibility for solving their marginalization and implicitly suggesting they haven't been entrepreneurial enough (Karnani, 2008). A decolonial perspective emphasizes the limits of the approach since it neglects structural inequalities produced by colonial history and patriarchy,[1] along with current practices of resource exploitation by Western powers. People cannot simply "entrepreneur themselves out of poverty" if the structures in which they operate continue to marginalize them and absolve the exploiters from the responsibility to right past (and current) wrongs (Hickey & Mohan, 2004). We accept this critique but continue to believe that entrepreneurship can be a mechanism for social change (Calás et al., 2009). By emphasizing personal agency, entrepreneurial methods encourage people to question existing structures and act to create new possibilities – entrepreneurship as a method has empowerment at its core. In addition, we believe that by providing resources (such as inclusive finance) and adapting entrepreneurial ecosystems to be more supportive, the constraints poor and marginalized actors face can be loosened somewhat. Together, these features can allow poor and marginalized actors to take some actions to improve their circumstances even when the power structures that oppress them make no move to change.

*Reinforcement of a Western Worldview*

Market-based interventions tend to use Western conceptions of entrepreneurship (Calás et al., 2009; Slade Shantz et al., 2018), privileging heroic, growth-oriented, individualistic entrepreneurs (Welter et al., 2017) and replicating exploitative and patriarchal Western business practices (Ng et al., 2022). A decolonial perspective suggests that pre-existing norms and practices in the context are not understood, appreciated, or even violated, leading to unintended consequences (Khan et al., 2007). Rich local traditions of entrepreneurship may be silenced as Western, patriarchal knowledge is privileged (Calás et al., 2009) in training programs designed by international development actors to fit their own (Western) frameworks and objectives (De Smet & Boroş, 2021). To avoid this problem, reflexivity and deep engagement with local actors are necessary to ensure that market-based interventions fit their contexts.

*Failure to Produce Lasting Impacts*

Market-based interventions have often not lived up to their promise to alleviate poverty despite resource investments (Alvarez & Barney, 2013). Development initiatives designed to support entrepreneurship through resource provision and training often fail to achieve substantial, lasting, and transformative impact because they neglect to address the root causes of poverty and inequality (Cornwall, 2016) and fail to embed changes in enduring social structures. Persistent biases from dominant groups hinder entrepreneurs' access to markets and resources (Alvarez & Barney, 2013; Mair et al., 2016) and saddle marginalized groups such as women and those of lower caste with domestic and other burdens that limit their ability to invest effort into their businesses (Chigunta et al., 2005; Fatoki & Chindoga, 2011). They also often fail to understand the reality of the people they try to help, both at the structural and epistemic levels (Brännvall, 2023; Konadu-Osei et al., 2022). Development organizations' misunderstandings of the lived experiences of poor people lead to interventions that are not tailored to the latter's needs (De Smet & Boroş, 2021). Again, reflexivity and deep engagement with local actors are necessary to ensure that market-based interventions are consistent with the needs of local actors.

*Both/and: Decolonized Market-Based Approaches?*

In summary, decolonial scholars argue that for true *empowerment,* local entrepreneurs must decolonize their own minds by reflecting on the structures of agency, power, and inequalities around them (Cornwall, 2016; Freire, 1996). This requires a deep engagement with the local cultural context (Rappaport, 1987) and the active participation of local entrepreneurs and their local supporters (Sholkamy, 2010) in the co-creation of place-based initiatives (Escobar, 2018; Uda, 2025; Wandersman et al., 2005; Zoogah et al., 2025). Initiatives should be embedded in social solidarity groups (Cornwall, 2016; McKague et al., 2015) and affect social norms around such entrepreneurs to ensure access to markets, resources, and time to invest in their businesses (Mair et al., 2012).

Despite intense debate between proponents of market-based approaches and those who mobilize decolonial lenses, both streams aim for the same objective – poverty alleviation – but believe in different means and mechanisms to achieve this goal. We acknowledge the importance of this intellectual debate but believe that, as scholars, we have the responsibility to push our research practice beyond dichotomies of right or wrong to seek plural perspectives. We seek to engage in research that allows us to alleviate poverty through market-based approaches, bearing in mind the important limits highlighted by a decolonial perspective. We believe that pragmatism, with its emphasis on acting for change and its belief in emancipation (Wegener et al., 2024), can guide us in this direction.

## A FRAMEWORK TO CLASSIFY RESEARCH APPROACHES ON MARKET-BASED INTERVENTIONS

We present a framework classifying market-based approaches in development settings based on two practices: *engagement with local actors* and *reflexivity* (Fig. 1).

*Engagement with local actors* involves interacting with local actors to build understanding and relationships, with the aim of co-designing research interventions. Previous research on pragmatist action has highlighted the importance of engaging with diverse actors over time to allow for the emergence of enriched, plural understandings of both problems and potential solutions (Ferraro et al., 2015). From a decolonial perspective, projects aimed at producing impact should place people at the center of the research process (Saldanha et al., 2022), building empowerment, defined by Kabeer (1999, p. 435) as "a process by which those who have been denied the ability to make strategic life choices acquire such an ability." This type of research requires extensive investment of resources and time in building shared understanding with local actors.

*Reflexivity* refers to an awareness of how power structures embedded in sociohistorical realities shape our perceptions and enable and constrain individual

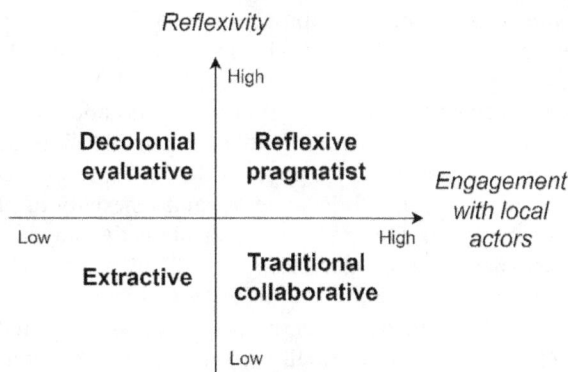

*Fig. 1.* Classifying Market-based Interventions with Marginalized Communities.

234 LUCIANO BARIN CRUZ ET AL.

opportunities (Bourdieu, 2004; Freire, 1996). Freire (1996) adds that reflexivity includes awareness of our capacity to transform our reality. Reflexivity among researchers has been defined as "the process of engaging in self-reflection about who we are as researchers, how our subjectivities and biases guide and inform the research process, and how our worldview is shaped by the research we do and vice versa." (Jamieson et al., 2023, p. 1).

Reflexivity enables researchers to be sensitive to the power structures both in the research process (Bhopal, 2010) and the research context of local actors in order to understand epistemic and cultural differences (De Smet & Boroş, 2021; Konadu-Osei et al., 2022), and avoid reproducing colonialist power structures in the research (De Smet & Boroş, 2021). Researchers can try to enhance research participants' own reflexivity, enabling them to become conscious of power structures and the possibility of transforming their own reality. For example, Chrispal (this volume) described how a research participant touched her feet to signal deference, and Chrispal responded by touching the participant's feet in turn to signal mutual respect.

We classify market-based interventions with marginalized communities into four quadrants based on these two dimensions.

In *"extractive"* research, researchers pursue their own objectives unreflexively with limited engagement with the local community. The power inequalities between researchers and the communities under study remain unmanaged because scholars perceive marginalized communities mainly as fieldwork opportunities (Auerbach Jahajeeah et al., 2025). Impacts for local actors are less likely to be positive and might be unintendedly negative: since the engagement of the local actors in designing the research intervention is low, it is unlikely to meet their needs.

A *"decolonial evaluative"* approach, featuring high reflexivity but low engagement, involves an evaluation of the interventions undertaken by others to assess how the interventions impact both desired outcomes and power structures. This approach, centered on a profound concern with power asymmetries, may yield valuable insights but become paralyzing, constraining positive impacts.

With *"traditional collaborative"* approaches, engagement with local actors is higher, but researchers lack reflexivity. The impact of the research might be to reproduce existing power structures (Kabeer, 1999/2011), potentially creating a cycle of dependency or creating interventions that do not endure beyond the research period since they fail to address root causes and local needs.

The approach we advocate in this paper is the *"reflexive pragmatist,"* which combines strong engagement with local actors and reflexivity to produce long-lasting and desired impacts. Our point of departure is the pragmatist theory of action, which emphasizes a situated, distributed, and processual approach to dealing with grand challenges (Ferraro et al., 2015; Gehman et al., 2022; Wegener et al., 2024). We build on its emphasis on distributed experimentation, defined as "iterative action that generates small wins, promotes evolutionary learning, and increases engagement while allowing unsuccessful efforts to be abandoned" (Ferraro et al., 2015, p. 376). This approach enables actors to incrementally

experiment on specific problems, learning collectively. We argue that when pragmatic efforts are undertaken reflexively by both researchers and their local partners, there is potential for empowerment (Kabeer, 2011).

When local actors are involved in design in an empowered and reflexive way,
they can ensure that interventions (a) address root causes, (b) resonate with them,
and (c) become embedded in social structures, allowing them to be sustained.
From the beginning, this approach integrates local knowledge with knowledge
from the West and other places. Therefore, our approach is grounded in the belief
that place-based approaches (Escobar, 2018; Uda, this volume) are necessary to
design and deliver effective interventions and to avoid harm and unintended consequences.

In what follows, we describe how we have been adapting our methodology over
time to perform research using a reflexive pragmatist approach.

## ADOPTING A "REFLEXIVE PRAGMATIST" APPROACH: IMPROVING REFLEXIVITY IN OUR ENGAGEMENT WITH LOCAL ACTORS

In this section, we present how we adopt a "reflexive pragmatist" approach with
our project SEED,[2] which we have been conducting for over 6 years. SEED partners include a multidisciplinary consortium of researchers from academic institutions, an international NGO (Desjardins International Development, DID) and
local organizations that promote or support entrepreneurship in each location
of intervention. Together, we have worked on projects in countries such as Sri
Lanka, Haiti, Tunisia, Colombia, and Senegal to better understand the conditions for effective micro-enterprise scaling, with the assumption that a favorable
entrepreneurial ecosystem and a stable economic base of micro-entrepreneurs
in local communities will reduce inequalities. SEED's objective is to co-create a
knowledge program with local ecosystem actors that assists micro-entrepreneurs
in increasing growth, empowerment, and innovation. The research relies on four
main phases, consistent with an abductive experimentation approach (Kistruck &
Slade Shantz, 2022). In what follows, we describe how to take a "reflexive pragmatist" perspective in each of these phases. We connect these practices with other
articles published in this volume (Fohim, 2025).

### *Exploratory Phase: Adopting a Place-based Approach*

An exploratory qualitative step is conducted to better understand the current
situation experienced by the marginalized entrepreneurs targeted by the intervention, adopting a place-based approach (Escobar, 2018; Uda, this volume;
Wandersman et al., 2005). In-depth interviews are conducted with beneficiaries
and local ecosystem actors that work with them. We rely on local partners and
translators to avoid the risks of epistemic violence, well described by Chrispal
(this volume). In the same vein, Ginting – Szczesny et al. (this volume) and Uda
(this volume) bring forward the idea of adopting a phenomenological posture

to resist epistemic coloniality. In their research about home-based work in rural Indonesia, Ginting-Szczesny et al. (2025) captured the unique interpretation of home through tangible (e.g., material objects, household members) and intangible elements (e.g., relationships, emotions).

In Sri Lanka, for example, we began our research with a qualitative diagnosis to understand innovation in the lives of rural entrepreneurs since we initially saw only limited innovation in their businesses. We found that at home, these entrepreneurs were quite innovative – in cooking and fashion, for example, and in solving the many problems of everyday life. Our intervention could then focus on drawing analogies between how they innovated at home, and how they could innovate in their businesses.

Adopting a reflexive pragmatist approach within the exploratory phase allowed us to make more informed and grounded decisions in subsequent steps. It increased our awareness of issues and enabled us to braid our knowledge with local knowledge (Kimmerer, 2013), a practice also advocated by James et al. (2025). Approaches that combine indigenous or local knowledge with knowledge from Western and other traditions have the potential to expand what each knows and create unforeseen integrative benefits. For example, farmers' local knowledge was finetuned by researchers using satellite data, AI, and expertise across a number of disciplines to predict the impacts of weather and climate on agriculture (and agricultural markets) in very specific local areas. The insights from the combined data, when customized to local farmers' epistemic cultures, enabled Senegalese herders to plan their seasonal migrations and helped farmers and herders in Burkina Faso and elsewhere prepare for weather events that are now more erratic due to climate change (Armstrong, 2024).

### Co-design Phase: Iterative Co-construction

Training interventions are co-designed iteratively. Researchers consult academic literature and prior practice and work together with international NGO staff, local entrepreneurship support organizations, and local trainers to co-create content and cases, pilot the training, and train other trainers. Our process thus answers Seremani and Bazana (2025) call for involving local actors as active participants in the research process rather than only involving them as a form of "politics of recognition," which perceives as a weak form of decolonizing, grounded mainly in diversity and inclusion. We propose to move beyond the simple dichotomy between the "Western savior" model and the "only local knowledge" model. Knowledge can be co-constructed and, as scholars, we feel, in line with what Asiedu et al. (2025) propose, we have the responsibility to find ways to foster collaboration and cross-fertilization – to braid different knowledge structures in a mutually respectful way (Kimmerer, 2013).

For instance, in Sri Lanka, we collaborated with a local professor of entrepreneurship in all phases of the project. He conducted qualitative interviews with us in the diagnosis and final phases and worked with us throughout the entire project. We co-designed the training with local trainers and entrepreneurship support organizations, and the local staff of the international NGO. In multiple iterations, we tested our assumptions about the problem and potential solutions, worked to develop more contextually appropriate materials, and tested resonance.

We see this co-creation movement with local actors as mutually beneficial. The participatory approaches we implement not only better ground knowledge and perspectives but also diminish the hierarchical relationships between researchers and participants (Konadu-Osei et al., 2022; Moore, 2015) and contribute to the reflexivity of both. In this way, we as researchers seek not to exploit local actors as field sites but attempt to create mutually beneficial projects that give voice to participants and address issues they see as important (Konadu-Osei et al., 2022). In Sri Lanka, our training materials were used after the intervention by local trainers in their own businesses because they were so moved by the resonance they had with micro-entrepreneurs, and micro-entrepreneurs wanted to share the ideas with others because they were directly applicable to their lives.

### *Intervention Phase: Experimenting Together*

Adopting a distributed experimentation mindset (Ferraro et al., 2015), our approach uses randomized trials to experiment with different types of intervention before the lead NGO[3] and local organizations scale their own interventions. While randomized experiments are often criticized by researchers of decolonization for having low engagement/low reflexivity (extractive approach in our classification), the first two phases of our research ensure that our approach is high in both. We collect baseline data and post-intervention data to see which interventions are more effective in achieving the results previously defined with the local partners. Experimenting together allows us to engage more deeply with our partners and learn together before deploying full interventions. In Sri Lanka, rural entrepreneurs felt empowered to innovate in their businesses because we linked conducting low-risk experiments in their businesses to the low-risk experiments they conducted when they cooked, which seemed to add playfulness to their experience of innovating –they claimed to enjoy it very much.

In this journey, clashes between different forms of knowledge became apparent, and despite being uncomfortable, we discussed them. As pointed out by James et al. (this volume), differences between the dominant Western entrepreneurship paradigm and other approaches are sometimes incompatible. They contend that we should strive to work with multiple knowledge systems in "ways where neither is subsumed by the other but allowing for the enrichment of each knowledge system independently." The only way this can be possible is with sustained engagement, where researchers and local actors learn from each other by studying reality from different perspectives. As Henry (2025) states, it is important to critically attend to the Western dimensions present in the researcher's frames and concepts. In Sri Lanka, local trainers deeply resisted our proposal to test the intervention that compared innovating in business to innovating in domestic areas – the examples we used did not fit their (arguably Western-inspired) conceptions of entrepreneurship. We took the time to understand their arguments and adapted our approach with their examples and ideas to make sure that the intervention would reflect their views, yet we also explained why we felt connecting to local domestic examples might be beneficial. We tested the domestic approach against the more traditional approach that they were more comfortable with, experimenting together (Slade Shantz et al., 2024). In the development of interventions, the right to speak (Spivak, 1988), to think (Moyo & Mutsvairo, 2018), and to act in line with one's own conceptualizations of meaningful change should be ensured (Saldanha et al., 2022).

### Learning and Scaling Phase

Achieving impact is a relational and recursive process (Wegener et al., 2024). To increase learning, all our projects incorporate a phase of post-mortem discussion with our partners to understand what worked well and what should be improved before scaling. Prior to recommending the scaling of the intervention, we conduct a final qualitative phase to better understand experimental results. Interviews are conducted with a sample of participants to refine results and understand root causes of changes in behavior through the training intervention. Results are then taken by the lead NGO and local partners and scaled to thousands of marginalized entrepreneurs in the same context experiencing similar challenges. In this sense, we as researchers are co-responsible for what is deployed later. For instance, our research project in Sri Lanka was developed in the first year of a 5-year project. Although we conducted our research on just 500 rural entrepreneurs, our results were used to inform the scaling of the intervention to another 8,000 Sri Lankan entrepreneurs.

This learning phase is key in the way we conduct partnerships and undertake reflexive practices. For instance, in Tunisia, the program we offered was marketed as a "women's empowerment" program. Some entrepreneurs faced barriers because of this labeling: their husbands would not allow them to participate. Our local partner took the time and the measures to provide the required support for those women in distress and secure their right of participation if they wanted. Even with these measures, some women could not continue the program. Learning from this experience made us think about how we can better work with families (particularly husbands) when we develop projects for women entrepreneurs. This is an example that reminds us of the risks that research in the Global South can have for individuals (Chrispal, this volume) and that we should learn from what went wrong to refine our assumptions (van Wijk et al., 2020).

Another important element in the scaling phase is that there are no property rights over the training programs. Local actors are free to use those materials to scale the programs in the ways they find appropriate. Our commitment to local impact drives our research efforts, and this practice ensures long-term engagement with local actors. We understand that much research with vulnerable populations has produced little benefit for them, increasing suspicions of future collaborations (James et al., this volume). Our own experience makes clear that research that aims to contest the root causes of grand challenges and make a significant impact is much more time and resource-consuming (Wegener et al., 2024), which probably inhibits many researchers from taking this approach (Auerbach et al., this volume). There may be trade-offs between practically addressing grand challenges such as poverty and producing research for top-tier journals, as the latter requires significant contributions to academic theory, which may not coincide with solutions to practical challenges (Kistruck & Slade Shantz, 2022). In addition, as Zoogah et al. (this volume) note, resources and efforts are needed to decolonize organizational theories and decenter their effects on the production and dissemination of knowledge from the Global South (Henry, this volume; Naude, 2019). It is not solely about enabling those labeled as "subaltern" to speak (Spivak, 1988), but also "to speak unproblematically", and allow for epistemic pluralism in terms of knowledge production and dissemination (Zoogah et al., this volume). Following Asiedu et al. (this volume), Western management research institutions should participate in this decolonial turn and enable economic, social, and cultural decolonial transformative processes.

## CLOSING REMARKS

We have proposed that researchers move beyond extractive, decolonial evaluative, and traditional collaborative types of research to more reflexive pragmatist approaches to enable more equitable research and more impactful, long-lasting, and contextually sensitive practice. Pairing a reflexive and engaged approach (Bhopal, 2010; Chrispal, this volume; De Smet & Boroş, 2021; Konadu-Osei et al., 2022; Uda, this volume) with a pragmatist orientation (Gehman et al., 2022; Wegener et al., 2024), we see our SEED research projects as a way to support international development organizations in co-developing and spreading knowledge that can be used again in future localized and co-created experiments. Taking seriously the idea that entrepreneurship is social change rather than simply economic development (Calás et al., 2009), we believe that it is possible to be reflexive and to co-create social change with local people, deliberately and cautiously, in a way that works with local values, practices and epistemologies *and* challenges marginalization and the power structures that reproduce it at the same time.

As scholars, we have the capacity and the responsibility to impact many lives in positive ways as we seek to address grand challenges like poverty. We need to accept this responsibility in a concerted effort with other stakeholders, not to impose Western practices but instead to braid local knowledge and Indigenous institutions, values, and practices (Zoogah et al., this volume) with what we know from other settings, in co-creation efforts with local actors (Henry, this volume). We will make mistakes along the way. Yet, let's not be afraid to assume this responsibility because of the risk of error or critique. We believe that experiments, whether successful or not, are learning opportunities (Ginting – Szczesny et al., this volume). They are a fundamental part of addressing grand challenges (Ferraro et al., 2015). As long as we adopt a continuous, incremental learning mindset (Asiedu et al., this volume), and a reflexive pragmatist approach involving both reflexivity and engagement with local actors, we can make progress on addressing grand challenges.

The intention of this paper was not to provide a complete roadmap for research as the sole form of intervention to alleviate poverty. Instead, it should be interpreted as principles we consciously apply to each new project we start. These principles are in constant evolution, and we purposefully build on our learnings with an outlook that improving reflexivity and real engagement with local actors is unfinished business.

## NOTES

1. As Kalei Kanuha & Colonization and Violence against Women (2002, pp. 4–5) noted, "Patriarchy and colonization go hand in hand". The systems of oppression and domination associated with colonization are equivalent to those that privilege men over women (Moane, 1966), and colonization changed the role of women in some societies (Bhatt et al., 2024).

2. SEED Research Project | IDEOS HEC Montréal.

3. Our lead NGO partner in this work is Développement International Desjardins (DID), which supports inclusive finance and entrepreneurship as a means of poverty alleviation in many countries around the world.

## REFERENCES

Alvarez, S. A., & Barney, J. B. (2013). Entrepreneurial opportunities and poverty alleviation. *Entrepreneurship Theory and Practice, 38*(1), 159–184.

Armstrong, H. R. (2024). The tech that helps these herders navigate drought, war, and extremists. *MIT Technology Review*, March 1. https://www.technologyreview.com/2024/03/01/1089006/high-tech-solutions-garbal-call-centers-herding-conflict-africa-sahel/

Asiedu, M., Mpabanga, D., Jacobs, C. D., & Lekorwe, M. (2025). Decolonizing through virtual exchanges? Reflections on an educational experiment between Botswana and Switzerland. In E. Fohim (Ed.), *Decolonizing management and organization studies: Why, how, and what (Research in the Sociology of Organizations)* (pp. 173–189). Emerald Group Publishing Limited.

Auerbach Jahajeeah, J., Gümüsay, A. A., Salvi, E., von Richthofen, G., & Kekana, L. (2025). Grand challenges, decoloniality and management scholarship. In E. Fohim (Ed.), *Decolonizing management and organization studies: Why, how, and what (Research in the Sociology of Organizations)* (pp. 83–101). Emerald Group Publishing Limited.

Bhatt, B., Qureshi, I., Shukla, D. M., & Hota, P. K. (2024). Prefiguring alternative organizing: Confronting marginalization through projective cultural adjustment and tempered autonomy. *Organization Studies, 45*(1), 59–84.

Bhopal, K. (2010). Gender, identity and experience: Researching marginalised groups. *Women's Studies International Forum, 33*(3), 188–195.

Bourdieu, P. (2004). *Science of science and reflexivity.* Polity.

Brännvall, R. (2023). (Un)successful scaling of social innovation. In G. Krlev, D. Wruk, G. Pasi, & M. Bernhard (Eds.), *Social economy science: Transforming the economy and making society more resilient* (pp. 260–283). Oxford University Press.

Calás, M., Smircich, L., & Bourne, K. (2009). Extending the boundaries: Reframing "Entrepreneurship as Social Change" through feminist perspectives. *Academy of Management Review, 34*(3), 552–569.

Chigunta, F., Schnurr, J., James-Wilson, D., Torres, V., & Creation, J. (2005). *Being "real" about youth entrepreneurship in Eastern and Southern Africa.* SEED working paper, 72.

Chrispal, S. (2025). Reducing epistemic violence in the pursuit of organization studies through reflective praxis: Some reflections. In E. Fohim (Ed.), *Decolonizing management and organization studies: Why, how, and what (Research in the Sociology of Organizations)* (pp. 105–118). Emerald Group Publishing Limited.

Cornwall, A. (2016). Women's empowerment: What works? *Journal of International Development, 28*(3), 342–359.

De Smet, S., & Boroş, S. (2021). Revisiting women empowerment through a cultural lens: An in-depth analysis of empowerment methodologies in horticulture in rural Ethiopia. *Frontiers in Psychology, 12*, 536656.

Elliot, D., Gibson, A., & Hitchins, R. (2008). Making markets work for the poor: Rationale and practice. *Enterprise Development and Microfinance, 19*(2), 101–119.

Escobar, A. (2018). *Designs for the Pluriverse: Radical interdependence, autonomy, and the making of worlds.* Duke University Press.

Fatoki, O., & Chindoga, L. (2011). An investigation into the obstacles to youth entrepreneurship in South Africa. *International Business Research, 4*(2), 161–169.

Ferraro, F., Etzion, D., & Gehman, J. (2015). Tackling grand challenges pragmatically: Robust action revisited. *Organization Studies, 36*(3), 363–390.

Fohim, E. (2025). Embarking on a journey toward decolonization. In E. Fohim (Ed.), *Decolonizing management and organization studies : Why, how, and what (Research in the Sociology of Organizations)* (pp. 1–14). Emerald Group Publishing Limited.

Freire, P. (1996). *Pedagogy of the Oppressed (revised).* Continuum.

Gabre-Madhin, E., & Nagarajan, N. (2004). "Making markets work for the poor", World scientific book chapters, In R. D. Christy (Ed.), *Achieving sustainable communities in a global economy alternative private strategies and public policies* (pp. 45–83), World Scientific Publishing Company Private Limited.

Gehman, J., Etzion, D., & Ferraro, F. (2022). Robust action: Advancing a distinctive approach to grand challenges. In A. A. Gümüsay, E. Marti, H. Trittin-Ulbrich, & C. Wickert (Eds.), In *Organizing for societal grand challenges* (pp. 259–278). Emerald Publishing Limited.

Ginting-Szczesny, B. A., Ginting-Carlström, C. E., Kibler, E., & Chliova, M. (2025). Taking context seriously through a phenomenology of place: An illustration of home-based work. In E. Fohim (Ed.), *Decolonizing management and organization studies: Why, how, and what (Research in the Sociology of Organizations)* (pp. 137–153). Emerald Group Publishing Limited.

Henry, E. (2025). Mātauranga Māori: A case of incorporating Indigenous Māori Knowledge in a business school minor. In E. Fohim (Ed.), *Decolonizing management and organization studies: Why, how, and what (Research in the Sociology of Organizations)* (pp. 157–172). Emerald Group Publishing Limited.

Hickey, S., & Mohan, S. (2005). Relocating participation within a radical politics of development. *Development and Change, 36*(2), 237–262.

James, A., Salamzadeh, A., & Dana, L. P. (2025). Decolonizing entrepreneurship: Time to open both eyes. In E. Fohim (Ed.), *Decolonizing management and organization studies : Why, how, and what (Research in the Sociology of Organizations)* (pp. 65–82). Emerald Group Publishing Limited.

Jamieson, M. K., Govaart, G. H., & Pownall, M. (2023). Reflexivity in quantitative research: A rationale and beginner's guide. *Social and Personality Psychology Compass, 17*(4), e12735.

Kabeer, N. (1999). Resources, agency, achievements: Reflections on the measurement of women's empowerment. *Development and Change, 30*(3), 435–464.

Kabeer, N. (2011). Between affiliation and autonomy: Navigating pathways of women's empowerment and gender justice in rural Bangladesh. *Development and Change, 42*(2), 499–528.

Kalei Kanuha, V. Colonization and Violence against Women (2002). Speech. Asian Pacific Institute on Gender-Based Violence.

Karnani, A. (2008). Help' don't romanticize, the poor. *Business Strategy Review, 19*(2), 48–53.

Khan, F. R., Munir, K. A., & Willmott, H. (2007). A dark side of institutional entrepreneurship: Soccer balls, child labour and postcolonial impoverishment. *Organization Studies, 28*(7), 1055–1077.

Kimmerer, R. (2013). *Braiding sweetgrass: Indigenous wisdom, scientific knowledge and the teachings of plants.* Milkweed editions.

Kistruck, G. M., & Slade Shantz, A. (2022). Research on grand challenges: Adopting an abductive experimentation methodology. *Organization Studies, 43*(9), 1479–1505.

Konadu-Osei, O. A., Boroş, S., & Bosch, A. (2022). Methodological decolonisation and local epistemologies in business ethics research. *Journal of Business Ethics, 186*(1), 1–12.

Mair, J., Marti, I., & Ventresca, M. J. (2012). Building inclusive markets in rural Bangladesh: How intermediaries work institutional voids. *Academy of Management Journal, 55*(4), 819–850.

Mair, J., Wolf, M., & Seelos, C. (2016). Scaffolding: A process of transforming patterns of inequality in small-scale societies. *Academy of Management Journal, 59*(6), 2021–2044.

McKague, K., Zietsma, C., & Oliver, C. (2015). Building the social structure of a market. *Organization Studies, 36*(8), 1063–1093.

McMullen, J. S. (2011). Delineating the domain of development entrepreneurship: A market–based approach to facilitating inclusive economic growth. *Entrepreneurship Theory and Practice, 35*(1), 185–215.

Meyer-Stamer, J. (2006). Making market systems work? For the poor? *Small Enterprise Development, 17*(4), 21.

Mignolo, W., & Escobar, A. (Eds.). (2010). *Globalization and the decolonial option. 580.* Routledge.

Moane, G. (1966). *Gender and colonialism: A psychological analysis of oppression and liberation.* St. Martin's Press.

Moore, E. (2015). Researching the private sphere: Methodological and ethical problems in the study of personal relationships in Xhosa families. In S. Van Schalkwyk & P. Gobodo-Madikizela (Eds.), *A reflexive inquiry into gender research: Towards a new paradigm of knowledge production & exploring* (pp. 149–170). Cambridge Scholars Publishing.

Moyo, L., & Mutsvairo, B. (2018). Can the subaltern think? The decolonial turn in communication research in Africa. In *The Palgrave handbook of media and communication research in Africa* (pp. 19–40).

Naude, P. (2019). Decolonising knowledge: Can Ubuntu ethics save us from coloniality? *Journal of Business Ethics, 159*(1), 23–37.

Ng, P. Y., Wood, B. P., & Bastian, B. L. (2022). Reformulating the empowerment process through women entrepreneurship in a collective context. *International Journal of Entrepreneurial Behavior & Research, 28*(9), 154–176.

Ramarajan, L., & Reid, E. (2020). Relational reconciliation: Socializing others across demographic differences. *Academy of Management Journal, 63*, 356–385.

Rappaport, J. (1987). Terms of empowerment/exemplars of prevention: Toward a theory for community psychology. *American Journal of Community Psychology, 15*(2), 121.

Saldanha, F. P., Pozzebon, M., & Delgado, N. A. (2022). Dislocating peripheries to the center: A tecnologia social reinventing repertoires and territories. *Organization*, 13505084221124192.

Seremani, T., & Bazana, S. (2025). In Emamdeen Fohim (Ed.), *Decolonizing management and organization studies: Why, how, and what (Research in the Sociology of Organizations)* (pp. 23–36). Emerald Group Publishing Limited.

Sholkamy, H. (2010). Power, politics and development in the Arab Context: Or how can rearing chicks change patriarchy? *Development, 53*(2), 254–258.

Slade Shantz, A., Kistruck, G., & Zietsma, C. (2018). The opportunity not taken: The occupational identity of entrepreneurs in contexts of poverty. *Journal of Business Venturing, 33*(4), 416–437.

Slade Shantz, A., Zietsma, C., Kistruck, G. M., & Cruz, L. B. (2024). Exploring the relative efficacy of 'within-logic contrasting' and 'cross-logic analogizing' framing tactics for adopting new entrepreneurial practices in contexts of poverty. *Journal of Business Venturing, 39*(1), 106341.

Spivak G. C. (1988). Can the subaltern Speak? In C. Nelson & L. Grossberg (Eds.), *Marxism and the interpretation of culture.* Macmillan.

Sutter, C., Bruton, G. D., & Chen, J. (2019). Entrepreneurship as a solution to extreme poverty: A review and future research directions. *Journal of Business Venturing, 34*(1), 197–214.

Uda, T. (2025). Access to the local lived experiences: A phenomenological approach to decolonize management and organization studies. In E. Fohim (Ed.), *Decolonizing management and organization studies: Why, how, and what (Research in the Sociology of Organizations)* (pp. 119–135). Emerald Group Publishing Limited.

van Wijk, J., van Wijk, J., Drost, S., & Stam, W. (2020). Challenges in building robust interventions in contexts of poverty: Insights from an NGO-driven multi-stakeholder network in Ethiopia. *Organization Studies, 41*(10), 1391–1415.

Wandersman, A., Snell-Johns, J., Lentz, B. E., Fetterman, D. M., Keener, D. C., & Livet, M. (2005). The principles of empowerment evaluation. In D. Fetterman & A. Wandersman (Eds.), *Empowerment evaluation principles in practice* (pp. 27–41). Guilford.

Wegener, F. E., Lee, J. Y., Mascena Barbosa, A., Sharma, G., & Bansal, P. (2024). EXPRESS: From impact to impacting: A pragmatist perspective on tackling grand challenges. *Strategic Organization*, 14761270241238915.

Welter, F., Baker, T., Audretsch, D. B., & Gartner, W. B. (2017). Everyday entrepreneurship – A call for entrepreneurship research to embrace entrepreneurial diversity. *Entrepreneurship Theory and Practice, 41*(3), 311–321.

Zoogah, B. D., Nkomo, S. M., & Kiggundu, M. N. (2025). The role of *Africa Journal of Management* in decolonizing management and organization studies. In E. Fohim (Ed.), *Decolonizing management and organization studies: Why, how, and what (Research in the Sociology of Organizations)* (pp. 191–207). Emerald Group Publishing Limited.

# DECOLONIZING AS AN EVER BEGINNING

Diane-Laure Arjaliès[a,1], Julie Bernard[a], Oana Branzei[a], Luciana Cezarino[b,f], Leanne Cutcher[c], Luke Fiske[d], Tauriq Jenkins[e], Lara Liboni[a], Lucas Stocco[f] and Gasodá Suruí[g]

[a]Ivey Business School, Western University, Canada
[b]Department of Management. Ca' Foscari University of Venice, Italy
[c]The University of Sydney Business School, The University of Sydney, Australia
[d]Rotterdam School of Management, Erasmus University, The Netherlands
[e]Faculty of Humanities, University of Cape Town, South Africa
[f]University of São Paulo, Brazil
[g]Rondonia State Superintendency of Indigenous Peoples, Brazil

## ABSTRACT

*The decolonial agenda calls for bringing the colonized and colonizers together to restore the past and recommit to the future. This essay accounts for the experiences of four research teams co-travelling the space-time continuum with a quest at once simple and complicated:* How do we begin decolonizing?

---

[1]As we sit in circle, our voices carry equal weight, and our message is shared. Our names are listed alphabetically.

---

Decolonizing Management and Organization Studies: Why, How, and What
Research in the Sociology of Organizations, Volume 93, 245–250
ISSN: 0733-558X/doi:10.1108/S0733-558X20250000093015

*Although each experience is unique and still unfolding, all four teams con-*
*verged on a shared insight: decolonizing is a succession of new beginnings.*
*As the river is never the same, each team's encounters led to many new*
*ways of seeing, being, and doing decolonizing. This essay invites us to begin*
*again. Decolonizing as an ever-beginning brings four intertwined aspects:*
*(1) the land, (2) the body, (3) the ethics, and (4) the politics. Together,*
*these continue to transform us profoundly and might offer some hope for new*
*beginnings toward decolonizing the colonial legacy of our fields.*

**Keywords:** Body; decolonial beginnings; ethics; land; politics

# ENTERING THE SPACE-TIME CONTINUUM

*My entry into the world of the Paiter Suruí was not just a crossing of physical boundaries but the*
*gateway to an entirely new paradigm of existence. Before setting foot in the Amazonian village*
*of the Paiter Suruí, my only knowledge of their world came from media snippets of their leader,*
*Gasodá Suruí, speaking at climate crisis roundtables and deforestation forums. However, I quickly*
*learned that no amount of information could prepare me for the richness, complexity, and profound*
*beauty that awaited me in their land.*

Decolonial beginnings start with an eagerness to listen, learn, and walk alongside
the people who preceded us. This walk is rife with vulnerability yet offers potential for deep transformation. Indigenous partners welcome us to a space-time
continuum where the past needs to be witnessed and understood before it can
begin to be corrected. In this space-time continuum, knowledge is asked for and
granted, inscribed on the land and the bodies, impregnated with not yet familiar
ethics that transcend generations' past and future, and overtly political in the aim
to expose and stop re-traumatization that has already gone on for far too long.
In this space-time continuum, the past's inhumanities, injustices, and indignities
teach us about the strangling of souls, the robbing of voices, and the violation of
decisions that have stewarded the good since times immemorial. Decolonizing
land to land, body to body, ethics to ethics, and politics to politics is much more
than a project. It is an invitation to relearn our worlds repeatedly.

*In Australian Aboriginal languages, "time and place are usually the same word – they are indivis-*
*ible" (Yunkaporta, 2020, p. 66). I recently glimpsed this indivisibility when I was invited by one*
*of my research partners to walk with them in their country. As I walked, my research partner, a*
*Darkinjung man, explained how, for thousands of years, his ancestors had walked the Songlines*
*of this Country, at times alongside some of my ancestors, the Awabakal people, as they gathered*
*to perform ceremonies in the shadow sacred Mount Yanko. Songlines are the invisible pathways*
*that crisscross Australia, tracks connecting communities and following ancient boundaries. Along*
*these lines, Aboriginal peoples pass the songs that reveal the land's creation and the secrets of its*
*past (Chapman, 1998). These Songlines are the repository of knowledge. As Yolŋu woman Sienna*
*Stubbs (2021) explains for her people, "Songlines can be looked at like a method or procedure.*
*They hold all of the information required to see the world and live as Yolŋu." The invitation offered*
*by my research partner to walk his ancestors' Songlines and listen to their stories was an invitation*
*to share knowledge. Walking the Songlines allowed me to honour my ancestors, and this honouring*
*lies at the heart of all my dialogues with Indigenous peoples.*

Our teams' beginnings were gently yet firmly guided, from first encounters with the land to progressive embodiments that carried us forward by opening and broadening a variety of ethical and political spaces.

# DECOLONIAL BEGINNINGS

## *The Land*

Decolonizing cannot begin without a relationship with the land. Land is kin. Land is the teacher. Land also holds us together – humans and beyond humans, past, present and future generations, and our responsibilities as stewards and settlers. The land was stolen and divided as colonization aimed to appropriate land not meant to be owned but cared for. Decolonizing is emplaced. It takes place not only on but for the land one's ancestors and successors care for – the land carries through time experiences that exceed the experience of a single or few generations. Non-Indigenous researchers can only enter the time-space continuum on the land. Learning to make kin with the land often requires multiple beginnings – appreciating how Indigenous partners care for the land much more.

> *It's hard to put into words how profoundly this project has transformed me and my relationship with/to the land. I always knew the land was underneath my feet but never fully acknowledged it. This connection goes beyond acknowledgment; it is about embracing my symbiotic relationship with the land. It is a journey of listening and learning, allowing the rhythms of nature to shape my thoughts and actions.*

The connection to the land is not merely symbolic; it is a relationship that must be grounded in dialogues sustained by reciprocity, respect, and refusal (Kirkness & Barnhardt, 1991). Engaging with the land requires embracing new ways of seeing, challenging entrenched beliefs, and reevaluating established paradigms. As one's kinship with the land develops, the wisdom, history, and narratives of generations embedded within the land become comprehensible in ways that extend beyond Western ways of knowing.

> *I realized that the tree was not merely a provider of sustenance but a sacred entity that sustained life in ways I had never imagined. It was a living embodiment of the people's connection to the land, its branches reaching into their cultural practices, social structure, and territorial relationships. The tree, once just an object in my Western understanding, now stood as a bridge between the physical and the spiritual, holding the key to an intricate human-nature balance that I was only beginning to comprehend.*

Comprehension is not a solo act but one guided on and for the land by Indigenous partners. Elders and knowledge keepers speak for the land, explaining its sacred meaning and defending its centrality against trespassers that violate its rights. Such guidance can be offered as one form of defense, as without comprehension, present-day colonization robs current generations of their heritage and future generations of the possibility of kinship. One of our teams was so strongly guided that in less than one hour, we went back hundreds of years and witnessed the sacrilege perpetrated on a river confluence in two-dimensional (360-degree views) and three-dimensional space. Our imaginations saw the relief and appreciated configurations of the stars and positions of the sun, even though access to the most sacred portion of the land was being physically colonized, abducted and restricted to Western ways to view and evaluate something that could not and should not be captured and contained.

## The Body

New beginnings move and shake every fiber of our bodies. We viscerally confront injustices as we sense and sense-make in the space-time continuum. Real-time injustices call forth the body by enrolling all senses at once. We witness the contrast between unbridled beauty and rhythms of life in reverence of nature on the one hand and the abomination of nature enslaved to modern dominion in the name of profit – the vistas of the few blocks out of the many. Heritage is bottled and sold to those on, but not for, the land.

Embodied metaphors stand in where senses no longer reach. Clouded by colonizing beliefs, the way of seeing the world is refined as abundant clear water is poured. As sediment settles, the transformation of our ways of seeing runs through our bodies, enabling us to embody a holistic engagement with the land that goes beyond what we can currently comprehend to what we can see, focus on, question, and discover anew. These revelations wash over us, clean remnants of biases, and make room for learning in and through kinship.

> The methodologies I had once relied upon were rendered obsolete by the sensory richness of the forest; my mind, body, and heart were all engaged in a harmonious dialogue with the land. The Brazil nut tree, in its grandeur, was no longer just a subject of research but a source of life, deeply respected and cherished. The sense of belonging I felt as I participated in the community's daily rhythms was a profound revelation, showing me that the sacred interaction between space, time, and nature could be understood without the need for structured knowledge.

The body is often guided. Non-Indigenous researchers come to discover their senses as they engage with the land and come to trust their senses as sensemaking devices that transcend prior ontologies, often impoverished by the priority given to thought.

> Walking the space colonized by the Amazon headquarters, the two of us learned to see the subjugation of the river. Its desecration by an abomination became comprehensible as our bodies climbed up steep hills to reclaim obstructed vistas, turned right and left to breathe in the difference, and followed the broken flight of migratory birds whose access had been curtailed.

## The Ethics

Entering the time-space continuum opens a dialogue with Indigenous people, requiring us to be prepared to sit without knowing. As our full bodies learn to partake in deep listening on the land, we appreciate the broader ethics of engagement that afford safety in shared vulnerability. The methodologies we employ must allow us to be open to "responding to what is not understood, to what unsettles existing knowledge, and to that which cannot be explained easily through causal relations and claiming to know the other person's intention" (Page, 2017, p. 19).

Most of us appreciate the imperative of ethical and safe spaces, but who creates these spaces in the first place? Who are we to foster inclusivity, respect, and trust? Can non-Indigenous researchers appreciate the vastness and diversity of lived experience as communities flourish in symbiosis with non-human ecosystems and suffer untold when existential bonds are severed? Perhaps not at first. Respectful interactions that progressively embody the ethics of the land have oriented our teams toward de- and co-constructing the very meaning of ethical and safe spaces (Ermine, 2007). Entering the space-time continuum is an invitation into dialogues, protocols and ceremonies interrupted by colonial ethics. Such interruptions are not benign. There are risks of re-traumatization in the name of what ethics may mean to some but not others. Some aspects are non-negotiable, but ceremony and protocol are not always available. And perhaps it should not be. Whom and how Indigenous communities welcome in their midst is not a matter of consent but a profound choice. These choices can be rethought and revoked; as teams work together, the meaning of ethics and safety cannot be assumed. The question becomes not how such spaces are created but rather what processes can be co-developed so that the requisite attention continues to be devoted to maintaining these ethical and safe spaces.

Commitment to ethical and safe practices is rooted in the constant pursuit of consent, arriving in this space with an open mind, working on oneself, and always seeing oneself as a learner. Entering those spaces transforms people forever; however, the necessity to constantly re-engage means remembering the past. Colonial legacies perdure and have present effects. The past is always reconstructed and restored, even in physical objects. The continuum of time and space obliges us to enter with humility, humanity and vulnerability – not presuming what is (or is not) ethical or safe.

## The Politics

*My research in the Australian context has led me on a journey where I have had to lay aside my pre-existing understandings of place and time and discover my connections to my ancestors, the Awabakal people. I am always becoming both a researcher and an Awabakal person.*

Beyond awareness, decolonizing is fundamentally political, but the politics of decolonizing are complex. Indigenous identity is deeply intertwined with political engagement, emphasizing the struggle for fundamental rights and greater inclusion of Indigenous perspectives in the political arena.

*As I delved deeper into this research, I became increasingly entangled in political engagement. I knew there were important issues and challenges; as a settler, I knew my understanding of the situation was limited. I did not fully grasp the complexity of the various issues and the extent of the situation, such as the profound struggle for fundamental rights, particularly concerning access to land and the inclusion of Indigenous perspectives in academic discourse. Still, I could not ignore my frustration when I saw silence perpetuated in the name of rules and business as usual.*

Our teams have learned to welcome politics as foundational to working together. Politics are not static, and there is a necessity to make room for changes, especially as team members confront layers of assumptions at various stages of the process. Bringing the political to the center of comprehension allows new ways to re-enter the time-space continuum.

## WHAT ABOUT THE END?

For our team, decolonizing is not an end but an ever beginning. Whatever has been (not) written, (not) done, or (not) said should always be questioned. As more academics engage in decolonizing work, we must create and commit to safe and ethical spaces for those involved and those left outside, particularly those who were – and still are – colonized. This cannot be achieved without constant re-engagement with what decolonizing means and asks of us in our particular contexts.

> *I find it hardest to hold myself in a place between prejudice and naivete, where I listen without past judgment, but also without blind hope. Is there such a place? Who will I be when I find it? Another worry: how can I avoid becoming the kind of academic who pats himself on the back for being an antiracist, yet still treats the decolonizing project as its own empty land, waiting for his stamp? How can I, in short, reach beyond myself?*

Constant re-engagement also means gifting the right to refuse to re-enter or to choose when or how to re-enter. Refusal should always exist alongside "Respect, Relevance, Reciprocity, Responsibility, Relationship, and Representation" (Kirkness & Barnhardt, 1991; McGregor, 2018). Without refusal, there can be no safety in an ethical space and no political project.

Decolonizing can be profoundly painful, evoking strong emotions of anger, shame, and injustice – particularly for the colonized. Decolonization requires us to see that there is an Other before us who has been deeply harmed both by past injustices and the ongoing effects of colonization. Although Indigenous partners do not (necessarily) hold us responsible for past harm, we bear responsibility for our present choices. Decolonizing is not an abstract, academic possibility but a deliberate practice in the continuum of space and time that begins on the land, enrolls our bodies, and (re)opens safe ethical spaces where political processes can begin again.

## REFERENCES

Chapman, B. (1998). *The songlines*. Vintage Press.
Ermine, W. (2007). The ethical space of engagement. *Indigenous LJ, 6*, 193.
Kirkness, V. J., & Barnhardt, R. (1991). First nations and higher education: The four R's—Respect, relevance, reciprocity, responsibility. *Journal of American Indian Education, 30*(3), 1–15.
McGregor, D. (2018). "From 'Decolonized' to reconciliation research in Canada: Drawing from indigenous research paradigms," 22.
Page, T. (2017). Vulnerable writing as a feminist methodological practice. *Feminist Review, 115*(1), 13–29.
Stubbs, S. (2021). *The past is in the present is in the future*. https://www.ngv.vic.gov.au/essay/the-past-is-in-the-present-is-in-the-future-the-knowledge-practice-and-tradition-of-the-yambirrpa-fish-traps/
Yunkaporta, T. (2020). *Sand talk: How indigenous thinking can save the world*. HarperCollins. https://books.google.ca/books?id=-7moDwAAQBAJ

# TOWARD "A CHARTA"

## Chintan Kella[a], Shaista E. Khilji[b], Leanne Hedberg[c], Medina Williams[d] and Jean-Pierre Imbrogiano[e]

[a] Rotterdam School of Management, The Netherlands
[b] George Washington University, USA
[c] MacEwan University, Canada
[d] Purdue University, USA
[e] University of Helsinki, Finland

## ABSTRACT

*This paper, "Toward a Charta," initiates a critical exploration aimed at confronting and recalibrating power imbalances within Management and Organization Studies (MOS), laying the groundwork for a decisive, action-oriented charter that catalyzes systemic change. Drawing upon a diversity of perspectives and the lived experiences of a group of scholars in this Research in the Sociology of Organizations volume, this work seeks to challenge and reimagine the entrenched colonial norms within the academic discipline. The proposed Charta serves as a preliminary framework, inviting further collaboration and iterative refinement to foster an inclusive and equitable scholarly environment. It emphasizes the importance of recognizing and rectifying the complicity of educational and scholarly practices in sustaining colonial structures and addresses the epistemic violence that systematically marginalizes non-Western knowledge systems. By advocating for epistemic justice and the integration of alternative knowledge systems, the paper outlines actionable points for decolonizing teaching strategies, business school curricula, conference themes, and*

Decolonizing Management and Organization Studies: Why, How, and What
Research in the Sociology of Organizations, Volume 93, 251–262
ISSN: 0733-558X/doi:10.1108/S0733-558X20250000093016

*journal policies. Thus, this document not only calls for action but also serves as a pledge to the dynamic, ongoing process of decolonization by challenging and reforming academic practices to foster a more inclusive and equitable discipline of Management and Organization Studies.*

**Keywords:** Epistemic justice; epistemic violence; equitable education; inclusive academia; power imbalance; scholarly reform; systemic change

# INTRODUCTION

This paper consolidates the diverse viewpoints expressed in this Research in the Sociology of Organizations volume (Fohim, 2025) that help management and organization studies (MOS) scholars comprehend the current state and the pathways forward in decolonizing the discipline. As a conclusion to this volume, we – a diverse group of scholars with individual experiences, origins, and interests – present a decolonizing Charta. Our mission for decolonizing MOS is based on a shared commitment toward its goals, regardless of whether we have directly experienced the impacts of colonization, borne witness to its effects, or unintentionally perpetuated them. Therefore, in this paper, we aim to pave the way for meaningful change and broaden the scope of consideration within the MOS literature by emphasizing also the need to end the colonial oppression of ecology and non-human living beings. We thus aspire to reimagine and reconstruct the MOS discipline toward an inclusive and equitable scholarly environment where different voices are valued and diverse, viable forms of knowing and living are respected, promoted, and protected.

We do not claim to be authorities on the decolonization of MOS. On the contrary, when we first convened to discuss the prospect of creating a Charta, we questioned our legitimacy in crafting such a document and pondered its purpose. We gravitated toward the concept of a "Toward a Charta" – a text that signifies progress rather than completion. In other words, this "Toward a Charta" document serves as a preliminary outline and an invitation for collaboration, expansion, and feedback on the decolonization of MOS.

# BEGINNING TO CHART

In pursuit of the aforementioned objectives, we undertook several steps that encompassed literature reviews and deliberations to find a suitable approach to a first outline of a Charta. These efforts culminated in the insight that such an endeavor is neither a simple task readily definable for implementation nor a process with clear starting and ending points for linear planning. Instead, decolonizing demands an understanding of how colonizations are enshrined in interpretive schemes and scripts guiding social behavior (e.g., in Western societies) and thus also shape the creation and maintenance of an academic discipline as an interactive social process (e.g., George et al., 2006; Scott, 2003). In other words, we contend that MOS scholarship has, irrespective of whether purposefully or non-purposefully, implicitly or explicitly, produced misrepresentations of the social world as part of its own making and remaking. The now widely acknowledged need for decolonizing affirms that this scholarship has been tuned toward the (re-)production of misrepresentations (Bastien et al., 2023), which can occur unconsciously for its members as one abides by the commonly accepted rules of professionalism (Giddens, 1979, 1984). Yet, this places the project of MOS decolonization and the formulation of its Charta on rugged terrain, as its purpose is to alter the interpretive schemes and scripts that guide knowledge production and diffusion within the discipline, thereby also delimiting academic relevance and success.

## WHAT THE CHARTA IS ABOUT

Debates surrounding the terms "decolonization" and "decoloniality" are rapidly evolving. We acknowledge this ongoing development when using the term "decolonization," recognizing that our language will likely evolve alongside our understanding. Furthermore, we acknowledge that colonialism encompasses not just territorial, economic, and political violence but also epistemic and cultural violence that erases or diminishes long-standing Indigenous and non-Western knowledge and cultural practices (Duvisac, 2022). Hence, this "Toward a Charta" reflects action through epistemic justice, i.e., decolonizing through "epistemic reconstitution and reparations: drawing on and centering alternative knowledge systems to reimagine the categories of thought and knowledge that underpin our social, economic, and political structures" (Duvisac, 2022, p. 2).

*Epistemic justice* is a cross-cutting concept in the decolonization literature. In MOS, the need for decolonization arises from its foundation in Western conceptions and values and corresponding biased representations of the world that are routinely applied to non-Western contexts, contributing to epistemic violence and erasure (Khan & Naguib, 2019). For instance, experiences and understandings of Indigenous communities are notoriously underrepresented in MOS elite journals (Salmon et al., 2023; see also Bastien et al., 2023; Murphy & Zhu, 2012). Instead, communities living and organizing by alternative conceptions and values are expected to conform to standards of Western progress and prosperity (e.g., Shantz et al., 2018). By highlighting the principle of epistemic justice, therefore, we portend that decolonizing MOS requires the facilitation of intellectual spaces that can enable a non-hierarchical "exchange of ideas and collaboration between mainstream and heterodox approaches to research" (Banerjee, 2022, p. 1083) as well as education (Allen & Girei, 2023; Woods et al., 2022). Epistemic justice, therefore, would contribute to expanding the scope and impact of different epistemological traditions and avoiding self-serving communities of practice. For effective pursuit, decolonizing would need to become centralized to a certain extent within the disciplinary rules of knowledge production and its diffusion.

Therefore, overcoming biases inherent in MOS requires, on the one hand, to probe Western knowledge structures that disseminate (Jaya, 2001) and "produce knowledge of the Other" (Banerjee, 2022, p. 1078) and, on the other hand, to disrupt any form of institutionalized superiority. We consider that the "Other" knowledge is equally important and that Western knowledge structures require dismantling, not maintaining and reproducing colonial differences (Banerjee, 2022). In line with suggestions presented by Seremani and Clegg (2016), MOS scholarship still needs to develop the capabilities to accommodate the epistemological space where open and serious discussion from various other knowledge viewpoints can occur.

Our project of outlining the status and ways of decolonizing MOS thus extends to different levels of human relations involving both the human and the non-human (i.e. nature). We seek to describe the structural and systemic mechanisms embedded in academic practices and institutions that perpetuate colonial biases. In doing so, we also address the power dynamics within the MOS and challenge the existing norms, latent biases, and institutional practices that contribute to the persistence of colonial legacy.

# WHAT WE PROPOSE

Based on our analysis of the prevalence of colonial institutions and structures in MOS scholarship through relevant literature, as well as taking inspiration from the Africa Charter for Transformative Research Collaboration,[1] we propose three constitutive elements toward a decolonizing Charta of MOS. First, we provide a checklist to help scholars inquire into potential power imbalances. Second, we outline guiding principles for decolonizing the scholarship. Third, we explicate what we have thus far synthesized about what a decolonizing Charta must achieve.

In the following sections, we walk the readers through a process of decolonizing, making sure scholars and their work benefits from a deeper introspection involving an assessment of their needs and subsequently establishing guiding principles for their work.

### Power Imbalances

After reviewing the literature and establishing a grounded understanding of the aforementioned concepts, we set out to formulate thought-provoking questions that summarize our analysis. We present these questions as a checklist in Table 1 that can be applied at any level, from individual researchers to faculties, journals, and other academic institutions. We argue that it is important to address decolonizing at all of these levels because they represent the institutions and structures of MOS knowledge dissemination and knowledge reproduction. The questions are intended to stimulate reflection on how colonial legacies continue to shape research and teaching.

Each set of questions addresses a power imbalance within MOS scholarship. As such, the table serves as a valuable instrument for gaining insights into the theoretical (including epistemology, language, concepts, etc.) and practical relevance of colonial thoughts as they prevail across the MOS research landscape.

***Table 1.*** Checklist for Assessing Power Imbalance to
Identify Needs for Decolonization.

**Epistemology:**
• Do I/we tend toward Western-centric epistemic orientations?
• Do I/we perpetuate Western-centric epistemic orientations, even unintentionally?
• Do I/we marginalize or ignore alternative epistemologies?

**Language:**
• Do I/we predominantly use Western languages as mediums for generating and disseminating new
  scientific knowledge?
• Do I/we overlook non-Western languages as valid mediums for scientific discourse?

**Theory & Concepts:**
• Do I/we primarily rely on Western-centric concepts and theories?
• Do I/we have an inherent bias toward considering 'the West' as the primary site for the generation
  of scientific theory for the world?
• Do I/we give adequate consideration to alternative knowledge systems and perspectives?

**The Development Frame:**
• Do I/we rely on a development frame as the basis for research in developing countries or the global
  South that leads to or perpetuates a one-sided view of "developing" regions as deficient and in
  need of investigation and intervention from 'developed' countries?
• Do I/we enable areas of research in the global South to be delimited by external agendas,
  neglecting other pressing issues formulated and prioritized by local communities?

**Institutional Resourcing:**
• Do I/we notice or promote significant differences in funding, infrastructure, and support that
  are based on programs' or institutions' geographical location, economic status, or historical
  background?

**Presenting and Disseminating:**
• Do I/we attend or promote conferences predominantly held in North America and Europe that
  limit the accessibility and representation of other geographic areas and their people?
• Do I/we commit or promote only research communication outlets that are governed by
  Western-centric rules and interests?

**The Non-human Other:**
• Do I/we attend to human-human dimensions only when considering the need for decolonizing?
• Do I/we engage with anthropocentrism when crafting perspectives on human-nature relationships?

Therefore, we propose Table 1 as an instrument for awareness building of the various needs where decolonizing needs to take place. We encourage scholars (the "I") and institutions (the "We") to use these questions to identify, reflect, and introspect the extent and scope of power imbalances and, hence, be better prepared to engage deeply with the decolonizing project.

Furthermore, we propose that the power imbalance checklist can ensure the cultivation of a scholarly environment that critically questions and thereby dismantles hegemonic perspectives, fostering inclusivity and embracing diverse epistemologies. It can also be used to spark dialogue and to guide actors toward actionable steps for fostering decolonial practices.

*Guiding Principles*

Since decolonizing involves a rigorous ongoing agenda, it is important to establish some guiding principles that establish key standards for scholars to pursue. These guiding principles could serve as the main tenets to that provide clarity of the future vision. With this in mind, we preface the *"Toward a Charta"* with a set of the following guiding principles focused on social justice, plurality of knowledge, crisis response, and human flourishing. These principles will help recenter our efforts to reimagine MOS with the aim of nurturing *an inclusive and equitable academic space that fuels human and environmental well-being.*

- *Social Justice*: A concerted and action-oriented effort is crucial, as a matter of social justice, to disrupt the continuation of unjust hierarchies within MOS. These hierarchies, rooted in colonial histories, perpetuate broader global political and economic inequities. Therefore, it is imperative to foster a clear, collaborative, and collective approach to address these issues effectively.
- *Knowledge Plurality*: Academic research must embrace diverse perspectives to challenge the dominance of Western scientific thought and address the adversities confronting the world.
- *Crisis Response and More-Than-Human Flourishing*: Academic research should prioritize addressing global crises, promoting human dignity across cultures, and the flourishing of all life on Earth.

## TOWARD A CHARTA

With the above guiding principles, we step closer *"Toward a Charta"*, which puts forth an initial set of commitments that orient scholars to propel MOS decolonization forward. These commitments inform the conceptualization and dissemination of research as well as other institutional domains.

Our approach "Toward a Charta" in Fig. 1 builds on the foundational insights from the power imbalances highlighted in Table 1. Yet, it ambitiously extends its scope to implement systemic changes across the MOS discipline. While the checklist in Table 1 effectively highlights specific areas where colonial biases manifest – such as in epistemology, language use, and resource allocation – the Charta transcends this initial diagnostic function. It proposes a more comprehensive blueprint not merely to identify but to actively dismantle and reconfigure the entrenched colonial structures within MOS. The Charta, therefore, serves as an evolutionary step toward deeper structural transformation.

In the construction of the Charta, we placed our focus on key areas of scholarly influence within MOS, specifically targeting teaching, business schools, conferences, and journals due to their roles as primary mechanisms for knowledge production, dissemination, and legitimization. These areas of scholarly influence not only shape the intellectual landscape but also act as platforms where colonial legacies are perpetuated or challenged, historically reinforcing colonial ideologies through curriculum design, research priorities, and knowledge dissemination that prioritize Western perspectives.

This led us to organize the Charta around seven core themes that commit to revising the theoretical foundation of the MOS discipline: furthering epistemic justice, upholding ethics of respect and de-anthropocentrism, committing to resources and collaborations, building global collaborations, demonstrating cultural sensitivity and educational transformation. Each of these themes is interconnected, targeting different aspects of the academic environment yet united in the overarching goal of dismantling colonial legacies. By focusing on these strategic intervention points, the Charta harnesses their transformative potential to foster a more inclusive, equitable, and diverse academic environment in MOS, initiating critical discussions, encouraging reflective practices, and facilitating a broader re-evaluation of how knowledge is created and valued in the discipline. Thus, the Charta moves beyond mere reflection on existing disparities to forge practical pathways for a reimagined, inclusive, and equitable academic discipline.

### Revising Theoretical Foundations

- We commit to critically examining existing epistemic positions and actively embracing diverse perspectives to enrich the academic discourse in MOS.
- We vow to challenge and revise foundational theories that perpetuate colonial and Western-centric biases in MOS.
- We advocate for the exploration and integration of Indigenous knowledge systems into MOS education, establishing curricula that transcend the Western worldview.

### Furthering Epistemic Justice

- We challenge dominant global perspectives in MOS and advocate for localized solutions, fostering authentic collaborations with Indigenous communities to co-create management knowledge across research, curriculum design, and policy-making.
- We promote initiatives that challenge colonial narratives and facilitate critical discussion to enhance awareness of colonialism's impacts on MOS.
- We pledge to explore and integrate a multitude of knowledge perspectives from diverse cultural contexts into MOS, recognizing especially the richness and validity of Indigenous knowledge systems and other alternative epistemologies.
- We commit to incorporating Indigenous knowledge systems and alternative epistemologies into all aspects of MOS curricula, research, and pedagogy, ensuring these perspectives are equally recognized and applied.
- We commit to transforming how management and organizing phenomena are understood and taught.

### Adopting Ethics of Respect and De-Anthropocentrism

- We vow to challenge assumptions about the Other, both the human and non-human, in the MOS literature and teaching.
- We advocate for stronger recognition of scholarship that dismantles biases about the Other, both human and non-human.
- We commit to developing ethical guidelines for respectful engagement with Indigenous knowledge and alternative epistemologies in MOS.
- We promote research methodologies that respect and incorporate alternative ways of knowing, fostering a broader and enhanced understanding of management and organizing phenomena and how they take place in the world.

*Fig. 1.* (*Continued*)

**Ensuring Resources and Collaboration**
• We advocate for resource allocation towards initiatives that support the integration of diverse knowledge systems, ensuring sustained progress in decolonization efforts in MOS.
• We encourage interdisciplinary collaboration that bridges MOS with disciplines like anthropology, post-colonial studies, and sociology to enrich and broaden perspectives.

**Establishing Global Networks and Accountability**
• We support the establishment of global networks for sharing best practices and fostering collaboration for decolonizing MOS.
• We commit to establishing benchmarks and mechanisms to evaluate the progress of decolonization in MOS, ensuring accountability and sustained commitment.

**Fostering Educational Transformation**
• We pledge to initiate programs within business schools that acknowledge, respect, and integrate Indigenous knowledge and other alternative epistemologies, fostering partnerships with communities for co-creation of curriculum content.
• We commit to developing training programs for educators that emphasize inclusive teaching practices, accommodating diverse learning styles and perspectives, and fostering culturally responsive classrooms.

**Committing for Cultural Sensitivity**
• We commit to providing more space and valence for local languages in all stages of MOS research and teaching to ensure inclusivity and effective communication across cultural boundaries.
• We advocate for the development and adherence to guidelines that promote ethical and culturally sensitive approaches in organizations, ensuring that management practices are inclusive and respectful of cultural diversity.

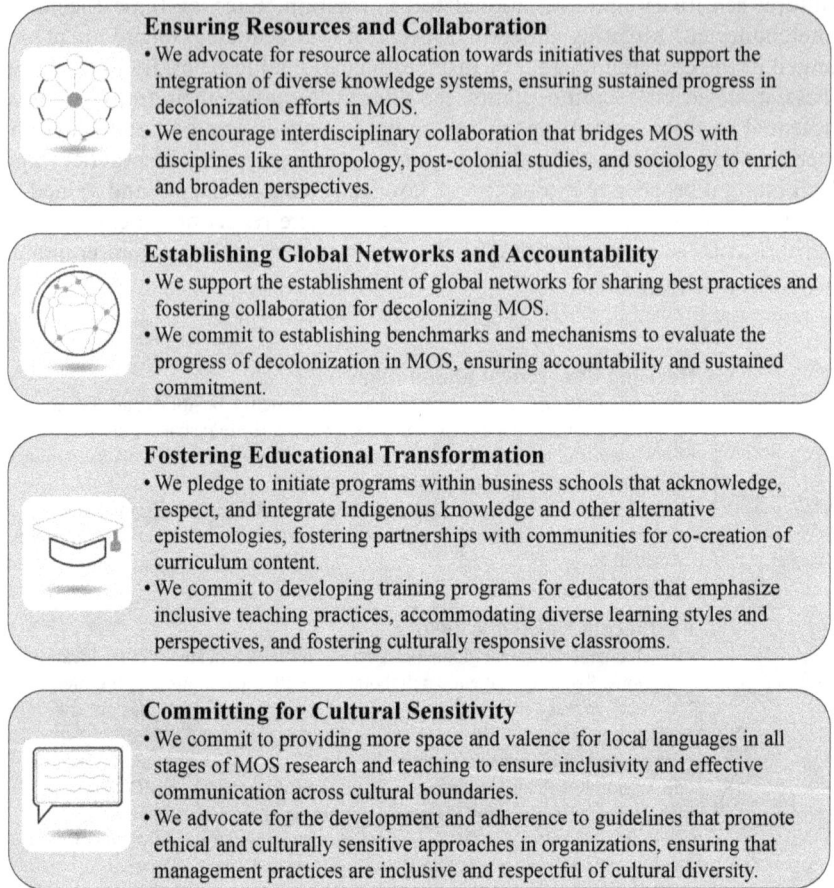

*Fig. 1.* "Toward a Charta" for Decolonializing MOS.[2]

Recognizing these areas as critical for implementing meaningful change, the Charta should, therefore, be used to identify teaching strategies, business school curricula, conference themes, and journal policies as actionable points for introducing decolonial practices to replace entrenched colonial norms. Moreover, the breakdown underscores the responsibility and complicity of these educational and scholarly activities and institutions in maintaining or dismantling colonial structures, compelling stakeholders to take responsibility for driving change. This table could be expanded to establish a clear and actionable framework for stakeholders, ensuring they can implement and adapt the Charta's principles effectively within the MOS discipline and beyond.

While we diligently chart our course toward a comprehensive Charta for decolonization of management and organization studies, decolonizing MOS should be viewed not as a static endpoint but as an ongoing process of reflexivity. This dynamic approach highlights the necessity of unlearning traditional frameworks and embracing a wide spectrum of ontologies and epistemologies. By prioritizing continuous critical reflection, the field can more effectively identify and dismantle the entrenched colonial legacies that shape its practices and theoretical underpinnings. This perspective ensures that decolonization remains an adaptive, inclusive process that is responsive to diverse academic and cultural contexts, avoiding the unintended reinforcement of the very structures we aim to dismantle.

We present this Charta as a paradigm shift toward decolonial practices that prioritize diverse representation, epistemic justice, and equitable access to knowledge. The Charta themes identified above serve as guidance to reshape the landscape of MOS education and scholarship. By advocating for transformative practices, pedagogical reforms, and revamped institutional frameworks, we anticipate the Charta to provide a roadmap for fostering a more inclusive and equitable academic environment within business schools, conferences, and journals. After thoroughly evaluating the principles set forth in the Charta and critically assessing the challenges confronting MOS scholarship, we urge colleagues to make a more informed decision.

## STARTING HERE, MOVING FORWARD

This paper serves as a call to action, inviting the MOS community to come together and play an active role in the decolonization of the MOS discipline. Much of what we derive from this paper depends on whether we as a research community will organize in global networks that further promote decolonizing MOS but also create targets, mechanisms, and benchmarks for accountability toward its goals. It is also clear that the dialogue about the need for these efforts and the value of a Charta, require to remain active and open for participation in relevant fora. With the proposed "Toward a Charta," therefore, we identify and call out the contributors to the colonial past while concurrently inviting and calling in the agents of decolonial change within our MOS community.

The proposed Charta above should be adopted, adapted, and discussed in light of our commitment to decolonizing MOS. Its construction is influenced by our (the authors') collective experiences and interpretations of our experiences and the literature we have reviewed. Hence, in conclusion, it is important to present our individual positionality to reflect and understand the various identities and worldviews with which we live, engage, and write.

## AUTHORS' POSITIONALITY

### *Chintan Kella*

I find myself navigating a complex intersection of minority identities within academia. As a scholar of Indian origin, I am acutely aware of how my skin color, sexual orientation, and recently diagnosed neurodivergence mark me as a triple minority (or a threat) in the West. Despite the corporate experience and an Indian perspective often overlooked in my career in the West, I persist. However, at times, having relocated from India to Rome and finally to the Netherlands, I feel I've arrived too late in Europe. While feedback on my academic writings' rigor persists, I've also launched a diversity and inclusion course at my school as one of the forms of my commitment to decolonizing MOS. Still, I wonder, is this burden mine to bear?

### Shaista E. Khilji

I have lived my life at the cusp of privilege and disadvantage. I come from a highly educated family where education served as a right, privilege, and calling. However, as a graduate student in the United Kingdom and later as an academic in Canada and the United States, I realized that some people only saw me through the stereotypes they carried about my religion, ethnicity, and skin color. These stereotypes conveniently intersected with gender. Their persistent questioning left me confused – until I learned to shrug it off. Years later, I realized they were trying to fit me in a neat box of a "good" or a "bad" Muslim (Oborne, 2022). My racialized, gendered, and intersectional experiences in Europe and North America commit me to decolonizing our mindsets and the academic discipline.

### Leanne Hedberg

I am a white settler and first-generation college student from a rural Ojibwe territory in Wisconsin, United States. My maternal grandmother grew up on an Indian reservation in Oklahoma. My daughters are registered, on their father's side, in the Muscogee, or Mvskoke, Creek Nation of Oklahoma, United States. I am neurodivergent and was raised in the context of generational addictions and poverty.

### Medina Williams

The downward pull of many facets (academic, vocational, personal) shapes my contributions here. I check so many marginalized and non-dominant boxes that I have lost count. Yet this is my attempt to resist the narratives that have become much entrenched, particularly in MOS and doing so violently, but in writing only.

### Jean-Pierre Imbrogiano

I have had the privilege of being born into and raised in an affluent Western society. My awareness and, thus, life orientation benefitted from stays abroad, where the immersion with nature became my focal point for existence. Thereby I learnt about different conceptions of the world, particularly how our Western approaches are limited, for instance, by conceiving of wealth as the access to goods and services. I am now convinced that, in the long run, this Western conception of wealth will have no future.

*Join us in embracing this transformative agenda aimed at decolonizing MOS education, research, and practice! Together, we can confront systemic barriers, amplify underrepresented voices, and champion epistemic justice. Your participation is crucial in shaping a more inclusive and equitable future! Share your perspectives and/or sign the "Toward a Charta" document by accessing it via this weblink (https://sites. google.com/view/charta/home) or by scanning the following QR code (see Fig. 2).*

*Fig. 2.* Your Commitment "Toward a Charta".

## NOTES

1. Africa Charter for Transformative Collaborations. (2023). *University of Bristol.* Retrieved from https://bpb-eu-w2.wpmucdn.com/blogs.bristol.ac.uk/dist/1/627/files/2023/07/Africa-Charter-for-Transformative-Collaborations.pdf

2. The graphic icons have been created by Marcel Imbrogiano, published with permission.

## REFERENCES

Allen, S., & Girei, E. (2023). Developing decolonial reflexivity: Decolonizing management education by confronting white skin, white identities, and whiteness. *Academy of Management Learning & Education, 00*(00), 1–19. https://doi.org/10.5465/amle.2022.0387

Banerjee, S. B. (2022). Decolonizing management theory: A critical perspective. *Journal of Management Studies, 59*(4), 1074–1087.

Bastien, F., Coraiola, D. M., & Foster, W. M. (2023). Indigenous Peoples and organization studies. *Organization Studies, 44*(4), 659–675.

Duvisac, S. (2022, July). *Decolonize: What does it mean?* Oxfam International. https://oxfamilibrary.openrepository.com/bitstream/handle/10546/621456/rrdecolonize-what-does-it-mean-151222-en.pdf

Fohim, E. (2025). Embarking on a journey towards decolonization. In E. Fohim (Ed.), *Decolonizing management and organization studies: Why, how, and what (Research in the Sociology of Organizations)* (pp. 1–324). Emerald Group Publishing Limited.

George, E., Chattopadhyay, P., Sitkin, S. B., & Barden, J. (2006). Cognitive underpinnings of institutional persistence and change: A framing perspective. *Academy of Management Review, 31*(2), 347–365.

Giddens, A. (1979). *Central problems in social theory: Action, structure and contradiction in social analysis.* University of California Press.

Giddens, A. (1984). *The constitution of society: Outline of the theory of structuration.* Polity Press.

Jaya, P. S. (2001). Do we really 'Know' and 'Profess'? Decolonizing management knowledge. *Organization, 8*(2), 227–233. https://doi.org/10.1177/1350508401082008

Khan, F. R., & Naguib, R. (2019). Epistemic healing: A critical ethical response to epistemic violence in business ethics. *Journal of Business Ethics, 156*, 89–104.

Murphy, J., & Zhu, J. (2012). Neo-colonialism in the academy? Anglo-American domination in management journals. *Organization, 19*(6), 915–927.

Oborne, P. (2022). *The fate of Abraham: Why the west is wrong about Islam?* Simon & Schuster.

Salmon, E., Chavez R, J. F., & Murphy, M. (2023). New perspectives and critical insights from Indigenous peoples' research: A systematic review of Indigenous management and organization literature. *Academy of Management Annals, 17*(2), 439–491.

Scott, W. R. (2003). Institutional carriers: Reviewing modes of transporting ideas over time and space and considering their consequences. *Industrial and Corporate Change, 12*(4), 879–894.

Seremani, T. W., & Clegg, S. (2016). Postcolonialism, organization, and management theory: The role of "epistemological third spaces." *Journal of Management Inquiry, 25*(2), 171–183.

Shantz, A. S., Kistruck, G., & Zietsma, C. (2018). The opportunity not taken: The occupational identity of entrepreneurs in contexts of poverty. *Journal of Business Venturing, 33*(4), 416–437.

Woods, B., Dell, K., & Carroll, B. (2022). Decolonizing the business school: Reconstructing the entrepreneurship classroom through indigenizing pedagogy and learning. *Academy of Management Learning & Education, 21*(1), 82–100.

www.ingramcontent.com/pod-product-compliance
Lightning Source LLC
Chambersburg PA
CBHW050339270326
41926CB00016B/3532